PRACTICAL FORENSIC MICROSCOPY

PRACTICAL FORENSIC MICROSCOPY

A Laboratory Manual

Second Edition

Barbara P. Wheeler
Forensic Science Consultant Lexington, KY, USA

WILEY

This second edition first published 2021

© 2021 John Wiley & Sons Ltd

Edition History
John Wiley & Sons Ltd (1e, 2008)

Registered Office(s)
John Wiley & Sons, Inc., 111 River Street, Hoboken, NJ 07030, USA
John Wiley & Sons Ltd, The Atrium, Southern Gate, Chichester, West Sussex, PO19 8SQ, UK

Editorial Office
The Atrium, Southern Gate, Chichester, West Sussex, PO19 8SQ, UK

For details of our global editorial offices, customer services, and more information about Wiley products visit us at www.wiley.com.

Wiley also publishes its books in a variety of electronic formats and by print-on-demand. Some content that appears in standard print versions of this book may not be available in other formats.

Library of Congress Cataloging-in-Publication Data

Names: Wheeler, Barbara, author.
  Title: Practical forensic microscopy : a laboratory manual / Barbara B.
  Wheeler, Eastern Kentucky University, Richmond, KY.
Description: Second edition. | Hoboken, NJ : Wiley, 2021. | Includes index.
Identifiers: LCCN 2020026988 (print) | LCCN 2020026989 (ebook) | ISBN
  9781119154495 (cloth) | ISBN 9781119154501 (adobe pdf) | ISBN
  9781119154518 (epub)
Subjects: LCSH: Medical jurisprudence–Laboratory manuals. |
  Microscopy–Laboratory manuals.
Classification: LCC RA1034 .W54 2020 (print) | LCC RA1034 (ebook) | DDC
  614/.1–dc23
LC record available at https://lccn.loc.gov/2020026988
LC ebook record available at https://lccn.loc.gov/2020026989

Cover Design: Wiley
Cover Image: © Westend61/Getty Images

Set in 10pt TimesLTStd by SPi Global, Chennai, India

SKYCCC3C8D7-D85B-47C0-A099-9CD41C157AF9_072221

Contents

Preface

In 2009, the National Academy of Sciences issued a report titled *Strengthening Forensic Science in the United States: A Path Forward*. Many strengths of the field were included, but also weaknesses found within various disciplines. Overall recommendations were made to improve methods, practice, and performance within forensic sciences. One area acknowledged was the state of forensic science education. While this broad topic includes undergraduate, graduate, and continuing education as well as in-service training, each education type presents various challenges.

As the popularity of forensic science has emerged, many colleges and universities have responded by creating forensic science programs. In 2002, American Academy of Forensic Science (AAFS) created an ad hoc committee, which in 2004 officially became Forensic Education Program Accreditation Committee (FEPAC). FEPAC created a manner of accrediting undergraduate and graduate forensic science programs using established standards within the field. In hopes of preparing graduates for careers in a forensic laboratory, these standards address both academic and practical concerns. AAFS recently acknowledged 135 undergraduate, 61 graduate, and 3 doctoral degree programs in the United States. Curricula of these degrees range from criminal justice to heavily science-based programs. Likewise, texts vary from general criminalistics to topics specific to forensic disciplines, for instance firearms, drugs, and DNA. In the past, forensic microscopy has had little distinction, being overshadowed by more visible disciplines. In more recent years, highly publicized criminal cases have brought forensic microscopy into the spotlight, creating the need for a text focused on this forensic discipline. In 2008, *Practical Forensic Microscopy: A Laboratory Manual* was published to address this need.

Since FEPAC recommends that academic training be paired with laboratory practices to acquire skills and experience, this updated text is again written with a balanced approach to the topic of forensic microscopy. Each chapter within the text begins with a list of simple objectives for the experiment topic. To assist the student in obtaining the objective, a general overview of the topic, selected reading references, and an experiment providing practical experience are utilized. Worksheets have also been included to compile analytical results. To test the student's knowledge, basic report requirements and questions are included. Additional educational aids are also available on the companion website.

While much of forensic microscopy remains the same, additional forensic topics, techniques, and references are included in this second edition. *Practical Forensic Microscopy* is a comprehensive lab manual that adapts microscopic procedures used in the forensic laboratory to practical experiments that can be taught in college laboratories. However, in some cases it is impractical to use forensic laboratory procedures in an educational setting due to the large number of students or when equipment and supplies such as controlled substances are not available. Every attempt was made to adapt forensic laboratory procedures to best address these concerns. If significant modifications were made for the educational setting, the scientifically accepted theory and principles of the forensic lab procedures were still covered thoroughly in the introduction. At times to address these concerns, it was necessary to make concessions for accuracy or precision. For example, the absolute measurement of density of glass evidence in a forensic laboratory would use a temperature-controlled system, whereas in this procedure students use standard laboratory glassware and balances. However, the need to cover the topic of measurement of the density of glass far outweighed the concessions made in accuracy and precision.

Once again, this second edition brings forensic microscopy to the student so that the future of this discipline within forensic science will continue to flourish. Forty-eight laboratory experiments have been developed to cover the variety of "microscopic" evidence disciplines within the forensic science field. The manual starts with the use of simple stereomicroscopes and gradually introduces more complex microscope systems used in a forensic laboratory. Many forensic science disciplines that use microscopes are covered so that the student will obtain a general understanding of the microscopes and microscopic techniques utilized in examinations. For example, impression evidence such as fingerprints, shoe print patterns, tool marks, and firearms will be analyzed using simple stereomicroscopic techniques. Biological evidence, drug evidence, and trace evidence (e.g., paint, glass, and hair fiber) will be covered by a variety of microscopes and specialized microscopic techniques.

I hope you utilize the "new and improved" version of *Practical Forensic Microscopy: A Laboratory Manual* to obtain the knowledge and skills to keep forensic microscopy alive.

Barbara P. Wheeler
Kentucky, 2020

Acknowledgments

Any author of a text knows the amount of people who assist and advise in preparation of a final manuscript, both text materials and also in the publication process. Numerous fellow practitioners, forensic faculty, and friends provided contributions, corroborations, and validations as I worked to update this text. My publishing team also provided support as I paused my work effort to allow time during my mother's final days. I am forever grateful to all.

And most of all, special thanks to my husband for his endless patience, encouragement, and support during the project.

BPW

Laboratory Safety

Laboratory work can be very interesting and exciting; however, certain safety concerns should always be taken into consideration. General laboratory safety rules follow. Each laboratory will have its own set of rules, so make sure that you have read those for your specific laboratory, understand them, and comply with them. When there is a question concerning laboratory safety, please ask the instructor.

1. Many materials in a laboratory may cause eye injury. Wear approved safety glasses to protect against chemical splashes and stray impacts.
2. Wear a protective laboratory apron or coat and close-toed shoes.
3. No eating, drinking, smoking, or applying makeup in the lab.
4. Keep your work area clean and free of clutter.
5. Be prepared to work while you are in the laboratory. No horseplay is permitted in the lab.
6. Do not perform any unauthorized experiments.
7. Handle scalpels and razor blades with extreme caution. Never cut materials toward you.
8. Use a fume hood for all substances that produce strong odors or fumes.
9. Do not remove any materials from the laboratory.
10. Dispose of all waste properly. Ask your instructor for directions if you are not sure what to do. To avoid contamination, never return chemicals to their original containers.
11. Do not work alone in the laboratory.
12. Check equipment to be sure that it is in good condition. Don't use chipped or cracked glassware.
13. Never pipette by mouth. Always use suction bulbs or disposable pipettes.
14. Never touch, taste, or smell a chemical. If you are instructed to note the smell, gently wave your hand over the opening to direct fumes toward your nose. Do not inhale the fumes directly from the container.
15. Rinse off any acid or base spills on your skin/clothing. Clean up all spills immediately and notify your instructor. Ask your instructor for assistance if you are not sure what to do.
16. Read labels carefully to be sure that you are using the correct reagent for an experiment.
17. Know the location and operation of the eyewash, safety shower, spill materials, and fire extinguisher in the lab.
18. Know the location of the safety kit.
19. All accidents and injuries should be reported to the instructor immediately.
20. Follow other safety rules as set by your laboratory.

Microscope Maintenance

The microscopes that you will be using in this class work on the same principles but vary greatly in their mechanical design and their various operating parts. If possible, make yourself familiar with the microscope's operational manual prior to using the microscope. It is important to inform the instructor of any problems. Most routine maintenance can be performed in the laboratory; however, some maintenance would require disassembly of the microscope, requiring a qualified service technician.

Basic Handling and Storage

The most critical step in microscope maintenance is prevention. Proper carrying, handling, use, and storage of the microscope is the greatest single thing that can be done to avoid major microscope repairs.

When microscopes are moved, always support them from the bottom. Only use the arm to balance the weight if necessary. When changing objectives, hold the nosepiece and not the objectives. Dust is the microscope's worst enemy, so keep the microscope covered when not in use. Plastic bags can be used if microscope covers are not available. Never store a microscope with the eyepiece or objective removed or uncovered. This also applies to the third ocular area if the microscope is equipped for setup with a camera. This would allow dust to collect in the body tube and will be very difficult to clean. Microscopes should always be stored clean and covered.

Optical Cleaning

All lenses in a microscope are made of coated, soft glass that can be easily scratched. Lenses should be treated with care. Never use a hard instrument or abrasive to clean a lens.

For the top of the eyepiece and the ends of the objectives, clean as follows: Use a camel's hair brush and an air aspirator or similar air source to remove all loose dust and dirt. Next try "fogging" by breath. If the eyepiece or objective is still dirty, use lens paper or moisten the end of a Q-tip™ with lens cleaning solution. Clean the optical surface with the moist end of the Q-tip using a circular motion. Remove any remaining dust and dirt using an air source. To determine which lens surfaces need cleaning, focus the microscope on a clean slide free of all dust. Moving the slide will determine if the visible dust is on the slide. Rotating the eyepiece will establish if dirt is on the eyepiece. If any dirt rotates, the eyepiece needs cleaning. Likewise, rotating objectives will establish if dirt is on a specific objective. Dust on a condenser lens can be detected in a similar fashion. If the dirt still persists, it may be necessary to clean the inside surfaces of the objective. If, after cleaning all optical surfaces carefully, dirt is still found in the field of view, it is possible that dirt is between the lenses of the objective. This dirt cannot be removed without disassembling the compound lens in the objective. Do not attempt this – call your microscope repair technician.

Mechanical Maintenance

Most microscopes require periodic cleaning, lubrication, and minor adjustments. *Never over-tighten or use force when doing any repair or maintenance of your microscope.* All high-quality microscopes are manufactured from brass or other soft metals and are easily damaged with excessive force.

The objective nosepiece can be adjusted if it becomes too tight or loose. The adjustment is often as simple as loosening or tightening the slot-headed screw in the middle of the nosepiece. Sometimes there is a two-hole ring nut. This requires using a round-nose pliers like a wrench to loosen or tighten the collar. On some microscopes, the stage must be removed to gain access to the nosepiece adjustment. Be sure to check the manual for your specific microscope.

Tension of the coarse and fine adjustment knobs can also be adjusted. Again, various mechanical methods have been designed. Some microscopes are adjusted by simply turning the knobs on each side of the microscope in opposite directions to tighten or loosen as desired. Others have adjustable collars on the shaft and require the use of specially designed collar-wrenches or allen wrenches to make the adjustments. Moving the collars out usually provides more tension. If your microscope requires unique collar-wrenches, obtain these from your microscope supplier.

Sliding surfaces on the microscope can be cleaned and lubricated. This should be done as needed or on an annual basis. Clean any grease and dirt from all sliding surfaces, using clean paper towels and a solvent such as alcohol. Wipe completely dry. Apply a thin layer of fresh grease to the sliding surfaces. Lithium-based grease or other grease specified by the manufacturer is recommended. Do not oil or grease the teeth of the rack and pinion gears.

Instructions for replacing the bulb in each specific microscope are found in its corresponding user's manual. Always allow a bulb to cool before attempting to replace it. When replacing bulbs, avoid touching the glass with your bare hands. Fingerprints left on the bulb will actually "burn into" the glass and reduce the bulb quality and life expectancy.

The Micro Kit

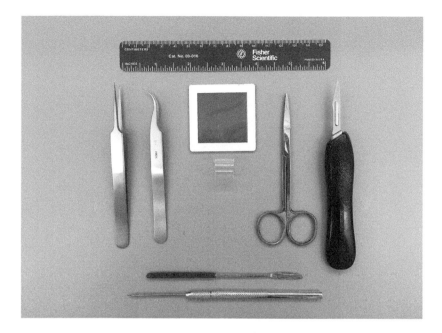

The micro kit contains various tools that are used in the experiments included in this manual. The contents of the kit are listed below. Possible sources for the more specialized items are also included.

  a. 6-inch ruler
  b. straight-end forceps, fine[1]
  c. curved-end forceps, fine[1]
  d. orange (589 nm) filter slide[1]
  e. ¼-inch glass ring (¼-inch thick)[1]
  f. scissors[2]
  g. scalpel with ability to accept straight-edge blade[2]
  h. microspatula
  i. needle probe[2]

Notes

1. Available from The McCrone Group, Attn: Order Department, 850 Pasquinelli Drive, Westmont, IL 60559-5539. (630) 887-7100. https://www.mccrone.com/instrument-sales/.
2. These items are part of a standard student classroom dissection kit, which may be purchased from companies such as Ward's Science, 5100 West Henrietta Road, PO Box 92912, Rochester, NY 14692-9102. (800) 962-2660. https://www.wardsci.com.

About the Companion Website

This book is accompanied by a companion website:

www.wiley.com/go/Wheeler/Forensic

For each experiment, this website includes:

- a listing of key words
- review questions to aid learning and understanding

Experiments

Chapter 1
Stereomicroscope

The stereomicroscope is utilized in most preliminary forensic examinations. This low-magnification microscope provides viewing of samples in a manner that is similar to the view observed by the human eyes. Our eyes function along with our brain to produce what is referred to as stereoscopic or three-dimensional vision. This occurs because of the brain's ability to interpret two slightly different images received from each of the eye's retinas. A distance of approximately 64–65 mm separates the human eyes. Because of this separation, each eye perceives an object from a somewhat different viewpoint. When the images are relayed to the brain, they are combined and still retain a high degree of depth perception. This provides spatial, three-dimensional images of the object. The stereomicroscope takes advantage of this ability to perceive depth by transmitting twin images that are inclined by a small angle (usually between 13°) to yield a true stereoscopic effect.

The stereomicroscope uses a combination of lenses to produce the low-magnification image. To accomplish this, the microscope has several components that redirect the light path so that a magnified image of the viewed object can be focused. A stereomicroscope has the following basic parts:

- light source
- sample stage
- objective
- focusing knobs
- oculars

There are two basic types of stereomicroscope: Greenough and Common Main Objective (CMO). Greenough stereomicroscopes utilize two identical optical systems within twin body tubes that are inclined to produce the three-dimensional effect. CMO stereomicroscopes use a single large objective that is shared between a pair of ocular tubes and lens systems to achieve the depth perception.

Stereomicroscopes offer low magnification, generally utilizing oculars and objectives that provide total magnification within the range of 0.7X to 40X. Step-type objective lenses or continuous variable zoom objective lenses are used to increase magnification in both Greenough and CMO stereomicroscopes. Because of the low total magnification, a large field of view and greater depth of field are obtained. Samples can be viewed with either reflected or transmitted light. Many forensic samples are often opaque in that they block visible light, and are most often viewed with reflected light. This allows the stereomicroscope to be mounted on a boom stand, allowing even greater flexibility of viewing large samples.

Practical Forensic Microscopy: A Laboratory Manual, Second Edition. Barbara P. Wheeler.
© 2021 John Wiley & Sons Ltd. Published 2021 by John Wiley & Sons Ltd.
Companion website: www.wiley.com/go/Wheeler/Forensic

In a forensic laboratory, the stereomicroscope is commonly used to view items and also to locate samples. The low-level magnification allows viewing of the initial characteristics of an item or sample. Samples can be collected and examined further with the stereomicroscope or by using additional microscopes and/or instrumentation.

Chapter 1

Experiment 1A: Familiarization with the Stereomicroscope

Recommended pre-lab reading assignment:

Schlueter GE, Gumpertz WE. The Stereomicroscope, Instrumentation and Techniques. *American Laboratory*. 1976; 8(4): 61–71.

Recommended website:

Flynn BO, Davidson MW. SMZ-1500 Stereoscopic Microscope [Java Interactive Tutorial; cited 2019]. Available from: http://www.microscopyu.com.

Objective

Upon completion of this practical exercise, the student will have developed a basic understanding of:

1. components of the stereomicroscope
2. magnification
3. field of view
4. depth of field
5. working distance

Introduction

A microscope is defined as an optical instrument that uses a combination of lenses to produce a magnified image of small objects. To accomplish this, a stereomicroscope utilizes several components, which gather light and redirect the light path so that a magnified image of the viewed object can be focused within a short distance.

Practical Forensic Microscopy: A Laboratory Manual, Second Edition. Barbara P. Wheeler.
© 2021 John Wiley & Sons Ltd. Published 2021 by John Wiley & Sons Ltd.
Companion website: www.wiley.com/go/Wheeler/Forensic

A stereoscopic microscope contains five basic components: light source, sample stage, objective(s), focusing knob, and oculars. This is somewhat different in construction than standard compound light microscopes, in the fact that there is no condenser.

There are two choices of illumination with the stereomicroscope. Reflected light, light that bounces off a surface, is used for objects that are opaque (objects impervious to light). If the sample is transparent it can be observed with transmitted light, light that is able to transfer through a material. Some samples are best observed with both reflected and transmitted light and can be viewed under both settings using a stereomicroscope.

Some stereomicroscopes use a simple platform for a sample stage (see Figure 1A-1), while others utilize the tabletop. The body of the stereomicroscope is the area that holds or contains the other components of the microscope: focusing knobs, objectives, and oculars. Knobs are used to raise and lower the body of the microscope so that various size samples can be viewed in focus. The objective lenses are typically built into the body of the stereomicroscope with a mechanism for changing magnifications from the outside. Older model stereomicroscopes and

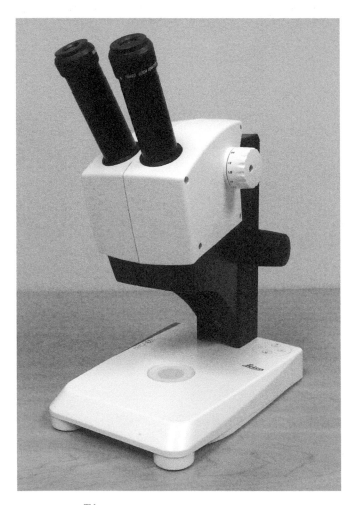

Figure 1A-1   The Leica EZ4™ microscope is capable of providing both reflected and transmitted light while utilizing continuous zoom magnification.

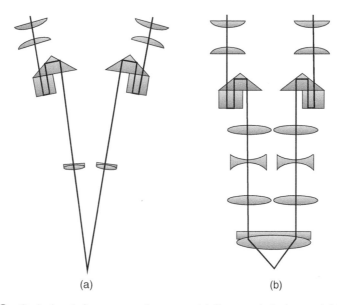

(a)   (b)

Figure 1A-2   Optical path for a stereomicroscope: (a) Greenough design, and (b) CMO design.

the less expensive newer stereomicroscopes employ a series of fixed objective lenses, which step up the magnification in discrete increments. The newer and typically better stereomicroscopes utilize a continuous zoom lens system, which allows any magnification within the range of the microscope. The objective collects the light from the sample and magnifies the focused image to the oculars, which further magnifies and refocuses the image to the viewer's eye.

There are two general designs of a stereomicroscope: Greenough and the Common Main Objective (CMO). The optical path for both stereoscope designs is shown in Figure 1A-2.

The Greenough design (Figure 1A-2a) utilizes two identical optical systems within twin body tubes. The CMO (Figure 1A-2b) utilizes a single objective that is shared between a pair of ocular tubes and lens assemblies. With a Greenough design stereomicroscope, the light initially interacts with the sample. Once it leaves the sample, it is collected by two identical optical systems. These systems are made up of an objective and a pair of image-inverting prisms, which de-rotate and invert the magnified sample image received from the back focal plane of the objectives to the oculars. The oculars re-focus the sample image to the viewer's eye. With a CMO stereomicroscope, the light interacts with the sample and is then collected by the common main objective. Light entering the objective is divergent light but once it leaves the objective it is parallel light, which is then split by a series of prisms redirecting the light to each of the oculars. The objective produces a sample image on its back focal plane. The oculars receive this sample image and re-focus it onto the viewer's eye. Most stereomicroscopes are CMO.

Magnification is the process by which lenses are used to make objects appear larger. A simple lens increases the refraction and in turn produces a virtual image that appears larger. Magnification of a simple lens is described by the equation:

$$M = \frac{25}{f} + 1 \qquad\qquad (1A\text{-}1)$$

where f is the focal length (the distance from a lens to its point of focus in centimeters), and 25 is the normal reading distance in centimeters.

Magnification of an image of a sample produced by a lens can be determined by the relationship:

$$\text{Magnification} = \frac{\text{height of image}}{\text{height of object}} = \frac{\text{image distance}}{\text{object distance}} \qquad (1A\text{-}2)$$

The portions of a microscope (oculars, objectives, etc.) that increase magnification usually have visible labeling noting the magnification power. To determine the combined magnification of a microscope, all magnification components must be taken into account. Total magnification is determined by multiplying all factors as shown in Equation (1A-3).

$$\text{Total magnification} = \text{ocular magnification} \times \text{objective magnification} \qquad (1A\text{-}3)$$

When using any microscope, the examiner must select the best magnification for viewing each sample. There are several factors that should be considered when determining magnification power. To start, it is important that sufficient detail can be viewed for the sample. In addition, when examining samples, a good microscopist always fills the viewing area to enhance detail but also to minimize white space. This often requires that the sample be viewed under a higher magnification. However, it is equally important to remember that when using high magnifications, a smaller portion of an overall sample is viewed. Field of view relates to that portion of the object that one is able to see when using the microscope. Field of view varies with magnification. A low power of magnification will provide the greatest field of view. Likewise, higher magnification restricts the field of view.

Depth of field is another factor to consider when choosing magnification. In photography if a lens focuses on a subject at a distance, all subjects at that distance are sharply focused. Subjects that are not at the same distance are out of focus and theoretically are not sharp. However, since human eyes cannot distinguish a very small degree of "unsharpness," some subjects that are in front of and behind the sharply focused subjects can still appear sharp. The zone of acceptable sharpness is referred to as the depth of field. Thus, increasing the depth of field increases the sharpness of an image. Just as in classical photography, depth of field is determined by the distance from the nearest object plane in focus to the farthest plane also simultaneously in focus. In microscopy, depth of field is very short and usually measured in units of microns. The term depth of field, which refers to object space, is often used interchangeably with depth of focus, which refers to image space. Once a focus has been obtained on a sample, areas lying slightly above and below will be blurred. The area or thickness of sample that remains in focus is the depth of field. Depth of field also varies with magnification.

The working distance of a stereomicroscope is another factor to bear in mind. The working distance is the distance between the objective lens and the sample. Stereomicroscopes generally have a large working distance and may also be placed on an adjustable stand, allowing for even more flexibility. The distance between the objective and the sample is determined by the focal length of the objective. To focus the sample, the distance is changed using the coarse focus for large increments and the fine focus for small changes in distance.

The stereomicroscope is a valuable tool in a forensic laboratory. The stereomicroscope combines low magnification, good depth of field, and a large working distance so that samples can be viewed three-dimensionally. These properties make it the "first instrument" used in many examinations.

Equipment and Supplies

Stereomicroscope

Micro kit

Samples:
Artificial Sweetener	Beard Hair
Black Pepper	Cigarette Ash
Cigarette Tobacco	Coffee
Glass	Graphite
Nutmeg	Oregano
Pencil Dust	Pencil Eraser Dust
Rosemary	Rust
Salt	Sand
Soap Powder	Soil
Tea	

Petri dish unknowns (various combinations of eight [8] samples from the Samples list)

Safety

Use standard laboratory safety procedures as described in guidelines set by your instructor.

Part I: Parts of a Stereomicroscope

1. Obtain a photograph of the stereomicroscope used in the laboratory.
2. Label the following parts of the microscope: light source, sample stage, objective(s), magnification knob, focusing knob, and oculars.

Part II: Operation of Stereomicroscope

Procedure

1. Familiarize yourself with the stereomicroscope. Locate each part of the stereomicroscope. Place a sample on the stage. After turning on the light source, manipulate the oculars of the stereomicroscope to adjust the interpupillary distance so that when viewing an object, the right and left eye images merge as one.
2. Adjust the focus up and down. Using the non-adjustable ocular, focus on a sample to obtain a clear image of the sample.
3. Focus the second ocular if necessary.
4. Try viewing the sample with both transmitted and reflected light (if both are available). What is the difference? _____
   _____
   _____

5. Adjust the magnification up and down to become familiar with the range of magnifications possible while looking at a metric ruler. Try to keep both eyes open.

6. Look at the side or the top of the oculars to determine the magnification factor of the ocular. An "X" usually follows the number designating the magnification power. Record the power here.

   Ocular lens power: _____

7. Look at the side of the low-power objective lens (for step-type objectives) or the zoom-controlling knob (for zoom objectives). The number designating the magnification power is usually a whole number followed by an "X" but can also be in fractions or may be a range of numbers when on a zoom control knob. Record the magnification of the low and repeat for high power.

   Low-power objective lens magnification: _____

   High-power objective lens magnification: _____

8. To calculate the magnification of the stereomicroscope, multiply the ocular lens power by the objective lens power according to Equation (1A-3). This will give you the total magnification of the stereomicroscope when using these two lens assemblies. Show the work below.

9. Total magnification of the stereomicroscope on low power: _____.

10. Total magnification of the stereomicroscope on high power: _____.

11. Now, place a metric ruler on the stage. Using the lowest magnification, look through the oculars (adjust the focus if necessary) and carefully move the ruler so that you are able to count the number of spaces it takes to view the entire field of view. Count or estimate any partial spaces also. This will give you the number of millimeters that equal the diameter of the field of view on low power.

    Diameter of the field of view: _____mm on low power

12. Repeat the measurement using the high-power objective:

    Diameter of the field of view: _____mm on high power

13. Using the lowest magnification, place a small piece of printed paper under the stereomicroscope. Make sure the section of paper has a letter "e" in it.

14. Use the focus adjustment to bring the letters into sharp focus. Adjust the printed section so that the "e" is in the center of the field of view.

15. Using the circle template located in Appendix E, make a drawing of the letter "e" on low and high power. Determine the magnification each time and record the total magnification. Try to fill the field of view when viewing under high power. Do you have greater field of view at high or low power?

16. Now, move the sample to the right, then toward you, and then away from you. Note the direction in which the "e" appears to move in respect to the original placement.

17. Next, examine samples of tea, cigarette tobacco, and cigarette ash under both low and high power. Try to distinguish features for each sample that can be used to identify that sample. Draw what you see for each sample under one of the magnifications (either low or high). Record the magnification. Do you have more depth of field at low or high power?

_____

18. Examine a dollar bill under low and high power on the stereomicroscope. At what magnification can you see more detail of the paper fibers? Are the fibers intertwined? What color fibers do you see? Draw what you see.

Part III: Trace Evidence Unknown

Procedure

Now use a stereomicroscope to examine an unknown sample, and determine the identity of the possible contents.

1. Examine the known samples, taking note of color, size, shape, texture, and any other characteristics that can be used to help identify that sample. Use the following worksheet or the circle templates in the appendix to describe or draw each sample.

    Artificial Sweetener _____
    Beard Hair   _____
    Black Pepper   _____
    Cigarette Ash   _____
    Cigarette Tobacco   _____
    Coffee   _____
    Glass   _____
    Graphite   _____
    Nutmeg   _____
    Oregano   _____
    Pencil Dust   _____
    Pencil Eraser Dust   _____
    Rosemary   _____
    Rust   _____
    Salt   _____
    Sand   _____
    Soap Powder   _____
    Soil   _____
    Tea   _____

2. Choose a petri dish containing an "unknown." Each dish contains a combination of eight samples.
3. Using the stereomicroscope, examine the unknown to determine which possible samples might be contained in the petri dish.

- -

Unknown number: _____

    1. _____   2. _____

    3. _____   4. _____

    5. _____   6. _____

    7. _____   8. _____

Report Requirements

Include all drawings, calculations, and other information obtained during the laboratory procedure. Notes and/or drawings should include the sample identification, magnification, and a complete description.

Report Questions

1. What are the five basic components of a stereomicroscope? What function does each component perform in the stereomicroscope?
2. Explain the optical light path utilized in a stereomicroscope.
3. What is the difference between a Common Main Objective and Greenough design stereomicroscope?
4. Name three types of forensic evidence that could be examined with a stereomicroscope. What would the examination consist of? (Hint: Would you use low- or high-power magnification?)
5. What are the two main benefits of using a stereomicroscope?
6. What are the limitations of a stereomicroscope?
7. Explain the correct way to set up and use a stereomicroscope.
8. Some stereomicroscopes have both reflected and transmitted light. Give an example of when you would use reflected light. Why?
9. Give an example of when you would use transmitted light. Why?
10. Using examples, define and explain the following terms: total magnification, field of view, depth of field, and working distance.
11. Calculate the magnification of a microscope that has an ocular lens magnification power of 10 and an objective lens magnification power of 4.
12. If using the microscope in the question above, when the objective is changed to 20X, what effect does this have on the field of view?
13. What effect does it have on the depth of field?

Recommended and Further Reading

Bradbury S. *An Introduction to the Optical Microscope*, rev. ed. Oxford: Oxford University Press and Royal Microscopical Society, 1989.

Chambers B. Today's Optical Techniques for Stereomicroscopes. *American Laboratory*. 2001; 33(8): 15–21.

De Forest PR. Foundations of Forensic Microscopy. In: Saferstein R, ed. *Forensic Science Handbook*, 2nd ed. Upper Saddle River, NJ: Pearson Education, 2002; 301–305.

Heath JP. *Dictionary of Microscopy*. Chichester, UK: John Wiley & Sons, Ltd, 2005.

Houck MM. *Mute Witnesses: Trace Evidence Analysis*. San Diego, CA: Academic Press, 2001.

Houck MM, Siegel JA. *Fundamentals of Forensic Science*, 3rd ed. Oxford: Elsevier Academic Press, 2015.

McCrone WC, McCrone LB, Delly JG. *Polarized Light Microscopy*, Ann Arbor, MI: Ann Arbor Science, 1997.

Saferstein R. *Criminalistics: An Introduction to Forensic Science*, 11th ed. Upper Saddle River, NJ: Pearson Education, 2015.

Walz M. Eye on Forensic Microscopy. *R&D Magazine*. 2005; 47(12): 33.

Chapter 2
Compound Light Microscope

Microscopes are used in many types of forensic examinations. The stereomicroscope discussed in Chapter 1 is used for lower magnification examinations, and the compound light microscope is generally used to obtain examinations under higher magnification.

Like the stereomicroscope, the compound light microscope uses a combination of lenses to produce a higher magnified image. To accomplish this, the compound light microscope has several components, which gather light and redirect the light path so that a magnified image of the viewed object can be focused within a very short distance. A compound light microscope has the following basic parts:

- light source
- condenser
- sample stage
- objective
- focusing knobs
- oculars

Basically, the light originates from the illuminator and is collimated by the condenser. The light then interacts with the sample on the sample stage, and is then collected by the objective. The objective re-focuses the image onto the back focal plane of the microscope. The oculars receive this image and re-focus it onto the viewer's eye.

Compound light microscopes offer higher magnification than a stereomicroscope, generally utilizing oculars and objectives that provide total magnification within the range of 40X to 400X. Because of the higher total magnification, a smaller field of view and less depth of field are obtained. Samples are viewed with transmitted light.

The compound light microscope is used to identify and characterize samples. The higher range of magnification allows viewing of the initial characteristics of an item or sample, with additional microscopic examinations and comparisons also possible. Further analysis of samples may also be performed with additional microscopes and/or instrumentation.

Practical Forensic Microscopy: A Laboratory Manual, Second Edition. Barbara P. Wheeler.
© 2021 John Wiley & Sons Ltd. Published 2021 by John Wiley & Sons Ltd.
Companion website: www.wiley.com/go/Wheeler/Forensic

Chapter 2

Experiment 2A: Familiarization with the Compound Light Microscope

Recommended pre-lab reading assignments:

Goldberg O. Kohler Illumination. *The Microscope*. 1980; 28: 15–21.
McCrone WC. Checklist for True Köhler Illumination. *American Laboratory*. 1980; 12(1): 96–98.
McCrone WC, McCrone LB, Delly JG. *Polarized Light Microscopy*. Ann Arbor, MI: Ann Arbor Science, 1978; 30–34.

Recommended website:

Parry-Hill MJ, Sutter RT, Davidson MW. Microscope Alignment for Kohler Illumination [Java Interactive Tutorial; cited 2020]. Available from: http://www.microscopyu.com.

Objective

Upon completion of this practical exercise, the student will have developed a basic understanding of:

1. components of a compound light microscope
2. use of the compound light microscope
3. numerical aperture
4. resolving power
5. centering objectives
6. proper techniques for setting up Köhler illumination

Practical Forensic Microscopy: A Laboratory Manual, Second Edition. Barbara P. Wheeler.
© 2021 John Wiley & Sons Ltd. Published 2021 by John Wiley & Sons Ltd.
Companion website: www.wiley.com/go/Wheeler/Forensic

Introduction

As with the stereomicroscope, a microscope is an optical instrument that uses a combination of lenses to produce a magnified image of small objects. To accomplish this, a compound light microscope utilizes several components that gather light and redirect the light path so that a magnified image of the viewed object can be focused within a short distance.

A compound light microscope has the following basic components: light source, condenser, sample stage, objective, focusing knobs, and oculars. There are two choices of illumination with the compound light microscope: transmitted or reflected light. If the sample is transparent, it can be observed with transmitted light. Most illuminators consist of a lightbulb (which may be centered and focused), a lens, and a diaphragm. Samples that are impervious to light use a specific type of reflected light, which will be discussed in Chapter 4. The main difference between a stereomicroscope and a compound light microscope is the presence of a substage condenser located directly below the sample stage (see Figure 2A-1). The substage condenser is a lens system that gathers the light from the illuminator, concentrating it so that the sample can be illuminated with uniform intensity. Stages can be either designed to rotate samples or equipped with a mechanical stage so that samples can be manipulated up and down as well as side-to-side. Most compound light microscopes are equipped with several objectives to provide a range of magnifications for viewing samples. The objective collects the light from the sample and magnifies the focused image to the oculars, which further magnifies and refocuses the image to the viewer's eye. Knobs are used to raise and lower the body of the microscope so that samples can be viewed in focus. These components are mounted in a well-designed base that lends itself to precision centering and alignment so that samples can be viewed with optimum magnification, resolution, and contrast.

The optics of a compound light microscope take advantage of two sets of conjugate planes. Conjugate planes are a set of planes at which a particular point is in focus in each plane. In a properly aligned and focused microscope, both illumination and image-forming planes are used. These are shown separately in Figure 2A-2; however, in a microscope, they are simultaneously in focus when observing a sample. The illuminating conjugate set consists of four aperture planes: lamp filament, condenser aperture, objective back focal plane, and the retina (see Figure 2A-2a). The orthoscopic image-forming conjugate set consists of four field planes: field diaphragm, sample plane, intermediate image plane, and retina (see Figure 2A-2b). The optical relationship between the conjugate planes is based on the fact that the illuminating ray wavefronts converge and are brought back into focus on the aperture planes, while the spherical waves of the image-forming ray converge into focused rays in the field planes. Focused light rays are nearly parallel when passing the image-forming planes. Because of this, when viewing a sample, the conjugate focal plane sets appear superimposed over another so that the light originates from the illuminator and is collimated by the condenser. The light then interacts with the sample and is then collected by the objective. The objective produces a real intermediate image onto the ocular front focal plane of the microscope. The oculars receive this image, magnify it, then re-focus it onto the viewer's eye.

The compound light microscope is used in various forensic applications. Generally, thin samples are prepared so that light is transmitted through the sample, allowing the image to be focused on the objective and then passed to the oculars. This microscope is generally utilized with total magnifications in the range of 40X to 400X power. Since there is only one light path in a compound light microscope, it produces a two-dimensional image. However, with greater magnification and resolution, the compound light microscope allows the image to be easily

Figure 2A-1 The LOMO™ compound light microscope is capable of providing a variety of magnification powers for viewing samples.

focused in successive planes so that a complete examination can be accomplished. This allows an examiner to learn morphological information about a sample. Both the visual appearance and the sample's internal construction can be examined because of the higher magnifications possible with the compound light microscope. Of similar importance is the ability to obtain analytical information. Classifying characteristics, such as colors and thickness, aids in the identification of unknown samples.

Several factors come into play when using a compound light microscope. Numerical aperture is a numerical measure of the ability of a lens or an objective to gather light and resolve fine sample detail at a fixed distance. Numerical aperture is related to the angular aperture by the following formula:

$$NA = n \ \sin \frac{AA}{2} \tag{2A-1}$$

where:

NA is the numerical aperture
n is the refractive index of the space between the cover slip and objective

Illumination path   **Image-forming path**

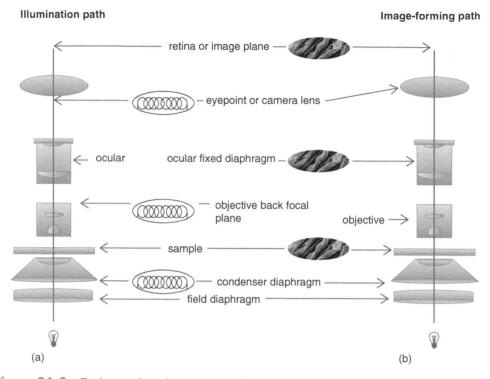

Figure 2A-2 Conjugate planes in a compound light microscope. Illumination planes (a) occur at the lamp filament, condenser diaphragm, objective back focal plane, and the eyepoint. Image-forming planes (b) occur at the field diaphragm, sample, ocular fixed diaphragm, and the retina of the eye.

AA is the angular aperture (the angle formed by the outermost rays of light that can be collected by the lens).

Lenses of short focal length (higher magnification) have greater angular aperture, which allows for the greatest angle for image-forming rays. This, in turn, relates to the microscope's resolution; therefore, the higher the NA, the greater the resolving power. Resolution is the smallest distance between two points on a sample that can still be distinguished as two separate entities. Resolution is a somewhat subjective value in microscopy, because at high magnification an image may appear unsharp but still be resolved to the maximum ability of the objective. Numerical aperture determines the resolving power of an objective, but the total resolution of a microscope system is also dependent upon the numerical aperture of the total system: condenser and objectives. The higher the numerical aperture of the total system, the better the resolution.

Magnification and good resolving power are important for good microscopy. While the optics on a microscope may be suitable, correct illumination is critical. Illumination should be evenly distributed over the entire viewing field, but also allow control of intensity, size of the illuminated field, and the angular aperture of the illuminating cone. The substage aperture diaphragm is used to control the light intensity and to obtain the best compromise between resolution and contrast. Neutral-density filters and a variable-voltage transformer on the light source can also control the light intensity; however, the latter method also affects the color of the light. The field diaphragm can control the size of the light field, and the substage iris can control the angular aperture.

Illumination is generally accomplished using one of three techniques: Nelsonian, Köhler, or diffuse. Most forensic laboratories utilize Köhler or modified Köhler illumination. This technique is based upon the positioning and alignment of various optical components in the microscope, such as the lamp condenser, substage condenser, objective, ocular, and light source, to produce two sets of image-forming planes. One image plane is observed orthoscopically (no Bertrand lens) and the other conoscopically (with the Bertrand lens). In the first, the conjugate planes in good focus and centered on the microscope axis are the field diaphragm, sample plane, intermediate image plane, and retina. In the conoscopic imaging, the conjugate planes in good focus and centered on the microscope axis are the lamp filament, substage aperture diaphragm, objective back focal plane, ocular focal plane, and retina. Many modern microscopes are equipped with ground-glass diffusers, allowing modified Köhler illumination. Köhler and modified Köhler illumination produce illumination that is uniformly bright and free from glare, which allows the examiner to utilize the microscope's full potential.

The compound microscope is another valuable tool in a forensic laboratory. The range of magnification powers provided by the compound microscope allows for samples to be viewed with greater detail. This property makes the microscope useful for many small-particle examinations.

Equipment and Supplies

Compound light microscope with objectives of various magnifications (e.g., 4X, 10X, 20X, and 40X)

McCrone Particle Reference Set™ (or something comparable)

This is a general reference set. It includes 100 prepared slides of the most commonly found particles, each mounted in Meltmount 1.662.

Safety

Use standard laboratory safety procedures as described in guidelines set by your instructor. Be cautious of microscope light levels to avoid eye damage.

Part I: Parts of the Compound Microscope

1. Obtain a photograph of the compound light microscope used in the laboratory.
2. Label the following parts of the microscope: light source, condenser, sample stage, objectives, field diaphragm, field diaphragm centering screws, field diaphragm focus knob, lamp aperture, focusing knobs, and oculars.

Part II: Operation of the Compound Microscope

Procedure

1. Familiarize yourself with the compound light microscope. Locate each part of the microscope. Place a prepared microscope slide on the stage. After turning on the light source,

manipulate the oculars of the microscope to adjust the interpupillary distance so that when viewing an object, the right and left images merge as one.

2. Adjust the focus up and down. Using the non-adjustable ocular, focus on a sample to obtain a clear image of the sample.

3. Focus the second ocular if necessary.

4. Adjust the magnification up and down to become familiar with the range of magnifications possible while looking at a prepared microscope slide from the McCrone Particle Reference Set. Try to keep both eyes open.

5. Calculate the total magnification for the microscope at low and high power.
Total magnification at low power: _____
Total magnification at high power: _____

Part III: Centering the Objectives

Procedure

1. Place a previously mounted sample from the McCrone Particle Reference Set (one with granular-shaped particles is best) on the microscope stage, and focus using the lowest power objective.

2. Place the mounted sample so that one particle is located in the center of the field of view (on the crosshairs).

3. Rotate the stage. The particle should stay essentially in the same spot. If it moves greatly or completely out of view, the objective requires centering.

4. To center the objective, rotate the particle again, paying special attention to the "path" of the particle as the stage is rotated. Note when the particle is at the greatest distance from the center of the field of view. Rotate the sample so the particle is now in that location.

5. Move the location of the viewed particle, by adjusting the centering screws located on the objective, until the particle is about halfway from its original location to the center of the field of view (on the crosshairs).

6. To check the newly aligned objective centering, move the mounted sample slide so that the particle is in the center of the field of view (on the crosshairs). Rotate the stage and note the "path" of the particle. Continue with steps 4 and 5 until the particle stays centered when rotating the stage.

7. Continue to center all the objectives on the microscope.

Part IV: Setting Up Köhler Illumination

Procedure

1. Place a previously mounted sample from the McCrone Particle Reference Set on the microscope stage, and focus using the 10X objective.

2. Close down the field diaphragm. The edges of the diaphragm will become multi-sided. Adjust the substage condenser, using the condenser focus knob, so that the edges are crisp and in focus.

3. Center the field diaphragm by adjusting the centering screws of the substage condenser.

4. Open the field diaphragm until it is just out of the field of view.

5. If the microscope has a ground-glass diffuser, you are finished setting up modified Köhler; proceed to step 6. If there is no diffuser or it can be removed, continue with the following steps.
   a. Insert the Bertrand lens. If there is no Bertrand lens, remove one ocular. This allows for viewing the image of the lamp filament.
   b. Focus and center the lamp filament by using the adjustment knobs and moving it back and forth.
   c. Remove the Bertrand lens (or replace the ocular). Focus on the sample.
6. Adjust the contrast and resolution by setting the substage condenser aperture to optimum appearance. Normally, this is approximately 70–80% open.
7. Köhler illumination should be checked with each sample.

Part V: Viewing Samples with the Compound Light Microscope

Procedure

1. From the McCrone Particle Reference Set, view and draw five of the following: diatoms, moth scales, seed hairs, insect parts, straw, cotton, table salt, and sawdust. Use various magnifications to become familiar with the microscope. Make sure to select magnifications that minimize the white space but allow you to view a significant portion of the sample.

Report Requirements

Include all drawings, calculations, and other information obtained during the laboratory procedure. Notes and/or drawings should include the sample identification, magnification, and a complete description.

Report Questions

1. What are the six basic components of a compound microscope? What function does each component perform in a compound microscope?
2. Explain the illuminating ray path utilized in a compound light microscope.
3. Explain the imaging ray path utilized in a compound light microscope.
4. Name three types of evidence that could be examined with a compound microscope. What would an examination consist of?
5. What types of evidence would not be examined with the compound microscope? Why?
6. What are the two main benefits of using a compound microscope?
7. What is numerical aperture? Why is this an important factor to take into consideration when purchasing a microscope?
8. Why is it necessary to center objectives? How is this done?
9. Describe Köhler illumination. Why is this technique used for most forensic microscopy work over Nelsonian or diffuse illumination?
10. How is Köhler illumination set up on a microscope? What determines whether true Köhler illumination or modified Köhler illumination has been set up?

Chapter 2

Experiment 2B: Measurements Using the Ocular Micrometer

> **Recommended pre-lab reading assignment:**
>
> McCrone WC, McCrone LB, Delly JG. *Polarized Light Microscopy*. Ann Arbor, MI: Ann Arbor Science, 1978; 96–99.
>
> **Recommended website:**
>
> Parry-Hill MJ, Fellars TJ, Davidson MW. Eyepiece Reticle Calibration [Java Interactive Tutorial; cited 2020]. Available from: http://www.microscopyu.com.

Objective

Upon completion of this practical exercise, the student will have developed a basic understanding of:

1. calibration of the ocular micrometer scale
2. measurements with the ocular micrometer scale

Introduction

The measurement of a sample size can also be an important portion of an examination. Very small linear distances can be measured accurately with a microscope. To determine the sample size, a specialized ocular is used. This ocular has a transparent scale graticule in the ocular that is superimposed onto the image being observed. This scale is arbitrary and so must be calibrated for each objective. Calibration requires a stage scale micrometer. While there are many types of stage scale micrometers, the most common is one that reads 0.01 mm per stage scale division.

Practical Forensic Microscopy: A Laboratory Manual, Second Edition. Barbara P. Wheeler.
© 2021 John Wiley & Sons Ltd. Published 2021 by John Wiley & Sons Ltd.
Companion website: www.wiley.com/go/Wheeler/Forensic

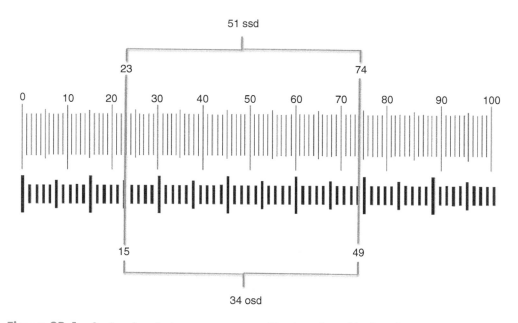

Figure 2B-1   Ocular view during measurement calibration of an objective. Counting the ocular and stage scale divisions between an aligned overlap area can be used to determine the calibration factor for each objective. This example shows 51 stage scale divisions per 34 ocular scale divisions.

The unit of length used for measurements obtained on the microscope is the micrometer (μm), so in this case each stage scale division equals 10 μm.

To calibrate the ocular scale, the stage scale is placed on the stage in a manner so that the scales are slightly offset from one another. Align the stage scale of the micrometer with the ocular scale so that there are two division lines that line up. This is illustrated in Figure 2B-1. The number of divisions between these two lines is then counted for both the stage scale (ssd) and ocular scale (osd). For accuracy purposes, it is best to choose two division lines far apart from one another. Since the stage scale is measured in millimeters (mm), this value must be converted to micrometers. This is done by multiplying the number of counted divisions by the factor as marked on the stage scale. In Figure 2B-1 there are 51 ssd between the lines 23 and 74. The number of micrometers is then calculated by using the following equation:

$$\text{ssd} \times \frac{10\,\mu\text{m}}{1\,\text{ssd}} = \text{ssd}\,\mu\text{m} \tag{2B-1}$$

So, for this example, when there are 51 stage scale divisions:

$$51\,\text{ssd} \times \frac{10\,\mu\text{m}}{1\,\text{ssd}} = 510\,\mu\text{m}$$

The calibration factor for the ocular scale is then determined by dividing the number of stage scale micrometers by the number of ocular scale divisions according to the following equation:

$$\text{calibration factor} = \frac{\text{ssd}\,\mu\text{m}}{\text{osd}} \tag{2B-2}$$

So, for this example, with 51 stage divisions and 34 ocular divisions:

$$\text{calibration factor} = \frac{510\,\mu\text{m}}{34\,\text{osd}} = 15.0\frac{\mu\text{m}}{\text{osd}}$$

When this ocular scale is used with this objective, each division of the ocular scale is equivalent to 15.0 μm. Accurate measurements of samples can now be obtained. For example, a particle observed with this objective and measuring 8.5 osd is 8.5×15.0 μm/osd or 127.5 μm in diameter.

The calibration factor obtained only applies to this calibrated objective. If there is a change in objective magnification, tube length, or any other part of the magnification system of the microscope, the ocular scale must be recalibrated.

The accuracy of the measurement depends on recognition of the edge of the particle when observing an image that may be slightly out of focus, and certainly involves errors introduced by the kind and quality of illumination as well as errors involved in the optical system itself. Even the refractive index of the mounting medium relative to the refractive index of the particle being measured has an effect on the apparent size. In all cases, the error will be minimized if the magnification of the optical system is sufficient to image the particle over at least ten ocular scale divisions. At worst, under these conditions, the edge of the particle can be measured accurately to within ± 0.25 divisions. Hence the overall error in measurement considering two sides of the particle could be ± 0.5 division, or 10%, for a ten-division particle. The error depends, of course, on the size and increases rapidly as the size decreases to the 1 μm range. The practical lower limit of accurate particle size measurement with the light microscope is about 0.5 μm.

Since various dimensions can be identified for many samples, it is a useful characteristic for small-particle examinations. When using the compound light microscope to determine measurements, it becomes another valuable tool in a forensic laboratory.

Equipment and Supplies

Compound light microscope with objectives of various magnifications (e.g., 4X, 10X, 20X, 40X, and focusing ocular with micrometer scale)

Stage micrometer; typically marked with 0.01 mm scale

McCrone Particle Reference Set™

Safety

Use standard laboratory safety procedures as described in guidelines set by your instructor. Be cautious of microscope light levels to avoid eye damage.

Part I: Calibration of the Ocular Micrometer

Procedure

1. After turning on the light source, adjust the microscope to obtain Köhler illumination.
2. Using the lowest magnification, place a stage micrometer on the microscope stage and bring the scale into focus.
3. Rotate to the objective that you have been assigned to calibrate, and re-focus on the stage micrometer.
4. Adjust the focus of the ocular micrometer so that both micrometer scales can now be visualized.

5. Line up the stage and ocular micrometer scales so that they are slightly offset. This makes it easier to read the values.
6. Select two locations on each scale that line up. It is best to choose one location on the east side of the field of view and one on the west side of the field of view.
7. Count the number of divisions of the stage scale (ssd) between the two lined-up divisions.
8. Next, count the number of ocular scale divisions (osd), which equals the same area for the stage scale divisions counted in step 7.
9. Calculate the number of micrometers for the stage scale. Remember: Most stage micrometers have a 1-millimeter-long scale subdivided into 100 divisions, which makes each division 0.01 mm or 10 μm.
10. Using Equation (2B-2), insert the values obtained for the ssd and osd. Calculate the calibration factor for the ocular scale divisions for that objective.
11. Repeat steps 3–10 to calibrate the ocular micrometer for the second objective you have been assigned. Record the objective magnification and the calibration factors in Table 2B-1.

Part II: Measurements Using the Calibrated Ocular Micrometer Scale

Procedure

You will now use the calibrated ocular scale to determine the diameter of a fiber.

1. You should now have an ocular scale calibration for two objectives. Measurements will be taken of the fiber diameter of a prepared slide of Dacron™ polyester from the McCrone Particle Reference Set, using each of the objectives.
2. Using the first calibrated objective, measure the diameter of the fiber in osd. Take four readings to the nearest 0.1 osd along the length of the fiber. Sharpen the focus to get good edge definition. Convert the osd to micrometers by multiplying by the appropriate calibration factor. Complete this portion for the first objective in Table 2B-1.

Table 2B-1 Calibration of two objectives and measurement of fiber diameter.

	Calibration Factor μm/osd	Ocular Scale Readings	Average × Calibration Factor = μm
Example		3.1 osd	
		3.3 osd	3.25 × 12.4 μm/osd =
4X	12.4 μm/osd	3.4 osd	40.3 μm
		3.2 osd	
		Avg = 3.25 osd	
Objective 1:			
Objective 2:			

3. Repeat this measurement with the second objective you calibrated. Complete Table 2B-1. Did you obtain the same diameter?
4. Select an objective and magnification that provide maximum detail. This does not have to be an objective you have calibrated. Draw what you see.

Report Requirements

Include all drawings, calculations, and other information obtained during the laboratory procedure. Notes and/or drawings should include the sample identification, magnification, and a complete description.

Report Questions

1. What is a stage micrometer? How is it used?
2. What is an ocular micrometer? How is it used?
3. Why is it necessary to determine the calibration factor for each objective?
4. If a calibration factor were found to be 17.3 µm/osd for a 10X objective, what would you estimate the calibration factor to be for a 20X objective?
5. If the stage scale had a label that said 0.05 mm per stage scale divisions and there were 17 ssd equivalent to 41 osd, what would the calibration factor be in µm/osd? If a pollen particle had a diameter of 2 osd, what would this be in micrometers? Show calculations.
6. Report your calibration factor for each objective from Part I. Make a label for the microscope you used to be placed on the base of the microscope. You will continue to use these calibration factors for future measurements.

Chapter 2

Experiment 2C: Microscopic Mounting Techniques

> **Recommended pre-lab reading assignments:**
>
> Cook R, Norton D. An Evaluation of Mounting Media for Use in Forensic Textile Fibre Examinations. *Journal of Forensic Sciences Society*. 1982; 22(1): 57–63.
>
> Grieve MC, Deck S. A New Mounting Medium for the Forensic Microscopy of Textile Fibers. *Science and Justice*. 1995; 35(2): 109–112.
>
> Loveland RP, Centifano YM. Mounting Media for Microscopy. *The Microscope*. 1986; (34): 181–242.
>
> Roe GM, Cook R, North C. An Evaluation of Mountants for Use in Forensic Hair Examinations. *Journal of Forensic Sciences Society*. 1991; 31: 59–65.

Objective

Upon completion of this practical exercise, the student will have developed a basic understanding of:

1. preparing dry mounts
2. preparing scale casts
3. preparing wet mounts (oils, semi-permanent and permanent mediums)

Introduction

In order to view samples with a compound microscope, samples must be mounted on a microscope slide. In a forensic laboratory, there are three general techniques used for mounting samples that are to be examined: dry mounts, scale casts, and wet mounts. The choice of the mounting technique is dependent on the sample.

Practical Forensic Microscopy: A Laboratory Manual, Second Edition. Barbara P. Wheeler.
© 2021 John Wiley & Sons Ltd. Published 2021 by John Wiley & Sons Ltd.
Companion website: www.wiley.com/go/Wheeler/Forensic

While scale casts and some dry mounts are viewed without a cover slip, wet mounts require the use of a cover slip. The cover slip is an important component of sample preparation and serves three purposes: (1) It protects the microscope's objective lens from contacting the specimen, (2) it creates an even thickness in wet mounts, and (3) it confines the specimen to a single plane and thereby reduces the amount of focusing necessary. Glass cover slips should be handled carefully as they are very fragile and break easily. Cover slips can be round, square, or rectangular and are available in two thicknesses: No. 1 and No. 2. No. 1 cover slips are 0.13–0.17 mm thick and are recommended for oil immersion; No. 2 cover slips are 0.17–0.25 mm thick and are used for general applications.

Dry mounting is the oldest mounting method and, as its name suggests, the sample is dry and mounted in air with or without a cover slip applied. Because dry-mounted samples are temporary, do not preserve the sample, and do not allow control of the refractive index of the mounting medium, they are not commonly used in forensic settings. Occasionally they are used to observe the external features of a sample, such as the color of fibers and hair. This can be performed with a stereomicroscope on large samples (as performed in earlier labs) or by viewing samples with a compound light microscope. Samples are placed directly on a microscope slide with or without a cover slip. Since a compound microscope uses transmitted light, the viewed dry mount sample must be transparent enough to allow light to pass when mounted on a microscope slide if both external and internal features are to be observed.

A scale cast mount can also be used to examine some external features of a sample. This mounting technique is commonly used to examine the cuticle scale pattern of animal hair. This technique is different than a dry mount, in the fact that the features are observed from a "cast" made of the sample, not from the sample itself. Since a clear substance is used to create the "cast" of the sample, the external features can be viewed using a compound microscope and transmitted light.

Most forensic samples are viewed with a compound microscope to determine their internal features or microscopic characteristics. This is performed on a compound microscope using transmitted light and wet microscope mounts. A mounting medium is a medium or solution into which the sample is placed. A variety of mounting mediums are available for microscopic use (see Table 2C-1). Samples are placed in mounting medium that has been positioned on a microscope slide. The sample is then covered with a cover slip. This helps to reduce the refraction of the light as it passes from air through the sample and back through air to reach the lenses of the microscope. This also allows for the best viewing of the internal features or microscopic characteristics of a sample. The degree to which the microscopic characteristics of a sample may be viewed depends on the actual mounting medium. A colorless transparent sample is visible because the light rays are refracted and reflected at the interface between the sample and the medium. However, if the colorless sample and medium are the same refractive index (RI), then the sample is invisible. The degree to which a transparent sample is visible is called relief. The greater the difference in the refractive index, the greater the relief.

Relief can be assigned to a particular sample mounting in terms of zero, low, medium, or high relief. Samples that are placed in a mounting medium that is the same RI as the sample will show zero relief, and will be invisible. Likewise, samples that are placed in a mounting medium that has a large difference in refractive index from the sample will show high relief. To view external features, it is best to use a mounting medium that has a different RI than that of the sample. However, excessive relief or contrast may obscure the internal features or microscopic characteristics. To view internal features, use a mounting medium with a refractive index near, but not the same as, the RI of the sample.

Table 2C-1   Common mounting mediums used for wet mounts.

Mounting medium	Refractive index
Water	1.33
Glycerol	1.46
Protex™	1.478
XAM™, neutral medium, improved white	1.491
Flo-texx™	1.495
Permount™	1.52
DPX™	1.5240
Canada balsam	1.5250
Cargille™ oils (numerous oils)	1.470–1.700
Norland™ (numerous mediums)	
65	1.524
68	1.54
MeltMount™ (numerous mediums)	
1.539	1.539
1.582	1.582
1.605	1.605
1.680	1.680

Equipment and Supplies

Compound light microscope with objectives of various magnifications (e.g., 4X, 10X, 20X, 40X, and focusing ocular with micrometer scale)

Micro kit

Fiber samples for mounting, such as acetate, nylon, rayon, silk, polyester, or cotton

Hair samples for mounting, such as various animal and human hairs

Various mounting mediums

Safety

Use standard laboratory safety procedures as described in guidelines set by your instructor. Be cautious of microscope light levels to avoid eye damage. Know the hazards associated with the mounting mediums, and use them with appropriate precautions as set by your instructor. Dispose of glass in an appropriate container.

Part I: Making Dry Mounts

Procedure

1. Label a microscope slide with identifying marks such as analyst initials, sample information, and date.
2. Using tweezers, position the sample on the microscope slide.
3. Place a cover slip over the sample.
4. Observe the sample. Note: If the sample is large, the cover slip will not remain horizontal and a wet mount should be made.
5. Repeat steps 1–3 for the assigned samples.

Part II: Making Scale Casts

Procedure

1. Label a microscope slide with identifying marks such as analyst initials, sample information, and date.
2. Apply a thin coating of clear nail polish.
3. While still wet, position a hair in the nail polish.
4. Let the nail polish dry completely.
5. Gently remove the sample to obtain the scale cast.
6. Observe the cuticle scale pattern of the hair.
7. Repeat steps 1–5 for the assigned samples.

Part III: Making Liquid Mounts: Semi-Permanent and Permanent Mounting Mediums

Procedure

1. Label a microscope slide with identifying marks such as analyst initials, sample information, and date.
2. Using an appropriate mounting medium from Table 2C-1, apply sufficient mounting medium to slide (see Figure 2C-1).
3. Using tweezers, position the sample on the microscope slide in the mounting medium. Note: For some samples, it may be easier to first position the sample and then add the mounting medium.
4. If additional mounting medium is needed, it may be added now (or along the edge of the cover slip after the cover slip is applied).
5. Gently apply the cover slip to even out the mounting medium. The procedure that best prevents the formation of bubbles is to position the cover slip so that it touches on one end of the microscope slide and then is allowed to gently fall over the mounting medium and sample, as shown in Figure 2C-1c and 2C-1d.
6. If bubbles form in the preparation, it may be possible to work them out by applying gentle pressure to the cover slip. Slight bumping of the slide may also encourage bubbles to move

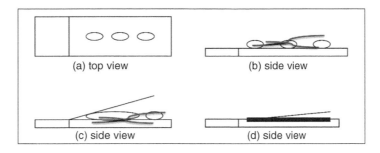

Figure 2C-1 Procedure for preparing liquid mounts. (a) Drops of mounting medium are distributed on slide. (b) Sample is added to mounting medium. (c) A cover slip is positioned above slide so that it is only touching on one side, and (d) the cover slip is allowed to gently fall over the mounting medium and sample.

to the edge. However, a sample preparation may still be usable if the bubbles occur away from the sample. It is essential that the sample be submerged in the mounting medium at all locations. If the bubbles prevent this, the sample may need to be mounted again.

7. Repeat steps 1–6 for the assigned samples, using different mounting mediums.

EXTRA CREDIT: What is the refractive index of the mounting medium used? What is the refractive index of the sample? Describe the relief viewed for the mounted samples. Is the relief observed what you would expect? Explain your answer.

Chapter 2

Experiment 2D: Determining Refractive Index

Recommended pre-lab reading assignments:

Koons RD, Buscaglia J, Bottrell M, Miller ET. Forensic Glass Comparisons. In: Saferstein R, ed. *Forensic Science Handbook*, 2nd ed. Upper Saddle River, NJ: Pearson Education, 2002; 188–189.

De Forest PR. Foundations of Forensic Microscopy. In: Saferstein R, ed. *Forensic Science Handbook*, 2nd ed. Upper Saddle River, NJ: Pearson Education, 2002; 301–305.

McCrone WC, McCrone LB, Delly JG. *Polarized Light Microscopy*. Ann Arbor, MI: Ann Arbor Science, 1978; 169–196.

Recommended websites:

Parry-Hill MJ, Sutter RT, Fellers TJ, Davidson MW. Refraction of Light [Java Interactive Tutorial; cited 2020]. Available from: http://www.olympusmicro.com.

Davidson MW. Refractive Index [Java Interactive Tutorial; cited 2020]. Available from: http://www.microscopyu.com.

Objective

Upon completion of this practical exercise, the student will have developed a basic understanding of:

1. refractive index
2. immersion oils
3. Abbe refractometer
4. dispersion staining
5. use of the compound light microscope to determine refractive index

Practical Forensic Microscopy: A Laboratory Manual, Second Edition. Barbara P. Wheeler.
© 2021 John Wiley & Sons Ltd. Published 2021 by John Wiley & Sons Ltd.
Companion website: www.wiley.com/go/Wheeler/Forensic

Introduction

Several interactions can occur when light falls upon matter. The first is that the light may simply bounce or reflect off of the matter with no other interaction. The manner in which it reflects is dependent on the sample's surface. Light that strikes a smooth surface and is reflected according to the "Law of Reflection" is referred to as specular reflection. Light that strikes a rough surface is reflected in random directions, and is referred to as diffuse reflection.

Light may also interact with matter. The interaction of light will be dependent on the specific nature of the material. When light strikes a transparent object, the light will continue to move through the material. An example of this is when light traveling through air strikes glass (see Figure 2D-1). Light will continue to pass through the glass; however, the direction of the light will change. This change in direction is called refraction. Refraction results from a change in the speed of light as it passes from one medium to another. Materials will refract light in differing degrees. The angle of refracted light is dependent upon both the angle of incidence and the material into which it is entering. We can define the normal as a line perpendicular to the boundary between two substances. Light will pass into the boundary at an angle to the normal and will be refracted according to Snell's Law:

$$\frac{\sin i}{\sin r} = \frac{n_2}{n_1} \tag{2D-1}$$

where n represents the refractive indices of material 1 and material 2, i is the angle of incident light with respect to the normal, and r is the angle of refracted light with respect to normal.

When light moves from one material to another with a slower speed of light, the light will be refracted or bent toward the normal. Likewise, when light moves from one material to another with a faster speed of light, the light will be refracted or bent away from the normal. When the two refractive indices are equal ($n_1 = n_2$), then the light is passed through without refraction.

As discussed, refraction occurs as light passes from one medium to another when there is a difference in the speed of light between the two materials. This can be described by a dimensionless number that describes how the light propagates through that medium called refractive index. Refractive index is defined as the relative speed at which light moves through material with respect to its speed in a vacuum. The refractive index of a vacuum is defined as having a value of 1.0. The index of refraction, n, of other transparent materials is defined through this equation:

$$n = \frac{c}{V_m} \tag{2D-2}$$

where c is the speed of light, and V_m is the velocity of light in that material.

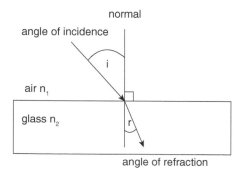

Figure 2D-1   Refraction occurs when light enters a medium with a different refractive index.

Because the refractive index of a vacuum is defined as 1.0 and a vacuum is devoid of any material, the refractive indices of all transparent materials are therefore greater than 1.0. For most practical purposes, the refractive index of light through air (1.0003) can be used to calculate refractive indices of unknown materials. Since light always travels faster in air than in any other medium (except a vacuum), n is always greater than one.

These refraction principles can be applied to forensic examinations. For instance, determining the refractive index for glass particles is one characteristic used in the comparison of glass samples. When a transparent object such as a glass chip is immersed in a mounting medium and viewed under a microscope, it is observed as having a light or colored boundary, a sort of "halo." This halo appears because of the internal reflection created at the boundary of the two mediums (glass and mounting medium), and it is called the Becke line. The intensity of this visible boundary around the glass depends on the difference in refractive index between the glass and the mounting medium. The greater the difference between the refractive index of a glass and that of the mounting medium, the more distinct the Becke line will appear. As the refractive indices of the glass and mounting medium approach equality, the Becke line will begin to disappear. If the refractive indices of a colorless glass and the mounting medium are equal, the glass may become practically invisible in monochromatic light. However, in this experiment, fragments rarely disappear because of a principle known as dispersion of refractive index. The dispersion of refractive index is a measure of the variation in refractive index with the wavelength of light. Because of this, refractive index measurements are typically recorded at sodium's D line (n_D, 589 nm, yellow), and hydrogen's C line (n_C, 656 nm, red) and F line (n_F, 486 nm, blue). The dispersion of refractive index, v, can be calculated by using:

$$v = \frac{n_D - 1}{n_F - n_C} \tag{2D-3}$$

where n_D is the refractive index at 589 nm, n_F is the refractive index at 486 nm, and n_C is the refractive index at 656 nm. The dispersion of refractive index can also be analyzed graphically, as described further here. The dispersion of a particle's refractive indices has evidentiary value since it is possible for particles with different compositions to have matching refractive indices at one wavelength but different refractive indices at other wavelengths. In this experiment, the glass particles will rarely disappear since we are using white light, light that contains all wavelengths. Experiment 19A explains the measurement of refractive index using monochromatic light to calculate the dispersion of refractive index.

An important advantage of the Becke line is not merely the fact that it indicates a difference between the refractive indices of the glass and mounting medium, but also that it indicates which medium possesses the higher value. Because of this phenomenon, it can be used with immersion oils of known refractive indices to determine the refractive indices of the sample. As the working distance is increased on a compound microscope, the Becke line will move toward the medium with the higher refractive indices. Likewise, as the working distance is decreased, the Becke line will move toward the lower refractive indices. This allows an examiner to select a series of mounting mediums to determine the refractive indices of a sample. There are a variety of immersion liquids that can be utilized for refractive index determinations. In forensic examinations, Cargille™ oils are commonly used because of their low volatility and chemically stable nature. They are commercially available with a variety of oils offered so that a wide range of refractive indices is possible. At times, it may become necessary to mix oils. To determine the actual refractive index of the oil mixture, an Abbe refractometer can be utilized.

Another method of determining refractive indices is through the use of a focal screening. This method takes advantage of the same phenomenon as the Becke line but uses a specialized

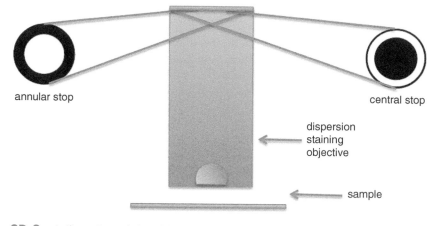

Figure 2D-2   A dispersion staining objective contains an outer stop called the annular stop and an inner stop called the central stop.

objective. When using immersion oils, a forensic scientist examines the entire cone of light. With the dispersion staining objective, portions of the light cone can be examined separately (see Figure 2D-2). The dispersion staining objective consists of a standard objective that has been modified with several positions. This allows a forensic scientist to choose a position that permits viewing of light coming from the center of the particle (annular) or another position that permits viewing of light from the outer edge of the particle (central). A final position is also included that contains a full aperture so that it can be used as an ordinary objective.

When the refractive indices of the mounting medium and sample are close, the edge of the sample acts as a dispersion prism and separates the white light into its color components. By viewing the light from the outer and inner parts of the sample separately, it is possible to determine the degree of dispersion of a given sample and also to determine the wavelength of light at which the particle's and mounting medium's refractive indices are the same. Table 2D-1 contains colors used to determine matching wavelengths for the annular and central stops.

After acquiring data using several oils, data points can be plotted on a Hartmann dispersion graph. Dispersion graphs, which plot refractive index versus wavelength for many compounds, exist in book form. The Becke line immersion method used with white light gives only a relative refractive index, whereas the dispersion staining technique can give a true refractive index for a given wavelength of light (e.g., n_D, n_F, or n_C).

Because density changes in condensed materials with changes in temperature, refractive index varies with temperature. To report a refractive index at a specific temperature, if temperature control is not possible, a temperature correction must be applied. The change per degree centigrade, $-dn/dT$, is called the temperature coefficient of refractive index. The commercially available Cargille refractive index liquids have their $-dn/dT$ marked on each bottle. Refractive index is commonly reported at 25°C; however, the immersion measurements may take place at room temperature, usually 23°C. To perform a temperature correction, the following formula would be applied:

$$n^{25} = n^{23} - (25 - 23)\frac{dn}{dT} \tag{2D-4}$$

Table 2D-1 Dispersion staining colors.

Matching λ (nm)	Annular position	Central position	
		in focus	Becke line
<420	blue-black	light yellow	faint gold + violet
430	blue-violet	yellow	faint gold + violet
455	blue	golden yellow	faint gold + violet
485	blue-green	golden magenta	yellow + violet
520	green	red-magenta	violet + orange
560	yellow-green	magenta	blue-violet + red-orange
595	yellow	blue-magenta	blue + red
625	orange	blue	blue
660	orange-red	blue-green	green
>680	brown-red	pale blue	pale green

Source: McCrone WC, McCrone LB, Delly JB. *Polarized Light Microscopy*. Ann Arbor, MI: Ann Arbor Science, 1978. Reproduced with permission from McCrone Associates, Inc.

where n^{25} is the index of refraction at 25°C; n^{23} is the index of refraction obtained at the measurement temperature of 23°C; and $-dn/dT$ is the temperature coefficient of refractive index for the liquid, which is found on the immersion oil bottle. Since temperature and refractive index are inversely related, it is important to check your answer using the rule that as temperature increases, refractive index decreases and vice versa.

Since refractive indices can be identified for various samples, it is useful for many small-particle examinations. When using the compound light microscope to determine refractive index, it becomes another valuable tool in a forensic laboratory.

Equipment and Supplies

Compound light microscope with objectives of various magnifications (e.g., 4X, 10X, 20X, 40X, and a dispersion staining objective)

Micro kit

Glass particles of known refractive indices

Unknown glass particles

Cargille™ refractive index liquid-mounting set (which would contain oils in the range of glass samples, 1.45–1.80)

Clove Oil and Olive Oil mixtures

Fifteen solutions of various refractive indices are made by mixing clove oil (refractive index: 1.5430) and olive oil (refractive index: 1.4667). Place these liquids in small labeled dropper bottles.

Solution #	1	2	3	4	5	6	7	8	9	10	11	12	13	14	15
Parts olive oil	all	13	12	11	10	9	8	7	6	5	4	3	2	1	–
Parts clove oil	–	1	2	3	4	5	6	7	8	9	10	11	12	13	all

Microscope slides

Cover slips

Abbe refractometer, with recirculating water bath (optional)

The Particle Atlas, Volume 3, 2nd edition (see "Recommended and Further Reading" section)

Safety

Use standard laboratory safety procedures as described in guidelines set by your instructor. Be cautious of microscope light levels to avoid eye damage. Know the hazards associated with the mounting mediums, and use them with appropriate precautions as set by your instructor. Dispose of glass in an appropriate container.

Part I: Refractive Index Determination of Glass Samples by Becke Line Oil Immersion Method

Procedure

Source: This procedure reproduced with permission of Lawrence J. Kaplan, Department of Chemistry, Williams College, Williamstown, MA 01267.

1. Choose a glass particle of known refractive index (RI), and mount it on a microscope slide with a cover slip using:
   a. Cargille oil of *higher* RI
   b. Cargille oil of *lower* RI
   For example: If you chose a glass with an RI of 1.52, put it in 1.500 and 1.540 oils.
2. Once the microscope is adjusted properly, use the 10X objective to focus on the edges of the glass particle. Use the orange filter in the Micro kit to obtain monochromatic light. This allows you to determine n_D.
3. Close the substage condenser to the minimum setting. Observe the Becke line, and then focus "upward" and "downward" to determine whether the glass fragment or the solution has the higher refractive index. Remember that as you focus up (raise the microscope lens away from the sample), the Becke line will move toward the substance with the higher refractive index. When the refractive indices of the glass and the immersion liquid are the same, the chip will become almost invisible, and it may be difficult to find and bring the edges of the chip into focus. What is your conclusion?
4. Repeat the steps above with a glass particle of a higher RI. What did you observe? What are your conclusions?
5. Choose two of the unknown glasses. Write down their numbers.
6. Following the flow chart in Figure 2D-3, choose clove–olive oil mixtures (which mimic what can also be accomplished with Cargille oils) to find an oil that provides minimum

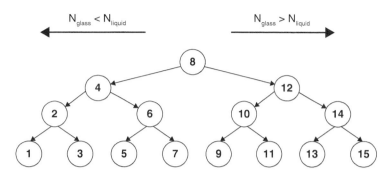

Figure 2D-3 Refractive index flow chart. Start with solution #8. If the index of refraction of the glass is greater than the liquid's, move on to solution #12. If the glass's index is greater still, try solution #14 next. If the index of the glass is less than that of solution #14, try solution #13. After this trial, the index of refraction for the fragment may be determined to be between the indices of solutions #13 and #14.

relief, otherwise known as a "match." Remember that the Becke line moves to the medium with the higher refractive index when the focal distance is increased. Note that even though there are 15 different immersion liquids, when using the flow chart, only four of them need to be used.

Part II: Determination of the Refractive Index of Samples by Identifying the Refractive Index of the Oil

Procedure

Note: The most common problem encountered with the refractometer is contamination of one liquid with another. Clean the prisms carefully between samples by washing with 95% ethyl alcohol and wiping with absorbent lens paper.

CAUTION: THE PRISMS ARE VERY DELICATE AND MUST NOT BE SCRATCHED. BE CAREFUL NOT TO TOUCH THEM WITH FINGERS OR DROPPERS!

1. Turn on the Abbe refractometer and the water bath so that the temperature will equilibrate to 25°C.
2. Using the clove oil that you were assigned, apply a small drop of oil between the prisms (but do not touch the prisms with the dropper). Allow it to spread so that a uniform layer is obtained when the prisms are closed.
3. Looking through the eyepiece, find the general light/dark area by rotating the small knob located on the right side of the refractometer. Until it is properly adjusted, this light/dark area will probably show highly colored fringes.
4. The color-compensating prism is adjusted by turning the knurled wheel on the front of the refractometer. When this is done, you will see a fairly sharp dividing line between the light and dark fields.
5. Rotate the small knob on the right side of the refractometer so that the cross hairs are exactly aligned on the light/dark dividing line, as illustrated in Figure 2D-4.

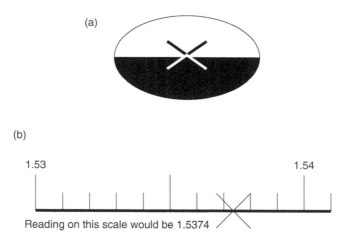

Figure 2D-4   (a) The dark and light field edges are sharpened and centered in the field of view. (b) After pushing a button, a scale is illuminated that can be read to five significant figures. This identifies the refractive index of the liquid.

6. Illuminate the scale by pressing the button on the left, rear side at the base of the refractometer. The numerical reading at the point where the cross hairs intersect the scale is the refractive index. Only each tenth division is numbered. Estimate the position of the cross hairs to the nearest one-tenth division. Read and record the refractive index to four decimal places (i.e., five significant figures; see Figure 2D-4).
7. Remember, if there is no circulating water bath, use a thermometer to obtain the room temperature. Correct the refractive index measured with the refractometer to report the refractive index at 25°C using Equation (2D-4).

Part III: Refractive Index Determinations of Particles Using Dispersion Staining

Procedure

1. After turning on the light source, rotate the objective turret until the dispersion staining objective is in place.
2. Prepare a microscope slide using quartz and a Cargille oil with a refractive index value of 1.544.
3. Place the sample on the microscope stage, and focus using the full aperture position. Adjust the microscope to obtain Köhler illumination.
4. Insert the Bertrand lens (or remove one eyepiece). Adjust the dispersion staining objective by rotating the selector disk until the central stop is selected (position marked by a dark center).
5. Close down the substage diaphragm until the field of view is just inside the central stop (background is dark).
6. Remove the Bertrand lens (or replace the eyepiece).
7. Insert the analyzer to establish a point of extinction for the quartz particle (the point at which the particle disappears).

8. Remove the analyzer.
9. Observe the colors visible in and slightly out of focus (Becke line) around the edges of the sample.
10. Insert the analyzer and rotate the sample to the next point of extinction. Remove the analyzer. Observe the colors visible in and slightly out of focus around the edges of the sample.
11. Insert the analyzer and return the sample to its original position (the first extinction point viewed). Remove the analyzer.
12. Insert the Bertrand lens (or remove one eyepiece). Adjust the dispersion staining objective by rotating the selector disc until the annular stop is selected (position marked by a bright center).
13. Close down the substage diaphragm until the field of view is just inside the annular stop (background is bright).
14. Remove the Bertrand lens (or replace the eyepiece).
15. Insert the analyzer to establish a point of extinction for the quartz particle (the point at which the particle disappears).
16. Remove the analyzer.
17. Observe the colors visible in and slightly out of focus (Becke line) around the edges of the sample.
18. Repeat this procedure (steps 3–17) with a Cargille oil with a refractive index of 1.554.
19. Repeat this procedure (steps 3–17) with a Cargille oil with a refractive index of 1.560.
20. Repeat this procedure (steps 3–17) with a Cargille oil with a refractive index of 1.568.
21. To determine the matching wavelength, compare the color observations to the dispersion staining colors in Table 2D-2.
22. Plot your data on the dispersion staining graph found in Appendix D. Compare these results to the known dispersion staining curve data for quartz found in *The Particle Atlas*.
23. When reporting a single refractive index for a sample, the refractive index is usually given as n_D. This can be obtained from the dispersion curve graph.

Report Requirements

Include all drawings, calculations, and other information obtained during the laboratory procedure. Notes and/or drawings should include the sample identification, magnification, and a complete description.

Report Questions

1. What is refractive index?
2. Define the Becke line. How is this used to determine the refractive index of a sample?
3. In which direction does the Becke line move when the particle is 1.49 and the oil used is 1.46? Why?
4. What are Cargille oils? How are they used in forensics?
5. What would you do if you wanted to test for a refractive index between two Cargille oils? How would you identify its refractive index value?
6. Describe how the Abbe refractometer determines a refractive index.
7. Why is it necessary for the Abbe refractometer to be temperature controlled?

8. A liquid has a refractive index of 1.532 at 25°C. It has a temperature coefficient of refractive index, −*dn/dT*, of 0.0004. What is the refractive index of the liquid at 20°C?

The following questions should also be answered if Part III was done.

9. Describe how a dispersion staining objective works.
10. If you were given a sample, how would you go about analyzing it using the dispersion staining method to prove that it is calcite?
11. How would you go about identifying an unknown crystal?

Recommended and Further Reading

Allen TJ. Modifications to Sample Mounting Procedures and Microtome Equipment for Paint Sectioning. *Forensic Science International.* 1991; 52(1): 93–100.

Almirall JR, Cole MD, Gettinby G, Furton KG. Discrimination of Glass Sources Using Elemental Composition and Refractive Index: Development of Predictive Models. *Science & Justice.* 1998; 38(2): 93–100.

Bennett RL, Kim ND, Curran JM, Coulson SA, Newton AWN. Spatial Variation of Refractive Index in a Pane of Float Glass. *Science & Justice.* 2003; 43(2): 71–76.

Bradbury S. *An Introduction to the Optical Microscope*, rev. ed. Oxford: Oxford University Press and Royal Microscopical Society, 1989.

Brown GA. Factors Affecting the Refractive Index Distribution of Window Glass. *Journal of Forensic Sciences.* 1985; 30(3): 806–813.

Carroll GR, Demers J. Technical Note: A New Method for Determining the Refractive Indices and Birefringence of Textile Fibers. *Canadian Society of Forensic Science Journal.* 1993; 26: 15–117.

Cassista AR, Sandercock PML. Precision of Glass Refractive Index Measurements: Temperature Variation and Double Variation Methods and the Value of Dispersion. *Canadian Society of Forensic Science Journal.* 1994; 27(3): 203–208.

Cook R, Norton D. An Evaluation of Mounting Media for Use in Forensic Textile Fibre Examinations. *Journal of Forensic Sciences Society.* 1982; 22(1): 57–63.

Cook R, Paterson MD. New Techniques for the Identification of Microscopic Samples of Textile Fibres by Infrared Spectroscopy. *Forensic Science International.* 1978; 12: 237–243.

Croft WJ. *Under the Microscope: A Brief History of Microscopy.* Hackensack, NJ: World Scientific, 2006.

Curran JM, Buckleton JS, Triggs CM. Commentary on Koons RD, Buscaglia J. The Forensic Significance of Glass Composition and Refractive Index Measurements. *Journal of Forensic Sciences* 1999; 44(3): 496–503. Journal of Forensic Sciences. 1999; 44(6):1324–1325.

Dabbs MDG, Pearson EF. The Variation in Refractive Index and Density across Two Sheets of Window Glass. *Journal of Forensic Sciences Society.* 1970; 10: 139–148.

De Forest PR. Foundations of Forensic Microscopy. In: Saferstein R, ed. *Forensic Science Handbook*, 2nd ed. Upper Saddle River, NJ: Pearson Education, 2002; 301–305.

Goldberg O. Köhler Illumination. *The Microscope.* 1980; 28: 15–21.

Heath JP. *Dictionary of Microscopy.* Chichester, UK: John Wiley & Sons Ltd, 2005.

Herman B, Lemasters JJ. *Optical Microscopy: Emerging Methods and Applications.* San Diego, CA: Academic Press, 1993.

Koons RD, Buscaglia J. The Forensic Significance of Glass Composition and Refractive Index Measurements. *Journal of Forensic Sciences.* 1999; 44(3): 496–503.

Koons RD, Buscaglia J, Bottrell M, Miller E. Forensic Glass Comparisons. In: Saferstein R, ed. *Forensic Science Handbook*, 2nd ed. Upper Saddle River, NJ: Pearson Education, 2002; 161–213.

Lambert JA, Satterthwaite MJ, Harrison PH. A Survey of Glass Fragments Recovered from Clothing of Persons Suspected of Involvement in Crime. *Science & Justice.* 1995; 35(4): 273–281.

Locke J. Improvements in the Use of Silicone Oils for the Determination of Glass Refractive Indices. *Journal of the Forensic Science Society.* 1982; 22: 257–262.

Loveland RP, Centifano YM. Mounting Media for Microscopy. *The Microscope*. 1986; (34): 181–242.

McCrone WC. Checklist for True Köhler Illumination. *American Laboratory*. 1980; 12(1): 96–98.

McCrone WC, Delly JG. *The Particle Atlas*. Ann Arbor, MI: Ann Arbor Science, 1978.

McCrone WC, McCrone LB, Delly JG. *Polarized Light Microscopy*. Ann Arbor, MI: Ann Arbor Science, 1978.

Newton AWN, Kitto L, Buckleton JS. A Study of the Performance and Utility of Annealing in Forensic Glass Analysis. *Forensic Science International*. 2005; 155(2–3): 119–125.

Parry-Hill MJ, Fellers TJ, Davidson MW. Eyepiece Reticle Calibration [Java Interactive Tutorial; cited 2020]. Available from: http://www.olympusmicro.com.

Parry-Hill MJ, Fellers TJ, Davidson MW. Microscope Alignment for Köhler Illumination [Java Interactive Tutorial; cited 2020]. Available from: http://www.olympusmicro.com.

Quadros J, Monteiro ELD. Collecting and Preparing Mammal Hairs for Identification with Optical Microscopy. *Revista Brasileira De Zoologia*. 2006; 23(1): 274–278.

Resua R, Petranco N. Fiber Optics: Illumination for Use in Dispersion Staining, the Microscope. *The Microscope*. 1980; 28: 51–55.

Roe GM, Cook R, North C. An Evaluation of Mountants for Use in Forensic Hair Examinations. *Journal of Forensic Sciences Society*. 1991; 31: 59–65.

Simon JM, Comastri SA. The Compound Microscope: Optical Tube Length or Parfocalization. *European Journal of Physics*. 2005; 26(6): 1101–1105.

Spencer M. *Fundamentals of Light Microscopy*. Cambridge, UK: Cambridge University Press, 1982.

Chapter 3
Polarized Light Microscope

Microscopes are utilized in many types of forensic examinations. Whereas the stereomicroscope and compound light microscope are used for many applications in a forensic laboratory, the polarized light microscope is generally used for specialized trace evidence examinations. When using higher magnification and the additional components found in a polarized light microscope, an analyst can identify important characteristics for a particular sample.

Like the compound light microscope, the polarized light microscope uses a combination of lenses to produce a magnified image. In addition to the basic components, several other parts are added to enhance the analytical ability of the microscope. A polarized light microscope has the following basic parts:

- light source
- condenser
- sample stage
- objective
- focusing knobs
- oculars

In addition, some or all of the following components may be added:

- polarizer
- analyzer
- compensators (first-order red, quarter-wave, quartz wedge)
- Bertrand lens

Basically, the light originates from the illuminator and is collimated by the condenser. It then passes through the polarizer, which only allows light to vibrate in a single plane. The now-polarized light interacts with the sample on the microscope stage, and is collected by the objective. As the light exits the objective, it passes through the analyzer (if allowed) and onto the oculars. The analyzer is similar to the polarizer in that it only allows light vibrating in a single plane to pass. The oculars receive this image and re-focus it onto the viewer's eye. Various compensators and a Bertrand lens can also be inserted for specific applications.

Polarized light microscopes generally use oculars and objectives that provide total magnification within the range of 40X to 400X. Because of the higher total magnification, a smaller

Practical Forensic Microscopy: A Laboratory Manual, Second Edition. Barbara P. Wheeler.
© 2021 John Wiley & Sons Ltd. Published 2021 by John Wiley & Sons Ltd.
Companion website: www.wiley.com/go/Wheeler/Forensic

field of view and less depth of field are obtained. Samples are viewed with transmitted light as well with crossed polars, an arrangement with the polarizer and analyzer oriented perpendicular to each other, to obtain their microscopic characteristics. The addition of compensators or a Bertrand lens also provides additional microscopic characteristics.

The polarized light microscope is used to identify and characterize samples. The higher level of magnification allows viewing of the initial characteristics of a sample, with additional comparison and microscopic examinations also possible.

Chapter 3

Experiment 3A: Familiarization with the Polarized Light Microscope

---

Recommended pre-lab reading assignments:

Brenner M. Understanding the Polarizing Microscope. *American Laboratory.* 1980; 42(4): 71.

De Forest PR. Foundations of Forensic Microscopy. In: Saferstein R, ed. *Forensic Science Handbook*, 2nd ed. Upper Saddle River, NJ: Pearson Education, 2002; 282–285.

Recommended website:

Abramowitz M, Davidson MW. Polarization of Light [Java Interactive Tutorial; cited 2020]. Available from: http://www.olympusmicro.com.

Objective

Upon completion of this practical exercise, the student will have developed a basic understanding of:

1. components of the polarizing light microscope
2. isotropic and anisotropic
3. birefringence
4. inherent color and interference colors
5. extinction points
6. pleochroism
7. use of the polarized light microscope to observe various optical properties

---

Practical Forensic Microscopy: A Laboratory Manual, Second Edition. Barbara P. Wheeler.
© 2021 John Wiley & Sons Ltd. Published 2021 by John Wiley & Sons Ltd.
Companion website: www.wiley.com/go/Wheeler/Forensic

Introduction

As with use of the stereomicroscope and compound microscope, a microscope is an optical instrument that uses a combination of lenses to produce a magnified image of small objects. To accomplish this aim, the polarized light microscope (PLM) uses several components that gather light and redirect the light path so that a magnified image of the viewed object can be focused within a short distance.

A compound light microscope has basic components mounted in a well-designed base that lends itself to precision centering and alignment so that samples can be viewed with optimum magnification, resolution, and contrast. However, in a PLM, there are additional parts that enhance the microscope's analytical ability. A PLM contains the basic components of a compound light microscope: light source, condenser, sample stage, objective, focusing knobs, and oculars, with the addition of a polarizer and an analyzer. The polarizer and analyzer are composed of the same type of specialized filter; however, the difference between them is the location and orientation within the microscope. A polarizer is placed below the sample, usually in a holder that is capable of rotating. An analyzer is placed above the sample, typically in a location near the back of the objective lens (see Figure 3A-1).

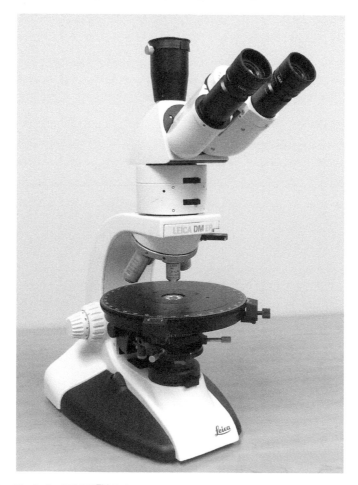

Figure 3A-1   The Leica DMEP™ light microscope is capable of providing polarized light with various magnification powers for sample viewing.

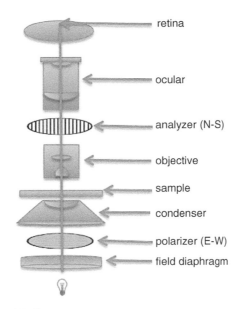

Figure 3A-2 Optical path for a polarizing light microscope.

The theory behind a polarizing light microscope is fairly simple. Both the polarizer and the analyzer are made of a polymer film that completely absorbs light vibrating in all but one direction. When these are positioned in a PLM, the light originates from the illuminator and passes through the polarizer (see Figure 3A-2). When the light passes through the polarizer, it is oriented in a specific vibrational direction, usually east-west (E-W). This "plane-polarized" light is collimated by the condenser, which allows the light to interact with the sample. This light is collected by the objective. The objective re-focuses the image through the analyzer (when used), which is oriented in the opposite vibrational direction from the polarizer, usually north-south (N-S), and onto the front focal plane of the ocular. The oculars receive this image and re-focus it onto the viewer's eye. The polarizer and analyzer are considered to be in the "crossed" position when their vibrational directions are oriented perpendicular to one another. In this orientation, the polarizer absorbs light in one direction (E-W) and the analyzer absorbs light perpendicularly (N-S); no light from the illuminator will pass to the oculars. Therefore, the field of view is black. However, when a sample is placed on the stage in the light path, it will react with the light in a variety of manners. Some particles will remain colorless or dark. These samples have no effect on polarized light regardless of their orientation and are considered isotropic. They exhibit similar optical properties in all directions (a single refractive index), so they produce no optical effect on the cross-polarized light. Others will appear brightly colored or seem to "glow." These samples are termed anisotropic and exhibit different optical properties in different orientations (they have more than one refractive index). Most anisotropic materials produce two polarized light components corresponding to the refractive indices: extraordinary and ordinary rays. Each of these rays will have a different refractive index.

The numerical difference in these refractive indices is called birefringence or B, and is shown in the following equation:

$$B = n_2 - n_1 \qquad\qquad (3A\text{-}1)$$

where n_1 and n_2 correspond to the refractive index of extraordinary and ordinary rays, respectively.

Anisotropic samples "glow" or produce interference colors that correspond to the retardation or slowing down of one ray with respect to the other. Retardation, Δ, depends on both the thickness, t, and the birefringence, B, according to the following equation:

$$\Delta = B \times t \qquad\qquad (3A\text{-}2)$$

Since retardation or interference colors are reported in nanometers and thickness is measured in micrometers (μm), it is often convenient to use the following equation:

$$\Delta = B \times t \times 1000 \frac{nm}{\mu m} \qquad\qquad (3A\text{-}3)$$

Interference colors should not be confused with natural or inherent color. Interference colors are observed under crossed polars, while inherent color is observed under plane-polarized light (with the analyzer out of the optical path). Both observations are important properties for identification and comparison of samples.

The orientation of samples with respect to the polarizer and analyzer filters may also cause samples to appear differently. Samples that are aligned with the polarizer's orientation will appear black (see Figure 3A-3a). This is because the vibration direction of the light passing through the sample is aligned perpendicular to the analyzer's vibration direction. These positions are called "extinction points." Extinction points occur every 90°, whereas points of maximum brightness occur every 45° (see Figure 3A-3b).

The extinction characteristics of samples can be useful in identification of materials. For example, cotton fibers never go completely dark upon rotation of the stage under crossed polars. This is due to the fiber's cellulose chains being oriented in a spiral manner relative to the long axis during the growth of the cotton fiber. Lack of extinction is considered a confirmatory test for cotton fibers.

Another common microscopic characteristic of materials is to determine whether or not a sample exhibits pleochroism. This is the phenomenon observed when a sample displays different

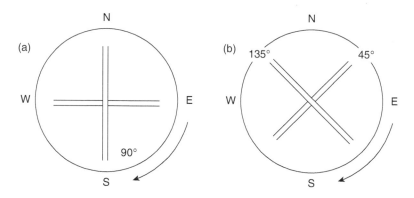

Figure 3A-3 A fiber is a typical anisotropic material. In this figure, a fiber is shown at different orientations on the rotating stage. (a) Under crossed polars, in the E-W and N-S positions, the fiber is in an orientation that allows light to pass that is parallel to the polarizer but perpendicular to analyzer. Because of this, the analyzer blocks the light, resulting in extinction. Extinction occurs every 90°. (b) When the fiber is oriented diagonally at 45° and 135°, the fiber interacts with the polarized light, producing two rays with two refractive indices. Some of the light is vibrating parallel to the analyzer and allowed to pass. Maximum birefringence occurs at 45° and 135°.

inherent colors depending on its orientation with the polarizer's vibration direction. The sample is viewed while rotating it under plane-polarized light (with the analyzer removed from the light path). A pleochloric sample will show a change in inherent color upon rotation of the stage. Since pleochroism is a unique property, it can be used to compare and distinguish otherwise similar samples. The range of pleochroism for samples may be anywhere from slight differences in color shade to a completely different color. Some materials show two colors or shades (dichroic), while others may show three (trichroic).

The optical properties of materials are used to characterize and distinguish different samples. Whether a sample is isotropic or anisotropic and its degree of birefringence are characteristics that are commonly determined for forensic samples. When using the polarized light microscope to determine these characteristics, along with others such as extinction points and degree of pleochroism, it becomes another valuable tool in a forensic laboratory.

Equipment and Supplies

Polarized light microscope (PLM) with objectives of various magnifications (e.g., 4X, 10X, 20X, and 40X)

McCrone Particle Reference Set™

Micro kit

Tetraphenylcyclopentadienone

Safety

Use standard laboratory safety procedures as described in guidelines set by your laboratory. Be cautious of microscope light levels to avoid eye damage. Know the hazards associated with the mounting mediums, and use them with appropriate precautions as set by your instructor. Dispose of glass in an appropriate container.

Part I: Parts of a Polarized Light Microscope

1. Obtain a photograph of the polarized light microscope used in the laboratory.
2. Label the following parts of the microscope: light source, condenser, sample stage, objectives, field diaphragm, field diaphragm centering screws, field diaphragm focus knob, lamp aperture, focusing knobs, polarizer, analyzer, and oculars.

Part II: Operation of the Polarized Light Microscope

Procedure

1. Familiarize yourself with the polarized light microscope. Locate each part of the microscope. Place a prepared microscope slide on the stage. After turning on the light source, manipulate the oculars of the microscope to adjust the interpupillary distance so that when viewing an object, the right and left images merge as one.

2. Adjust the focus up and down. Using the non-adjustable ocular, focus on an item to obtain a clear image of an item.
3. Focus the second ocular if necessary.
4. Set up Köhler illumination and have your instructor check the microscope for correct illumination.

Part III: Isotropic versus Anisotropic

Procedure

1. Using the polarized light microscope, set the polarizer and analyzer so that you have obtained "crossed polars." If the filters are properly aligned, the field of view should go completely black when the analyzer is introduced into the light path of the microscope (without a sample on the stage). If the field of view does not go perfectly black, the filters are not oriented perpendicular to each other, and either the polarizer or the analyzer must be adjusted to correct this. On most microscopes, the polarizer may be adjusted by simply rotating it. It should be left in the position that results in the darkest field of view possible.
2. Examine the following prepared microscope slides, documenting what you see. Make sure you note the sample, the magnification, the orientation of polarizing filters (crossed/uncrossed), and the sample orientation for each drawing done on a circle template from Appendix E:

Quartz	Olivine
Calcite	Ground glass
Mineral wool	Diatoms

Drawings should be made in both plane-polarized light and crossed polars. Record whether the particles in each of the prepared slides are isotropic (I) or anisotropic (A).

Part IV: Extinction Points and Birefringence

Procedure

1. Place a prepared slide of nylon on the microscope stage.
2. Align the fiber with the orientation of the polarizer.
3. Place the analyzer in position. The field of view should be black, including the fiber.
4. Rotate the fiber 90°. Does the fiber go to extinction?
5. Place the fiber at a 45° angle. Describe and draw what you see.
6. Repeat steps 2–5 with acetate fibers.

Part V: Color and Pleochroism

Procedure

1. Mount a few crystals of tetraphenylcyclopentadienone (TPCP).
2. View the sample using crossed polars. Pick a bright grain and rotate the stage so that the particle goes to extinction. Remember: Not all grains will be oriented in the same manner, so make sure you focus on ONE grain.
3. Take the analyzer out. Note the inherent color of the sample and the orientation in the field of view. Draw what you see.
4. Rotate the stage 90°. Note the color of the sample. If the crystal did not exhibit pleochroism, the color would be the same regardless of the orientation.
5. Draw the sample in the second orientation.
6. Did the sample exhibit pleochroism?

Report Requirements

Include all drawings, calculations, and other information obtained during the laboratory procedure. Notes and/or drawings should include the sample identification, magnification, and a complete description.

Report Questions

1. What are the eight basic components of a PLM? What function does each component perform in a PLM?
2. Explain the optical light path utilized in a polarized light microscope.
3. Name three types of evidence that could be examined with a PLM. What would the examination consist of?
4. What types of evidence would not be examined with the PLM? Why?
5. Explain plane-polarized light. How do you set this up?
6. Define crossed polarized light. How do you set this up?
7. Define isotropic. How can you determine if something is isotropic?
8. Define anisotropic. How can you determine if something is anisotropic?
9. What is birefringence?
10. What is pleochroism? How is this observed?
11. During a given rotation of the stage, how many times does a sample exhibit extinction?
12. What are the locations of maximum birefringence during a complete stage rotation? How many times does this occur during one stage rotation?
13. Do a web search of the items in Part III. State their chemical composition. Where are they likely to be found in casework? Why are they isotropic or anisotropic?

Chapter 3

Experiment 3B: Determining Refractive Index of Anisotropic Materials

---

Recommended pre-lab reading assignments:

Bell S. *Forensic Chemistry*. Upper Saddle River, NJ: Pearson Education, 2006; 580–586.

De Forest PR. Foundations of Forensic Microscopy. In: Saferstein R, ed. *Forensic Science Handbook*, 2nd ed. Upper Saddle River, NJ: Pearson Education, 2002; 305–309.

Objective

Upon completion of this practical exercise, the student will have developed a basic understanding of:

1. difference between isotropic and anisotropic materials
2. use of polarized light to orient anisotropic materials
3. measurements of two refractive indices for fibers (n-parallel and n-perpendicular)
4. calculation of birefringence of fibers

Introduction

When samples are placed on the stage of a polarizing light microscope (PLM) in the optical light path, they will react in a variety of manners. Some samples have no effect on a polarized light beam regardless of their orientation and are said to be isotropic. Isotropic materials have no repeating crystal structure and therefore have only one refractive index. An example of an isotropic material commonly encountered in forensics is glass. The Becke line immersion method was used to determine the refractive index of isotropic materials in Experiment 2D.

Practical Forensic Microscopy: A Laboratory Manual, Second Edition. Barbara P. Wheeler.
© 2021 John Wiley & Sons Ltd. Published 2021 by John Wiley & Sons Ltd.
Companion website: www.wiley.com/go/Wheeler/Forensic

As demonstrated in Experiment 3A, some samples will react in a variety of manners when viewed under plane-polarized or crossed polarized light. Anisotropic materials have more than one refractive index and "glow" or exhibit interference colors under cross-polars. Many common forensic samples are anisotropic and produce two polarized light components corresponding to the extraordinary ray (e-ray) and ordinary ray (o-ray). When the material has more than one refractive index, the refractive index is found to vary with the orientation of the material with respect to the vibration direction of the light. This is because anisotropic materials contain a repeating structure that differs by direction, creating two or more paths for light to travel. The Becke line immersion method can also be used to measure multiple refractive indices within a single sample; however, the procedure now requires control of the orientation of the sample. It is the use of polarized light that allows the orientation of the sample to be controlled with respect to the vibration direction of light.

With fibers, the orientation of the sample is relatively easy to control. Fibers are composed of repeating monomer units so that they vary in density in two directions. This creates the two axes, causing light to be separated into two rays within the fiber. One direction is parallel to the length of the fiber, or "n-parallel." The other is perpendicular to the length of the fiber, or "n-perpendicular." For anisotropic fibers, it will always be true that in one direction, light will encounter a higher density of atoms. This causes the light to be retarded or slowed in that direction. Light moving in this direction is called the slow ray. Perpendicular to this direction, light encounters a lower density of atoms and moves at a faster velocity. Light moving in this direction is called the fast ray. Refractive index has been defined in Chapter 2 by Equation 2D-1, and it can easily be shown that the slower ray has a higher refractive index and vice versa. Since fibers demonstrate this characteristic, determination of both the n-parallel and n-perpendicular refractive indices can be used to help identify fibers.

The polarizing light microscope can be used to determine both refractive indices for fiber samples. The polarizer allows light to pass in only one vibrational direction, typically E-W polarized. Since plane-polarized light is necessary for this procedure, the polarizer is in place but the analyzer is removed from the light path. To determine n-parallel, the mounted fiber is oriented on the stage so that the length of the fiber is parallel to the polarizer (see Figure 3B-1a).

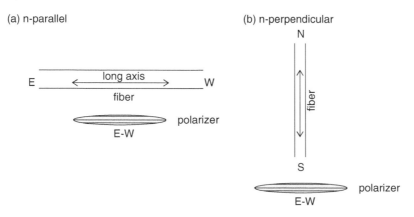

Figure 3B-1   In order to properly orient the fiber to determine refractive index, the vibration direction of the polarizer must be known. For most microscopes: (a) A fiber oriented with its length parallel to the vibration direction of the polarizer allows n-parallel to be measured. (b) A fiber oriented with its long axis perpendicular to the vibration direction of the polarizer allows n-perpendicular to be measured.

Once in this orientation, the Becke line is used to determine if the immersion oil has a higher or lower refractive index than the fiber's n-parallel value. As in the case of determining refractive index for a glass particle, the Becke line will move to the medium of higher refractive index when the focal distance is increased. This is repeated with various Cargille™ oils until minimum relief is observed in this direction, allowing the refractive index to be identified. To determine n-perpendicular, the fiber is rotated so that the length is perpendicular to the polarization direction of the polarizer (see Figure 3B-1b). For an E-W polarizer, this results in a N-S orientation of the fiber. The Becke line is once again used to determine if the immersion oil has a higher or lower refractive index than the fiber's n-perpendicular. This is also repeated with various Cargille oils until minimum relief is observed in this orientation. Once n-parallel and n-perpendicular have been determined, the birefringence can be determined by subtraction according to Equation (3B-1). Birefringence is an optical property of a material having a refractive index that depends on the polarization and vibrational direction of light.

$$\text{Birefringence of fibers} = n_{\parallel} - n_{\perp} \tag{3B-1}$$

For fibers, it is fairly easy to orient the fiber with the polarizer or perpendicular to the polarizer. However, for some anisotropic materials, the orientation of crystal must be known in order to determine the respective refractive indices. This represents a more complicated situation since it is possible for the crystal to have up to three refractive indices. Orientation of crystals with respect to vibration direction is determined using conoscopic illumination and is covered in Experiment 21A.

The optical properties of materials are used to characterize and distinguish different samples. When using the polarized light microscope to determine refractive index, it becomes another valuable tool in a forensic laboratory.

Equipment and Supplies

Polarized light microscope with objectives of various magnifications (e.g., 4X, 10X, 20X, and 40X)

McCrone Particle Reference Set™

Unknown fibers

Microscope slides and cover slips

Cargille™ oils

Safety

Use standard laboratory safety procedures as described in guidelines set by your instructor. Be cautious of microscope light levels to avoid eye damage. Know the hazards associated with the mounting mediums, and use them with appropriate precautions as set by your instructor. Dispose of glass in an appropriate container.

Part I: Observing n-Parallel and n-Perpendicular

Procedure

1. Set up the polarizing light microscope for Köhler illumination.

2. Determine the vibration direction of the polarizer on your microscope. Using a 10X objective, focus on a prepared slide of Dacron™ polyester from the McCrone Particle Reference Set. Select a straight portion of the fiber. With the polarizer in and no analyzer, rotate the fiber so that you observe its relief in both the E-W and N-S orientations. Since the mounting medium of the slide is near the n-parallel refractive index of Dacron, it will exhibit minimum relief when it is parallel to the vibration direction of the polarizer. If this occurs when the fiber is oriented in the E-W direction, then your polarizer allows light vibrating in the E-W direction to pass.

3. OPTIONAL: Adjust the polarizer to match the cross hairs of your microscope. Rotate the Dacron fiber to align directly with the orientation of the polarizer. For example, rotate the fiber until it is perfectly E-W if your polarizer is E-W polarized. Now rotate your polarizing filter until you obtain minimum birefringence. This requires that the polarizer not be in a fixed position.

4. Remove the analyzer. Determination of n-parallel and n-perpendicular is performed using plane-polarized light.

5. Close down the condenser aperture to increase contrast and to prevent the formation of a false Becke line. A false Becke line may be observed as a second bright line, which moves in the opposite direction of the Becke line. This is visible when the difference between the refractive index of a sample and the immersion liquid is low and the true Becke line is faint.

6. Place a single polyester fiber on a microscope slide, and add a cover slip.

7. Choose a Cargille oil close to one of the known refractive indices for polyester (n-parallel: 1.720, n-perpendicular: 1.540). Allow a drop of the oil to be drawn under the cover slip.

8. Place the microscope slide on the stage with the length of the fiber parallel to the plane of polarized light. Examine the fiber under high power. Explain what you see in this orientation.

9. Place the microscope slide on the stage with the length of the fiber perpendicular to the plane of polarized light. Examine the fiber under high power. Explain what you see in this orientation.

10. At what orientation does it disappear? Why?

11. Rotate the fiber to the direction (either parallel or perpendicular) that is not a match. Using the focus, adjust the position while observing the edges of the fiber. When the fiber is slightly out of focus, the Becke line will appear either inside or outside the fiber edge. The Becke line will move toward the higher refractive index when the focal distance is increased. Does the Becke line move into or out of the fiber? Why?

12. Repeat step 11 using a Cargille oil close to the other known refractive indices for polyester (n-parallel: 1.720, n-perpendicular: 1.540).

Part II: Determining n-Parallel and n-Perpendicular of an Unknown Fiber

Procedure

1. Obtain an unknown fiber.
2. Using the polarizing light microscope, check the lighting to ensure that samples will be viewed using Köhler illumination.

3. Place the unknown fiber on a microscope slide, and add a cover slip. Place a drop of Cargille oil on the edges of the cover slip, and allow it to be drawn up under the cover slip.
4. Place the microscope slide on the stage, and focus using high magnification and plane-polarized light.
5. Rotate the fiber so that the length of the fiber is parallel to the plane of polarized light. For most microscopes, this would be E-W.
6. Close down the condenser to prevent the formation of a false Becke line. A false Becke line may be observed as a second bright line, which moves in the opposite direction of the Becke line. This is visible when the difference between the refractive index of a sample and the immersion liquid is low and the true Becke line is faint.
7. Using the focus knob, adjust the focus while observing the edges of the fiber. When the fiber is slightly out of focus, the Becke line will appear either inside or outside the fiber edge. The Becke line will move toward the higher refractive index when the focal distance is increased. Document which medium has the higher refractive index.
8. Rotate the fiber so it is oriented perpendicular to the plane of polarized light. For most microscopes, this would be N-S.
9. Once again, focus the edges to determine which medium has the higher refractive index. Document which medium has the higher refractive index.
10. Repeat with various Cargille oils until you are able to determine the refractive indices for your fiber. Determine which liquid to use next by depending on your previous results. Remember: If the Becke line moved toward the fiber when the focal distance is increased, it had a higher refractive index, so a higher Cargille oil should be used next to find a match point.
11. Continue until you have determined the minimum relief for the two directions of your fiber. Report n-parallel and n-perpendicular for the room temperature.
12. Using the temperature coefficient on the bottle of Cargille oil that was a match, report the refractive index at 25°C.
13. Calculate the birefringence of the fiber at 25°C.

Report Requirements

Include all drawings, calculations, and other information obtained during the laboratory procedure. Notes and/or drawings should include the sample identification, magnification, and a complete description.

Report Questions

1. Define isotropic and anisotropic.
2. Are there any fibers that are isotropic? How would you determine this?
3. Why do fibers have more than one refractive index?
4. Explain the difference between plane-polarized light and crossed polars.
5. If a fiber is oriented in the N-S direction, which refractive index is being measured using E-W polarized light? Why?
6. If you have a Kodel™ polyester fiber oriented in the E-W direction and are using a microscope with a polarizer that is oriented in the E-W direction, what refractive index would you be trying to measure? If it were mounted in 1.700 Cargille oil, would you

expect this to be a "match"? If not, if you increased the focal distance, in which direction would the Becke line move?

7. If you had a Qiana™ nylon fiber mounted in 1.546 Cargille oil, what would you expect to see when viewing the fiber in the E-W direction? What would you expect to see when rotating the fiber into the N-S direction? Why? How would you finish your examination to determine the refractive indices for this fiber?

8. Why was the analyzer removed from the light path to determine refractive index?

9. Can this procedure be used on any compound light microscope?

10. Calculate the birefringence of the polyester fiber used in Part I, step 7. Assuming the room temperature was 22°C, report the refractive indices and birefringence for 25°C.

Chapter 3

Experiment 3C: Determining Sign of Elongation and Birefringence

---

Recommended pre-lab reading assignment:

De Forest PR. Foundations of Forensic Microscopy. In: Saferstein R, ed. *Forensic Science Handbook*, 2nd ed. Upper Saddle River, NJ: Pearson Education, 2002; 284–285.

Recommended website:

Griffin JD, Johnson ID, Davidson MW. Specialized Microscopy Techniques—Polarized Light Microscopy—Compensators and Retardation Plates [Java Interactive Tutorial; cited 2020]. Available from: http://www.olympusmicro.com.

Objective

Upon completion of this practical exercise, the student will have developed a basic understanding of:

1. common compensators
2. sign of elongation of fibers
3. birefringence of fibers
4. use of the polarizing light microscope to determine sign of elongation
5. use of compensators to determine birefringence of fibers

Introduction

Many optical properties can be determined for samples with the aid of a polarizing light microscope and a compensator. As learned in the previous experiments, birefringence is the

---

Practical Forensic Microscopy: A Laboratory Manual, Second Edition. Barbara P. Wheeler.
© 2021 John Wiley & Sons Ltd. Published 2021 by John Wiley & Sons Ltd.
Companion website: www.wiley.com/go/Wheeler/Forensic

numerical difference between the refractive indices for a given sample. This can be determined by Equation 3A-1 or by several other methods with the aid of a compensator. The sign of elongation of anisotropic samples is another characteristic that can be determined with a polarized light microscope. Sign of elongation is a term that refers to how a sample is elongated in relation to its refractive indices. If the refractive index for light parallel to the long axis of the sample (n-parallel) exceeds that of the refractive index of light perpendicular to the long axis of the sample (n-perpendicular), the elongation is said to be positive. This means that the slow component vibrates in the longest direction of the fiber. If the reverse is true, the sign of elongation is negative.

Sign of elongation can be determined by two methods:

1. by measuring both refractive indices followed by mathematical subtraction to determine the birefringence and sign of elongation according to Equation 3B-1; or
2. by interpreting observations when inserting a compensator into the optical path.

In Experiment 3B, you used the Becke line immersion method to determine the refractive index of n-parallel and n-perpendicular for a fiber. These values can be applied using Equation 3B-1 to obtain the birefringence. If the value obtained was a positive value, the sign of elongation is deemed to be positive. Likewise, if the value obtained was a negative value, the sign of elongation is deemed to be negative. This method of determining sign of elongation and birefringence is dependent on the correct identification of n-parallel and n-perpendicular for a fiber. In this experiment, a compensator is used to determine both the sign of elongation and birefringence.

Compensators are made of various anisotropic crystalline materials. The amount of retardation is marked on the compensator. They are also marked to identify their slow direction, which is the higher refractive index direction. First-order compensators, also called full-wave plates, are made of selenite or quartz and produce a retardation of approximately 550 nm. Quarter-wave compensators are usually made of mica or quartz and produce a retardation of approximately 137 nm. A quartz wedge is another type of compensator in which a "wedge" of quartz of variable thickness is used to compensate the retardation produced by a sample. First-order compensators and quartz wedges are most commonly used for forensic applications. When inserted into the light path under crossed polars, a compensator will either add or subtract retardation according to their thickness and refractive indices. For example, first-order red compensators add or subtract approximately 550 nm. A change in the interference color observed when the compensator is inserted is caused by either "addition" or "subtraction" to the light path. If the slow components of both the sample and the compensator are aligned or parallel, addition occurs. If the slow components of both the sample and the compensator are perpendicular to each other, then subtraction will occur. The Michel-Lévy chart located in Appendix C can be used to determine if the change in color after insertion of a compensator is due to addition or subtraction. If the insertion of the compensator causes a resulting new color that corresponds to a higher retardation color, addition has occurred and the color is said to have "moved up the chart." If the color change results in a lower retardation color, subtraction has occurred and the color is said to have "moved down the chart." As known from Equation 3A-3, retardation is related to birefringence. If the thickness of a sample can be determined, the interpretation of retardation colors obtained when using a compensator can also provide a value for birefringence.

Sign of elongation and birefringence are characteristics that are commonly determined to identify and compare fiber evidence. A fiber has two optical axes in that light is separated into two rays when it interacts with the fiber. One ray is parallel to the long axis of the fiber, while the other is perpendicular to the long axis. Light will travel at different speeds in the two directions, due to the fiber's internal organization. Light that is retarded in one direction is said to be the slow ray, and that direction will have a higher refractive index. Likewise, light traveling in the other direction, the fast ray, will have a lower refractive index. Fibers are first observed in the NE-SW or 45° position under crossed polars. If the fiber has a gray color when first observed in the NE-SW position under crossed polars, it can have a negative sign of elongation or a positive sign of elongation coupled with very low birefringence. If interference colors other than gray are observed, the fiber has a positive sign of elongation. That is, the slow ray is parallel to the length of the fiber, and the refractive index in the elongated direction is greater than the refractive index in the perpendicular direction. Sign of elongation and birefringence can be determined by addition of a "known" thickness compensator to the optical path, which also has the effect of changing the retardation of light. To obtain specific information about the birefringence value, it is possible to add enough thickness to the compensator, so that the fast ray is completely retarded to match the speed of the slow ray. This causes the fiber to appear dark and mimics an isotropic sample. A quartz wedge has a variable thickness and allows the analyst to estimate the retardation needed to equalize the speed in the two directions. This retardation is used to calculate the birefringence, provided the thickness can be determined using Equation 3A-3.

The optical properties of materials are used to characterize and distinguish different samples. When using the polarized light microscope to determine sign of elongation and birefringence, it becomes another valuable tool in a forensic laboratory.

Equipment and Supplies

Polarized light microscope with objectives of various magnifications (e.g., 4X, 10X, 20X, and 40X)

McCrone Particle Reference Set™

Prepared slides of unknown fibers

First-order compensator

Quartz-wedge compensator

Michel-Lévy chart

Safety

Use standard laboratory safety procedures as described in guidelines set by your instructor. Be cautious of microscope light levels to avoid eye damage. Know the hazards associated with the mounting mediums, and use them with appropriate precautions as set by your instructor. Dispose of glass in an appropriate container.

Part I: Sign of Elongation Using the First-Order Compensator

Procedure

1. Obtain a prepared slide of acrylic.
2. After turning on the light source, adjust the microscope to obtain Köhler illumination.

3. Using the lowest magnification, place the prepared sample on the microscope stage and bring it into focus.
4. Observe the acrylic fiber under crossed polars. Rotate this fiber into a NE-SW orientation (upper right–lower left). Using the circle template in Appendix E, draw what you see. Remember: If interference colors other than gray are observed, the fiber should have a "+" sign of elongation.
5. Insert the first-order compensator, and redraw the sample.
6. Consult the Michel-Lévy chart (Appendix C), and determine if addition or subtraction of interference colors is occurring. Is this a positive or negative fiber?
7. Rotate the stage 90°, and redraw the colors. Why has there been a change in the interference colors?
8. Next, obtain a prepared slide of acetate fibers.
9. Observe the fiber under crossed polars. Rotate the fiber into a NE-SW orientation. Draw what you see.
10. Insert the first-order compensator, and redraw the colors. Is this a positive or negative fiber?
11. Rotate the stage 90°, and redraw the colors. Why has there been a change in the interference colors?

Part II: Sign of Elongation Using the Quartz Wedge

Procedure

1. Obtain a prepared slide of polyester.
2. Observe the fiber under crossed polars. Rotate the fiber into a NE-SW orientation. Draw what you see.
3. Insert the quartz wedge and observe the color change.
4. Continue inserting the wedge until the center of the fiber becomes black. As you insert the quartz wedge, you are increasing the retardation of the light. When the fiber goes black, you have slowed down the fast ray until it equals the speed of the slow ray. The sample and the quartz wedge are now isotropic (equal in all directions).
5. Rotate the stage 90°, and observe what happens to the black color. Draw what you see. Because the slow direction of the quartz wedge is known, you can determine the slow and fast directions of the sample. Likewise, the elongation can be determined since you will know if n-parallel or n-perpendicular is greater. Is this a positive or negative fiber?
6. Repeat steps 1–5 with a prepared slide of rayon and a prepared slide of nylon.

Part III: Birefringence Measurement Using a Quartz Wedge

Procedure

1. Obtain a prepared slide of your unknown fiber.
2. Observe the fiber under crossed polars. Rotate the fiber into a NE-SW orientation.
3. Determine if the unknown fiber is positive or negative using the procedure in Part I or Part II.
4. Measure the diameter of the unknown fiber using your calibrated ocular micrometer.

5. Using crossed polars, rotate the fiber into a NE-SW orientation.
6. Insert the quartz wedge while observing the color change at the center of the fiber. This is the location that corresponds to colors on the Michel-Lévy chart. Continue inserting the wedge until the center of the fiber becomes black. As you insert the quartz wedge, you are increasing the retardation of the light. When the fiber goes black, you have slowed down the fast ray until it equals the speed of the slow ray. The sample and the quartz wedge are now isotropic, and the center color of the fiber is said to be distinguished.
7. Read the amount of retardation from the quartz wedge. If your wedge is not calibrated (as is more often the case), you can determine the retardation by counting the number of red bands that pass on the outside of the fiber as you are inserting the quartz wedge on its way to being distinguished. Each red band corresponds to 550 nm.
8. From the retardation obtained, calculate the birefringence of the fiber using Equation 3A-3. For example, a nylon fiber is found to be 49 μm in diameter. Upon insertion of the quartz wedge, the color in the center of the fiber is distinguished in between five and six orders of a quartz wedge. Its retardation is therefore 5.5 orders × 550 nm, or 3025 nm. The birefringence is determined using Equation 3A-3:

$$3025 \text{ nm} = B \times 49 \text{ μm} \times 1000 \text{ nm/μm}$$

$$B = 0.061$$

From Appendix B, this fiber can be identified as nylon 6,6.
9. Compare the sign of elongation and birefringence to the table found in Appendix B to identify your unknown. Justify your answer with both drawings and a short discussion.

Report Requirements

Include all drawings, calculations, and other information obtained during the laboratory procedure. Notes and/or drawings should include the sample identification, magnification, and a complete description.

Report Questions

1. Define the sign of elongation. How can it be determined?
2. What is the difference between sign of elongation and birefringence?
3. How is the sign of elongation used in forensic examinations?
4. What are the advantages and disadvantages of this optical property for forensic samples?
5. Two compensators were used in this experiment.
   a. Draw a quartz wedge, and explain what happens when it continues to be inserted.
   b. How many wavelengths of retardation are added for a full-wave plate compensator?
   c. How many wavelengths of retardation are added for a quarter-wave plate compensator?
6. A fiber is viewed in the NE-SW position under crossed polars. The background is black. The fiber has a positive sign of elongation.
   a. Explain why the background changes from black to red upon insertion of the first-order red compensator.
   b. With the first-order red compensator in position, the fiber is rotated 90° to the NW-SE position. Would the color change be (a) no change, (b) higher order, or (c) lower order? Fully explain your answer.

7. If you have an Acrilan 36™ acrylic fiber mounted in 1.514 Cargille™ oil, how would you determine the sign of elongation?

8. If you were given a positive sign of elongation fiber that appeared first-order red when viewed in the NE-SW orientation under crossed polars, what color on the Michel-Lévy chart would the fiber be after the insertion of a quarter-wave plate? What color would the fiber be after the insertion of a full-wave plate? When still using the full-wave plate, what color would the fiber appear if it were rotated to the NW-SE orientation?

9. Explain why the center of the fiber went dark upon insertion of the quartz wedge in Parts II and III.

10. You have a nylon fiber that extinguishes at fifth-order green using a quartz wedge. If the thickness is 45 mm, what is the birefringence?

Recommended and Further Reading

Abramowitz MJ. The Polarizing Microscope. *American Laboratory*. 1990; 22(9): 72.

Bell S. *Forensic Chemistry*. Upper Saddle River, NJ: Pearson Education, 2006.

Benedetti-Pichler AA. *Identification of Materials via Physical Properties, Chemical Tests and Microscopy*. New York: Springer, 1964.

Brenner M. Understanding the Polarizing Microscope. *American Laboratory*. 1980; 42(4): 72.

DeForest PR. Foundations of Forensic Microscopy. In: Saferstein R, ed. *Forensic Science Handbook*, 2nd ed. Upper Saddle River, NJ: Pearson Education, 2002; 301–305.

Dobos SK. Polarized Transmitted-Light and Reflected-Light Microscopy in the Earth, Materials, and Related Sciences. *American Laboratory*. 1986; 18(4): 64.

Eyring MB, Gaudette BD. An Introduction to the Forensic Aspects of Textile Fiber Examination. In: Saferstein R, ed. *Forensic Science Handbook*, 2nd ed. Upper Saddle River, NJ: Pearson Education, 2002; 245–281.

Laughlin GJ. Counterterrorism and the Polarized Light Microscope. *American Laboratory*. 2003; 35(8): 10.

McCrone W. Refractive Indices and Birefringence of Fibers. *The Microscope*. 1991; 39: 57–58.

McCrone WC. The Case for Polarized Light Microscopy. *American Laboratory*. 1996; 28(9): 12.

McCrone WC. Why Use the Polarized-Light Microscope? *American Laboratory*. 1992; 24(6): 17–21.

McCrone WC, McCrone LB, Delly JG. *Polarized Light Microscopy*. Ann Arbor, MI: Ann Arbor Science, 1978.

Robinson P, Bradbury S. *Qualitative Polarized Light Microscopy*. Oxford: Oxford Science Publications (RMS), Oxford University Press, 1992.

Weaver R. Rediscovering Polarized Light Microscopy. *American Laboratory*. 2003; 35(20): 55.

Chapter 4
Fluorescence Microscope

In the previous chapters, we have discussed microscopes used in many types of forensic examinations as well as many different sections of a forensic laboratory. Similar to the polarized light microscope, the fluorescence microscope is generally used for specialized examinations in the trace section. Using high magnification and the additional components found in a fluorescence microscope, an analyst is able to identify many important characteristics for a sample, which can be used for identification and comparison purposes.

Like other microscopes, the fluorescence microscope uses a combination of lenses to produce a magnified image. In addition to the basic components, several additional parts are added to enhance the analytical ability of the microscope. A fluorescence microscope has the following basic parts:

- visible light source
- condenser
- sample stage
- objective
- focusing knobs
- oculars

In addition, the following components are added:

- ultraviolet light source
- excitation filters
- barrier filters

Basically, the short-wavelength light in a fluorescence microscope originates from a specialized illuminator. The light from the illuminator then passes through an excitation filter. The excitation light is redirected through the objective by a mirror so that it reaches the sample. Part of this light is absorbed by the sample and re-emitted as fluorescence. The re-emitted light then passes through a barrier filter. This filter allows light to pass that is in the visible range (fluorescence from the sample), permitting it to reach the oculars. Since the barrier filter blocks light emitted by the excitation filters, the background will appear black, allowing only fluorescence from a sample to be viewed.

Fluorescence microscopes generally utilize oculars and objectives that provide total magnification within the range of 40X to 400X. Because of the higher total magnification, a smaller

Practical Forensic Microscopy: A Laboratory Manual, Second Edition. Barbara P. Wheeler.
© 2021 John Wiley & Sons Ltd. Published 2021 by John Wiley & Sons Ltd.
Companion website: www.wiley.com/go/Wheeler/Forensic

field of view and less depth of field are obtained. Samples may initially be viewed with trans-mitted light; however, reflected filtered light is sometimes used to obtain certain microscopic characteristics.

The fluorescence microscope is used to identify and characterize samples. The high-level magnification allows viewing of the initial characteristics of an item or sample, with additional comparison and microscopic examinations also possible.

Chapter 4

Experiment 4A: Familiarization with the Fluorescence Microscope

Recommended pre-lab reading assignment:

Siegel JI. Fluorescence Microscopy. *American Laboratory*. 1982; April: 65–69.

Recommended website:

Abramowitz M, Herman B, Murphy DB, Davidson MW. Anatomy of a Fluorescence Microscope [Java Interactive Tutorial; cited 2020]. Available from: http://www.olympusmicro.com.

Objective

Upon completion of this practical exercise, the student will have developed a basic understanding of:

1. components of the fluorescence microscope
2. fluorescence
3. use of the fluorescence microscope to observe sample fluorescence

Introduction

As with the polarized light microscope, components can be added to a microscope so that particular sample characteristics can be examined. The fluorescence microscope allows the forensic scientist to observe sample fluorescence.

The theory behind a fluorescence microscope is fairly simple. Some materials possess the property that when specific wavelengths of light fall upon them, they absorb this light and in turn re-emit light of a longer wavelength. This property is called fluorescence. The fluorescence microscope allows the forensic scientist to observe this property by selectively irradiating the sample and viewing the resultant fluorescence. Although many samples fluoresce, the fluorescence properties of fibers will be examined in this experiment. Fiber evidence is considered class evidence (i.e., not unique) because many fibers from different sources could be indistinguishable. The discovery of a fiber and its identification as a particular fiber type (e.g., acrylic, cotton, nylon, polyester) may not, of itself, provide much support for a forensic investigation. However, the probative value of particular fibers found at a crime scene depends on their uniqueness relative to the background of fibers normally encountered. What is often required to aid in the characterization of a fiber is information that makes the trace evidence more specific and discriminating. Since the fluorescent property of a questioned fiber may be unique, it may be easily distinguished from other similar fibers if this characteristic is examined.

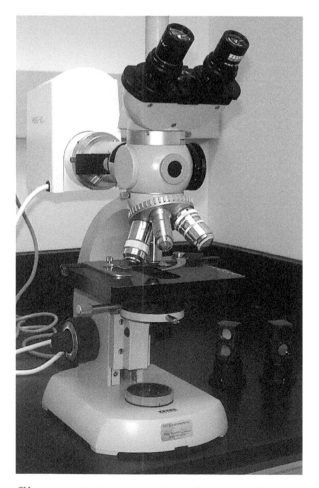

Figure 4A-1 Zeiss™ compound microscope with epi-fluorescence lighting. Additional filter cubes can be inserted for viewing samples over various wavelength ranges.

A microscope is an optical instrument that uses a combination of lenses to produce a magnified image of small objects. Just like a compound or polarized microscope, the fluorescence microscope utilizes several basic optical components that gather light and redirect the light path so that a magnified image of the viewed object can be focused within a short distance. These basic optical components are: light source, condenser, sample stage, objective, focusing knobs, and oculars. In addition, the fluorescence microscope uses additional components that enhance the microscope's analytical ability. These additional components are excitation and barrier filters and a specialized light source that extends into the ultraviolet (UV) region of the spectrum for sample excitation (see Figure 4A-1). High-intensity light consisting of a narrow band of wavelengths is required to excite the sample. Typically mercury or xenon arc lamps are used to provide the high-intensity multispectral light. To obtain a narrow band of specific wavelengths, excitation filters are placed in the optical path between the illuminator and the sample. However, to view sample fluorescence, unwanted excitation wavelengths must be blocked from reaching the viewer's eye. This is accomplished by the placement of a barrier filter between the sample and the oculars. Excitation and barrier filters may be short-pass filters (filter that rejects longer wavelengths and passes shorter wavelengths) or bandpass filters (filter that passes frequencies within a certain range and rejects frequencies outside that range). In most fluorescence microscopes, both the excitation filter and the barrier filter are contained in a filter cube. This cube also contains a dichroic mirror that directs the light. This arrangement, where both the illuminated (excitation filter light) and emitted light (barrier filter light) travel through the same optical path, is referred to as epi-fluorescence microscopy.

The optical path of the fluorescence microscope is shown in Figure 4A-2. In a fluorescence microscope, the short-wavelength light originates from a specialized illuminator. Since fluorescence is easily examined with reflected light, the illuminator is usually mounted at the top of the microscope. A high pressure xenon or mercury lamp is most often utilized. The light from

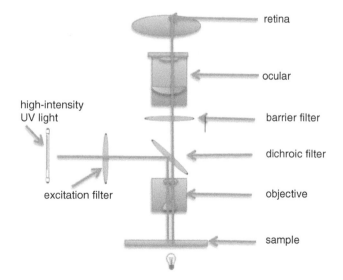

Figure 4A-2 Fluorescence excitation of the sample occurs when UV light travels from the high-intensity light source through an excitation and dichroic filter to the specimen. Fluorescence excitation is detected by observing the light coming off the specimen. Only fluorescence from the sample is observed, since UV light from the light source is blocked by a barrier filter.

the lamp is passed through an excitation filter that allows only a narrow band of specific wavelengths to pass through. Excitation filters are normally in the UV range of light. The excitation light is redirected through the objective by a dichroic mirror. This mirror or beamsplitter efficiently directs the light by reflecting shorter wavelength light and passing longer wavelength light so that it reaches the sample. Part of this light is absorbed by the sample and re-emitted as fluorescence. The re-emitted light then passes back through the objective to the dichroic mirror that once again directs the light. Because the re-emitted light consists of longer wavelengths than the excited light, it is able to pass through the mirror or beamsplitter to the barrier filter. The barrier filter restricts any residual excitation light but continues to allow the longer re-emitted wavelengths to pass to the oculars. Since the barrier filter blocks light emitted by the excitation filters, the background will appear black, allowing any fluorescence from a sample to be easily viewed.

Samples may initially be viewed with transmitted light; however, reflected filtered light is utilized to obtain a sample's fluorescent characteristics. A series of four filter cubes – ultraviolet, violet, blue, and green – are usually recommended for forensic use. It is important to note that glass microscope slides and most mounting mediums can absorb UV radiation or fluoresce in and of themselves. A strongly fluorescing sample may still be visible with a glass cover slip, but weak fluorescence might be missed. In order to minimize this interfering fluorescence, it is best to use quartz microscope slides and cover slips. Since most of the common mounting mediums also fluoresce, it is important to use mounting mediums such as methanol, glycerin, xylene, Norland 65^{TM}, and XAM^{TM}, which do not fluoresce.

The optical properties of materials are used to characterize and distinguish different samples. When using the fluorescence light microscope to determine a sample's fluorescent characteristics, it becomes another valuable tool in a forensic laboratory.

Equipment and Supplies

Fluorescence microscope with objectives of various magnifications (e.g., 4X, 10X, 20X, and 40X) and various excitation and barrier filters

Micro kit

Fibers with known fluorescence

Quartz microscope slides

Quartz cover slips

Mounting medium such as methanol, glycerin, xylene, Norland 65^{TM}, or XAM^{TM}

Safety

Use standard laboratory safety procedures as described in guidelines set by your instructor. Mercury or xenon lamps generate extreme heat and may explode. Do not look at the lamp directly to avoid eye damage. Use the safety shield if it is provided. Be cautious of microscope light levels to avoid eye damage. Know the hazards associated with the mounting mediums, and use them with appropriate precautions as set by your instructor. Dispose of glass in an appropriate container.

Part I: Parts of a Fluorescence Microscope

1. Obtain a photograph of the fluorescence microscope used in the laboratory.
2. Label the following parts of the microscope: light source, high-intensity light source, condenser, sample stage, objectives, field diaphragm, lamp aperture, focusing knobs, filter cubes, and oculars.

Part II: Initial Operation of the Fluorescence Microscope

Procedure

1. Familiarize yourself with the fluorescence microscope. Locate each part of the microscope. Place a prepared microscope slide on the stage. After turning on the transmitted light source, manipulate the oculars of the microscope to adjust the interpupillary distance so that when viewing an object, the right and left images merge as one.
2. Adjust the focus up and down. Using the non-adjustable ocular, focus on an item to obtain a clear image of an item.
3. Focus the second ocular if necessary.
4. Set up Köhler illumination and have your instructor check the microscope for correct illumination.
5. Determine the location of the specialized illuminator.
6. Determine the location of the excitation/barrier filter cubes.

Part III: Observing Sample Fluorescence

Procedure

1. Turn on the power supply for the specialized illuminator. Slide the lamp diaphragm into the closed position while the lamp warms up.
2. Prepare the sample using non-fluorescent microscope slides, cover slips, and mounting medium.
3. Turn on the power supply for the transmitted light illuminator. (Steps 3 and 4 are only necessary if the transmitted light will be used to aid in the visualization of samples.) Adjust the microscope to obtain Köhler illumination.
4. Using the lowest magnification, place the prepared sample on the microscope stage and bring it into focus. Lower the intensity of the transmitted light and room lighting. Open the lamp diaphragm on the specialized illuminator. Refocusing of the sample may be necessary.

5. Observe the sample and note the color of any light being emitted. Change excitation/barrier filter cubes, and note your observations. In your notes, fully describe the fluorescent characteristics of your sample.
6. Repeat this examination with three more samples.

Report Requirements

Include all drawings, calculations, and other information obtained during the laboratory procedure. Notes and/or drawings should include the sample identification, magnification, and a complete description.

Report Questions

1. Explain how a fluorescence microscope is used in forensic science. Discuss the purpose and value of a fluorescence examination.
2. What is fluorescence? How is fluorescence initiated?
3. What are the advantages and disadvantages of this optical property for forensic samples?
4. Explain the optics utilized in a fluorescence microscope.
5. What function does each component perform in the fluorescence microscope?
6. If a forensic scientist has a polarizing microscope such as a Leica DMEP, which they want to convert to a fluorescence microscope, could they use the same illumination? Why or why not?
7. What is the purpose of the excitation and barrier filters?
8. How are excitation and barrier filters paired?
9. Does the color of light emitted from a fluorescent sample have any significance in distinguishing and identifying the sample?
10. Why were quartz microscope slides and cover slips used?
11. Name two types of evidence that could be examined with a fluorescence microscope. What would the examination consist of?
12. What types of evidence would not be examined with the fluorescence microscope? Why?

Recommended and Further Reading

Bell S. *Forensic Chemistry*. Upper Saddle River, NJ: Pearson Education, 2006.

Fong W. Analytical Methods for Developing Fibers as Forensic-Science Proof – a Review with Comments. *Journal of Forensic Sciences*. 1989; 34(2): 295–311.

Herman B. *Fluorescence Microscopy*. 2nd ed. Oxford: Bios Scientific Publishers, Springer in Association with the Royal Microscopical Society, 1998.

Wang XF, Herman B. *Fluorescence Imaging Spectroscopy and Microscopy*. New York: John Wiley & Sons Inc., 1996.

Wiggins K, Holness JA. A Further Study of Dye Batch Variation in Textile and Carpet Fibres. *Science & Justice*. 2005; 45(2): 93–96.

Chapter 5
Phase Contrast Microscope

The stereomicroscope and compound light microscope are utilized for many applications in different sections of a forensic laboratory. Similar to the polarized light microscope and fluorescence microscope, the phase contrast microscope is used for specialized examinations in the trace section. Using high magnification and additional components, a phase contrast microscope allows the analyst to identify important characteristics of a forensic sample.

Like other optical microscopes, the phase contrast microscope uses a combination of lenses to produce a magnified image. In addition to the basic components, several additional parts are added to enhance the analytical ability of the microscope. A phase contrast microscope has the following basic parts:

- light source
- condenser
- sample stage
- objective
- focusing knobs
- oculars

In addition, the following components are added:

- phase annulus
- phase plate

Basically, the light from the illuminator is passed to the condenser. In the phase contrast microscope, the condenser is modified by replacing the substage iris with a phase annulus. The phase annulus is a centerable mechanical device that allows only a ring of light to pass into the condenser. The purpose of the phase annulus is to separate the light into direct rays and diffracted rays that are then focused upon the sample. Once the light has exited the sample, it is once again modified by a phase plate. A phase plate is a standard objective modified with a ring of material that retards the light coming through the objective. This directly corresponds to the light being allowed through by the phase annulus. This phase retardation interferes destructively with the direct light and reduces its amplitude, usually by $\lambda/2$. The light being diffracted by the sample does not go through this ring, and its amplitude is therefore not affected. The net effect of this light diffraction is that there is a bigger difference in the amplitude of the direct and diffracted rays, which in turn makes the image more visible.

Practical Forensic Microscopy: A Laboratory Manual, Second Edition. Barbara P. Wheeler.
© 2021 John Wiley & Sons Ltd. Published 2021 by John Wiley & Sons Ltd.
Companion website: www.wiley.com/go/Wheeler/Forensic

Phase contrast microscopes generally utilize oculars and objectives that provide total magnification within the range of 40X to 400X. Because of the higher total magnification, a smaller field of view and less depth of field are obtained. Samples are viewed with transmitted light.

The phase contrast microscope is used to identify and characterize samples. The high-level magnification allows viewing of the initial characteristics of an item or sample, with additional comparison and microscopic examinations also possible.

Chapter 5

Experiment 5A: Familiarization with the Phase Contrast Microscope

Recommended pre-lab reading assignment:

McCrone WC, McCrone LB, Delly JG. *Polarized Light Microscopy*. Ann Arbor, MI: Ann Arbor Science, 1978; 61–64.

Recommended website:

Abramowitz M, Davidson MW. Specialized Microscopy Techniques—Phase Contrast [Java Interactive Tutorial; cited 2020]. Available from: http://www.olympusmicro.com.

Objective

Upon completion of this practical exercise, the student will have developed a basic understanding of:

1. components of the phase contrast microscope
2. use of the phase contrast microscope to determine refractive index

Introduction

As with the polarized light microscope and fluorescence microscope, components can be added to a microscope so that particular sample characteristics can be examined. The phase contrast microscope allows the forensic scientist to observe images with enhanced contrast.

A microscope is an optical instrument that uses a combination of lenses to produce a magnified image of small objects. The phase contrast microscope accomplishes this using several components that gather light and redirect the light path so that a magnified image of the viewed object can be focused within a short distance. In a phase contrast microscope, there

Practical Forensic Microscopy: A Laboratory Manual, Second Edition. Barbara P. Wheeler.
© 2021 John Wiley & Sons Ltd. Published 2021 by John Wiley & Sons Ltd.
Companion website: www.wiley.com/go/Wheeler/Forensic

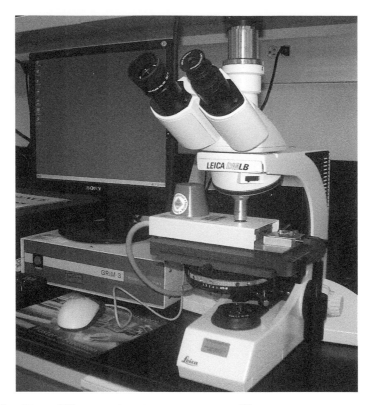

Figure 5A-1   GRIM 3™ system featuring a Leica DMLB™ phase contrast microscope with a hot stage attachment.

are additional parts that enhance the microscope's analytical ability. This microscope contains the basic components of light source, condenser, sample stage, focusing knobs, and oculars, with the addition of a phase annulus or ring that modifies the condenser, and an objective with a phase plate (see Figure 5A-1).

The microscopist uses the difference in the refractive index of the mounting medium and the sample to enhance the contrast in the images seen. If the microscopist cannot improve the contrast of a sample by changing the mounting medium, as is the case with biological samples or when working with very tiny particles, they may need to work with a phase contrast microscope. The theory behind a phase contrast microscope is fairly simple. Since most transparent samples diffract light, a phase shift occurs in the rays of light that pass through them. When the sample being observed is either very thin or has a refractive index close to the mounting medium, this phase difference is undetectable by a routine compound light microscope. Phase contrast microscopes take advantage of this shift by transforming the differences in light waves into differences in the observed image.

Most phase contrast microscopes use the Zernike contrast method. When using a phase contrast microscope, the phase differences between light passing through the sample and light passing through the mounting medium are converted into amplitude differences. This provides a difference in brightness between the sample and the background. The phase contrast microscope renders undetectable phase differences into easily observed light and dark areas. This makes the image appear as if it has been "stained," which in turn enhances the ability to view the sample.

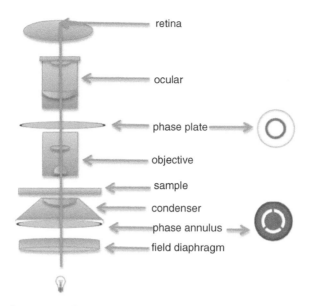

Figure 5A-2 Optical path of a phase contrast microscope.

This phenomenon takes place in the phase contrast microscope by the special placement of a phase annulus and phase plate in the optical path, as illustrated in Figure 5A-2. The phase annulus, placed under the lower lens of the condenser, separates the light passing to the objective. The phase annulus is a mechanical device that allows only a ring of light to pass from the condenser and, in turn, to be focused upon the sample plane. This allows both direct light (background) and diffracted light (by the sample) to fill the focal plane of the objective and the complementary phase plate that is located in the back focal plane of the objective.

A phase plate, mounted in or near the objective back focal plane, contains a ring of material that either retards or advances the light coming through. This area of the phase plate corresponds directly to the light being allowed through by the phase annulus, causing a phase shift of the light. At this point, the light is either slowed because the ring area of the phase plate is thicker (negative phase contrast) or speeds up because the ring area of the phase plate is thinner in the area (positive phase contrast). This results in either constructive or destructive interference when the direct and diffracted light from the sample recombine.

If the phase plate is negative, the light passing through the phase plate is retarded. Since the phase annulus and the phase plate are complementary, direct light is affected, but the diffracted light from the sample is unaffected. This results in constructive interference since the direct and diffracted waves are now in phase. This produces an increase in amplitude that creates an enhanced contrast between a bright image and a darker background. Likewise, if the phase plate is positive, the light passing through the phase plate is advanced. Once again, since the phase annulus and the phase plate are complementary, direct light is affected, but the diffracted light from the sample is unaffected. This results in destructive interference since the direct and diffracted waves are now out of phase. This produces a decrease in amplitude that creates a darker image for samples with a lighter background.

The optical properties of materials are used to characterize and distinguish different samples. The phase contrast microscope allows the forensic scientist to observe samples with greater contrast that can be defined as the difference in brightness between the light and dark areas of an image. When using the phase contrast microscope to determine a sample's optical characteristics, it becomes another valuable tool in a forensic laboratory.

Equipment and Supplies

Phase contrast microscope with objectives of various magnifications (e.g., 4X, 10X, 20X, and 40X)

Micro kit

Glass samples

Microscope slides

Cover slips

Cargille™ oils

Safety

Use standard laboratory safety procedures as described in guidelines set by your instructor. Be cautious of microscope light levels to avoid eye damage. Know the hazards associated with the mounting mediums, and use them with appropriate precautions as set by your instructor. Dispose of glass in an appropriate container.

Part I: Parts of a Phase Contrast Microscope

1. Obtain a photograph of the phase contrast microscope used in the laboratory.
2. Label the following parts of the microscope: light aperture, light source, condenser, phase annulus centering screws, sample stage, objectives, focusing knobs, and oculars.

Part II: Operation of the Phase Contrast Microscope

Procedure

1. Familiarize yourself with the phase contrast microscope. Various brands of phase contrast microscopes are available. Familiarize yourself with the operations manual of the microscope so that you are able to center the phase rings prior to use.
2. Locate each part of the microscope. Place a prepared microscope slide on the stage. After turning on the light source, manipulate the oculars of the microscope to adjust the interpupillary distance so that when viewing an object, the right and left images merge as one.
3. Adjust the focus up and down. Using the non-adjustable ocular, focus on an item to obtain a clear image of an item.
4. Focus the second ocular if necessary.
5. Set up Köhler illumination, and have your instructor check the microscope for correct illumination.

6. Determine the location of the phase annulus.
7. Determine the location of the phase plate.

Part III: Using the Phase Contrast Microscope

Procedure

1. Obtain a glass sample. Mount a small portion of the sample on a microscope slide, and cover with a cover slip. Choose a Cargille™ oil close to the estimated refractive index of the glass sample. Place a drop of the oil next to the cover slip so that it is drawn under the cover slip. Turn on the power supply for the base light illuminator, and adjust the light to provide an even, bright illumination over the entire field of view.
2. With the microscope set on the lowest magnification, adjust the interpupillary distance for the oculars, so that the right and left images merge into one.
3. Place the mounted glass samples on the stage and focus; if necessary, focus (using the non-adjustable ocular) on the sample by using the coarse and fine focus knobs. Next, adjust the second ocular so that a crisp, clear image is viewed.
4. Check alignment of the phase annulus and phase plate.
5. Observe the sample, looking at the Becke line. Using the focus knob, adjust the focus while observing the edges of the glass sample. When the glass is slightly out of focus, the Becke line will appear either inside or outside the fiber edge. The Becke line will move toward the higher refractive index when the focal distance is increased. Document which medium has the higher refractive index.
6. Repeat with an oil of different refractive index until you are able to determine the refractive index of the glass sample. Determine which liquid to use next by depending on your previous results.
7. Repeat steps 3–6 for all assigned samples.

Report Requirements

Include all drawings, calculations, and other information obtained during the laboratory procedure. Notes and/or drawings should include the sample identification, magnification, and a complete description.

Report Questions

1. What are the specialized components of a phase contrast microscope? What function does each component perform in a phase contrast microscope?
2. Name two types of specimens that would be best to be viewed with a phase contrast microscope. What would the examination consist of?
3. Why do biologists commonly use this microscope?
4. Give an example of how this microscope is used by forensic scientists.
5. Explain the optics utilized in a phase contrast microscope.

6. Name two types of evidence that could be examined with a phase contrast microscope. What would the examination consist of?
7. What are the advantages and disadvantages of using this microscope for forensic samples?

Recommended and Further Reading

Allen R, Brault J, Zeh R. Image Contrast and Phase Modulation Light Methods in Polarization and Interference Microscopy. *Advances in Optical and Electron Microscopy.* 1966; 1: 77–114.

De Forest PR. Foundations of Forensic Microscopy. In: Saferstein R, ed. *Forensic Science Handbook*, 2nd ed. Upper Saddle River, NJ: Pearson Education, 2002; 301–305.

Determann H, Lepusch F. Phase Contrast Microscopy. In: *The Microscope and Its Application*. Deerfield, IL: Ernst Leitz Wetzlar, 1988; 19–22 and 47–48.

Gerlovin BY. Calculation of the Optimum Dimensions of the Phase Rings of Phase-Contrast Microscope Objectives. *Soviet Journal of Optical Technology.* 1987; 54(10): 596–599.

Goldstein D. Extension of the Abbe Theory to Transparent Objects (Zernike's Phase Contrast). In: *Understanding the Light Microscope*. New York: Academic Press, 1999; 45–55.

Hostounsky Z, Pelc R. Phase-Contrast Versus Off-Axis Illumination: Is a More Complex Microscope Always More Powerful? *Advances in Physiology Education.* 2007; 31(2): 232–235.

Kong XG, Feng TS, Jin GF. Reflection Zernike Phase-Contrast Microscope. *Applied Optics.* 1990; 29(10): 1408–1409.

Murphy D. Phase Contrast Microscopy. In: *Fundamentals of Light Microscopy and Electronic Imaging*. New York: Wiley-Liss, 2001; 97–112.

Ojena SM, De Forest PR. Precise Refractive Index Determination by the Immersion Method Using Phase Contrast Microscopy and the Mettler Hot Stage. *Journal of the Forensic Science Society.* 1972; 12: 315–329.

Ross KFA. *Phase Contrast and Interference Microscopy for Cell Biologists*. London: Edward Arnold, 1967.

Application
Experiments

Chapter 6

Experiment 6: Physical Match Examinations

Recommended pre-lab reading assignments:

Thornton JI. Fractural Surfaces as Models of Physical Matches. *Journal of Forensic Sciences*. 1986; 31(4): 1435–1438.

Adolf FP. Physical Fits Between Textiles. In: *Proceedings of the 3rd Meeting of the European Fibres Group*, Linkoping, Sweden. 1995; 36–41.

Objective

Upon completion of this practical exercise, the student will have developed a basic understanding of:

1. physical match examinations

Introduction

A comparative examination is the process of ascertaining whether two or more objects have a common origin. One way that this is accomplished is by a physical match examination. Once a comparative examination has been completed, the forensic scientist must be prepared to render a conclusion with respect to the origins of the samples. Do they or do they not originate from the same source? Evidence is said to possess class characteristics when it can be associated with a group and not with a single source. Evidence that can be associated with a common source with an extremely high degree of probability is said to possess individual characteristics. When a physical match is obtained, it is considered unique, or an individual characteristic, and an analyst can determine that two portions were one at an earlier time.

Physical matching of broken, cut, or torn objects can be encountered in many types of forensic investigations. These types of examinations are performed to associate an item with the material

Practical Forensic Microscopy: A Laboratory Manual, Second Edition. Barbara P. Wheeler.
© 2021 John Wiley & Sons Ltd. Published 2021 by John Wiley & Sons Ltd.
Companion website: www.wiley.com/go/Wheeler/Forensic

from which it is thought to have originated. Physical match determinations may be performed in situations in which an item has been cut, torn, broken, or has otherwise undergone a separation into two or more pieces. If a separation is the result of a random process, the particular separation would not be expected to be repeated and should be considered unique. It is therefore possible that broken pieces could be fit together in a unique fashion to demonstrate a common origin.

The process of determining a physical match depends on the actual items themselves. For most items that have been cut or torn, a forensic scientist is able to determine whether or not the items were one piece at an earlier time by using edge shapes and surface features, as shown in Figure 6-1. These items are typically examined as a whole with low magnification on a stereomicroscope. Edge shapes are examined for a physical "fit," similar to what is done when working on a jigsaw puzzle. Cut edges will appear sharp and crisp, allowing edges to be easily examined and aligned. Torn edges may be frayed or rough, so in some instances, a closer examination with slightly higher magnification may be necessary. Surface features can also be used when performing a physical match. Surface features such as colored or molded patterns

Figure 6-1 This section of fabric displays a physical match that can be determined by both cut edges and surface features.

may also be useful in determining the actual placement of a section. Unique surface markings such as manufacturing striations or polishing scratches can also be helpful. In some cases, it may be necessary to use surface features only, since items that have been separated by "sawing" have actually had small portions of the newly formed edge removed.

Items that have been broken may also be examined using edge shapes and surface features. However, at times additional examinations are also necessary. Prior to breaking, some items tend to bend or stretch. This can cause unique stress markings perpendicular to the break edge. These markings, which will appear as mirror images, can also be examined to determine whether or not two items were one piece at an earlier time.

Several conclusions can be reached for physical match examinations. First, if a physical match is obtained, it can be determined that the items were one at an earlier time. Sometimes a physical match is not possible. This may be a result of differences or the lack of characteristics to make a determination. In these situations, no indication should be given as to whether or not the items were one at an earlier time. However, when appropriate, further testing may be suggested to either prove or disprove similarities between the items.

Equipment and Supplies

Stereomicroscope

Previously prepared sets of plastic pieces, cut up

Previously prepared sets of playing cards, cut up

Previously prepared sets of matchbooks and matches

Previously prepared sets of fabric, cut up

Previously prepared sets of broken microscope slides

Safety

Use standard laboratory safety procedures as described in guidelines set by your instructor.

Part I: Physical Match Examinations Using Edge Shape

Procedure

1. Obtain a set of plastic pieces.
2. Using the stereomicroscope, examine the edges of the pieces.
3. Describe the pieces. Any physical characteristics, such as color, edge, shape, and so on, should be noted.
4. Using the circle template in Appendix E, draw what you see for each piece.
5. Determine if the pieces were "one" at an earlier time. If you obtain a physical match, draw and state what you see. If you do not obtain a physical match, state the differences you found.
6. As a forensic scientist, you must learn to draw a conclusion and be able to communicate your conclusion verbally and in writing. Clearly state if you found a physical match between the plastic pieces. Explain how you reached this conclusion. If you do not obtain a physical match, state the differences you found.

Part II: Physical Match Examinations Using Edge Shape and Surface Features

Procedure

  A. Playing Cards
    1. Obtain a set of playing card pieces.
    2. Using the stereomicroscope, examine the edge shapes and surface features of the pieces.
    3. Describe the playing card pieces. Any physical characteristics, such as color, patterns, edge shapes, and so on, should be noted.
    4. Draw what you see for each piece.
    5. Determine if the pieces were "one" at an earlier time. If you obtain a physical match, draw and state what you see. If you do not obtain a physical match, state the differences you found.
    6. Clearly state if you found a physical match between the playing card pieces. Explain how you reached this conclusion. If you do not obtain a physical match, state the differences you found.
  B. Matches and Matchbook
    1. Obtain a match and matchbook set.
    2. Using the stereomicroscope, examine the edge shapes and surface features of the match and matchbook.
    3. Describe the match and matchbook in your notes. Any physical characteristics, such as color, width, length, thickness, and so on, should be noted. Most matchbooks are made from reprocessed paper. Sheets of paper are cut and dipped. Examination of the sides of the match and the edge where it was separated from the matchbook should be performed. Examination of these edges may reveal fibers that can be traced from one piece to another. Inclusions consisting of a large variety of colored fibrous material, aluminum foil, and other contaminants that were involved in the production of the paper may also be visible.
    4. Draw what you see for the match.
    5. Draw what you see for the matchbook.
    6. Determine if the match and the matchbook were "one" at an earlier time. If you obtain a physical match, draw and state what you see. If you do not obtain a physical match, state the differences you found.
    7. Clearly state if you found a physical match between the match and matchbook. Explain how you reached this conclusion. If you do not obtain a physical match, state the differences you found.
  C. Fabric
    1. Obtain a set of fabric pieces.
    2. Using the stereomicroscope, examine the edge shapes and surface features of the pieces.
    3. Describe the fabric pieces. Any physical characteristics, such as color, patterns, edge, shapes, and so on, should be noted.
    4. Draw what you see for each piece.
    5. Determine if the pieces were "one" at an earlier time. If you obtain a physical match, draw and state what you see. If you do not obtain a physical match, state the differences you found.

6. Clearly state if you found a physical match between the fabric pieces. Explain how you reached this conclusion. If you do not obtain a physical match, state the differences you found.

Part III: Physical Match Examinations and "Mirror Images"

Procedure

1. Choose a broken glass microscope slide set.
2. Using the stereomicroscope, examine the edge shapes and actual edge of the glass pieces. Glass is a super-cooled liquid. It will bend and stretch before it breaks. This creates "rib" markings on the edge upon breaking.
3. Draw the "rib" markings on one piece of glass.
4. Determine if the pieces "fit" together. Make a drawing of the fit. (Some maneuvering is necessary.) Write a statement about whether or not the pieces fit together next to your drawing.
5. Clearly state if you found a physical match between the glass pieces. Explain how you reached this conclusion. If you do not obtain a physical match, state the differences you found.

Report Requirements

Include all drawings, calculations, and other information obtained during the laboratory procedure. Notes and/or drawings should include the sample identification, magnification, and a complete description.

Report Questions

1. What is a physical match?
2. Explain why physical matches are possible.
3. Explain how a physical match examination is conducted. Give an example.
4. Give an example of how an examination is performed for items that might display "mirror images" when separated.
5. Explain the three characteristics that are used when performing physical examinations and how examinations are performed for each. Give an example of another item besides what you examined in lab for each type of comparison analysis.
6. A glass examiner examines a small piece of glass and is able to make a physical fit to a windowpane found at the crime scene. The glass examiner makes an opinion as to whether or not the piece of questioned glass came from the windowpane. Which one of the following opinions can be made? Fully explain your choice.
   a. Positive opinion of identity
   b. Opinion of probable common source
   c. Positive opinion of nonidentity
   d. Opinion that no conclusion could be reached

7. A broom handle has been sawed in half. One piece is used to break a window at a crime scene (and left behind), and the other piece is still at the suspect's garage. Can a physical match be made between the two pieces? Explain your answer.

Recommended and Further Reading

Adolph FP. Physical Fits between Textiles. *Proceedings of the 3rd Meeting of the European Group,* Linkoping, Sweden. 1995.

Bisbing RE. Fractured Patterns: Microscopical Investigation of Real Physical Evidence. *The Locard Exchange.* 2004; January 29: 1–5.

Farmer NL, Ruffell A, Meier-Augenstein W, Meneely J, Kalin RM. Forensic Analysis of Wooden Safety Matches – a Case Study. *Science & Justice.* 2007; 47: 88–98.

Inman K, Rudin N. The Origin of Evidence. *Forensic Science International.* 2002; 126(1): 11–16.

Lee HC, Harris HA. *Physical Evidence in Forensic Science.* Tucson: Lawyers & Judges Publishing, 2000.

McJunkins SP, Thornton JI. Glass Fracture Analysis: A Review. *Forensic Science.* 1973; 2(1): 1–27.

Thornton JL. Fractural Surfaces as Models of Physical Matches. *Journal of Forensic Sciences.* 1986; 31(4): 1435–1438.

Tsach T, Wiesner S, Shor Y. Empirical Proof of Physical Match: Systematic Research with Tensile Machine. *Forensic Science International.* 2007; 166(1): 77–83.

Chapter 7

Experiment 7: Construction Examinations of Evidence

Recommended websites:

Contractors Rope LLC. [Home page] [cited 2017]. Brookfield, IL: Contractors Rope LLC. Available from: http://www.contractorsrope.com.

The Carpet and Rug Institute. [Home page] [cited 2017]. Dalton, GA: The Carpet and Rug Institute. Available from: http://www.carpet-rug.org.

Objective

Upon completion of this practical exercise, the student will have developed a basic understanding of:

1. examinations to determine construction features of evidence
2. common construction features for ropes, carpets, and duct tape

Introduction

A construction examination is the process of ascertaining how an item is made, and in some situations, what it is composed of. Many times, this examination provides indications as to whether or not two items originated from the same source. Evidence is said to possess class characteristics when it can be associated only with a group and not with a single source. However, evidence that can be associated with a common source with an extremely high degree of probability is said to possess individual characteristics. Once a construction examination is completed, the forensic scientist is able to determine whether additional testing is required.

Various compositions and methods of construction can be identified when performing a simple construction examination. These types of examinations are performed to associate an item with a similar item from which it is thought to have originated. For instance, a section

Practical Forensic Microscopy: A Laboratory Manual, Second Edition. Barbara P. Wheeler.
© 2021 John Wiley & Sons Ltd. Published 2021 by John Wiley & Sons Ltd.
Companion website: www.wiley.com/go/Wheeler/Forensic

of duct tape retrieved from a victim may be compared back to a roll of duct tape. The process of determining construction depends on the actual item itself. For most items, this involves examining the item to such a degree that details can be obtained to determine identifying characteristics about the construction and composition.

Rope

Ropes are classified into two categories: twisted or braided. Twisted ropes usually consist of three strands. Strands are composed of twisted yarns that are sections of fibers that have been spun together. Strands may be either right-laid, Z twist or left-laid, S twist, as shown in Figure 7-1.

(a)   (b)

Figure 7-1   Twists for yarns: (a) Z-twist is right-laid, and (b) S-twist is left-laid.

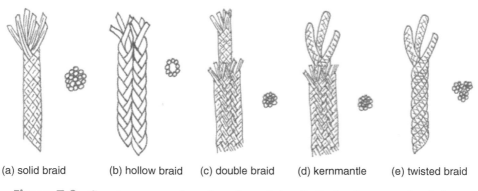

(a) solid braid   (b) hollow braid   (c) double braid   (d) kernmantle   (e) twisted braid

Figure 7-2   Common rope configurations shown in longitudinal and cross-sectional views.

The interweaving of three or more strands that occur in a diagonal overlapping pattern makes braided ropes. Braided ropes are found in a variety of patterns: solid braid, braid with or without a core, and twisted braid. Solid braid is the simplest braid, formed by interweaving numerous strands. Diamond braid without a core (also called hollow braid) is a looser braid with no core. Diamond braid with a braided core is a doubly braided rope: a braid over a braid. Kernmantle braid is a braided rope with long twisted fibers as a core. Plaited ropes are composed of twisted strands that have been braided. Common rope configurations are shown in Figure 7-2.

Carpet

Characteristic details can also be learned about the backing and method of construction for carpets. Carpets are usually woven, knitted, or tufted. Woven carpets are produced on a loom, similar to cloth production. Materials produced on a loom are composed of warp and weft yarns. Warp yarns are the lengthwise or longitudinal yarns, while weft yarns are the crosswise yarns. Weft yarns can also be called fill yarns. Interweaving the surface pile and the backing creates the carpet. This may be produced by a variety of different methods. Figure 7-3 shows side views of Wilton™, Axminster™, velvet, and chenille woven carpets. These carpets are produced on different style looms, or as in chenille carpets, on several looms. A process that loops the backing yarn, the stitching yarn, and the pile yarn creates knitted carpets. Tufted carpets are produced on a tufting machine. After the backing has been woven, yarns are introduced that may either be cut or left as loops. Most carpets manufactured today are either woven or tufted. Figure 7-4 shows yarns that have been tufted into two different backings.

Woven and tufted carpets are most commonly examined in forensics laboratories. They are constructed to provide a variety of textures. Differences in the yarn construction, fiber count, and whether or not the yarns are sheared or unsheared provide various textures for carpet. Each

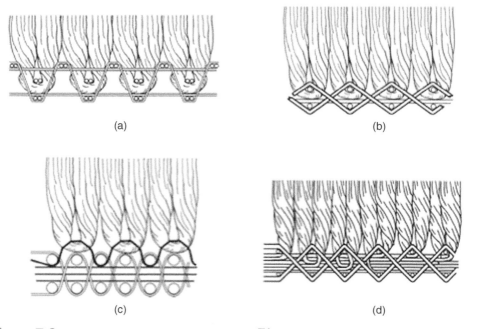

(a)

(b)

(c)

(d)

Figure 7-3 Common woven carpets: (a) Axminster™, (b) velvet, (c) chenille, and (d) Wilton™.

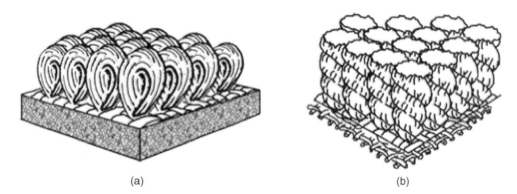

(a)   (b)

Figure 7-4   Tufted carpets with (a) foam backing or (b) double-woven backing.

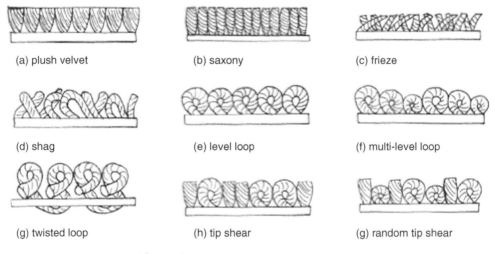

(a) plush velvet   (b) saxony   (c) frieze

(d) shag   (e) level loop   (f) multi-level loop

(g) twisted loop   (h) tip shear   (g) random tip shear

Figure 7-5   Common tufted carpet styles.

loop or tuft can be examined for more detail as to yarn construction and fiber count. Figure 7-5 shows various types of tufted carpets that provide a wide assortment of textures. In addition to the construction of the carpet, backing materials and adhesives holding the actual loops or tufts of the carpet yarns themselves may also be examined.

Duct Tape

Duct tape may also be composed of various constructions. The simplest duct tape is composed of a vinyl backing with an adhesive. Many duct tapes are now reinforced with fibers. Fiber reinforcements may also be constructed in a variety of manners. Yarn count and whether or not the fiber reinforcement is woven or non-woven should be considered. When the fibers are loosely woven, they are called scrim. Scrim can have one of four different weave patterns. These are shown in Figure 7-6: plain weave, plain weave with inserted weft bundles, warp knit with inserted weft thread, or warp knit with inserted weft bundles. A plain weave consists of successive spun yarns in both warp and weft directions that are varied over and under each other

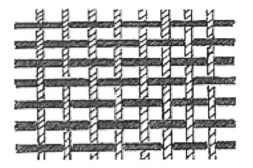

(a) Plain weave

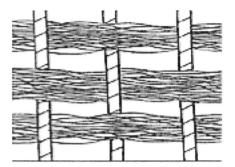

(b) Plain weave with inserted weft bundles

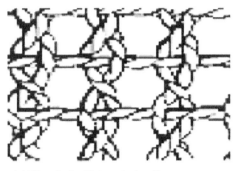

(c) Warp knit with inserted weft thread

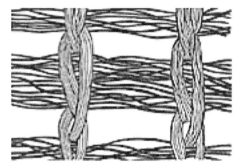

(d) Warp knit with inserted weft bundles

Figure 7-6 Common scrim weave patterns used as fiber reinforcement on tapes.

(see Figure 7-6a). A plain weave with inserted weft bundles consists of successive yarns in both warp and weft directions that are varied over and under each other; however, the warp yarns are spun, while the weft yarns are filament bundles (see Figure 7-6b). Scrim can also be woven as warp knit with inserted weft thread. This type of scrim consists of two or more spun warp yarns crossing over each other and interlacing with one or more spun weft yarns (see Figure 7-6c). And, finally, warp knit with inserted weft bundles can also be woven for scrim. This consists of spun yarns in a chain stitch interlacing with weft filament bundles inserted (see Figure 7-6d).

Since most construction examinations involve comparison to a known sample, conclusions are generally simple. If the construction and composition are similar, a conclusion may be reached that would indicate that the items might have originated from the same source. Further testing would be recommended to prove or disprove these similarities. At times, differences are also found that indicate more than one source.

Equipment and Supplies

Stereomicroscope

Micro kit

Previously prepared sections of rope

Previously prepared sections of carpet

Previously prepared sections of duct tape

Safety

Use standard laboratory safety procedures as described in guidelines set by your instructor.

Part I: Construction Examinations Using the Stereomicroscope

Procedure

Worksheets for examination notes may be found at the end of the experiment.

A. Rope
   1. Obtain a sample of rope.
   2. Determine the construction of the sample under the stereomicroscope.
      Using the worksheet, draw the construction with further details about each portion. Include any physical characteristics, such as: color, diameter, type of construction (twisted or braided), number of strands, direction of twist (Z or S; see Figure 7-1), type of braid (see Figure 7-2), and core and/or sheaths present.
   3. Repeat steps 2 and 3 using a second rope sample.
B. Carpet
   1. Obtain a carpet sample.
   2. Using the stereomicroscope, determine the construction of the sample.
   3. Draw the construction with further details about each portion. Any physical characteristics, such as color, type of construction, texture and style, and carpet components (including details of the backings and tufts), should be noted (see Figures 7-3, 7-4, and 7-5).
   4. Repeat steps 2 and 3 using a second carpet sample.
C. Duct Tape
   1. Obtain a duct tape sample.
   2. Using the stereomicroscope, determine the construction of the sample.
   3. Draw the construction with further details about each portion. Any physical characteristics, such as color, type of construction, backing, adhesive, width, thickness, yarn count, and weave pattern of fiber reinforcement, should be noted (see Figure 7-6).
   4. Repeat steps 2 and 3 using a second tape sample.

Report Requirements

Include all drawings, calculations, and other information obtained during the laboratory procedure. Notes and/or drawings should include the sample identification, magnification, and a complete description.

Report Questions

1. Explain why construction examinations are important.
2. Describe one type of rope construction besides the type that you determined your samples to be. How would you examine this?
3. What fibers are commonly used for rope production?
4. Describe one method of carpet construction besides the type that you determined your samples to be.
5. What components are commonly used for backings, bonding agents, and fiber in carpet production?
6. Describe one method of tape construction besides the type that you determined your samples to be.
7. How would you conduct an examination on a fiber-reinforced tape?
8. What components are commonly used for backings, adhesives, and fiber reinforcements in duct tape production?

Recommended and Further Reading

David SK, Pailthorpe MT. *Classification of Textile Fibres: Production, Structure, and Properties*, 2nd ed. London: Francis & Taylor, 1999.

Joseph ML. *Joseph's Introductory Textile Science*, 6th ed. New York: International Thomson Publishing, 1992.

Laux DL. Identification of a Rope by Means of a Physical Match between the Cut Ends. *Journal of Forensic Sciences*. 1984; 29(4).

Wiggins K. *Ropes and Cordage*, 2nd ed. London: Francis & Taylor, 1999.

Wiggins KG. Recognition, Identification and Comparison of Rope and Twine. *Science & Justice*. 1995; 35(1): 53–58.

ROPE WORKSHEET

Physical Characteristics:

Color_____ Diameter_____

Construction type: twist_____ : Z or S

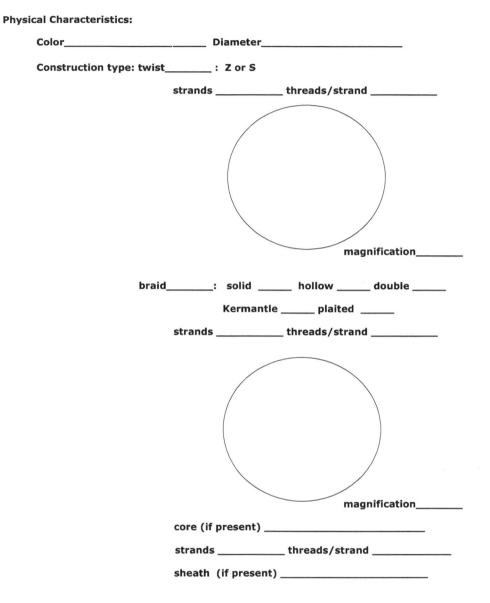

strands _____ threads/strand _____

magnification_____

braid_____: solid _____ hollow _____ double _____

Kermantle _____ plaited _____

strands _____ threads/strand _____

magnification_____

core (if present) _____

strands _____ threads/strand _____

sheath (if present) _____

CARPET WORKSHEET

Physical Characteristics:

    Color_____

    Construction type: texture and style _____

        tufts/inch: warp _____ **fill** _____

        adhesive _____

        primary backing _____

            Warp: count _____ **twist** _____
            Fill: count _____ **twist** _____

        secondary backing _____

            Warp: count _____ **twist** _____
            Fill: count _____ **twist** _____

magnification_____   **magnification**_____

DUCT TAPE WORKSHEET

Physical Characteristics:

      Backing color_____   **Adhesive Color**_____

      Width _____

      Fiber Reinforcement/Weave_____
          Warp: count _____ **fiber type** _____ **twist** _____
          Fill: **count** _____ **fiber type** _____ **twist** _____

Microscopic Test:
      Warp: _____
             _____
             _____

      Fill: _____
             _____
             _____

             magnification_____   **magnification**_____

Chapter 8

Experiment 8: Lamp Filament Examinations

> **Recommended pre-lab reading assignments:**
>
> Baker JM, Fricke LB, Baker KS, Ayock TL. *Traffic Collision Investigation*, 9th ed. Evanston, IL: Northwestern University Center for Public Safety, 2001; 301–366.
> Becker T. *Lamp Examination for Traffic Collision Investigators*. Jacksonville, FL: Institute of Police Technology and Management, 1995.

Objective

Upon completion of this practical exercise, the student will have developed a basic understanding of:

1. lamp filaments
2. lamp filament examinations

Introduction

At times, it may be necessary for a forensic scientist to examine a lamp filament from a vehicle to determine whether or not a filament was illuminated when a collision occurred. These examinations of filaments can be performed using the stereomicroscope. However, prior to discussing filament examinations, it is important to understand how a lamp is constructed and how it works.

Nearly all lamps are incandescent electric lamps. When a filament produces light, it is at approximately 4000°F. At this temperature, the electric current produced by the lamp raises the filament's temperature until it reaches incandescence or produces "white light." Tungsten is generally used for the filament because it does not melt at incandescent temperatures. Wires are used to support the filament and carry the electrical current through the lamp. Since tungsten will

Practical Forensic Microscopy: A Laboratory Manual, Second Edition. Barbara P. Wheeler.
© 2021 John Wiley & Sons Ltd. Published 2021 by John Wiley & Sons Ltd.
Companion website: www.wiley.com/go/Wheeler/Forensic

oxidize rapidly in air at incandescent temperatures, the filaments and supports must be enclosed in a glass bulb that has had the air removed and replaced with either nitrogen or another inert gas. Many newer vehicles use halogen gas technology for headlamps. This makes the tungsten filaments more effective producers of light—more lumens out per watt in—and gives drivers more light than was available from non-halogen filaments at the same power consumption. However, even in normal use, the tungsten will gradually "boil off." This produces weak spots in the filament. Over time the heat continues to weaken the filament until a gap develops, leading to lamp failure.

Another type of failure can be caused by fracture of the filament. This failure can be produced by accidental breakage, or by vibrations or force, which is applied while the filament is either hot or cold. Filament examinations identify the microscopic characteristics that can be associated with each type of lamp failure, allowing the forensic scientist to determine whether or not a lamp was incandescent at the time of impact.

The majority of lamp filament examinations involve vehicle lamps; however, these examinations can be performed on any type of lamp filament. Lamps come in a variety of sizes and shapes and may be used for more than one purpose. Vehicle lamps may also have one or more filaments in many different shapes and sizes, and they can serve many purposes. Headlamps,

Table 8-1 Characteristics of normal lamps.

NEW	Bright luster to the filament
	Bright luster to the filament supports
	Evenly spaced coils to the filament
	Longitudinal draw lines in the filament
	Normal arch to the filament
	No darkening of the glass enclosure
	Working circuit
AGED	Bright luster to the filament
	Bright luster to the filament supports
	Evenly spaced coils of the filament
	Rough or pitted filament
	Downward sag in the filament arch
	Possible darkening of the glass enclosure
	Working circuit
BURNOUT	Bright luster to the filament
	Bright luster to the filament supports
	Evenly spaced coils of the filament
	Separated filament
	Separated ends are usually rounded or "balled," but may also have a slight taper
	Possible darkening of the glass enclosure
	Open circuit

which are the most commonly examined, come in two varieties. Sealed beam headlamps can have one or two filaments contained within the glass enclosure. Semi-sealed beam headlamps contain a halogen bulb that is placed in a plastic lens assembly. Many other lamps are also used in vehicles and may at times be necessary to examine. Some have single filaments, and others may be dual-purpose filaments.

A lamp filament examination involves a careful examination of the entire lamp. Knowledge of the lamp's actual placement in the vehicle is extremely important with respect to the final conclusions that can be reached. To begin the microscopic examination, it is necessary to be able to view the bulb and filaments. Special care should be taken if it is necessary to open a sealed beam headlamp or halogen bulb since these are highly pressurized. An initial examination should be performed to determine the condition of the bulb. This includes a test of the electrical circuit if the filament is intact and a simple visual examination of the bulb. An ohmmeter can be used to determine the continuity of the electrical circuit.

Visual characteristics will vary depending on the actual circumstances of the lamp. Characteristics that indicate a normal lamp are included in Table 8-1. It is important to recognize

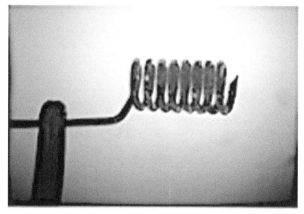

(a)

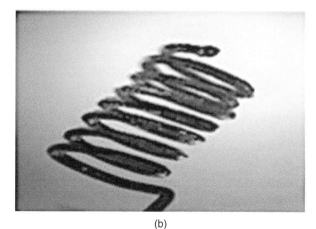

(b)

Figure 8-1   Filament ends from a normal burned-out bulb. Coils are evenly spaced with distinct shaped ends: (a) slight tapered end, or (b) round balled end.

aged and normal burnout filament characteristics, since they can be misinterpreted at times. The easiest way to distinguish these filament characteristics from impact characteristics is the even coil spacing. With aged filaments, coils will remain evenly spaced, even though there may be a downward sag in the filament arch. With normal burnout, the filament ends are separated with a tapered or balled shape (see Figure 8-1). The "boiling off" of the tungsten wire, which causes the short, or burnout, causes this shape.

There are additional characteristics often associated with an impact. These may occur when a lamp is "hot" (incandescent) or "cold" (off) during impact. If the lamp was on, the characteristics that may be present are referred to as "hot shock." Table 8-2 summarizes the characteristics associated with "hot shock." The most common characteristic for "hot shock" is the greatly stretched or distorted coils of the filament (see Figure 8-2). If the lamp was off during impact, the characteristics are referred to as "cold shock." Table 8-3 summarizes the characteristics associated with "cold shock." The most common characteristic for "cold shock" is the fractured brittle ends to an evenly spaced filament (see Figure 8-3). Keep in mind that, in some situations,

Table 8-2 Characteristics of incandescence at impact (hot).

GLASS UNBROKEN, filament intact	Bright luster to the filament
	Bright luster to the filament supports
	Greatly stretched or distorted coils of the filament
	If filament is separated, ends would appear tapered
	Possible darkening of the glass enclosure (depending on age)
	Working circuit is possible
GLASS BROKEN, filament intact	Coloring or blackening to the filament
	Coloring to the filament supports
	Greatly stretched or distorted coils of the filament
	If filament is separated, tapered ends
	Possible darkening of the glass enclosure (depending on age)
	Possible fusing of glass on the filament and supports
	Oxidation on the filament and supports
	Open circuit
GLASS BROKEN, filament missing	Coloring or blackening to filament fragment
	Coloring to the filament supports
	Possible darkening of the glass enclosure (depending on age)
	Possible fusing of glass on the supports
	Oxidation on the supports
	Open circuit

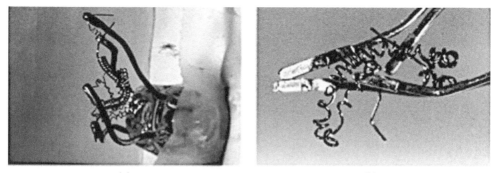

(a) (b)

(c) (d)

Figure 8-2 Examples of "hot shock" with the glass broken and the filament present.

Table 8-3 Characteristics of non-incandescence at impact (cold).

GLASS UNBROKEN, filament intact	Bright luster to the filament
	Bright luster to the filament supports
	No distortion of the coils of the filament
	If filament is separated, fractured brittle ends
	Possible darkening of the glass enclosure (depending on age)
	Working circuit is possible
GLASS BROKEN, filament intact	Bright luster to the filament
	Bright luster to the filament supports
	No distortion of the coils of the filament
	If filament is separated, fractured brittle ends
	Possible darkening of the glass enclosure (depending on age)
	Open circuit
GLASS BROKEN, filament missing	Bright luster to filament fragment
	Bright luster to the filament supports
	Possible darkening of the glass enclosure (depending on age)
	Open circuit

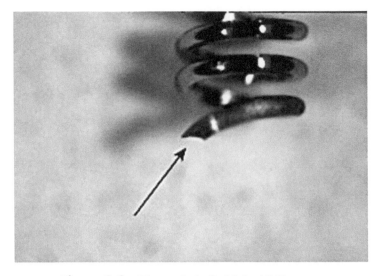

Figure 8-3   Blunt end of a "cold shock" filament.

only a portion of these characteristics may be present. This is especially true when the filament is a distance from the impact area. In these circumstances, an inconclusive conclusion may be reached.

Three conclusions are generally reached for filament examinations. Firstly, a filament may be identified as incandescent at impact when indications are found of "hot shock" distortion, fused glass particles, or oxidation. Secondly, a filament may also show no indications of incandescence. In this situation, a filament may exhibit "cold shock," or it may have been too far from the impact to introduce characteristics. Thirdly, a filament may lack enough characteristics for a determination to be made.

Equipment and Supplies

    Stereomicroscope

    Micro kit

    Scribe

    Propane torch to open pressurized headlamps

    Previously prepared lamp filaments

Safety

Use standard laboratory safety procedures as described in guidelines set by your instructor. Be cautious when opening lamps, since they are highly pressurized. Dispose of glass in an appropriate container.

Part I: Lamp Filament Examinations

Procedure

Worksheets for examination notes may be found at the end of the experiment.

1. Obtain a lamp.
2. Using the stereomicroscope, initially examine the lamp.
3. Using the worksheet, describe the overall condition of the bulb, noting any markings on the bulb.
4. If possible, check the electrical circuit to determine if the lamp is operational.
5. If necessary, clean the glass enclosure so that the filament can be visualized.
   If the filament cannot be viewed, it may be necessary to open the enclosure. *Proceed with caution, since lamps can be highly pressurized.* Lamps that are contained in a plastic lens assembly may be cut open. To open glass enclosures, place the lamp face down (onto a towel) and use the scribe to make a circular scratch around the base. Next, use a propane torch in a continuous motion to apply heat to the lamp and the area around the scratch. Immediately place a towel that has been "iced" onto the hot headlamp in the area of the scratch. The glass should pop open where the stress has been created by the scribe.
6. Determine whether the lamp is a single- or double-filament lamp.
7. Examine the color of the filament.
8. Examine the shape of the filament.
9. If the filament is broken, examine the ends of the filament.
10. Determine if there are any particles *fused* to the filament.
11. Next, examine the color and shape of the filament supports.
12. Determine if there are any particles *fused* to the supports.
13. Repeat steps 7–12 if the lamp is a double-filament lamp.
14. Draw what you see.
15. Determine whether or not the lamp was incandescent at impact.
16. Repeat steps 2–15 using two more lamps.
17. For each lamp filament examination, you were asked to evaluate evidence. As a forensic scientist, you must learn to draw a conclusion and be able to communicate your conclusion verbally and in writing. Clearly state your results. Explain how you reached the conclusions.

Report Requirements

Include all drawings, calculations, and other information obtained during the laboratory procedure. Notes and/or drawings should include the sample identification, magnification, and a complete description.

Report Questions

1. Using a single-filament lamp as an example, explain how it creates light.
2. Explain how a double-filament lamp works. Give an example of a double-filament lamp and what each filament is used for.
3. Explain "hot shock" and differentiate it from "cold shock."

4. Give an example of when a lamp filament examination would be valuable information in an investigation.
5. Is it possible for a driver-side lamp filament to show characteristics of incandescence and the passenger-side lamp filament (of the same vehicle) to show no characteristics? Explain your answer.
6. If the vehicle being examined has extensive damage to the front so that no headlamps or side lights are able to be examined, how could you determine if the lights were on or off at impact?

Recommended and Further Reading

Badger JE. Casting New Light on Lamp Investigation. *Law Enforcement Technology*. 1989; September: 38–53.

Baker JS, Aycock TL, Lindquist T. Lamp Examination for On or Off in Traffic Accidents. In: *Traffic Accident Investigation Manual*. Evanston, IL: Northwestern University Traffic Institute, 1987.

Baker JS, Fricke LB. *The Traffic Accident Investigation Manual: A Technical Follow-Up*. Evanston, IL: Northwestern University Center for Public, 1986.

Baudoin P, Lavabre R, Vayne F. An Unusual Oxidation Type on Bulb Filaments after a Car Crash Dive. *Journal of Forensic Sciences*. 2002; 47(2).

Coldwell BB, Melski TB. Motor Vehicle Lights as Evidence in Traffic Accident Investigation. *RCMP Gazette*. 1961: 3.

Dolan DN. Vehicle Lights and Their Use as Evidence. *Journal of Forensic Science Society*. 1971; 11: 2.

Ehmann R, Yu JCC. Determination of Energization State of Xenon High Intensity Discharge Automobile Headlights. *Forensic Science Journal*. 2009; 8(1): 13–28.

Fu L, Leutz R, Ries H. Physical Modeling of Filament Light Sources. *Journal of Applied Physics*. 2006; 100(10).

Greenlay W, Juzkow M, Mikkelsen S, Beveridge A. The Effect of Impact on the Filaments of Quartz Halogen Headlamps. *Canadian Society of Forensic Science Journal*. 1986; 19(2): 77–82.

Lavabre R, Baudoin P. Examination of Light Bulb Filaments after a Car Crash: Difficulties in Interpreting the Results. *Journal of Forensic Sciences*. 2001; 46(1): 147–155.

Mathyer J. Evidence Obtained from the Examination of Incandescent Electric Lamps, Particularly Lamps of Vehicles Involved in Road Accidents. *International Criminal Police Review*. 1975; January: 2–18.

Menon VJ, Agrawal DC. A Theory of Filament Lamp's Failure Statistics. *European Physical Journal-Applied Physics*. 2006; 34(2): 117–121.

Powell GFL. Interpretation of Vehicle Globe Failures: The Unlit Condition. *Journal of Forensic Sciences*. 1977; 22(3): 628–635.

Severy DM. Headlight-Taillight Analyses from Collision Research. In: *Proceedings of the 10th STAPP Car Crash Conference*, November 8–9, Holloman Air Force Base, New Mexico, 1966.

Thorsen KA. Examination of Bulb Filaments by the Scanning Electron Microscope. *Canadian Society of Forensic Science*. 1981; 14(2): 55–69.

SINGLE FILAMENT WORKSHEET

Bulb
location:_____

Bulb
type/markings:_____

Bulb condition:
        Glass intact _____
                Darkened_____
                White deposit _____
        Glass broken _____
                Darkened_____
                White deposit   _____

Electrical Circuit: _____

Single filament condition
        Shiny _____   Colored _____
        Evenly stretched _____   Distortion _____
        Broken_____
                ends _____
        Deposits _____   Fused glass _____
        Other _____
        Missing:
Filament supports:
        Bent _____
        Broken _____
        Colored _____
        Deposits _____
        Other _____

magnification _____

DOUBLE FILAMENT WORKSHEET

Bulb
location:_____

Bulb
type/markings:_____

Bulb condition:
    Glass intact _____
           Darkened_____
           White deposit _____
    Glass broken _____
           Darkened_____
           White deposit _____
Electrical Circuit: _____

Double filament condition—thick filament
    Shiny _____   Colored _____
    Evenly stretched _____   Distortion _____
    Broken_____   magnification _____
          ends _____
    Deposits _____   Fused glass _____
    Other _____
    Missing _____
Filament supports:
    Bent _____
    Broken _____
    Colored _____
    Deposits _____
    Other _____

Double filament condition—thin filament
    Shiny _____   Colored _____
    Evenly stretched _____   Distortion _____
    Broken_____
          ends _____   magnification _____
    Deposits _____   Fused glass _____
    Other _____
    Missing _____
Filament supports:
    Bent _____
    Broken _____
    Colored _____
    Deposits _____
    Other _____

Chapter 9

Experiment 9: Fingerprint Examination and Comparison

Recommended pre-lab reading assignments:

U.S. Department of Justice. *The Science of Fingerprinting*. Washington, DC: Government Printing Office, 1990.
U.S. Department of Justice. *Fingerprint Training Manual*. Washington, DC: Government Printing Office, 1993.

Objective

Upon completion of this practical exercise, the student will have developed a basic understanding of:

1. general characteristics of fingerprints
2. use of the stereomicroscope to visualize the characteristics of fingerprints
3. fingerprint comparison

Introduction

Fingerprints are an impression of friction ridges found on the tips of the palm side of fingers and thumbs. Fingerprints may be found in three forms: patent, plastic, or latent. Patent prints are those that are easily viewed with the naked eye and created by transfer of foreign material from a finger to a surface. Examples of patent prints are ridge patterns on surfaces created by the transfer of blood, grease, or ink. Plastic prints are those that are left as an impression in a material. Examples of plastic prints are ridge patterns found in a soft substrate such as the adhesive on duct tape, or solid substances such as melted candle wax that will harden to an impression. Latent prints are those that are hidden or invisible until viewed with the aid of a visualizing agent. Common visualizing agents are dusting powders (black, colored, fluorescent,

---

Practical Forensic Microscopy: A Laboratory Manual, Second Edition. Barbara P. Wheeler.
© 2021 John Wiley & Sons Ltd. Published 2021 by John Wiley & Sons Ltd.
Companion website: www.wiley.com/go/Wheeler/Forensic

or magnetic), ninhydrin, and cyanoacrylate ester. In addition, various wavelengths of light can also be utilized as visualizing agents. A resulting fluorescent latent print is photographed.

Friction ridges are formed during the third and fourth months of fetal development. They are formed as the result of the fusion of the main two layers of the epidermis: the stratum corneum and the stratum mucosum. The stratum corneum covers the surface, and the stratum mucosum is a portion of the basal layer. It is the combination of these two layers that forms friction ridges. Cells in the stratum mucosum divide, causing folds to form ridges that will run lengthwise and correspond to the surface ridges. However, these are twice as numerous since the deeper ridges that correspond to the middle of the surface ridges alternate with smaller ones that correspond to the furrows. As the fetus develops, ridges are further "stretched," causing breaks, dots, forks, and other individual characteristics. Sweat pores run in single rows along the ridges. Through these pores, perspiration releases and deposits on the skin. Fingerprint impressions are created through direct contact of the friction ridges with wet or soft surfaces (patent or plastic prints) or when the perspiration deposits and any oil that is also on the skin are transferred to items (latent prints).

Friction ridge patterns are stable, complex patterns and are recognized as valuable and reliable characteristics that can be used for personal identification. Generally speaking, when an individual bruises or slightly cuts the outer layer of the skin of the finger, the ridges will not be permanently changed. However, if a more serious injury is inflicted on the tip of the finger that damages the stratum mucosum, the friction skin will heal but not in its original formation. A scar will appear in the area of injury, changing the friction ridge pattern. Fingerprints offer a dependable means of personal identification. Other personal characteristics may change, but fingerprints are formed prior to birth and remain constant until death and decomposition. Even identical twins, which have the same DNA, do not have the same fingerprints! Individuals may have the same pattern types; however, the ridge detail of every fingerprint of every person is different. This is also true of the palms of the hands, the toes, and the soles of the feet.

Prints are classified into three main categories: arch, loop, and whorl. These patterns may be further divided into subgroups by means of the smaller differences existing between the patterns in the same general group. First, a pattern area must be determined. The pattern area is the part of the print in which the cores, deltas, and ridges appear. The pattern areas of arches are open. The pattern area of loops and whorls are enclosed by type lines. Type lines may be defined as the two innermost ridges that run parallel from the lower corners of the pattern and flow inward and upward, diverge and separate, and finally surround or tend to surround the pattern area.

Within the pattern areas, focal points may be used to classify them. These points are called the core and the delta (see Figure 9-1). The core is the approximate center of the fingerprint impression. The core is placed upon the innermost sufficient recurve. When the innermost sufficient recurve contains an uneven number of rods rising as high as the shoulders, the core is placed upon the end of the center rod, whether it touches the looping ridge or not. When the innermost sufficient recurve contains an even number of rods, the core will be placed upon the end of the farther one of the two center rods. The delta is the point on a ridge at or in front of and nearest the center of the divergence of the type lines. It may be a bifurcation, ending ridge, dot, short ridge, meeting of two ridges, or a point on the first recurving ridge located nearest to the center and in front of the divergence of the type lines.

An arch is a ridge pattern that is characterized by lines that enter the print from one side and exit from the other with no recurving. As it crosses the pattern area, there is a rise in the ridge pattern. The difference in this rise determines whether it is classified as a plain arch or a tented arch (see Figure 9-2). A plain arch is the simplest of all fingerprint patterns. There are no recurving ridges or deltas. While the ridge pattern will follow a general contour, various ridge

(a)   (b)

Figure 9-1   Core and delta are two characteristics used to classify fingerprints. (a) The core is the approximate center of a fingerprint. (b) A delta is the point on a ridge where a divergence occurs.

(a)   (b)

Figure 9-2   The arch classification has ridges that enter the print from one side and exit on the other. Arches may be either (a) plain or (b) tented.

formations such as ending ridges, bifurcations, dots, and islands may also be involved in this type of pattern. For a tented arch, most of the ridges enter one side of the print and exit out the other side; however, the ridge or ridges at the center do not. One or more ridges that are not continuous at the center form an upthrust. An upthrust is an ending ridge of any length rising at a sufficient degree from the horizontal plane at 45° or more. Tented arches are sometimes confused with loops. Approximately 5% of the population has arch patterns.

A loop is a ridge pattern that is characterized by lines that enter on one side of the print and recurve, touch, or pass an imaginary line drawn from the delta to the core, and terminate or tend to terminate on or toward the same side of the print from which such ridge or ridges entered (see Figure 9-3). A loop is distinguished as being "radial" or "ulnar." The terms "radial" and "ulnar" are derived from the radius and ulna bones of the forearm. Loops that flow in the direction of the ulna bone (toward the little finger) are called ulnar loops, and those that flow in the direction of the radius bone (toward the thumb) are called radial loops. A loop pattern will always have a delta. Approximately 60% of the population has loop patterns.

A whorl is a ridge pattern that is generally rounded in shape and has at least two deltas (see Figure 9-4). A whorl may be further subdivided into four categories: plain, central pocket loop, double loop, or accidental. The plain whorl has two deltas and at least one ridge making a complete circle, which may be spiral, oval, circular, or any variant of a circle. An imaginary line drawn between the two deltas must touch or cross at least one of the recurving ridges within the inner pattern area. The central pocket loop type of whorl has two deltas and at least one ridge that makes or tends to make a complete circle. The circle may be spiral, oval, circular, or any variant of a circle. An imaginary line drawn between the two deltas must not touch or cross any recurving ridges within the inner pattern area. The double loop consists of two separate loop formations, with two separate and distinct sets of shoulders, and two deltas. The accidental whorl

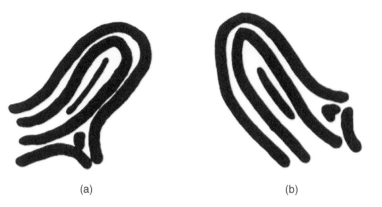

(a)   (b)

Figure 9-3   Loops are classified as either radial or ulnar. (a) Loops that form toward the right are radial loops, and (b) loops that form toward the left are ulnar loops.

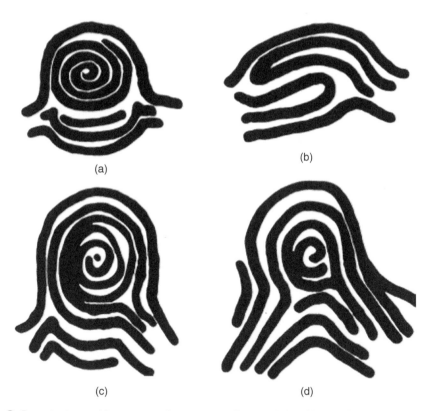

(a)   (b)

(c)   (d)

Figure 9-4   Whorls are ridge patterns that are generally rounded and have at least two deltas: (a) plain whorl, (b) double-loop whorl, (c) central pocket loop whorl, and (d) accidental whorl.

is a pattern consisting of a combination of two different types of patterns, with the exception of the plain arch, with two or more deltas; or a pattern that possesses some of the requirements for two or more different types; or a pattern that conforms to none of the definitions. Approximately 35% of the population has whorl patterns.

Once the main ridge patterns have been determined, comparisons may next be considered. To compare fingerprints, note the ridge characteristics in two fingerprint impressions (exemplars to either plastic, patent, or latent prints) to determine whether or not they match. An identification is established when a number of these characteristics occupy the same relative position in the two fingerprint impressions. When making a comparison, the first observation would be using a magnifying glass or stereomicroscope to determine if the fingerprints are of the same pattern type (for example, arch, loop, or whorl).

If the pattern types are the same, the next step is to examine the fingerprint for specific characteristics: bifurcations, short ridges, ridge endings, and/or enclosures. These characteristics are called minutia features (see Figure 9-5). A ridge ending is the point at which a friction ridge stops. Enclosures are a ridge that completely encloses another. Short ridges are ridges that are significantly smaller than the average ridge length of the print. Bifurcations are points at which a single ridge splits into two ridges. The examiner begins by looking for the most obvious points

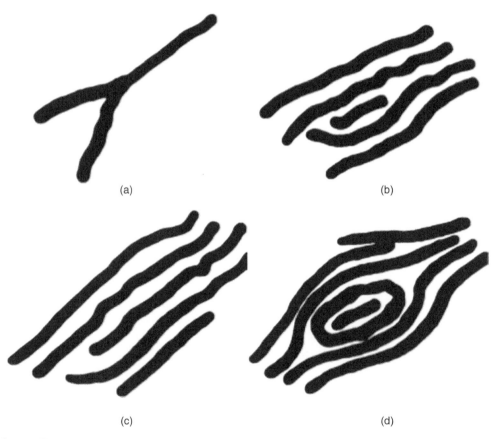

(a)   (b)

(c)   (d)

Figure 9-5   Minutia features used in fingerprint classifications: (a) bifurcation, (b) short ridge, (c) ridge ending, and (d) enclosure.

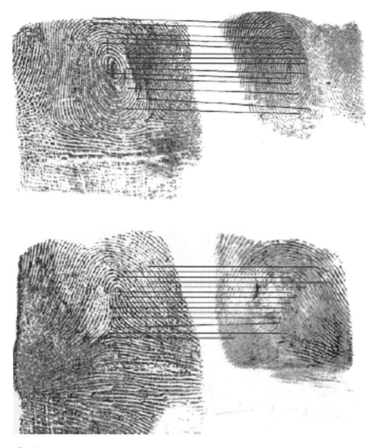

Figure 9-6   Fingerprint comparisons for two latent lifts to known fingerprint samples.

of identification. This would be the characteristic that captures one's attention when first looking at the fingerprint. This characteristic or point is compared to the same area of the suspect print to make a potential match. If the same characteristic or point is present in both prints, the number of ridges is counted from the first characteristic or point to the second characteristic; continue this process until you have determined that the two fingerprint impressions are either the same (see Figure 9-6) or different.

There is no standard number of characteristics required to establish identification. The fingerprint examiner must determine when enough points have been located to make identification. This number may vary due to clarity, uniqueness of formations, experience, and ability.

Equipment and Supplies

Fingerprint ink

Print cards

Stereomicroscope

A set of known prints

Unknown latent prints

Safety

Use standard laboratory safety procedures as described in guidelines set by your instructor. Be cautious of microscope light levels to avoid eye damage.

Part I: Fingerprint Examination

Procedure

1. Obtain a fingerprint card.
2. Using the fingerprint ink, ink and roll each of your fingers on the card.
3. Using the stereomicroscope or a magnifying glass, determine the pattern type and subdivision for each finger.
4. Locate any delta(s) of the prints, if applicable.
5. Locate any cores of the prints, if applicable.
6. Draw the main characteristics that you see to determine the pattern type and subdivision. Include any cores or deltas found.

Part II: Fingerprint Comparison

Procedure

1. Obtain a set of known prints.
2. Obtain a set of unknown prints.
3. Determine if any of the unknown prints match the known prints using the above procedure.
4. Draw the comparison of any prints that you have considered a match.

Report Requirements

Include all drawings, comparisons, and other information obtained during the laboratory procedure. Notes and/or drawings should include the sample identification, magnification, and a complete description.

Report Questions

1. What is a patent print? How would you compare this to known samples?
2. What is a latent print? How would you compare this to known samples?
3. List and explain at least two methods of visualizing latent prints. What are the limitations?
4. What are the main groups of fingerprints? Describe each.
5. What are the two subgroups of arches?
6. What are the two subgroups of loops?
7. What are the four subgroups of whorls?
8. What is a delta?
9. What is the core?
10. What are the four types of minutia used to compare fingerprints? Describe each.

11. Can partial prints be compared?
12. How many characteristics must match in order to make a positive identification? Explain.
13. Would identical twins be able to be distinguished by their fingerprints? Can they be distinguished by their DNA?

Recommended and Further Reading

Ashbaugh D. *Quantitative-Qualitative Friction Ridge Analysis: An Introduction to Basic and Advanced Ridgeology.* Boca Raton, FL: CRC Press, 1999.

Champod C. Friction Ridge Skin Impression Evidence: Standards of Proof. In: Siegel J, Saukko P, ed., *Encyclopedia of Forensic Sciences*, 2nd ed. Amsterdam: Elsevier Academic Press, 2013; 111–116.

Champod C, Lennard C, Margot P, Stoilovic M. *Fingerprint and Other Ridge Skin Impressions.* Boca Raton, FL: CRC Press, 2004.

Cole SA. Grandfathering Evidence: Fingerprint Admissibility Rulings from Jennings to Llera Plaza and Back Again. *American Criminal Law Review.* 2004; 41(3): 1189–1276.

Cole SA. More Than Zero: Accounting for Error in Latent Fingerprint Identification. *Journal of Criminal Law & Criminology.* 2005; 95(3): 985–1078.

Cole SA. What Counts for Identity? The Historical Origins of the Methodology of Latent Fingerprint Identification. *Science in Context.* 1999; 12(1): 139–172.

Cole SA. Witnessing Identification: Latent Fingerprinting Evidence and Expert Knowledge. *Social Studies of Science.* 1998; 28(5–6): 687–712.

Egli NM, Champod C, Margot P. Evidence Evaluation in Fingerprint Comparison and Automated Fingerprint Identification Systems: Modeling within Finger Variability. *Forensic Science International.* 2007; 167(2–3): 189–195.

Grant A, Wilkinson TJ, Holman DR, Martin MC. Identification of Recently Handled Materials by Analysis of Latent Human Fingerprints Using Infrared Spectromicroscopy. *Applied Spectroscopy.* 2005; 59(9): 1182–1187.

Houck MM, Siegel JA. *Fundamentals of Forensic Science*, 3rd ed. Amsterdam: Elsevier Academic Press, 2015; 493–517

Kahn HS. Enhanced Collection of Fingerprints and Ridge Counting. *American Journal of Human Biology.* 2005; 17(3): 383.

Kempton JB, Sirignano A, Degaetano DH, Yates PJ, Rowe WF. Comparison of Fingernail Striation Patterns in Identical-Twins. *Journal of Forensic Sciences.* 1992; 37(6): 1534–1540.

Kulkami JV, Patil BD, Holambe RS. Orientation Feature for Fingerprint Matching. *Pattern Recognition.* 2006; 39(8): 1551–1554.

Saferstein R. *Criminalistics: An Introduction to Forensic Science*, 11th ed. Upper Saddle River, NJ: Prentice Hall, 2015; 1125–1147.

Wilson JD, Cantu AA, Antonopoulos G, Surrency MJ. Examination of the Steps Leading up to the Physical Developer Process for Developing Fingerprints. *Journal of Forensic Sciences.* 2007; 52(2): 320–329.

Zhu E, Yin JP, Hu CF, Zhang GM. A Systematic Method for Fingerprint Ridge Orientation Estimation and Image Segmentation. *Pattern Recognition.* 2006; 39(8): 1452–1472.

Zhu Y, Dass SC, Jain AK. Statistical Models for Assessing the Individuality of Fingerprints. *IEEE Transactions on Information Forensics and Security.* 2007; 2(3): 391–401.

Chapter 10

Experiment 10: Tool Mark Examinations

Recommended pre-lab reading assignments:

Burd D, Kirk PL. Tool Marks: Factors Involved in Their Comparison and Use as Evidence. *Journal of Police Science*. 1942; 32(6): 465.

Miller J. An Introduction to the Forensic Examination of Tool Marks. *AFTE Journal*. 2001; 33(3): 233–248.

Objective

Upon completion of this practical exercise, the student will have developed a basic understanding of:

1. tool mark examinations
2. use of the comparison stereomicroscope for tool mark examinations

Introduction

A tool mark is any impression, cut, gouge, or abrasion caused by a tool coming into contact with another object. Because the tool is usually the harder surface, when it comes into contact with a softer object, it will impart its unique marks on that object.

Tool mark identifications involve the basic principle of uniqueness, where all objects are unique to themselves and thus can be differentiated from each other. The mechanism for differentiating tool marks depends on class and individual characteristics, both of which involve a tool's working surface. The working surface is the portion of the tool that contacts a surface and produces the tool mark. The number of working surfaces will vary for tools depending on the working action of the tool. The working action can be described as the mechanical advantage

---

Practical Forensic Microscopy: A Laboratory Manual, Second Edition. Barbara P. Wheeler.
© 2021 John Wiley & Sons Ltd. Published 2021 by John Wiley & Sons Ltd.
Companion website: www.wiley.com/go/Wheeler/Forensic

that is obtained by the tool: compression, crimping, flat action, gripping, shearing, pinching, or slicing. Compression tools are tools that compress by pressure or impact and have one working surface, such as hammers and die stamps. Crimping, gripping, flat action, and slicing tools have two working surfaces. Crimping tools are tools that have two opposing jaws designed to bend or crease materials: for example, wire crimpers and vial crimpers. Gripping tools impart a squeeze or hold on an object by two opposing jaws, like pliers and pipe wrenches. Flat action tools have a flat blade that has two surfaces, such as screwdrivers and pry bars. Slicing tools are tools that impart a cutting action using a blade or cutting surface with two sides that move in the direction of the cut: for example, a knife or a razor edge. Shearing and pinching tools have four working surfaces. Shearing tools have two blades, both with two sides, on adjacent planes that pass each other and are designed to cut: for example, scissors and tin snips. Pinching tools have opposing jaws, both with two sides that use a pinching action to cut, such as wire cutters and bolt cutters.

Tool mark class characteristics are intentional or design characteristics that would be common to a particular group of items. The size and shape of a tool's working surface is an example of a class characteristic. For instance, a significantly larger impression may be left by one flat-head screwdriver than another. The shape can also leave varying impressions, as shown by flat-head and Phillips-head screwdrivers. The distance between a toothed instrument's teeth is also considered a class characteristic.

Tool mark individual characteristics are marks produced by random imperfections or irregularities of a tool surface. These characteristics may be produced through the machining process or by random imperfections or irregularities that are produced incidental to manufacture and/or caused by use, corrosion, or damage. For instance, small irregularities left in the edge of the tool as a result of the machining process used to cut and finish edges provide individual characteristics. The shape and pattern of such irregularities are also modified by wear and damage to the tool. This can create a unique pattern for every tool, allowing for the possibility of performing tool mark examinations.

A microscopic examination of tool markings reveals irregularities that can be compared to the working surface of the suspected tool. Usually a reverse image of the tool or tool mark must be made so that comparisons can be performed. Silicone casting materials are used to obtain the reverse images. In some situations, the investigator may request identification of the possible tool. For this, the examiner determines the class characteristics of the impression. From this information, a class of tools can usually be determined.

In other situations, a complete examination may be requested. In these cases, if the class characteristics are consistent with a suspected tool, test marks are then made using lead sheets. The test marks are initially compared to each other to ensure that the tool produces unique, consistent individual markings. This examination is done on a comparison stereomicroscope with a special stage. A comparison stereomicroscope is composed of two stereomicroscopes that are connected by an optical bridge. The bridge contains prisms and mirrors that are used to direct the light to a common set of oculars. A set of knobs is used to adjust the field of view, so that items can be viewed from either microscope independently or combined. In the combined field of view, the image is split, showing portions of the field of view from each microscope. The stage used for tool mark identifications will allow the sample to be moved and rotated so that markings can be easily compared on various surfaces (see Figure 10-1). This allows the examiner to view two items side-by-side on a microscopic scale.

If unique, consistent markings are found with the test marks, comparisons can then be performed with the evidence samples. When comparisons are performed, the forensic examiners usually reach one of three conclusions: (1) An identification: the exhibit was produced by contact with the tool, and a sufficient correlation between individual characteristics is found;

Figure 10-1   This specialized stage holds tool mark samples for viewing on a comparison stereomicroscope. Since the sample area of the stage is positioned on a ball-and-socket joint, samples can be easily maneuvered for comparison examinations.

(2) a non-identification or elimination: the exhibit was not produced by the tool because class or individual characteristics disagree; and (3) inconclusive: class characteristics agree, but there is an insufficient correlation between individual characteristics.

Equipment and Supplies

Comparison stereomicroscope

Unknown tool mark impressions

Casting material (Mikrosil™, Duplicast™, or Epse Impregum™)

Tools

Lead sheets

Safety

Use standard laboratory safety procedures as described in guidelines set by your instructor.

Part I: Casting a Tool Mark

Procedure

1. Mix the casting material according to the manufacturer's instructions.
2. Apply the casting material over the tool or tool mark to be cast.

3. When the casting material has sufficiently set (or cooled), gently tap the area to loosen the cast. Some casting materials may require more force to separate the cast from the area.

Part II: Tool Mark Comparison

1. Examine the tool mark that you have been assigned. Make a cast, if necessary.
2. Identify the class characteristics to determine a possible tool.
3. Obtain a possible tool and, using the tool, make several test tool marks using lead sheets.
4. Attach the test tool marks to the stages of the comparison microscope. Examine the test tool marks to determine if the tool produces unique, consistent markings.
5. If consistent, compare these markings to those of your cast. Not only must the size and shape match up, but also the irregularities or longitudinal striations on each must coincide. Comment on the striations and, using the circle template located in Appendix E, draw regions that appear similar. Is there anything unusual with any of the knowns or unknowns?

Report Requirements

Include all drawings, calculations, and other information obtained during the laboratory procedure. Notes and/or drawings should include the sample identification, magnification, and a complete description.

Report Questions

1. For tool mark evidence, what properties are class characteristics? Using a tool, describe its class characteristics.
2. What are the individual characteristics for tool mark evidence? Using a different tool than in the previous question, describe its individual characteristics.
3. Write a statement about your comparison with the "known tool." Could the tool have produced the tool mark impression? Back up your written statement with a discussion of why you think they match or don't match, referring to your drawings if necessary.

Recommended and Further Reading

Burd D, Kirk PL. Toolmarks: Factors Involved in Their Comparison and Use as Evidence. *Journal of Police Science.* 1942; 32(6): 465.

Liukkonen M, Majamaa H, Virtanen J. The Role and Duties of the Shoeprint/Toolmark Examiner in Forensic Laboratories. *Forensic Science International.* 1996; 82(1): 99–108.

Miller J. An Introduction to the Forensic Examination of Tool Marks. *AFTE Journal.* 2001; 33(3): 233–248.

Nichols RG. Defending the Scientific Foundations of the Firearms and Tool Mark Identification Discipline: Responding to Recent Challenges. *Journal of Forensic Sciences.* 2007; 52(3): 586–594.

Nichols RG. Firearm and Toolmark Identification Criteria: A Review of the Literature. *Journal of Forensic Sciences.* 1997; 42(3): 466–474.

Nichols RG. Firearm and Toolmark Identification Criteria: A Review of the Literature, Part II. *Journal of Forensic Sciences.* 2003; 48(2): 318–327.

Novoselsky Y, Tsach T, Klein A, Volkov N, Shor Y, Vinokurov A. Unusual Contact Marks: Connecting the Hubcap to the Wheel of the Car. *Journal of Forensic Sciences.* 2002; 47(3): 630–632.

Petraco N, Petraco ND, Pizzola PA. An Ideal Material for the Preparation of Known Toolmark Test Impressions. *Journal of Forensic Sciences.* 2005; 50(6): 1407–1410.

Chapter 11

Experiment 11: Firearms Examinations

Recommended pre-lab reading assignments:

Hamby J. Identification of Projectiles. *AFTE Journal*. 1974; 6(5–6): 22.
Nicols R. Firearms and Toolmark Identification Criteria: A Review of the Literature. *Journal of Forensic Sciences*. 1997; 42(3): 466–474.
Nicols R. Firearms and Toolmark Identification Criteria: A Review of the Literature—Part 2. *Journal of Forensic Sciences*. 2003; 48(2): 18–327.

Recommended website:

FirearmsID. [Home page] [cited 2020]. Louisville, KY: FirearmsID. Available from: http://www.firearmsid.com.

Objective

Upon completion of this practical exercise, the student will have developed a basic understanding of:

1. firearm examinations
2. use of the comparison stereomicroscope for firearms examinations

Practical Forensic Microscopy: A Laboratory Manual, Second Edition. Barbara P. Wheeler.
© 2021 John Wiley & Sons Ltd. Published 2021 by John Wiley & Sons Ltd.
Companion website: www.wiley.com/go/Wheeler/Forensic

Introduction

Firearms identification is actually a form of tool mark identification. A tool mark is any impression, cut, gouge, or abrasion caused by a tool coming into contact with another object. For firearms examinations, the firearm itself acts as the tool. Since the components of the firearm are harder than the ammunition, it leaves impressed or striated marks on the ammunition components with which it comes into contact. Studies have shown that no two firearms, even those with the same make and model, will produce the same unique markings on fired bullets and cartridge cases.

As a firearm is fired, several actions occur that make firearms examinations possible. First, the cartridge enters the chamber. Then the firing pin strikes the primer of the cartridge case, igniting it. The spark from the primer ignites the propellant. The burning gases from the propellant expand the cartridge case to seal it against the chamber wall. This causes the projectile to be pushed in the direction that releases the pressure, down the barrel. Once the projectile leaves the barrel, the pressure is released, allowing the cartridge case to be removed from the chamber. These actions cause unique impressions or markings on the bullet and cartridge case that firearms examiners use for identifications.

During the manufacturing process of a rifled firearm, the barrel goes through a rifling process. Rifling of a barrel can occur through several methods. The most common methods used are broach rifling, button rifling, hammer-forged rifling, and electrochemical rifling. Broach rifling uses a hardened steel rod with evenly spaced cutting rings that are successively larger. The rod is twisted as it passes down a barrel, creating the spiraled lands and grooves. Button rifling is the most common rifling method. A "shaped" button is forced down a barrel, creating the engraved spiraled lands and grooves. Hammer-forged rifling is the newest rifling method. A "shaped" mandrel is inserted into the barrel, which is then machine hammered to force the barrel against the mandrel. This creates a polygonal-shaped hill-and-valley rifling pattern. Electrochemical rifling uses wet-etching of the interior of the barrel to create the grooves. These rifling processes create the unique spiral lands and grooves (hills and valleys) that the firearms examiner uses for identification of bullets. The raised portions of the rifled barrel are called lands, and the recessed portions are called grooves. With polygonal rifling, there is not a distinct transition, so the areas are referred to as hills and valleys. Firearms can be manufactured with any number of lands and grooves (hills and valleys) in their barrels. They vary in widths and also vary in the degree and direction of twist, spiraling either left or right.

The final class characteristic is the size of the firearm. Caliber is the size of a rifled firearm. This is the distance measured between opposing lands and grooves. Gauge is the size of a smooth-barrel firearm. It is the number of solid spheres of a diameter equal to the inside diameter of the barrel that could be made from a pound of lead.

To perform an examination, the firearms examiner deals with class and individual characteristics. Class characteristics are intentional or design characteristics that would be common to a particular group of items. The class characteristics that the firearms examiner must take into consideration are: number of lands and grooves, width of lands and grooves, direction of twist, degree of twist, and caliber (or gauge).

Individual characteristics are marks produced by random imperfections or irregularities of a tool surface. These characteristics may be produced through the machining process or by random imperfections or irregularities that are produced incidental to manufacture and/or caused by use, corrosion, or damage. The individual characteristics that the examiner must take into consideration are: rifling impressions, striated action marks, and impressed action marks. For projectiles, a closer examination is done of the rifling impressions. Imperfections on the interior of the barrel leave microscopic striations or scratches on the projectile as it passes through the barrel. For cartridges, a closer examination is done of the striated action marks and impressed action marks. Striated action marks are scratches produced as the cartridge case moves laterally against the chamber. These may be in the form of chamber marks, shear marks, firing pin drag marks, extractor marks, or ejector marks. Chamber marks are scratches produced by the walls of the chamber as the cartridge is loaded and removed from the chamber. Scratches resulting from the movement of the primer area of the cartridge case against the firing pin aperture are called shear marks. Firing pin drag marks are scratches produced as the firing pin drags across the primer during extraction. Extractor marks are scratches resulting from the extractor "hook" removing a cartridge from the chamber, and ejector marks are striated marks created as the cartridge contacts the ejector during ejection. Impressed action marks are the result of sufficient impact by a portion of the firearm causing impressed or indented marks. These may be in the form of firing pin marks, breech marks, or ejector marks. Firing pin marks are indentations produced when the firing pin strikes the primer. Impressions resulting from the head of the

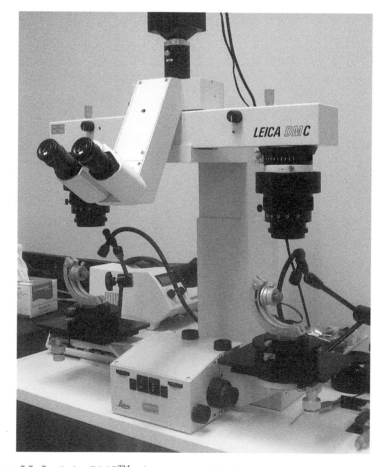

Figure 11-1 Leica DMC™ microscope used for firearms comparative examinations.

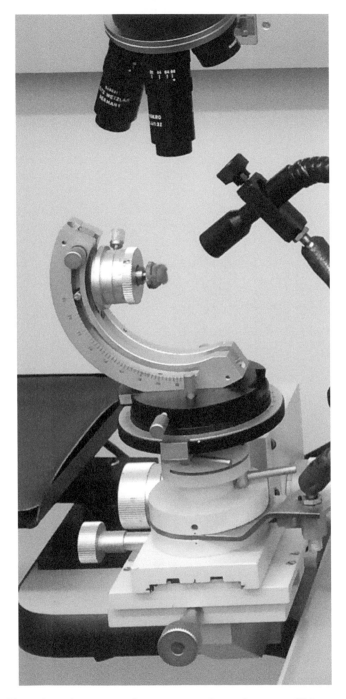

Figure 11-2   The universal stage on a firearms comparison microscope. This stage allows complete movement in all directions of the sample.

cartridge striking the breech face of the firearm are called breech marks. Ejector marks are indentations created as the cartridge is ejected from the chamber.

In some situations, the investigator may request identification of the possible weapon. For this, the examiner determines the class characteristics of the projectile or cartridge case. From this information, possible weapons can be determined. In other situations, a complete examination may be requested. In these cases, if the class characteristics are consistent with a suspected firearm, test fire samples are made using similar ammunition. The test fires are then compared to each other to ensure that the firearm produces unique, individual markings. This examination is done on a comparison stereomicroscope (see Figure 11-1). A comparison stereomicroscope is composed of two stereomicroscopes that are connected by an optical bridge. The bridge contains prisms and mirrors that are used to direct the light to a common set of oculars. A set of knobs is used to adjust the field of view, so that items can be viewed from either microscope independently or combined. Samples are placed on a universal bullet stage. This stage is designed to allow the sample to be moved and rotated so that markings can be easily compared on various surfaces (see Figure 11-2). This accommodates the numerous sizes and shapes of bullets, cartridge casings, and shot shell casings. The combined field of view shows

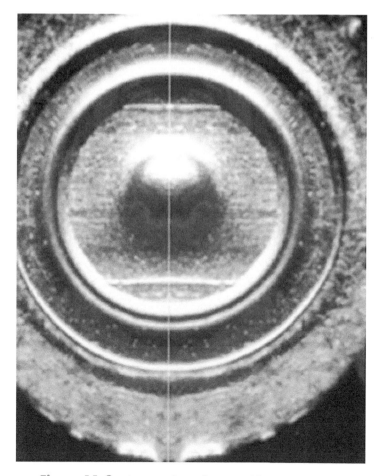

Figure 11-3 A comparison of two cartridge case samples.

portions from each microscope's field of view. This allows the examiner to examine two items side-by-side on a microscopic scale (see Figure 11-3).

If unique, consistent markings are found, comparisons can then be performed with the evidence samples. When comparisons are performed, the firearms examiners usually reach one of four conclusions: (1) The exhibit was identified as having been fired from or in the suspected weapon, (2) the exhibit could neither be identified nor eliminated as having been fired from the weapon, (3) the exhibit was eliminated as having not been fired from or in the suspected weapon, and (4) the exhibit was identified as having passed through the action of the suspected weapon.

Equipment and Supplies

> Comparison stereomicroscope
>
> Previously prepared known and unknown bullet sets
>
> Previously prepared known and unknown cartridge case sets
>
> Micrometer

Safety

Use standard laboratory safety procedures as described in guidelines set by your instructor. Be cautious of microscope light levels to avoid eye damage.

Part I: Parts of the Comparison Stereomicroscope

1. Obtain a photograph of the comparison microscope used in the laboratory.
2. Label the following parts of the microscope: light source, optical bridge, sample stage, objectives, focusing knobs, X-Y alignment knobs, knobs for adjusting field of view, and oculars.

Part II: Bullet and Cartridge Casing Comparisons

Procedure

You will use a stereomicroscope to compare bullets and cartridge casings shot from several weapons. This procedure will be followed for both the knowns (A, B, and C) and your assigned unknown.

A. Bullets
1. Examine the unknown bullet for the number of lands and grooves. Hold the bullet with the tip end away from you, and look at it under the stereomicroscope.
2. Mark one of the lands with a pen or marker. Use something that can be washed off after examination is complete.
3. Using a micrometer, measure the diameter of the bullet to determine the caliber.
4. Using wax, press the bullet onto the rotating stage mount. Rotate the bullet to count the number of land impressions until the bullet is rotated completely around to your mark. This is the number of lands and grooves. Remember: When the bullet passes through

the barrel, the impressions left on the bullet are reversed from the barrel—lands are recessed, and grooves are raised.

5. Next, examine the bullet for the direction of twist. Holding the bullet with the tip end away from you, determine the direction of twist. If the land and groove impressions go toward the right, the bullet has a right twist; if they go toward the left, the bullet has a left twist.

6. Using a micrometer, measure the width of the lands and grooves.

7. Examine the known bullets for the caliber, the number and width of lands and grooves, and the direction of twist, as performed in steps 1–6. Determine if your unknown bullet shares class characteristics with any of the known bullets.

8. Finally, using the comparison stereomicroscope, examine the unknown bullet for the rifling striations.

9. Look at the striations for comparison to any possible knowns. Not only must the lands and grooves of the questioned and known bullets match, but also the longitudinal striations on each must coincide. Comment on the striations, and draw regions that appear similar using the circle template in Appendix E. Is there anything unusual with any of the knowns or unknowns?

B. Cartridges

1. A cartridge casing can be compared for both striated action marks (chamber marks, shear marks, extractor marks, and ejector marks) and impressed action marks (firing pin impressions, breech marks, and ejector marks).

2. Draw the firing pin impression or other individual characteristics found for each cartridge examined (known and unknown).

3. Determine if any of the cartridge casings were fired from the same weapon.

Report Requirements

Include all drawings, calculations, and other information obtained during the laboratory procedure. Notes and/or drawings should include the sample identification, magnification, and a complete description.

Report Questions

1. For firearm evidence, what are the class characteristics that should be considered? Discuss each.

2. How can the caliber of a firearm be determined from a fired bullet?

3. What are the individual characteristics for firearm evidence? Discuss each.

4. What function does each component perform in the comparison stereomicroscope used for firearms identifications?

5. Write a statement about your comparison with the "known bullet samples." Could the weapon from which they (known samples) had been fired also be the weapon from which the unknown was fired? Back up your written statement with why you think they match, referring to your drawings if necessary.

6. Write a statement about your comparison with the "known cartridge case samples." Could the weapon from which they (known samples) had been fired also be the weapon from which the unknown was fired? Back up your written statement with why you think they match, referring to your drawings if necessary.

Chapter 11

Experiment 11A: Gunshot Residue Examinations

Recommended pre-lab reading assignments:

Anon. Gunshot Residues and Shot Pattern Test. *FBI Law Enforcement Bulletin*. 1970; 39(9): 7.

Dillon J. The Modified Griess Test: A Chemically Specific Chromophoric Test for Nitrate Compounds in Gunshot Residues. *AFTE Journal*. 1990; 22(3): 248.

Dillon J. The Sodium Rhodizonate Test: A Chemically Specific Test for Lead in Gunshot Residues. *AFTE Journal*. 1990; 22(3): 26.

Fiegel F, Anger V. *Spot Tests in Inorganic Analysis*, 6th ed. Amsterdam: Elsevier, 1972.

Lekstrom JA, Koons RD. Copper and Nickel Detection on Gunshot Targets by Dithiooxamide Test. *Journal of Forensic Sciences*. 1986; 31(4): 1283.

Recommended website:

FirearmsID. [Home page] [cited 2020]. Louisville, KY: FirearmsID. Available from: http://www.firearmsid.com.

Objective

Upon completion of this practical exercise, the student will have developed a basic understanding of:

1. gunshot residue
2. chemical tests used for gunshot residue examinations
3. chemical tests performed on gunshot residue for distance determinations
4. chemical tests performed on samples for copper determination

---

Practical Forensic Microscopy: A Laboratory Manual, Second Edition. Barbara P. Wheeler.
© 2021 John Wiley & Sons Ltd. Published 2021 by John Wiley & Sons Ltd.
Companion website: www.wiley.com/go/Wheeler/Forensic

Introduction

At times, it may be important to examine an item for gunshot residue to determine a muzzle-to-target distance. When a gun is fired, the firing pin strikes the back of the cartridge and sparks the primer that ignites the "gunpowder" and causes it to burn. This results in the formation of gaseous vapors that force the bullet down the barrel of the gun and out the muzzle. The majority of the vapor proceeds out the muzzle, but the vapor can also escape from the cylinder gap in a revolver or the ejection port in a pistol. The vapor and any unburnt particles that escape from these areas are called gunshot residue (GSR). This includes primer and gunpowder residues, plus metallic residues from projectiles.

To understand GSR, we must first discuss some of the components of ammunition, since this is where the constituents for gunshot residue originate. A modern cartridge consists of: a bullet (projectile), the casing (which holds all the parts together), the propellant (powder), the rim (the portion of the casing used for loading), and the primer (which ignites the propellant). A modern shotgun shell consists of: shot (projectile), the casing (which holds all the parts together), the wad (which separates the shot from the propellant), the propellant (powder), and a brass head that includes a primer (which ignites the propellant). It is typically the projectile (bullet or shot), propellant, and primer that supply the components that are identified when doing muzzle-to-target determinations.

Bullets, either non-jacketed or jacketed, are usually made of a metal alloy or a layered combination of metals. Non-jacketed bullets are usually an alloy of lead and antimony, which is added to lead to provide additional hardness to the bullet; however, copper, brass, or tungsten may also be used. Non-jacketed bullets may have a thin coating of copper or even Teflon to provide specific performance requirements. Jacketed bullets are a typically a laminate of lead with a harder jacket covering. Jacket coverings may be copper or other metals such as aluminum or steel. Steel jackets are usually plated with either nickel or copper to prevent rusting. At times, jacketed bullets may contain small lead pellets or sections with a silicone rubber. Shot can be made of lead or steel. A propellant is a chemical that is used to move an object by applying a force. Black powder and smokeless powder are used in ammunition as propellants. Black powder contains charcoal, potassium nitrate, and sulfur. Smokeless powder may either be single-based or double-based. Single-based smokeless powder contains cellulose nitrate with a stabilizer and modifier. Double-based smokeless powder contains cellulose nitrate and nitroglycerin, with stabilizers and modifiers. Stabilizers react with the nitrogen oxides. If these not removed, the propellants are extremely unstable and prone to auto-ignition. Common stabilizers are diphenylamine and ethyl centralite. Modifiers are either plasticizers or flash suppressants. Plasticizers soften the powder. This prevents the powder from fracturing. Flash suppressants interrupt the reaction of muzzle gases. Common modifiers are nitroglycerin, ethyl centralite, dibutyl phthalate, 2,4-dinitrotoluene, and triacetin. Common flash suppressants are potassium nitrate and potassium sulfate. The ignition component of a cartridge is the primer. Originally mercury fulminate and potassium chlorate were used as primers. However, these compounds deteriorated the weapons. Currently lead azide, lead styphnate, antimony sulfide, barium nitrate, and tetracene are used.

While most laboratories will perform instrumental techniques to identify barium, lead, and antimony in GSR (Experiment 32), chemical spot testing can also be performed to help identify GSR and ammunition components. Three elements are associated with GSR: barium, lead, and antimony. The sodium rhodizonate test is specific for lead. The Harrison-Gilroy test is used to identify antimony. Gunpowder used in most ammunition is smokeless powder made of

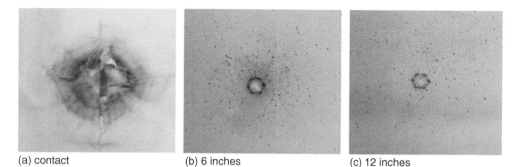

(a) contact   (b) 6 inches   (c) 12 inches

Figure 11A-1   Visible residue is shown from distance determination samples from a .40 caliber pistol.

nitrocellulose or a nitroglycerin–nitrocellulose combination. The modified Griess test is used to detect the presence of nitrite residues. Diphenylamine (DPA) may be used to test for the presence of the nitrate ion. These tests are generally used to determine the physical characteristics of bullet holes, which aids in muzzle-to-target distance determinations. Chemical spot tests may also be performed for copper. Since many bullets are copper coated, this in combination with the sodium rhodizonate test may give an analyst important information about the entrance or exit holes produced by bullets. It can also provide information about the type of bullet used to produce the holes. Unburned nitrocellulose and nitroglycerin particles can also be identified with the modified Griess test or DPA.

Objects or materials may be examined to determine if any of the GSR components are present. Bullets that are fired through clothing or items will often leave traces of lead and/or copper. The lead may come from the surface of the bullet, from the barrel of the weapon, or from primer components. Copper may come from the bullet itself. Examinations may also be performed for the presence of barium, antimony, nitrates, or other components of the ammunition that are released upon firing. When these examinations are done in combination, distance determinations can sometimes be made. It is important to perform the tests in a particular sequence, so that reagents won't interfere with results. The modified Griess test is performed first, with the dithiooxamide test second, followed by the sodium rhodizonate test. A distance determination is done when it is important to determine the possible distance from a weapon muzzle to the target. Known test fire samples are made from various distances; for instance, from 12 inches (30 cm) away from the target, from 18 inches (45 cm) away from the target, and from 24 inches (60 cm) away from the target. Visible residue patterns can initially be examined (see Figure 11A-1). These samples are then processed using the color spot tests to give additional visual patterns. The closer the weapon is to the target, the more pattern there will be. Likewise, when distances greater than three feet (90 cm) are tested, patterns become less visible. The unknown sample is chemically treated and compared to the known test fire samples to determine a possible weapon-to-target distance.

Chemical spot tests are used because they are both inexpensive and easy to perform. They can be very effective, and their ease of use allows them to be performed by personnel with very minimal training. As with all presumptive tests, these spot tests must be confirmed with additional testing (see Experiment 32).

Equipment and Supplies

Reagents and samples as listed with each test

Safety

Use standard laboratory safety procedures as described in guidelines set by your instructor. Students should know the hazards associated with the solvents used in the procedures, and use them with appropriate precautions as set by your instructor.

Refer to your safety data sheet (SDS) as needed. Students should wear personal protective equipment, such as goggles and nitrile gloves, for all parts of this lab. All work done with organic solvents should be completed in a hood or with adequate ventilation. Several of the reagents are hazardous and should be handled with caution.

Part I: Color Tests for Nitrate and Nitrite

These spot tests will test for nitrates and nitrite ions commonly found in GSR. Since nitrates are ubiquitous compounds commonly found in many consumer products, positive results must be interpreted with caution. These tests are commonly used to identify gunpowder patterns so that distance determinations can be made. You will perform the modified Griess test and the diphenylamine test (DPA).

Modified Griess Test for Nitrites

Equipment and Supplies

Reagents:
1. Griess Reagent A: Prepare 10 mL of 1% (w/w) solution of sulfanic acid (MW = 173.84 gm/mol). Place in a dropper bottle, and label.
2. Griess Reagent B: Prepare 10 mL of 0.1% (w/w) 1-napthylamine (MW = 143.19 gm/mol) in methanol. Place in a dropper bottle, and label.

Known sample: Nitrite solution: Dissolve 0.6 gm of sodium nitrite in 100 mL of distilled water. Place in a dropper bottle, and label.

Unknown sample: Obtain an unknown sample from your instructor, and record its number in your notes.

Procedure

1. First, perform a positive control. Add a few drops of the nitrite solution to a cotton swab. Use a hot air gun or hair dryer to dry the swab.
2. Next, add a few drops of Griess Reagent A to the swab. Follow this with a few drops of Griess Reagent B. Note the reaction. An orange-red color indicates the presence of nitrites. Record your observations.
3. Perform a negative control. Place a few drops of dilute HCl (about 1.5 M) on a blank swab. Next, add a few drops of Griess Reagent A followed by a few drops of Griess Reagent B to the swab. No color change should result. Record your observations.

4. To test your unknown, add a few drops of Griess Reagent A followed by a few drops of Griess Reagent B to the swab. A positive result indicating the presence of nitrate is an orange-red color. Record your observations.

Diphenylamine (DPA) Test for Nitrates

Equipment and Supplies

Reagent:
1. DPA reagent: Add 10 mL concentrated sulfuric acid to 2 mL distilled water under constant stirring. Add to this solution 0.05 gm diphenylamine, and stir until the solid is completely dissolved. Store in a dark glass bottle. Place into a dropper bottle, and label.

Known sample: Sodium nitrate ($NaNO_3$).

Unknown sample: Obtain an unknown sample from your instructor, and record its number in your notes.

Procedure

1. To test the reagent, first add a couple of crystals of $NaNO_3$ to a test tube. Add a few drops of water, and mix until the $NaNO_3$ dissolves. Dip a clean dry cotton swab into the solution, and let it absorb. Remove the swab, and add a drop of DPA reagent. Note the reaction. A positive result indicating the presence of nitrate is a blue-purple color.
2. Record your observations.
3. Perform a negative control. Place a few drops of DPA on a blank swab. No color change should result. Record your observations.
4. To test your unknown, add a few drops of the reagent to the swab. Record your observations.

Part II: Color Tests for Lead and Antimony

Spot tests to detect the presence of antimony (Sb), barium (Ba), and lead (Pb) from the bullet primer were developed in the 1960s. These tests are considered more conclusive than the test for nitrates and nitrites because, in combination, these three elements are rarely found in the natural environment. When all three of these elements are found in significant levels on a person, recent exposure to GSR is probable.

Sodium Rhodizonate Test for Pb

Equipment and Supplies

Reagents:
1. Sodium rhodizonate: Prepare the sodium rhodizonate solution by adding 0.2 gm of sodium rhodizonate to 100 mL of distilled water, then stirring. This reagent has a short shelf life and should be made fresh. Discard any portions not used. Place in a spray bottle, and label.

2. Buffer solution, pH 2.8: Dissolve 1.9 gm of sodium bitartrate and 1.5 gm of tartaric acid in 100 mL of distilled water. This solution may be stored. Place in a spray bottle, and label.

3. Hydrochloric acid: Combine 5 mL of concentrated hydrochloric acid in 95 mL of distilled water. This solution may be stored. Remember to gently pour the acid into the water. Calculate the molarity of the HCl, and place in a labeled spray bottle.

Known samples: 1 mg/mL Pb standard solution.

Unknown sample: Obtain an unknown sample from your instructor, and record its number in your notes.

Procedure

1. First, perform a positive control. Obtain a large circle of filter paper pre-treated with acetic acid. Add 1–2 drops of the lead standard solution. Use a hot air gun or hair dryer to dry the filter paper. Note any color changes. Saturate, by spraying, the test papers with the sodium rhodizonate solution.

2. Allow the papers to sit for approximately one minute. The test area should turn a yellowish-orange color.

3. Next, spray the area with the buffer solution. The test area for lead should turn pink.

4. To confirm the presence of lead, spray the area with the hydrochloric acid solution. Test areas that turn deep blue-violet indicate the presence of lead. Record your observations.

5. Next, perform a negative control. Using a blank section of paper, saturate the paper with the sodium rhodizonate solution.

6. Continue with steps 2–4. Record your observations.

7. Obtain an unknown. Saturate the sample with the sodium rhodizonate solution.

8. Continue with steps 2–4. Record your observations.

Harrison-Gilroy (Triphenylmethylarsonium Iodide) Test for Sb

Equipment and Supplies

Reagent:

1. Triphenylmethylarsonium iodide: Dissolve 10 gm of triphenylarsine and 10 gm of methyl iodide in 20 mL of absolute ethanol. Reflux the solution for three hours. To reflux, place the solution in a round-bottom flask and attach a fractionating column and condenser, so that the refluxed liquid can be trapped. Add ether to the trapped liquid to precipitate the triphenylmethylarsonium salt. The salt can be purified by re-dissolving in ethanol and precipitating with ether.

Known sample: 1 mg/mL Sb standard solution.

Unknown sample: Obtain an unknown sample from your instructor, and record its number in your notes.

Procedure

1. Perform a positive control. Obtain a large circle of filter paper that has not been pre-treated with acetic acid. Divide it in half. Label one half as Sb and the other as negative control. Add 1–2 drops of the appropriate standard solution. Use a hot air gun or hair dryer to dry the filter paper. Note any color changes.

2. Add 1–2 drops of triphenylmethylarsonium iodide solution where the Sb standard was placed. If Sb^{3+} is present, an orange precipitate will appear in about 30 seconds. No further color development will occur after two minutes. Record your observations.
3. Perform a negative control. Place a few drops of distilled water on the blank filter paper. Add 1–2 drops of triphenylmethylarsonium iodide at the location you want to test. No color change should result. Record your observations.
4. To test your unknown, add 1–2 drops of the triphenylmethylarsonium iodide solution. Record your observations.

Part III: Color Test for Copper

This spot test will test for copper. Simple cast lead slugs are the simplest form of bullets. At times, the lead may be blended with another metal to give the bullet additional hardness. It is not uncommon to have leaded bullets with a thin coating of copper plating. These bullets are referred to as "copper-washed." This test provides important information about the entrance or exit holes produced by bullets. It can also provide information about the type of bullet used to produce the holes.

Dithiooxamide (DTO)

Equipment and Supplies

Reagents:
1. Dithiooxamide solution: Dissolve 0.2 gm of dithiooxamide in 100 mL of ethanol. This solution should be stored in a tightly sealed container to prevent evaporation. Transfer to a spray bottle just before use.
2. Ammonia solution: Dilute 50 mL of concentrated ammonium hydroxide with 50 mL of distilled water. Always use a ventilated hood when mixing ammonium hydroxide solutions. Place in a spray bottle, and label.
Known samples: 1 mg/mL Cu standard solution or a copper-washed bullet.
Unknown sample: Obtain an unknown sample from your instructor, and record its number in your notes.

Procedure

1. Perform a positive control. Obtain a large circle of filter paper. Divide it in half. Label one half as Cu, and the other as negative control. Add 1–2 drops of the Cu standard solution, or swipe the copper-washed bullet over the paper several times. If the solution is used, dry the area with a hot air gun or hair dryer. Note any color changes.
2. Spray the test area with the ammonia solution.
3. After one minute, spray the area with DTO. A green color is a positive reaction for copper. (The presence of a yellow color may indicate the presence of lead.)
4. Perform a negative control. Place a few drops of ammonia followed by the DTO solution, as performed in steps 2 and 3, to a blank filter paper. No color change should result. Record your observations.
5. To test your unknown, add a few drops of the reagents to the swab. Record your observations.

Report Requirements

Include all drawings, calculations, and other information obtained during the laboratory procedure. Notes and/or drawings should include the sample identification, magnification, and a complete description.

Report Questions

1. Write a paragraph describing how a color test is performed, including the value and purpose of the test.
2. Define "false positive." Give an example of a false-positive color test.
3. What could be said if antimony and lead were confirmed on a test sample, but no barium was present? Can this still be attributed to GSR?
4. What are "significant levels"?
5. How is the Griess test used for distance determinations?
6. What effect would a bloody shirt have on the testing of a bullet hole? What can be done to compensate for this?
7. Is it important to test both sides of a test sample?

Recommended and Further Reading

Banno A, Masuda T, Ikeuchi K. Three Dimensional Visualization and Comparison of Impressions on Fired Bullets. *Forensic Science International.* 2004; 140(2–3): 233–240.

Basu S, Boone CE, Denio DJ, Miazga RA. Fundamental Studies of Gunshot Residue Deposition by Glue-Lift. *Journal of Forensic Sciences.* 1997; 42(4): 571–581.

Biasotti A. A Statistical Study of the Individual Characteristics of Fired Bullets. *Journal of Forensic Sciences.* 1959; (4): 35–50.

Coumbaros J, Kirkbride KP, Kobus H, Sarvas I. Distribution of Lead and Barium in Gunshot Residue Particles Derived from 0.22 Caliber Rimfire Ammunition. *Journal of Forensic Sciences.* 2001; 46(6): 1352–1357.

Degaetano D, Siegel JA. Survey of Gunshot Residue Analysis in Forensic-Science Laboratories. *Journal of Forensic Sciences.* 1990; 35(5): 1087–1095.

D'Uffizi M, Falso G, Ingo GM, Padeletti G. Microchemical and Micromorphological Features of Gunshot Residue Observed by Combined Use of AFM, SA-XPS and SEM + EDS. *Surface and Interface Analysis.* 2002; 34(1): 502–506.

Emmons RC. *The Universal Stage (with Five Axes of Rotation)* (Memoir 8). Washington, DC: Geological Society of America, 1943.

Hamby J, Brundage D, Thorpe J. The Identification of Fired Bullets from 10 Consecutively Rifled 9mm Ruger Pistol Barrels: A Research Project involving 507 Participants from 20 Countries. *AFTE Journal.* 2009; (41): 99–110.

Houck MM, Siegel JA. *Fundamentals of Forensic Science*, 3rd ed. Amsterdam: Elsevier Academic Press, 2015; 545–572.

Klein A, Nedivi L, Silverwater H. Physical Match of Fragmented Bullets. *Journal of Forensic Sciences.* 2000; 45(3): 722–727.

Meng HH, Caddy B. Gunshot Residue Analysis – a Review. *Journal of Forensic Sciences.* 1997; 42(4): 553–570.

Nichols RG. Defending the Scientific Foundations of the Firearms and Tool Mark Identification Discipline: Responding to Recent Challenges. *Journal of Forensic Sciences.* 2007; 52(3): 586–594.

Romolo FS, Margot P. Identification of Gunshot Residue: A Critical Review. *Forensic Science International.* 2001; 119(2): 195–211.

Rowe W. Firearms Identification. In: Saferstein R, ed. *Forensic Science Handbook*, vol. 2. Englewood Cliffs, NJ: Prentice Hall, 1988; 393–449.

Saferstein R. *Criminalistics: An Introduction to Forensic Science*, 11th ed. Upper Saddle River, NJ: Prentice Hall, 2015; 167–181.

Tillman WL. Automated Gunshot Residue Particle Search and Characterization. *Journal of Forensic Sciences.* 1987; 32(1): 62–71.

Tugcu H, Yorulmaz C, Bayraktaroglu G, Ulner HB, Karslioglu Y, Koc S, et al. Determination of Gunshot Residues with Image Analysis: An Experimental Study. *Military Medicine.* 2005; 170(9): 802–805.

Tugcu H, Yorulmaz C, Karslioglu Y, Uner HB, Koc S, Ozdemir C, et al. Image Analysis as an Adjunct to Sodium Rhodizonate Test in the Evaluation of Gunshot Residues – an Experimental Study. *American Journal of Forensic Medicine and Pathology.* 2006; 27(4): 296–299.

Wilber CG, Lantz RK, Sulik PL. Gunshot Residue, 10 Years Later. *American Journal of Forensic Medicine and Pathology.* 1991; 12(3): 204–206.

Zeichner A. Is There a Real Danger of Concealing Gunshot Residue (GSR) Particles by Skin Debris Using the Tape-Lift Method for Sampling GSR from Hands? *Journal of Forensic Sciences.* 2001; 46(6): 1447–1455.

Zeichner A, Levin N. More on the Uniqueness of Gunshot Residue (GSR) Particles. *Journal of Forensic Sciences.* 1997; 42(6): 1027–1028.

Chapter 12

Experiment 12: Shoe and Tire Impression Examinations

Recommended pre-lab reading assignments:

Bodziak WJ. *Footwear Impression Evidence*, 2nd ed. Boca Raton, FL: CRC Press, 2000.
McDonald P. *Tire Imprint Evidence*. Boca Raton, FL: CRC Press, 1993.

Objective

Upon completion of this practical exercise, the student will have developed a basic understanding of:

1. shoe and tire impression examinations
2. use of the stereomicroscope for shoe and tire impression examinations

Introduction

Similar to tool mark impressions, shoe and tire impression examinations involve the basic principle of uniqueness: that all objects are unique to themselves and thus can be differentiated from each other. The mechanism for differentiating shoe or tire impressions depends on class and individual characteristics. Class characteristics are intentional or design characteristics that would be common to a particular group of items. The size and shape of a shoe or tire surface is an example of a class characteristic. For instance, a significantly larger shoe impression may be left by a size 13 tennis shoe than a size 8 tennis shoe. The pattern design and manufacturing characteristics of tire tread can also leave varying impressions, as shown by different tire brands. General wear patterns to both shoes and tires are also considered class characteristics. Individual characteristics are marks produced by random imperfections or irregularities of the tread surface. These characteristics may be produced through the machining process or by

---

Practical Forensic Microscopy: A Laboratory Manual, Second Edition. Barbara P. Wheeler.
© 2021 John Wiley & Sons Ltd. Published 2021 by John Wiley & Sons Ltd.
Companion website: www.wiley.com/go/Wheeler/Forensic

random imperfections or irregularities, which are produced incidental to manufacture or caused by use or damage. For instance, small irregularities left in the edge of the tire as a result of the machining process used to cut and finish edges provide individual characteristics. More commonly, the shape and pattern of both shoe and tire treads are modified by wear and damage to the tire or shoe. Foreign material such as stones or sticks may become attached or wedged into a shoe or tire, which may also provide individual characteristics in an impression. This can create a unique pattern for every shoe or tire, allowing for the possibility of individualizing the evidence.

When several objects are pressed or stamped against one another, allowing the objects to transfer and retain characteristics from one another, impression evidence is created. Although soil is the most common example, any material that can be manipulated with some degree of force may contain impression evidence. Impression evidence such as shoe or tire impressions can be divided into two general categories: (1) two-dimensional impressions and (2) three-dimensional surfaces. Prints made by depositing or removing material from the "plane" of a hard surface are considered to be two-dimensional, and as such only length and width of the impression can be examined. Shoes or tires that come into contact with a liquid (for example, blood or oil) may leave a stain or pattern, creating a two-dimensional impression when further movement occurs. These prints are usually photographed and/or lifted. Impressions made in a pliable material are considered three-dimensional. Three-dimensional impressions involve examinations of length, width, and depth for the impression. Wet cement and snow, for example, may provide a surface for three-dimensional impressions. They should be photographed and cast (see Figure 12-1). Spray impression wax can be used prior to casting materials for impressions left in snow.

Many prints and impressions can be enhanced to improve the quality of the visible impression. This may involve various photographic techniques such as the use of filters, oblique lighting, ultraviolet lighting, infrared lighting, and high-contrast lighting. An Electrostatic Dust Print Lifter may also be used to enhance outline prints, impressions on paper, or dust prints. Fingerprint powders may enhance some prints and impressions that have been left by wet surfaces. Gelatin and adhesive lifters can also be utilized to lift visible prints and impressions. Chemical enhancements can be done to visualize trace blood prints and impressions.

In some situations, the investigator may request identification of the possible shoe or tire. For this, the examiner determines the class characteristics of the impression. From this information, a class of shoes or tires can sometimes be determined using a reference database.

In other situations, a complete examination may be requested. In these cases, if the class characteristics are consistent with a suspected shoe or tire, test marks are then made. The test marks are then compared to each other to ensure that the shoe or tire produces unique, consistent individual markings. This examination is done visually and with a stereomicroscope. If unique, consistent markings are found, comparisons can then be performed with the evidence samples. When comparisons are performed, the forensic examiners usually reach one of three conclusions: (1) an identification, where the exhibit was found to be produced by contact with the shoe or tire, and a sufficient correlation between individual characteristics was found; (2) a non-identification or elimination, where the exhibit was found not to be produced by the shoe or tire, and class characteristics did not match; and (3) inconclusive, where class characteristics agree but there is an insufficient correlation between individual characteristics.

Figure 12-1 A plaster cast made from a partial footprint in soil. The soil can be cleaned from this cast, so that comparisons to a suspect's shoe can then be performed.

Equipment and Supplies

Stereomicroscope

Micro kit

Unknown shoe and tire prints

Unknown shoe and tire impressions

Casting material (Dental Stone™ or Die Stone™)

Cardboard (or another firm material to frame the impression)

Hair spray

Inkless print kit (paper and ink may also be used)

Shoes

Tires

Safety

Use standard laboratory safety procedures as described in guidelines set by your instructor.

Part I: Casting an Impression

Procedure

1. Make a frame or dam around the impression area.
2. If the foundation of the impression is in a loose material (for example, dry soil), spray the area with hair spray to firm up the top layer of the impression.
3. Mix the casting material according to the manufacturer's instructions. The ideal mixture should be the consistency of a batter, not watery, but also not too thick.
4. Apply the casting material over the impression to be cast. To prevent the casting material from breaking up the impression, divert the casting material by gently pouring the mixture over a spatula. For large impressions, more than one cast may be necessary.
5. When the casting material has begun to set, mark an area with identifying marks.

Part II: Two-dimensional Print Comparison

Procedure

1. Examine the unknown print that you have been assigned.
2. Identify the class characteristics to determine a possible shoe or tire.
3. Obtain a possible shoe or tire, and make several test prints using the inkless print kit. After pressing the shoe or tire on the print coater, press it again onto the chemically treated paper. Black prints will become visible.
4. Examine the test prints with the naked eye or stereomicroscope to determine if the shoe or tire produces unique, consistent markings.
5. Compare these markings to those of your unknown print. Not only must the size and shape match up, but also the irregularities or longitudinal striations on each must coincide. Comment on the striations and, using the circle template in Appendix E, draw regions that appear similar. Is there anything unusual with any of the knowns or unknowns?

Part III: Three-dimensional Impression Comparison

Procedure

1. Examine the unknown impression that you have been assigned.
2. Make a cast of the impression.
3. Once it has thoroughly dried (this could take 48 hours), clean off the cast with water and a soft brush. Take special care not to damage the cast.
4. Identify the class characteristics to determine a possible shoe/tire.
5. Obtain a possible shoe or tire. Make several test prints using the inkless print kit. After pressing the shoe or tire on the print coater, press it again onto the chemically treated paper. Black prints will become visible. If necessary, test impressions or casts can also be made of the known shoe/tire.
6. Examine the test prints with the naked eye or stereomicroscope to determine if the shoe or tire produces unique, consistent markings.
7. Compare these markings to those of your unknown print. Not only must the size and shape match up, but also the irregularities or longitudinal striations on each must coincide. Comment on the striations, and draw regions that appear similar. Is there anything unusual with any of the knowns or unknowns?

Report Requirements

Include all drawings, calculations, and other information obtained during the laboratory procedure. Notes and/or drawings should include the sample identification, magnification, and a complete description.

Report Questions

1. For shoe or tire print/impression evidence, what properties are class characteristics? Using a shoe, describe its class characteristics.
2. What are the individual characteristics for shoe or tire print/impression evidence? Using a tire, describe individual characteristics.
3. Write a statement about your print comparison with the "known." Could the shoe/tire have produced the print? Back up your written statement with a discussion as to why you think they match or don't match, referring to your drawings if necessary.
4. Write a statement about your impression comparison with the "known." Could the shoe/tire have produced the impression? Back up your written statement with a discussion as to why you think they match or don't match, referring to your drawings if necessary.

Recommended and Further Reading

Abbott JR. *Footwear Evidence*. Springfield, IL: Charles C. Thomas, 1964.

Bodziak WJ. Evidence Photography of Shoe and Tire Impressions. *The Professional Photographer*. 1985; 43–44.

Bodziak WJ. Manufacturing Processes for Athletic Shoe Outsoles and Their Significance in the Examination of Footwear Impression Evidence. *Journal of Forensic Sciences*. 1986; 31(1): 153–176.

Cassidy M. *Footwear Identification*. Ottawa: Royal Canadian Mounted Police, 1980.

DuPasquier E, Hebrard J, Margot P, Ineichen M. Evaluation and Comparison of Casting Materials in Forensic Sciences – Applications to Tool Marks and Foot/Shoe Impressions. *Forensic Science International*. 1996; 82(1): 33–43.

Grogan R. Tyres and Crime. *Journal of Forensic Sciences*, 1971; 11(1).

Houck MM, Siegel JA. *Fundamentals of Forensic Science*, 3rd ed. Amsterdam: Elsevier Academic Press, 2015; 578–590.

Kerstholt JH, Paashuis R, Sjerps M. Shoe Print Examinations: Effects of Expectation, Complexity and Experience. *Forensic Science International*. 2007; 165(1): 30–34.

Kovac F. *Tire Technology*, 5th ed. Akron, OH: Goodyear Tire & Rubber Company, 1978.

Liukkonen M, Majamaa H, Virtanen J. The Role and Duties of the Shoeprint/Toolmark Examiner in Forensic Laboratories. *Forensic Science International*. 1996; 82(1): 99–108.

Majamaa H, Ytti A. Survey of the Conclusions Drawn of Similar Footwear Cases in Various Crime Laboratories. *Forensic Science International*. 1996; 82(1): 109–120.

Novoselsky Y, Tsach T, Klein A, Volkov N, Shor Y, Vinokurov A. Unusual Contact Marks: Connecting the Hubcap to the Wheel of the Car. *Journal of Forensic Sciences*. 2002; 47(3): 630–632.

Robbins LM. The Individuality of Human Footprints. *Journal of Forensic Sciences*. 1978; 23(4); 778–785.

Saferstein R. *Criminalistics: An Introduction to Forensic Science*, 11th ed. Upper Saddle River, NJ: Prentice Hall, 2015; 191–199.

Shor Y, Kennedy RB, Tsach T, Volkov N, Novoselsky Y, Vinokurov A. Physical Match: Insole and Shoe. *Journal of Forensic Sciences*. 2003; 48(4): 808–810.

Shor Y, Weisner S. A Survey on the Conclusions Drawn on the Same Footwear Marks Obtained in Actual Cases by Several Experts throughout the World. *Journal of Forensic Sciences*. 1999; 44(2): 380–384.

Willshire B, Hurley N. Development to Two-Dimensional Footwear Impressions Using Magnetic Flake Powders. *Journal of Forensic Sciences*. 1996; 41(4).

Chapter 13

Experiment 13: Botanical Examinations

Recommended pre-lab reading assignments:

Clarke RC. *Marijuana Botany: Propagation and Breeding of Distinctive Cannabis*, 2nd ed. Berkeley, CA: Ronin Publishing, 1993.

Core HA, Cote WA, Day AC. *Wood Structure and Identification*, 2nd ed. Syracuse, NY: Syracuse University Press, 1979; 64–89, 98–122.

Hauber DJ. Marijuana Analysis with Recording Botanical Features Present and without the Environmental Pollutants of the Duquenois-Levine Test. *Journal of Forensic Sciences*. 1992; 37(6).

Small E. Morphological Variation of Achenes of Cannabis. *Canadian Journal of Botany*, 1974; 53: 978–987.

Summitt R, Siliker A. *CRC Handbook of Materials Science*. Boca Raton, FL: CRC Press, 1980; 11–19.

Objective

Upon completion of this practical exercise, the student will have developed a basic understanding of:

1. general characteristics of marijuana samples
2. use of the stereomicroscope to identify microscopic characteristics for marijuana
3. general characteristics for hard and soft woods
4. use of the compound microscope to identify microscopic characteristics for hard and soft woods

Practical Forensic Microscopy: A Laboratory Manual, Second Edition. Barbara P. Wheeler.
© 2021 John Wiley & Sons Ltd. Published 2021 by John Wiley & Sons Ltd.
Companion website: www.wiley.com/go/Wheeler/Forensic

Introduction

At times, it may be necessary for a forensic scientist to examine plant material. The most common botanical examinations involve the examination of plant material to identify marijuana, a controlled substance containing delta 9-tetrahydrocannabinol (THC); or hard and soft woods, commonly found during various crimes. These examinations can be performed using the stereomicroscope and the compound light microscope.

Marijuana

Marijuana is one of the most common drugs. Because of this fact, examinations must be performed on plant material to identify marijuana and the chemical component contained within, THC. Marijuana examinations involve both microscopic and chemical tests. To understand the identifying morphological features of marijuana, we must first discuss the plant itself. The species, *Cannabis sativa* L., has many varieties; however, the identifying features are the same. The plant itself is a tall, weedy plant, sometimes growing to 18 feet (5.5 m) high. Marijuana plants are considered dioecious, having either male or female flowers. Male pre-flowers have a shape similar to that of the spade on a playing card. These grape-shaped balls fill with pollen. Male flowers will grow in elongated clusters. Female pre-flowers are longer and shaped like a wispy flickering flame. They start showing one or two wispy white hairs where their buds are going to start forming, which is where the main stem connects to the individual nodes or "branches." Because of this fact, female flowers are initially more inconspicuous and are usually found hidden among small leaves at the ends of stalks and branches. They have more of a spike-like cluster and generally grow in pairs. Pistils may be present on female flowers growing from a bract (seed covering) near the base of the leaf stem. Leaves are arranged opposite one another on an erect, branching stem. Leaves are compound palmate (i.e., they appear hand-like), radiating from a common origin with numerous leaflets. The number of leaflets is usually an odd number and is most often found to be 7; however, numbers between 3 and 9 have also been found. Leaflets are green, brown-spotted, or brown in color. Leaflets vary in length up to 6 inches and are typically 1.5 inches wide. They are lanceolate (lance-like) shaped, with serrated (saw-tooth) edges. There is a single central vein with further venation from the central vein, ending at the sharp point or notch of the serrated edge. This is best viewed from the underside of the leaflet. Seeds are typically greenish-yellow to brown in color. They are oval in shape, with a distinct ridge along one side. They have a mottled tortoise-shell appearance. Stems and roots may also be present in some samples. Male plants are usually taller but less robust than female plants.

The identifying microscopic characteristics for marijuana are found on the leaflets. The identifying characteristics involve the hair found on each leaflet. Cystolithic hair is found on the top of the leaflet, while simple hairs are found on the bottom side. Cystolithic hairs are claw-shaped and point toward the end of the leaflet. At times, particles of calcium carbonate may be found at the base of the hair (see Figure 13-1a). Simple hairs have a wooly appearance, are not tapered, and are longer. They are more numerous and appear as a downy mass (see Figure 13-1b). Both cystolithic and simple hairs must be present on the same leaflet for a microscopic marijuana identification. In most situations, it is also necessary to perform further confirmatory tests. This is usually done by the modified Duquenois-Levine test described in Experiment 27, "Microscopic Analysis of Controlled Substances."

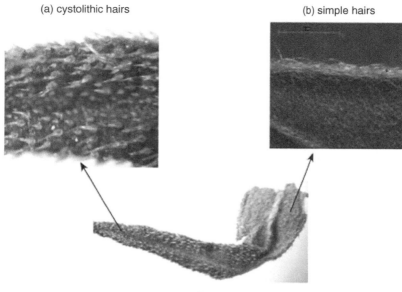

(a) cystolithic hairs

(b) simple hairs

marijuana leaf

Figure 13-1 A marijuana leaf showing the location of cystolithic and simple hairs. (a) Cystolithic hairs are found on the top of marijuana leaves, while (b) simple hairs are found on the bottom of the leaves. Both hair types must be present on a sample leaf for a positive identification.

One of two conclusions is generally reached for marijuana examinations: A sample may be identified as containing delta 9-tetrahydrocannabinol (THC), a controlled substance; or no controlled substances may be identified in a sample.

Soft and Hard Woods

Wood is used for many purposes. Its common use in furniture, tools, cutlery, and construction materials exposes the potential of it becoming evidence in almost every crime. A forensic scientist may also be asked to examine botanical samples to determine the species of various wood particles.

Wood samples can initially be classified into either soft (coniferous or non-porous) or hard (non-coniferous or porous) woods. This is done by examining the cellular structure of three planes of reference for a sample: cross section, radial section, and tangential section (see Figure 13-2). Cutting the wood perpendicular to the direction of growth produces the cross section. The radial section is the vertical plane from the pith at the center of the tree, heading out toward the bark. The tangential section is the plane perpendicular to the long axis of the rays and tangential to the growth rings. By using these three planes of reference, various macroscopic and microscopic characteristics allow identification of species for wood particles.

Wood is composed of several cellular structures. In soft woods, the longitudinal tracheid functions for both support and fluid conduction. Tracheid cells are elongated narrow cells found in the xylem. In soft woods, they are elongated, providing support, and have larger prominent bordered pits on their radial walls, allowing the transfer of water and mineral salts within the plant. When viewing the cross section of soft woods, the latewood tends to be dark, dense and with small-diameter tracheid pores. The earlywood of soft woods is light and soft, and has

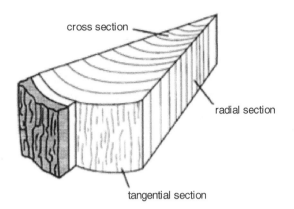

cross section

radial section

tangential section

Figure 13-2   Planes of reference for a wood sample.

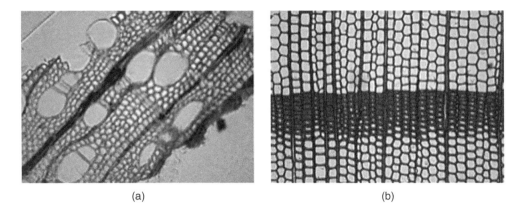

(a)   (b)

Figure 13-3   (a) A microtome cutting of birch (hardwood), which shows vessel elements present. (b) A microtome cutting of Douglas fir (softwood); note the lack of vessel elements. To make the cellular structure more easily viewed, the samples have been stained with food coloring. Source: Photographs reproduced with permission of Lara Mosenthin Steidel.

slightly larger diameter tracheid pores. Since soft woods are approximately 90% tracheid cells, and both latewood and earlywood have very similar-sized tracheids, the cross section has a more uniform appearance. However, in hard woods, there are two main cell structures, which provide a different cross-sectional appearance. Fiber tracheids are used for support, but vessels are used for water conduction. Fiber tracheids in hard woods are shorter. Vessel cells have thin walls but a relatively large diameter. It is also the vessels in hard woods that may possess small bordered pits, allowing for the transfer of water and mineral salts within the plant. When cross sections of hard woods are viewed for latewood, smaller and less frequent pores are found, and the earlywood has larger and more numerous pores. In cross-sectional samples, the major difference between soft and hard woods is the presence of vessel elements or pores (see Figure 13-3).

To further distinguish soft and hard wood species, additional microscopic examinations must be performed. Radial and tangential sections should be examined with a polarized light microscope to identify the various microscopic features present within the sample. Details of the cross-field pits, the shape of parenchyma cells, the shape and organization of the rays, and the presence of resin canals can provide information that can aid in the identification of specific soft wood species. Likewise, the details of vessel pits, shape and arrangement of fiber tracheid pits and ends, shape and arrangement of parenchyma, and shape and arrangement of rays can provide information that can aid in the identification of specific hard wood species.

One of three conclusions is generally reached for wood examinations. A sample may be identified as a particular soft wood, as a particular hard wood, or the species may not be able to be determined for the sample.

Equipment and Supplies

Stereomicroscope

Compound light microscope with objectives of various magnifications (e.g., 4X, 10X, 20X, and 40X) and focusing ocular with micrometer scale

Micro kit

Microscope slides and coverslips

Mounting medium (a colorless mounting medium in the refractive index range of 1.50–1.60)

Various plant samples, including marijuana

Hard and soft wood samples

Safety

Use standard laboratory safety procedures as described in guidelines set by your instructor. Be cautious of microscope light levels to avoid eye damage.

Part I: Marijuana Examinations

Procedure

1. Obtain a plant sample.
2. If possible, weigh the sample.
3. Using the stereomicroscope, examine the sample.
4. Describe the overall condition of the sample.
5. Observe whether or not the following features are present: palmate leaflets, lanceolate-shaped leaflets, serrated edges, alternate venation or pinnate venation, seeds, stems, bracts, husks, female flowers, and male flowers.
6. Continue to examine the leaflet under the stereomicroscope, using slightly higher magnification.
7. Observe whether or not the following features are present: cystolithic hair, simple hair, and resin glands. Using the circle template found in Appendix E, draw what you see.
8. Determine whether or not the sample contains marijuana.
9. Repeat steps 1–9 using five more samples.

Part II: Wood Examinations

Procedure

1. Obtain a wood sample.
2. Prepare a cross section for viewing by making a thin, clean cut perpendicular to the growing length of the sample.
3. Mount the sample so that it can be examined using the compound light microscope. Examine the surface for the presence or absence of vessel elements.
4. If necessary, enhance the image by soaking the cross section in green food coloring. Allow to dry, and re-examine the surface.
5. Draw what you see.
6. Identify the sample as either hard or soft wood.
7. Repeat steps 1–6 with five additional samples.

Report Requirements

Include all drawings, calculations, and other information obtained during the laboratory procedure. Notes and/or drawings should include the sample identification, magnification, and a complete description.

Report Questions

1. What are the microscopic characteristics used to identify marijuana?
2. Describe the difference between the hairs found on marijuana samples.
3. What is the difference between male and female marijuana plants?
4. What is the difference between soft and hard woods? Use examples of each in your discussion.
5. What are the identifying characteristics for soft woods? Use examples in your discussion.
6. What are the identifying characteristics for hard woods? Use examples in your discussion.

Recommended and Further Reading

Clarke RC. *Marijuana Botany*. Berkeley, CA: And/Or Press, 1981.

Clarke RC. *Marijuana Botany: Propagation and Breeding of Distinctive Cannabis*. Berkeley, CA: Ronin Publishing, 1993.

Core HA, Cote WA, Day AC. *Wood Structure and Identification*, 2nd ed. Syracuse, NY: Syracuse University Press, 1979.

Hauber DJ. Marijuana Analysis with Recording Botanical Features Present and without the Environmental Pollutants of the Duquenois-Levine Test. *Journal of Forensic Sciences*. 1992; 37(6): 1656–1661.

Hoadley RB. *Identifying Wood – Accurate Results with Simple Tools*. Newton, CT: Taunton Press, 1990.

Houck MM, Siegel JA. *Fundamentals of Forensic Science*, 3rd ed. Amsterdam: Elsevier Academic Press, 2015; 337–339.

Robards AW, *Botanical Microscopy*. Oxford: Oxford University Press and Royal Microscopical Society (Great Britain), 1985.

Schultes RE, Hoffman A. *The Botany and Chemistry of Hallucinogens*. Springfield, IL: Charles C. Thomas, 1980.

Small E. Morphological Variation of Achenes of Cannabis. *Canadian Journal of Botany.* 1974; 53: 978–987.

Summitt R, Siliker A. CRC *Handbook of Materials Science.* Boca Raton, FL: CRC Press, 1980.

US Treasury Department. *Marijuana and Its Identification.* Washington, DC: US Government Printing Office, 1948.

Welch MJ, Ellerbe P, Tai SSC, Christensen RG, Sniegoski LT, Sander LC, et al. NIST Reference Materials to Support Accuracy in Drug-Testing. *Fresenius Journal of Analytical Chemistry.* 1995; 352(1–2): 61–65.

Wheeler EA, Baas P. Wood Identification – A Review. *IAWA Journal.* 1998; 19(3): 241–264.

Chapter 14

Experiment 14: Paint Examinations

Recommended pre-lab reading assignments:

Thornton J, Kraus S, Lerner B, Kahane D. Solubility Characterization of Automotive Paints. *Journal of Forensic Science.* 1983; 28(3): 1004.
Thornton JI. Forensic Paint Examinations. In: Saferstein R, ed. *Forensic Science Handbook*, 2nd ed. Upper Saddle River, NJ: Pearson Education, 2002; 458–473.

Objective

Upon completion of this practical exercise, the student will have developed a basic understanding of:

1. general characteristics of paint samples
2. cross sections of paint and techniques that can be used to produce them
3. paint solubility testing
4. use of the stereomicroscope to visualize paint characteristics

Introduction

For many years, mankind has used colored substances contained within some type of a substrate to either adorn or protect surfaces. Decorative effects are produced by color, gloss, texture, lighting, or a combination of these properties. The protective function of paint includes resistance to air, chemicals, and water, in addition to properties such as hardness and abrasion resistance. Because of these decorative and protective features, the average person is surrounded by painted items. The main uses of paint include: automobiles, architectural or structural, and other miscellaneous uses (e.g., tools, non-automotive vehicles, appliances, artistic media, and cosmetic coatings). Since there is the possibility of contact with these items, microscopic examination of paint presents itself as indirect or circumstantial evidence in a court of law. Paint examinations are performed to determine possible associations between people, places, and objects. This evidence is generally used in conjunction with other forensic evidence.

In forensics, paint is usually considered to be a pigment or extender that has been dispersed in a suitable vehicle or binder, and reduced to an application viscosity with the addition of solvents. Pigments, which may be organic or inorganic, provide color and concealing properties to paint. They furnish the dried paint film with color, opacity, gloss, and permeability. Extenders may be added to the formulation to disperse the pigment. These compounds are held together with the aid of a vehicle, or binder. Paint vehicles are made of chemicals, generally resins, which form the thin film. The vehicle gives the adhesive, durability, flexibility, and reinforcement properties to the paint film. The thickness of the film may be adjusted with various solvents that are either water-based or organic-based. Solvents provide the properties that affect drying time and flow. Other additives may also be incorporated to modify the paint properties or application. At times components are added to increase gloss, hardness, and chemical resistance of the paint. UV and anti-mold components may also be added.

Paint examinations use of a variety of microscopes, techniques, and instruments. Examinations have two goals: (1) Identify a paint type, and (2) compare a paint sample to a possible paint source when possible. Initially a stereomicroscope is used to examine the paint sample for layer structure and solubility properties. Fourier transform infrared (FTIR) microspectrophotometry (see Experiment 29), UV-VIS microspectrophotometry (see Experiment 30), scanning electron microscopy (see Experiment 32), and pyrolysis gas chromatography are additional techniques that may be performed on paint.

Examination and comparison of layer structure are integral parts of a paint examination. A cross section is usually obtained to observe this, by making a "slice" of that solid. The shape can vary according to the orientation of the slice. A true cross section is obtained with a 90° cut; however, at times, to view the cross section of a paint sample, a 45° cut is preferred. With paint samples, a cross section is used to identify the various layers of the paint sample and, at times, other characteristics within these layers. The layer structure is a characteristic of a paint sample and at times may be very unique. The sequence of the layers also provides valuable information. Automotive paints are applied in layer sequences that may be related to specific manufacturing companies. For instance, some manufacturers use a combination of three paint coats (clear coat, color coat, and primer), while others use four (clear coat, color coat, and two primer layers). The individual layers may also provide additional manufacturer information. Thickness and texture of paint layers may help indicate the application method utilized. Original automotive paints are very thin; however, most repaints are applied slightly thicker, and at times unevenly. The thickness of layers may also give indications as to whether the paint is from a vehicle, a painted object, or a structural paint sample. Surface defects due to weathering and aging, and any contaminants, may also be noted during a cross-sectional examination.

To visualize the layers, a cross-sectional sample can be obtained using a scalpel. This can be done by cutting the paint sample at an angle (either 45° or 90°). While a 90° cut is considered a true cross section, a 45° cross-sectional cut exposes more surface of each layer of the paint sample, assisting in viewing thin layers. Clear layers can also be visualized by placing the cross-sectional cut sample into a porcelain dish, along with a solvent such as methanol to cover the sample. Further examination of each individual layer by solubility testing, and the instrumental methods listed above, also provide the examiner with additional chemical information.

Solubility determinations can also be an important part of paint examinations. Although this method of testing is destructive, valuable information can be obtained from solubility testing.

Table 14-1   Solubility and reactions for common solvents used in paint examinations.

Solvent	Solubility and reactions
Chloroform	Enamels remain insoluble. Acrylics will soften. Acrylic enamels will smoke and leave an oily residue. Latex softens. Alkyds show no reaction. Lacquers are soluble or soften. Nitrocellulose lacquer is insoluble.
Acetone	Most acrylics will soften. Acrylic lacquers are generally soluble. Lacquers are almost always soluble. Nitrocellulose is soluble or softens. Enamels are insoluble. Latex softens.
DPA: (reagent is a mixture of .5 grams diphenylamine, 100 ml of concentrated sulfuric acid, 20 ml distilled water)	A color change to blue may indicate the presence of an oxidizing agent or nitrocellulose paint. Some paints containing carbonate will also effervesce.

Determining the solubility of the different layers in paint samples has been used to discriminate between paint samples of differing pigment and binder composition that are otherwise similar in visual and macroscopic appearance. These tests are based on the solubility of the paint binders, in addition to the pigment and binder color interactions of oxidation, dehydration, and reduction. Solubility testing of paints involves a possible reaction of the paint with a variety of solvents. Since paints are made of different components and processes, they will react differently in certain solvents. Common reactions include: (1) The paint may be soluble or partially soluble; (2) it may leach or change color; or (3) it may swell, curl, discolor, soften, sink, and/or float. Occasionally the paint sample may react with the solvent, which provides additional limited information concerning the type of paint being tested. Table 14-1 lists the solubility and reaction properties for three common solvents used in forensic laboratories. Chloroform is used to distinguish acrylic lacquers. Acetone is used to distinguish acrylic lacquers and nitrocellulose lacquers. Diphenylamine (DPA) is used to determine oxidizing ions: nitrates, nitrites, chlorates, and ferric ions. This assists in identifying nitrocellulose paints. Since chloroform and acetone readily evaporate, they are typically used prior to DPA if a single paint chip is being tested.

The examination of cross sections and solubility determinations are only one portion of a paint examination. From these examinations, determinations can be made to identify the type of paint. When necessary, further analytical testing can be performed to detect significant similarities or differences between samples.

Equipment and Supplies

Stereomicroscope

Paint samples

Micro kit

Spot plate

Solvents (chloroform, methanol, acetone, and DPA)

Safety

Use standard laboratory safety procedures as described in guidelines set by your instructor. Be cautious of microscope light levels to avoid eye damage. The solvents should be handled with care. Proper ventilation, gloves, and eye protection should be used at all times. Refer to the safety data sheet (SDS) if necessary.

Part I: Cross Sections

Procedure

1. Obtain a paint sample.
2. Using the stereomicroscope, turn the paint chip up on edge.
3. Using the circle template in Appendix E, draw the layer structure.
4. Cut a small chip from your sample. Using a spot plate, immerse the paint chip on edge in methanol. (Using methanol helps visualize clear layers.)
5. Draw the layer structure.
6. Lay the paint chip back down. Using a scalpel, slowly cut the edge of the paint chip at approximately a 45° angle to expose the underneath layers. Check the layer structure against your previous findings. Draw your findings.

Part II: Solubility

Procedure

1. Obtain two paint samples.
2. Cut three small sections from one of the paint samples.
3. Place each section in a separate spot well.
4. Add a drop (or two) of chloroform to the spot well.
5. Observe and document any reaction with the paint sample (paying attention to each layer).
6. To the second spot well, add a drop (or two) of acetone.
7. Observe and document any reaction with the paint sample.
8. To the third spot well, add a drop (or two) of DPA.
9. Observe and document the reaction with the paint sample.
10. Repeat steps 2–9 with the second paint sample.
11. Create a chart with your findings.

Report Requirements

Include all drawings, calculations, and other information obtained during the laboratory procedure. Notes and/or drawings should include the sample identification, magnification, and a complete description.

Report Questions

1. What are the main components of paint? What is the purpose for each portion?
2. What is a cross section?
3. What information does a cross section give an examiner for paint samples?
4. How can an examiner determine if an automotive paint sample is a repaint?
5. Describe the principle behind solubility testing.
6. Define solubility. Why is solubility testing performed during a paint examination?
7. What are the advantages of solubility testing?
8. What are the disadvantages of solubility testing?
9. What is the correct procedure for performing solubility testing on evidence?

Recommended and Further Reading

Allen TJ. Modifications to Sample Mounting Procedures and Microtome Equipment for Paint Sectioning. *Forensic Science International.* 1991; 52(1): 93–100.

Allen TJ. The Examination of Thin-Sections of Colored Paints by Light-Microscopy. *Forensic Science International.* 1992; 57(1): 5–16.

Allen TJ, Schnetz B. The Removal of Paint Smears from Tools and Clothing for Microscopic Examination and Analysis. *Forensic Science International.* 1991; 52(1): 101–105.

ASTM. *Standard Guide for Forensic Paint Examination (ASTM E-1610-14).* West Conshohocken, PA: ASTM International, 2014.

Beam TL, Willis WV. Analysis Protocol for Discrimination of Automotive Paints by SEM-EDX Using Beam Alignment by Current Centering. *Journal of Forensic Sciences.* 1990; 35(5): 1055–1063.

Bender L. Architectural Paints. In: Siegel J, Saukko P, ed. *Encyclopedia of Forensic Sciences*, 2nd ed. Amsterdam: Elsevier, 2013; 250–256.

Bender L. Automotive Paints. In: Siegel J, Saukko P, ed. *Encyclopedia of Forensic Sciences*, 2nd ed. Amsterdam: Elsevier, 2013; 257–264.

Bender L. Overview (Paints). In: Siegel J, Saukko P, ed. *Encyclopedia of Forensic Sciences*, 2nd ed. Amsterdam: Elsevier, 2013; 245–249.

Caddy B. *Forensic Examination of Glass and Paint: Analysis and Interpretation.* London: Ellis Horwood Ltd., 2001.

Castle DA. The Forensic Examination of Paint. *Jocca-Surface Coatings International.* 1992; 75(7): 247.

Crown DA. *The Forensic Examination of Paints and Pigments.* Springfield, IL: Charles C. Thomas, 1968.

Giang YS, Wang SM, Cho LL, Yang CK, Lu CC. Identification of Tiny and Thin Smears of Automotive Paint Following a Traffic Accident. *Journal of Forensic Sciences.* 2002; 47(3): 625–629.

Goldstein J, Newbury D, Joy D, Lyman C, Echlin P, Lifshin E, Sawyer L, Michael J. *Scanning Electron Microscopy and X-Ray Microanalysis.* New York: Plenum, 2003.

Houck MM, Siegel JA. *Fundamentals of Forensic Science*, 3rd ed. Amsterdam: Elsevier Academic Press, 2015; 405–425.

Laing DK, Locke J, Richard RA, Wilkerson JM. The Examination of Paint Films and Fibers as Thin-Sections. *Microscope.* 1987; 35: 233–248.

Muehlethaler C, Gueissaz L, Massonnet G. Forensic Paint Analysis. In: Siegel J, Saukko P, ed. *Encyclopedia of Forensic Sciences*, 2nd ed. Amsterdam: Elsevier, 2013; 265–272.

Ryland S., Kopec J. The Evidential Value of Automotive Paint Chips. *Journal of Forensic Sciences.* 1979; 26: 64–74.

Ryland S., Kopec J, Somerville P. The Evidential Value of Automotive Paint Chips: Part II. *Journal of Forensic Sciences.* 1981; 24: 140–147.

Schweitzer P. *Paint and Coatings.* Boca Raton, FL: CRC Press, 2005.

Stoecklein W. *The Role of Colour and Microscopic Techniques for the Characterization of Paint Fragments.* London: Taylor & Francis, 2001.

Thornton J. Forensic Paint Examination. In: Saferstein R, ed. *Forensic Science Handbook*, vol. 1. Englewood Cliffs, NJ: Prentice Hall, 2002; 429–478.

Thornton J, Shemuel K, Lerner B, Kahane D. Solubility Characterization of Automotive Paints. *Journal of Forensic Sciences.* 1983; 28(3): 1004.

Zieba-Palus J. Selected Cases of Forensic Paint Analysis. *Science & Justice.* 1999; 39(2): 123–127.

Chapter 15

Experiment 15: Cigarette Butt Examinations

Recommended pre-lab reading assignment:

Bourhill B. *Cigarette Butt Identification Guide*, 14th ed. Salem, OR: Oregon
Department of Forestry, 1994.

Recommended websites:

Cigarette Production [video tour: cited 2017]. Available from: http://www.pmi.com.
Making Our Cigarettes [cited 2017]. Available from: http://www.altria.com.

Objective

Upon completion of this practical exercise, the student will have developed a basic understanding of:

1. general characteristics of cigarette butts
2. use of the stereomicroscope to visualize cigarette butt characteristics

Introduction

A tobacco cigarette is a small paper cylinder that has been filled with a finely ground tobacco blend. The cigarette is one of the most common methods of smoking and, because of this, is commonly found at crime scenes. Comparison and identification of cigarette butts can provide important leads to an investigation and at times save time and money, since unnecessary DNA analysis is not performed.

Cigarettes are produced by a variety of American and international companies. Each company produces numerous brands, and each brand may have various options available to the consumer. Most cigarettes have four main portions: tobacco, cigarette paper, tip paper, and filter

Practical Forensic Microscopy: A Laboratory Manual, Second Edition. Barbara P. Wheeler.
© 2021 John Wiley & Sons Ltd. Published 2021 by John Wiley & Sons Ltd.
Companion website: www.wiley.com/go/Wheeler/Forensic

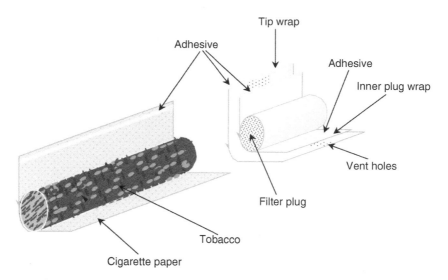

Figure 15-1   Portions of a cigarette used during a forensic examination.

(see Figure 15-1). The tobacco is usually a blend of bright, burley, and oriental tobacco. Various additives are typically mixed with the tobacco to enhance the end product. Sugars are added to mask the bitter flavor of tobacco. Ammonia is added to raise the pH of the smoke. This frees the nicotine from its salt form so that the body more readily absorbs it. Flavors such as licorice or cocoa are added to enhance the end product, but they also act as "bronchodilators." This opens the breathing passages, allowing more exposure of the nicotine to the surface area of the lungs. Humectants such as propylene glycol or glycerol are added to keep the tobacco blend moist. Menthol or other fragrances may also be added to enhance the perfume-like flavor.

The construction of a cigarette provides many characteristics that can be used for a forensic examination. The tobacco blend is encased in a paper wrapper. The paper is typically composed of flax or wood fibers (see Experiment 16) to which calcium carbonate is added for color. The paper may vary in porosity to allow for ventilation of the burning ember. These bands or "speed bumps" in the paper design decrease the flow of oxygen, which in turn slows the rate at which the cigarette burns. Some solid or unbanded cigarette paper contains sodium or potassium citrate. This also helps to control the burning rate of the cigarette and the stability of the ash product. The paper wrapper may contain colored writing, motifs, or bands.

The tip paper attaches the filter, when present, to the paper-wrapped tobacco blend. Tip paper comprises several layers of paper: an inner plug wrap to encase the filter, and the tipping wrap to attach the wrapped filter to the encased tobacco blend. The inner plug wrap moderates the burning of the cigarette as well as the delivery of the smoke. The more air is allowed to mix with the smoke as it passes through the filter, the less impact the tobacco and toxic gases will have on the smoker. The inner plug wrap paper is similar to cigarette paper in composition. The tipping wrap connects the wrapped filter to the wrapped tobacco blend. This paper is treated with chemicals to stabilize the filter from saliva, which prevents it from sticking to the lips of the smoker. The tipping wrap paper is similar to cigarette paper in composition, but denser. It is usually white or formulated to look like cork. Many tipping wraps contain vent holes. This increases the efficiency of the filter by allowing air to enter with the smoker's puff. The tipping wrap may also contain writing, motifs, or bands.

Filters are used to modify the toxic particulate smoke phase by particle retention. Manufacturers have used various filters over the years; however, most filters are now made of cellulose acetate fibers. Since a number of tar components (including acetaldehyde, acetone, acetic acid, and phenols) were more chemically active with moist cellulose acetate, long-lasting humectants are added to the cellulose acetate fibers. Triacetin is also added to make the filter flexible and durable. Some manufacturers also adjust the pH of the filter to produce greater discoloration in the filter during smoking.

Cigarette butt examinations use a stereomicroscope to identify various manufacturing characteristics so that brand identifications and comparisons can be performed. Initially a stereomicroscope is used to examine the cigarette butt for its overall physical dimensions. The length of a full non-smoked cigarette is 70–120 mm; however, most are 85–100 mm. Smokers tend to smoke cigarettes similarly, so the length of cigarette butts and the manner in which they have been extinguished should be noted. The circumference of a cigarette can vary from 17 to 27 mm, with the average cigarette being 25 mm. The color of both the cigarette paper and the tipping wrap paper should be noted. Measurements should be taken to the highest visible marking. Writing size, location, alignment, style, and color should also be described. Likewise, the size, location, alignment, style, and color should also be recorded for any numerals or motifs. The size, location, number, and color of bands should be noted. Finally, details of the tip paper, including length measurements for tipping wrap, inner plug wrap, and overlap area (tipping wrap and cigarette paper), should be recorded. The size, shape, location, and number of vents should also be detailed. These characteristics can be compared to known samples so that a brand and subcategory can be determined.

While this experiment concentrates on the physical characteristics of cigarette butts and specifically the identification of brand and type, other possible evidence types should also be considered for additional investigative information. When lip balm or lipstick are present on the tip paper, they can be analyzed and compared to possible sources. Latent fingerprints may also be recovered and identified. Finally, cellular tissue (from saliva or fingerprints) may be deposited on the cigarette butt. DNA profiles can be obtained from this cellular tissue and may be compared to possible individuals involved.

Equipment and Supplies

Stereomicroscope

Cigarette butt samples

Micro kit

Safety

Use standard laboratory safety procedures as described in guidelines set by your instructor. Be cautious of microscope light levels to avoid eye damage.

Part I: Cigarette Butt Examination

A worksheet for examination notes may be found at the end of the experiment.

Procedure

1. Obtain a cigarette butt sample.
2. Note the length and diameter of the cigarette butt.
3. Observe and record the color of the cigarette paper and tip end wrap papers.
4. Measure to the highest visible marking.
5. Observe and note the presence of writing; the size, location, alignment, style, and color should also be described.
6. Observe and record the size, location, alignment, style, and color for any numerals or motifs present.
7. Observe and note the size, location, number, and color of any bands present.
8. Measure the length of the tipping wrap and inner plug wrap.
9. Measure the area of overlap between the tipping wrap and cigarette paper.
10. Using the stereomicroscope, record the size, shape, location, and number of vents present in the tipping wrap.
11. Draw the main characteristics of the cigarette butt.
12. Repeat steps 2–11 using a second cigarette butt sample.

Report Requirements

Include all drawings, calculations, and other information obtained during the laboratory procedure. Notes and/or drawings should include the sample identification, magnification, and a complete description.

Report Questions

1. What are the main portions of a cigarette? What is the purpose for each portion?
2. What information does a cigarette butt examination provide to an investigation?
3. What are the advantages of doing this type of examination?
4. List and explain four characteristics that can be used to differentiate cigarette butts.
5. Are there any precautions that should be taken when doing a cigarette butt examination?

Recommended and Further Reading

Browne CL. *The Design of Cigarettes*. Irving, TX: Hoechst Celanese, 1990.

Claflin W, Houck J. *Control of Smoking Delivery through Cigarette Paper Porosity*. Rye Brook, NY: Philip Morris Inc., 1975.

Gentry JS, Womble KM, Banerjee CK, Blakley RL. *Cigarette Filter*. Winston-Salem, NC: RJ Reynolds Tobacco Company, 1996.

Gentry JS, Womble KM, Banerjee CK, Blakley RL, Barnes RD, Calleson DA, Ridings HT. *Cigarette Filter*. Winston-Salem, NC: RJ Reynolds Tobacco Company, 1996.

Grise V. *The U.S. Tobacco Industry*. Washington, DC: US Department of Agriculture Economics Research Service, 1988.

Hoffmann D, Djordjevic MV, Brunnemann K. Changes in Cigarette Design and Composition over Time and How They Influence the Yields of Smoke Constituents. In: Shopland D, ed. *The FTC Cigarette Test Method for Determining Tar, Nicotine, and Carbone Monoxide Yields of US Cigarettes: Report of the*

NCI Expert Committee (NCI Smoking and Tobacco Control Monograph No. 7). Bethesda, MD: National Institutes of Health, National Cancer Institute, 1996; 15–37.

Milford EC, Guess HE, Chapman PS, Dunn RS, Perfetti PF. *Cigarette and Paper Wrapper Therefor*. Winston-Salem, NC: RJ Reynolds Tobacco Company, 1991.

Norman V. The Effect of Perforated Tipping Paper on the Yields of Various Smoke Components. *Beitrage zur Tabakforschung*. 1974; 7: 282–287.

Owens WF Jr. Effect of Cigarette Paper on Smoke Yield and Composition. *Recent Advances in Tobacco Science*. 1978; 4: 3–24.

CIGARETTE BUTT WORKSHEET

Physical Characteristics:

Overall Length: _____   **Diameter**_____

Paper color: _____ white _____ banded _____non-banded _____ other color

Filter color: _____no filter _____ common brown _____ white _____ gold

_____ very dark brown _____ black _____ pale brown _____ other

Highest visible marking: _____

Writing: _____ distance from tip _____ width _____ height _____

Writing alignment: _____ vertical _____straight _____ slanted down

_____ slanted up _____ curved outward _____ curved inward

Writing style: _____ capitals _____ lowercase _____ block _____ script

Writing color: _____ red _____ blue _____ gray _____ green _____ purple

_____ gold _____ silver _____ brown _____ black

Numerals: _____ distance from tip _____ width _____ height _____

Numerals color: _____ red _____ blue _____ gray _____ green _____ purple

_____ gold _____ silver _____ brown _____ black

Motif: _____ crest _____monogram _____crown _____ stars _____ circle

_____ box _____animal _____ other

distance from tip _____ width _____ height _____

Motif color: _____ red _____ blue _____ gray _____ green _____ purple

_____ gold _____ silver _____ brown _____ black

Bands: _____ 1 _____ 2 _____ 3   _____ vertical _____horizontal

distance from tip _____ height _____ spacing between _____

Tip wrap: height _____   **Inner plug wrap: height _____**

Overlap: height of tip wrap/cigarette paper _____

Vents: _____ 1 _____ 2 _____ 3 _____ 4 _____5   distance from tip: _____

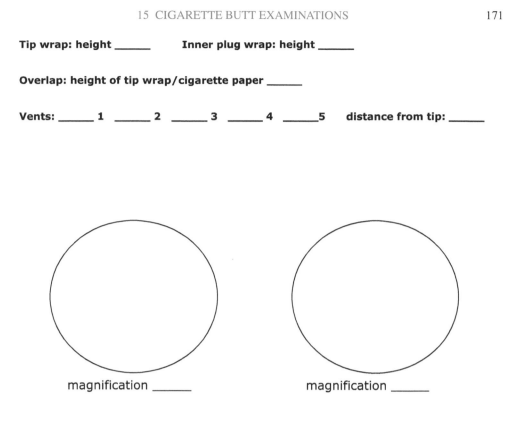

magnification _____   magnification _____

Chapter 16

Experiment 16: Document Examinations

Recommended websites:

SWGDOC. Standard for Test Methods for Forensic Writing Ink Comparison [cited 2017]. Available from: http://www.swgdoc.org.
What Is Paper? [cited 2017]. Available from: http://www.paperonline.org.

Objective

Upon completion of this practical exercise, the student will have developed a basic understanding of:

1. manufacture of paper and the fibers used
2. use of the compound light microscope to identify paper fibers
3. ink types
4. spots tests to identify ink dyestuffs

Introduction

A document is any material that conveys a message, whether invisible, partially visible, or visible. When a question such as authorship or authenticity of a document arises, a forensic examination is necessary. Document examinations involve a scientific and systematic examination and comparison of the document to known exemplars. Typically, this involves both paper and the writings. This can encompass a variety of examinations: the paper and its components, the method or type of writing (handwritten, typewritten, printed, or photocopied documents), the ink, and, in some cases, the alterations to the document (erasures and obliterations). This experiment will focus on the microscopic examination of paper and ink.

Practical Forensic Microscopy: A Laboratory Manual, Second Edition. Barbara P. Wheeler.
© 2021 John Wiley & Sons Ltd. Published 2021 by John Wiley & Sons Ltd.
Companion website: www.wiley.com/go/Wheeler/Forensic

Paper

Most documents are produced on paper. Paper can be defined as a thin material that has been manufactured from either wood fibers or another cellulose-based fibrous substance. Since analytical testing can be done for its components, it is important to understand how paper is made. To produce paper, softwoods, hardwoods, or other cellulose-based plants are chemically treated (sulfate [kraft], soda, and sulfite [acid process]) or mechanically treated (ground wood; thermomechanical—with heat; or thermochemimechanical—with heat and chemicals) to create pulp. Pulp is the fibrous material that remains once other plant matter such as sap, resin, or lignin have been removed. The choice of the pulp fiber affects the final nature of the paper. The highest quality paper contains a high percentage of rag pulp (cotton and linen fibers). A cheaper quality of paper is made of ground wood pulp. The pulp flows into machines called refiners, where the pulp fibers are cut to a uniform size. "Loaders," such as kaolin, china clay, calcium sulfate, or

Table 16-1   Results of Graff "C" stain on paper fibers.

Pulp fiber	Chemical pulp method	Raw	Cooked	Unbleached	Bleached
Softwood	Sulfite	Vivid yellow	Light greenish-yellow		Light purple-gray to weak red-purple
	Sulfate	Greenish-yellow	Yellowish-brown to dark greenish-gray		Dark bluish-gray to dusty purple
Hardwood	Sulfite	Pale yellow-green		Pale yellow-green	Weak purplish-blue to purplish-gray
	Sulfate	Pale blue-green		Weak blue-green	Dusty blue to dusty purple
Cotton, flax, hemp, ramie		Reddish-orange			
Abaca		Light greenish-yellow			Yellowish-gray to light blue
Jute		Yellowish-orange		Vivid yellow-orange	Light yellow-green
Straw, bamboo, bagasse, esparto		Light yellow to greenish-yellow		Light greenish-gray to dark bluish-gray	Light greenish-gray to dark bluish-gray
Gampi, mitsumata		Light greenish-yellow to light bluish-green			
Kozo		Pinkish-gray			

barium sulfate, are added to fill the pores of the pulp fibers, giving the final product a smoother surface. Other additives (gelatin, rosins, starch, wax, etc.) are also included to make the final paper suitable for accepting ink. At this point, the pulp mixture contains approximately 99% water. It is passed onto a Fourdrinier wire that vibrates side-to-side, so that the fibers intertwine and the liquid drains, creating "sheets." The sheets go through a long series of dryers, which press the fibers and remove any remaining liquid. Additional calendering or coating steps may also be done, depending on the final product.

The examination of paper can often answer investigative questions such as the identity of the paper, its source or origin, and its date of manufacture. In most instances, the analysis is a comparative examination of the chemical and physical properties of the paper. Physical properties such as thickness, weight, color, opacity, fluorescence, and the presence of watermarks are initially determined. Chemical properties such as the fiber composition and the chemical composition of fillers, additives, coatings, and pigments also characterize the paper.

The fiber composition of paper can be determined by observing the fibers with the aid of a compound light microscope. Once the fibers have been separated from the fillers, coatings, and additives, the morphological appearance can be observed (see Experiment 13). This, in combination with staining characteristics, can be used to distinguish and identify the paper fibers. Common stains used for paper fiber examinations include Graff "C" stain, Herzberg stain, and Selleger stain. These stains give color reactions that help to differentiate the pulping method and the fiber type.

Graff "C" stain is the most commonly used paper fiber stain. It is used to differentiate both fiber types and pulping methods. The color reaction also varies with the degree of cooking and whether the fiber has been bleached. Stain colors can be observed from vivid yellow to bluish purple. Yellow indicates high lignin content when Graff "C" stain is used, while red indicates the

Table 16-2 Results of Herzberg stain on paper fibers.

Pulp fiber	Raw	Unbleached	Bleached
Softwood	Light olive-gray to olive-gray	Dark bluish-gray to weak purplish-blue	Dark purplish-gray to dark reddish-purple
Hardwood	Weak olive to dusty blue-green	Dark purplish-gray to deep reddish-purple	Dark purplish-gray to deep reddish-purple
Cotton, flax, hemp, ramie	Purplish-pink to red-purple		
Abaca	Yellow	Dark purplish-gray to purplish-pink	Dark purplish-gray to purplish-pink
Jute	Yellowish-orange		Greenish-yellow
Straw, bamboo, bagasse, esparto	Light yellow	Light purplish-gray to purplish-pink	Light purplish-gray to purplish-pink
Gampi, mitsumata	Light greenish-yellow		
Kozo	Pinkish-gray		

Table 16-3 Results of Selleger stain on paper fibers.

Pulp fiber	Chemical pulp method	Raw	Unbleached	Bleached
Softwood	Sulfite		Yellow	Red
	Sulfate		Yellow	Blue-gray
Hardwood	Sulfite			Bluish-red
	Sulfate		Blue	Blue
Cotton, flax, hemp, ramie		Red		
Abaca				Claret red
Straw, esparto				Blue

absence of lignin. Cooking changes fiber colors to shades with green or brown tints, depending on the method. Bleaching tends to add shades of red to the color. Table 16-1 shows expected results when using Graff "C" stain. While some fibers may give similar color reactions, they can easily be distinguished by their morphology.

Herzberg stain is also useful to differentiate between fiber types and pulping methods and is typically used to confirm results from the Graff "C" stain test. In general, the colors appear bluer than with Graff "C" stain. A drop of Herzberg stain solution will turn lignin-containing fibers bright yellow, while most non-lignin-containing fibers turn red. Table 16-2 shows expected results when using Herzberg stain. While some fibers may give similar color reactions, they can easily be distinguished by their morphology.

Selleger stain is used to differentiate between softwood and hardwood pulp. Selleger stain is also helpful in differentiating between chemically pulped bleached softwoods. Pulps that contain lignin will give yellow colors. Non-lignin pulps give colors with Selleger stain that tend to have more pink or red shades. Table 16-3 shows expected results when using Selleger stain.

Other stains that are less commonly used on paper fibers are Wilson stain, Alexander stain, Green-Yorston stain, Kantrowitz-Simmons stain, Lofton-Merritt stain, NCR stain, and DuPont stains. Combining morphology characteristics and information gained from staining examinations allows an analyst to identify paper fiber compositions.

Ink

Many document examinations also involve analytical testing of the ink. Ink is a complex liquid, which contains various pigments and/or dyes that can be used for coloring a surface. Solvents, resins, surfactants, lubricants, organic additives, and other materials may be added to provide the desired characteristics for the ink type.

There are two main types of ink, ballpoint and fluid inks. Ballpoint ink is thick, high-viscosity ink with an oil (pre-1950) or glycol base. Ballpoint ink is easy to recognize because of its frequent appearance of ink deposits (gooping) and striations caused by the ball that is used as the delivery method for the ink. Fluid inks are generally thinner and may be either water or solvent based. Since fluid inks (fountain pens, rollerballs, gel pens, felt-tip pens, and markers) tend to be thinner, the ink has a tendency to "bleed" into the paper fibers.

Ballpoint pens work on the principle of the ball staying coated with the ink. Because of this, the ink tends to be fairly thick. The dye composition of ballpoint pen ink is a large percentage of the total formulation and is typically synthetic compounds. Solvents, fatty acids, resins, surfactants, organic additives, viscosity adjustors, and other materials may be added to provide the desired characteristics for the ink type.

Fluid inks are generally water and water-soluble organic solvent mediums to which other additives have been added to provide the desired characteristics for the ink type. Of the fluid inks, fountain pen, rollerball, gel pen, and felt-tip inks are generally water based. Markers and permanent markers are usually solvent based. Fountain pen inks, which work on a capillary action, are thin and water based. There are two types of fountain pen ink: iron-gallotannate and aqueous solutions of synthetic dyes. Iron-gallotannate inks gradually darken, giving credence to the name "blue-black ink." Most fountain pen inks are now aqueous solutions of synthetic dyes. Various additives may also be included in the formulation to provide the desired characteristics for the ink. Rollerball pens combine the technology of the ballpoint and fountain pens. The pressurized ink is deposited on the interior of the ball, and with its rotation during writing, ink is relayed to the paper. The inks are usually water based and contain glycols and formamide to slow the drying out of the ball. Dyes used in these inks are typically acidic dye salts. Gel pens have recently gained more popularity. Gel pens use similar mechanisms as the ballpoint or rollerball pens; however, the difference is once again in the ink. Pigment is suspended in the water-based ink; however, it is highly viscous liquid. The physical property of pigments makes it practically impossible to analyze by traditional methods. Felt-tip pens and markers have a tip that is commonly made of felt, nylon, or ceramic. Glycol and formamide are used to adjust the surface tension that keeps the tip from drying out. The ink is generally water or xylene based, combined with dyes and additives similar to those in either rollerball or fountain pen inks.

Solubility testing and spot testing can provide information about the ink. Since these tests do minimal damage to a document, photographs should be taken prior to any testing. Solvents can be used to help differentiate ballpoint and non-ballpoint inks. Ballpoint inks are either oil or glycol based, and they will be soluble in pyridine. Fluid inks are generally water or alcohol based, and they are readily soluble in an ethanol and water solution (1:1). Samples may also be spot tested to help identify the pigment or dye coloring. Table 16-4 indicates some common dyestuffs used in inks. Reactions with hydrochloric acid and sodium hydroxide can aid in the identification of the dyestuffs (see Table 16-5).

While this experiment concentrates on the microscopic characteristics of paper fibers and spot tests for ink dyestuffs, other possible testing can be considered for additional investigative information. Elemental analysis can provide information concerning fillers, coating, and additives of paper. Use of Fourier transform infrared (FTIR), pyrolysis–gas chromatography (PGC), or gas

Table 16-4 Common pigments and dyes used in ink.

Color	Dyestuffs
Green-blue pigment	Phthalocyanines
Blue pigment	Iron blues, ultramarine blue
Blue dye	Victoria blue, alkali blue, phthalocyanines
Red dye	Rhodamine B, eosin
Violet and purple dye	Methyl violet, crystal violet, indulines

Table 16-5 Common spot test results for ink dyestuffs (*no reaction).

Dyestuffs	HCl	NaOH	HCl Neutralized with NaOH
Phthalocyanines	Bright green		Deep green
Victoria blue	Brown	Brown	Pale blue
Methyl blue			Pale blue with purple
Alkali blue	*	Reddish-brown	Deep green
Rhodamine B	Faint orange-yellow	*	
Eosin	Faint yellow	Orange	
Methyl violet	Yellow-brown		Purple
Crystal violet	Yellow-brown		Purple
Indulines	*	*	

*No color change.

chromatography–mass spectrometry (GCMS) can also aid in identification of these paper components. Ink dyestuffs can be further differentiated by separation and identification by thin-layer chromatography (TLC) or high-performance liquid chromatography (HPLC). A video spectral comparator (VSC) can also be used to discriminate between different inks.

The examination of paper fibers and spot tests for ink is only one portion of a document examination. Determinations can be made from the information gained by the fiber examinations as to the possible source of paper. Analysis of the ink and ink dyestuffs helps to identify the type of ink and the specific dye or pigment used to produce the color of ink. These examinations can be used to detect significant similarities or differences between samples, but should be followed up with additional confirmatory testing.

Equipment and Supplies

Compound light microscope with objectives of various magnifications (e.g., 4X, 10X, 20X, and 40X) and focusing ocular with micrometer scale

Micro kit

Microscope slides and coverslips

Mounting medium (a colorless mounting medium in the refractive index range of 1.50–1.60)

Paper samples

UV light box

Beaker and test tubes

Spot plate

Hot plate

Graff "C" stain: Place 20 mL of Solution A, 10 mL of Solution B, 10 mL of Solution C, and 12.5 mL of Solution D in a tall narrow container. Place in a darkened area for 12–24 hours.

Once precipitate has settled, pipette off the clear portion into a dark bottle, and add one leaf of iodine. Store in darkness.

Solution A: 40 gm of aluminum chloride in 100 mL distilled water

Solution B: 100 gm of calcium chloride in 150 mL distilled water

Solution C: 50 gm of zinc chloride in 25 mL distilled water

Solution D: 0.90 gm potassium iodide and 0.65 gm iodine in 50 mL distilled water

Herzberg stain: Place 25 mL of Solution A with Solution B in a tall narrow container. Place in a darkened area for 12–24 hours. Pipette off the supernatant liquid into a dark bottle, and add one leaf of iodine. Store in darkness.

Solution A: 50 gm zinc chloride in 25 mL distilled water

Solution B: 0.25 gm iodine, 5.25 gm potassium iodide, and 12.5 mL distilled water

Selleger stain: Place Solution A, 3 mL of Solution B, and 1 g of iodine in a dark container. Let stand for 1 week prior to use.

Solution A: 100 gm calcium nitrate in 50 mL distilled water

Solution B: 8 gm potassium iodide in 90 mL distilled water

5% Hydrochloric acid

0.05N Hydrochloric acid

5% Sodium hydroxide

1% Sodium hydroxide

Safety

Use standard laboratory safety procedures as described in guidelines set by your instructor. Be cautious of microscope light levels to avoid eye damage. Know the hazards associated with the mounting mediums, and use them with appropriate precautions as set by your instructor. Dispose of glass in an appropriate container. Refer to the safety data sheet (SDS) if necessary.

Part I: Paper Fiber Separation

Procedure A

1. Obtain a paper sample.
2. Observe and record the thickness, weight, color, and opacity of the paper.
3. Using a UV light box, observe the fluorescence of the paper under short (250 nm) and long (320–400 nm) UV light.
4. Using transmitted light, observe the presence of any watermarks.
5. Place a small amount of the paper in a beaker, covering it with distilled water.
6. Heat to a boil. Decant the water, and place the paper sample in a clean test tube.
7. Add distilled water, and shake vigorously until the fibers separate.

Procedure B: For Paper Samples That Will Not Disintegrate with Procedure A

This should not be used on roofing paper or papers that might contain wool.

1. Place the sample in a beaker, covering it with 1% sodium hydroxide solution.
2. Heat to a boil. Decant the liquid, and wash sample with distilled water.
3. Cover the sample with 0.05N hydrochloric acid, and let stand several minutes.
4. Decant the liquid, and wash with distilled water.
5. Add distilled water, and shake vigorously until the fibers separate.

Part II: Paper Fiber Staining

Paper fibers should also be examined for morphological characteristics (see Experiment 13).

Reagents: Graff "C" stain, Herzberg stain, and Selleger stain

Procedure

1. Using tweezers, position a few DRY paper fibers on a microscope slide that has been labeled with identifying marks (analyst initials and sample). The fibers must be dry so they will absorb the stain and not dilute it.
2. Add three drops of a stain, then place a cover slip over the sample.
3. Allow the slide to stand approximately 1–2 minutes, then drain off any excess stain.
4. Compare the color to known data to identify your possible fiber type.
5. Repeat for remaining stains.

Part III: Ink Spot Tests

Procedure

1. Obtain an ink sample. Using the stereomicroscope, determine the color and ink type (ballpoint or fluid) by noting the characteristics of the ink sample.
2. Cut a small portion of the ink sample, and place it in a well of a spot plate.
3. Add a drop of 5% hydrochloric acid. Observe, and note any color change.
4. Neutralize the sample with a drop of 5% sodium hydroxide. Observe, and note any color change.
5. Cut another small portion of the ink sample, and place it in a clean well of the spot plate.
6. Add a drop of 5% sodium hydroxide. Observe, and note any color change.
7. Determine the possible dyestuff.

Report Requirements

Include all drawings, calculations, and other information obtained during the laboratory procedure. Notes and/or drawings should include the sample identification, magnification, and a complete description.

Report Questions

1. Explain the possible fiber differences between construction paper and lined writing paper.
2. How would you determine whether a paper contained softwood or hardwood fibers?
3. How would you determine whether a paper contained cotton or jute fibers?
4. From the staining procedures, what is the composition of fiber types within your paper sample? How did you determine this?
5. What are the main characteristics that can be used to identify ballpoint pen ink?
6. What is the difference between ballpoint pen ink and rollerball pen ink?
7. How would you *identify* Victoria blue as a dyestuff in an ink?
8. From the ink spot tests, what type colorant did you determine for each of your ink samples? Include your notes and results from each testing.
9. What are the other common components for this ink type? How would you go about testing or identifying these components?
10. Are there ways to date a document by the ink sample? Explain your answer.

Recommended and Further Reading

Brunelle RL, Pro MJ. A Systematic Approach to Ink Identification. *Journal of Official Analytical Chemistry.* 1972; 55: 823–826.

Brunelle RL, Reed W. *Forensic Examination of Ink and Paper.* Springfield, IL: Charles C. Thomas, 1984.

Crown DA, Brunelle RL, Cantu AA. Parameters of Ballpoint Ink Examination. *Journal of Forensic Sciences.* 1976; 21: 917–922.

Crown DA, Conway JV, Kirk PL. Differentiation of Blue Ballpoint Pen Inks. *Journal of Criminal Law and Criminology.* 1961; 52(3): 338–343.

Ellen D. *The Scientific Examination of Documents: Methods and Techniques*, 2nd ed. Philadelphia: Taylor & Francis, 1997.

Graff JH. *Color Atlas for Fiber Identification.* Appleton, WI: The Institute of Paper Chemistry, 1940.

Graff JH. New Stains and Their Use for Fiber Identification. *Paper Trade Journal.* 1935; 16: 45–50.

Harris J. Developments in the Analysis of Writing Inks on Questioned Documents. *Journal of Forensic Sciences.* 1992; 37(2): 612–619.

Hilton O. *Scientific Examination of Questioned Documents.* Boca Raton, FL: CRC Press, 1992.

Isenberg IH. *Pulp and Paper Microscopy*, 3rd ed. Appleton, WI: The Institute of Paper Chemistry, 1967.

Kelly JD, Cantu AA. Proposed Standard Methods for Ink Identifications. *Journal of Official Analytical Chemistry.* 1975; 58: 122–125.

Robertson EW. *Fundamentals of Document Examinations.* Chicago: Nelson-Hall, 1991.

Souder W. Composition, Properties and Behavior of Ball Pens and Inks. *Journal of Criminal Law and Criminology.* 1955; 45(6): 743–747.

Tappolet JA. Comparative Examination of Ink Strokes on Paper with Infrared and Visible Luminescence. *Forensic Science Society.* 1986; 26: 293–299.

Wayne NJ. *Identification of Pigments by Spot Tests* (Bulletin 2-5-12). West Paterson, NJ: American Cyanamid Company, 1963.

Woodward J. Stains for the Determination of Paper Components and Paper Defects. *Microscopy and Microanalysis.* 2002; 8(2): 196–197.

Chapter 17

Experiment 17: Hair Examinations

Recommended pre-lab reading assignment:

Ogle RR, Mitosinka GT. A Rapid Technique for Preparing Hair Cuticle Scale Casts. *Journal of Forensic Sciences.* 1973; 18–82.

Recommended websites:

Deedrick DW, Koch SL. Microscopy of Hair Part I: A Practical Guide and Manual for Human Hair. *Forensic Science Communications.* 2004; 6(1). Available from: http://www.fbi.gov.

Deedrick DW, Koch SL. Microscopy of Hair Part II: A Practical Guide and Manual for Animal Hairs. *Forensic Science Communications.* 2004; 6(3). Available from: http://www.fbi.gov.

Objective

Upon completion of this practical exercise, the student will have developed a basic understanding of:

1. general characteristics of hair
2. use of the stereomicroscope to visualize the characteristics of hair
3. use of the compound or comparison light microscope to visualize the characteristics of hair
4. preparation of scale casts
5. identification of animal hair
6. identification of human hair

Practical Forensic Microscopy: A Laboratory Manual, Second Edition. Barbara P. Wheeler.
© 2021 John Wiley & Sons Ltd. Published 2021 by John Wiley & Sons Ltd.
Companion website: www.wiley.com/go/Wheeler/Forensic

Introduction

Humans and most other mammals have hair located over their bodies. While animal hair is limited in characteristics to determine specific species and somatic origin, human hair possesses characteristics that make these identifications and further comparisons possible at times. Because of this fact, a microscopic examination of hair presents itself as indirect or circumstantial evidence in a court of law. This evidence is generally used in conjunction with other forensic evidence. Hair examinations are performed to determine possible associations between people, places, and objects.

The hair is divided into several regions for examination purposes (see Figure 17-1a). The root is the structure at the proximal end of a hair. This portion of the hair is the active growing site when attached to the hair follicle. The tip is the most distal end of a hair. The section in the middle is the hair shaft, composed of three main sections: cuticle, cortex, and medulla (see Figure 17-1b).

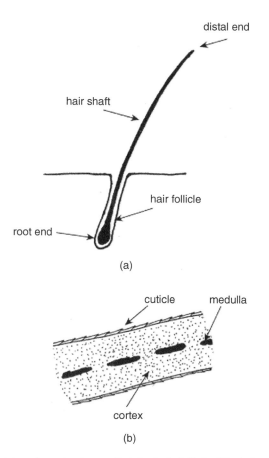

Figure 17-1 (a) Hair grows in a structure called the hair follicle. The hair can be divided into three regions; root, shaft, and tip (distal end). Hair grows from the root end, which is attached to the follicle during growth. (b) The three sections of the hair are the cuticle, medulla, and cortex.

Microscopic analysis of hair includes using a stereomicroscope and a compound microscope. Examinations are performed to identify characteristics of the hair. These characteristics may include more obvious macroscopic features such as color, shaft form, diameter, and length of the hair, but also microscopic features such as cuticle scales, cortex characteristics including pigment granules, shape of medulla, and root and tip characteristics. Many times, the medullary index (MI) is also determined. The MI is simply the diameter of the medulla divided by the diameter of the hair shaft.

$$\text{medullary index} = \text{MI} = \frac{\text{diameter of medulla}}{\text{diameter of hair}} \tag{17-1}$$

Among other things, the MI is used to distinguish animal hair from human hair. Animals have a medullary index ranging from 0.5 to 0.9, while humans have a medullary index less than 0.3.

Macroscopic Characteristics

Characteristics such as the color, shaft form, diameter, and length of the hair are considered macroscopic characteristics. Various colors, either natural or artificial, are found in hair: white or gray, blonde, red, brown, black, and other. These colors may range in various shades and also intensities. Visible coloring or banding patterns may also be present. Other macroscopic characteristics such as the shaft form, diameter, and length of the hair are considered descriptions of the hair structure. Hair may display various shaft forms or shapes. Straight, waved, curled, kinked, and curved are examples of shaft form. The shaft diameter is another macroscopic characteristic of the hair structure. Diameter can be recorded either as a measurement or with terms such as fine, medium, coarse, and varying. Finally, the shaft length is also measured for each hair sample. This is generally measured in inches or centimeters and described as a range for a sample.

Microscopic Characteristics

The reflected color of hair can also be described while viewing the hair microscopically. Colorless, blonde, red, brown, black, and other are terms used to describe the microscopic color of hair. These colors may also be in various shades (e.g., gray-brown, yellow-brown, or red-brown) and varying intensities: light, medium, and dark. Description of the pigmentation further defines the coloring of the hair microscopically. Natural pigment granule color, size, shape, density, and distribution, in addition to pigment aggregation and aggregate size and density, can provide additional information about the microscopic characteristics of a hair. Artificially colored hair can also be described with similar details.

The microscopic structure of hair can also be divided into several categories during a hair examination. Shaft forms such as buckling, convoluting, shouldering, undulating, twisting, and uniform can be determined from microscopic examinations. Hairs that display buckling (see Figure 17-2a) have a disruption of the hair shaft, resulting in an abrupt change in direction without a twist. Convoluting hairs show an abrupt rotation of the hair shaft. Shouldering on hairs (see Figure 17-2b) is viewed as a partial variation of the diameter along the hair shaft. Undulating describes hairs with changes in the diameter along the hair shaft.

The cross-sectional appearance can also provide additional information about a hair. Round, oval, flattened, and triangular cross sections are commonly found for hair samples. The diameter of a hair is described in micrometers during a microscopic examination. This should be measured

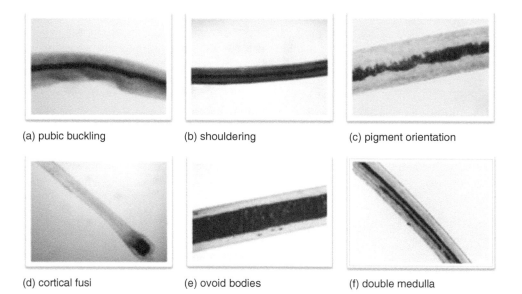

(a) pubic buckling   (b) shouldering   (c) pigment orientation

(d) cortical fusi   (e) ovoid bodies   (f) double medulla

Figure 17-2 Several microscopic characteristics of hair that can be noted to "individualize" a hair sample.

at several points along the hair shaft (from root to tip end) with an objective containing a calibrated micrometer.

A hair can be divided into three main regions: the root, the shaft, and the tip. The root (proximal end) of a hair can provide numerous microscopic characteristics. A hair lost from the scalp during the anagen stage (actively growing) will typically have an epithelial sheath adhering to the elongated pigmented root. A hair lost during the catagen stage (transition) will generally have a slightly enlarged root and may have bits of epithelial tissue adhering to the root. Hairs that are shed during the telogen (resting) stage typically have an enlarged root that lacks pigment and has no epithelial tissue attached. Shriveled, stretched, or damaged follicular tags may also provide information as to how or why the hair was shed. Postmortem changes in a hair root can also provide important information. The absence of a root may also provide information. The missing root end may be square cut, angular cut, angular cut with elongated

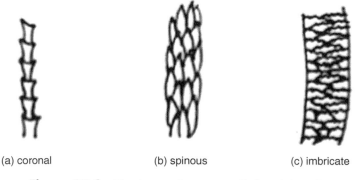

(a) coronal   (b) spinous   (c) imbricate

Figure 17-3 The three main patterns of hair cuticle scales.

tail, crushed, broken, and singed. Postmortem changes may also be described when the root end is missing.

Many microscopic characteristics are also found within the shaft (central portion) of a hair. The shaft can be divided into three sections: cuticle, cortex, and medulla.

Cuticle: This portion of the hair consists of the multiscale outer layer, which may be present or absent. The scales overlap to form a variety of patterns. There are three main patterns of scales: coronal, spinous, and imbricate (see Figure 17-3). The coronal scale pattern is created by the overlapping of scales that are shaped like small crowns or cups, stacked on top of each other. The spinous or petal-shaped scales are created by the overlapping of scales that are shaped like small triangular tiles, stacked on top of each other. Imbricate scales have irregular borders and margins. Once again, they are stacked on top of each other. Various scale patterns may be found in animal hair; however, human hair is always imbricate or irregular waved. Figure 17-4 contains several variations of spinous and imbricate scale patterns. When present, the thickness and color of the cuticle should be noted. Thin is generally considered 2.5 μm or less. Thick generally refers to 2.5 μm or greater. Colors are generally referred to as transparent, translucent, or yellow. The condition of the outer cuticle margin may also display a variety of microscopic differences. Smooth, flattened,

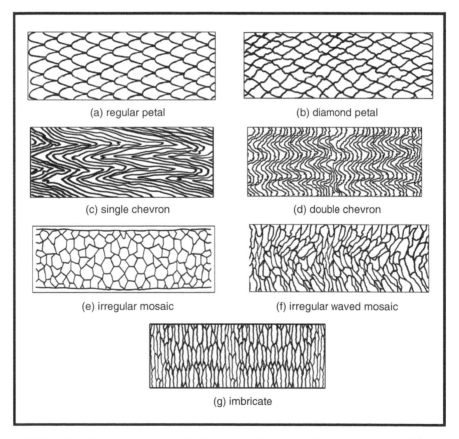

(a) regular petal

(b) diamond petal

(c) single chevron

(d) double chevron

(e) irregular mosaic

(f) irregular waved mosaic

(g) imbricate

Figure 17-4 Variations of spinous and imbricate scale patterns. Scale patterns specific to the deer family and antelope are shown in Figure 17A-2.

serrated, looped, ragged, and cracked are examples of the possibilities for the appearance of the outer margin of a cuticle. The inner cuticle margin may be distinct or indistinct, with pigment granules absent or present.

Cortex: This portion is the main body of the hair. It is composed of elongated and fusiform keratinized cells. Many of the microscopic characteristics are found within this portion of the hair. The cellular texture of the cortex may be apparent, extreme, or not visible. Color and pigmentation details are visualized in the cortex portion of the hair (see Figure 17-2c). Cortical fusi, which are small fusiform bodies that contain air, are sometimes found in the cortex. They are more commonly found near the root and the proximal portion of the hair (see Figure 17-2d), but may be seen at times toward the distal portion. Their size, shape, location, and abundance should be noted. Ovoid bodies, which are large aggregates of pigment that have a spherical or oblong shape, may also be present (see Figure 17-2e). They range in diameter from 3 to 20 μm. When present, the size, shape, location, and abundance should also be noted.

Medulla: This is the innermost portion of the hair. A medulla is located in the center of the hair, which may or may not be visible in each hair. There are several cellular patterns or medulla forms that are found in human and animal hair. These may appear clear or dark. Animal hair may have uniserial, multiserial, lattice, vacuolated, or amorphous medullas, which are shown in Figure 17-5. Human hair medulla is generally amorphous in appearance. The distribution of the medulla is also an important microscopic characteristic. This describes the presence of the medulla along the hair shaft. Absent, continuous, or discontinuous are several terms used to describe the medulla distribution. The

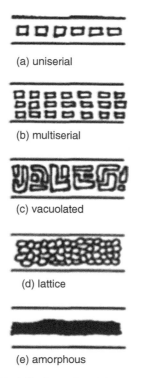

(a) uniserial

(b) multiserial

(c) vacuolated

(d) lattice

(e) amorphous

Figure 17-5 Medulla forms found in animal or human hair.

appearance of the medulla may be opaque, translucent, or absent. If the medulla is air filled, it will appear black or opaque with transmitted light (see Figure 17-2b). If the medulla is filled with a liquid, it will appear clear or translucent. The relative width of the medulla should also be noted using the medullary index that is calculated by using Equation (17-1).

The tip of the hair also displays microscopic characteristics. Natural or uncut tips may be referred to as tapered. Cut tips may appear square, angular, or angular with a tail. Tips may also be broken, split, frayed, rounded, crushed, abraded, or singed.

Animal and human hair can easily be differentiated by macroscopic and microscopic characteristics. Animal hairs may contain various colors and color banding patterns, while human hair tends to be more consistent in color. Hair shaft diameter changes along the shaft are commonly found in animal hairs. Various scale patterns are found in animal hairs, whereas human hair displays an imbricate or irregular-waved scale pattern. Various medullary patterns are found in animal hairs. Human hair generally has an amorphous medulla that may be either absent, discontinuous, or continuous. In addition to medullary patterns, the medullary index can also be a determining factor of whether hair is human or animal. Finally, various distinct root shapes are found in some animal hairs.

Animal hair: The forensic scientist uses numerous characteristics to identify animal hair. These are summarized in Table 17-1. Pigmentation, shaft diameter, scale patterns, medullary patterns, and root shapes provide valuable information to the forensic hair examiner. Various pigmentation and color banding patterns are commonly found in animal hairs. These patterns provide information for specific identifications of animal hair. Shaft diameter and changes along the shaft are also important factors to take into consideration when identifying animal hair. Numerous scale patterns are found in animal hairs. Use of scale cast mounting preparations makes viewing scale patterns easier for the hair examiner. The size, shape, and scale pattern arrangement of the hair provide distinctive characteristics for certain animals. Several medullary patterns are also found in animal hairs. These patterns provide additional information for certain animal hair identifications. Various root shapes are found in some animal hairs. These root shapes provide information for specific identifications of animal hair. Once a hair has been identified as animal, further characterization of the hair can be done to identify a species. Animal hair is not routinely compared in forensic casework.

Human hair: The hair examiner utilizes numerous characteristics to identify human hair. These are summarized in Table 17-1. Pigmentation, shaft diameter, scale pattern, medullary pattern, and root characteristics also give information to aid in the identification of human hair. Natural color is generally constant. Shaft diameter is generally moderate with gradual changes. The scale pattern for human hair is imbricate or irregular waved. The medulla is amorphous when present, and distributed either continuously or discontinuously. Root shape may also give an indication for human hair. Once a hair has been identified as human, further characterization of the hair can be done.

Hair examinations involve the use of a variety of microscopes and techniques. Examinations are usually performed to identify a hair and then, when necessary, to compare the hair back to a possible hair source. Initially a stereomicroscope is used to examine the hair for macroscopic

Table 17-1 Comparison of animal and human hair characteristics.

Characteristic	Animal	Human
Color	Often has color changes along shaft; may be in specific banding patterns	Color remains consistent
Pigmentation distribution	Pigment is denser toward medulla	Pigment is even or denser toward cuticle
Cuticle	Various scale patterns; some changes along shaft	Imbricate pattern
Cortex	Width is thinner than the medulla	Width is the majority of the hair shaft
Medulla	Width is greater than 1/3 of hair shaft; usually continuous	Width when present is thin; mostly continuous
Medulla form	Various patterns	When present: amorphous
Root shape	Various shapes	Bulbous
Diameter of hair	Variation along shaft, "shield"	Diameter moderate; changes gradual along shaft

characteristics such as color, length, and form. Further testing can be performed using a compound or comparison light microscope to determine the microscopic characteristics of the hair sample. To do this, either scale casts or semi-permanent/permanent mounts are utilized.

Since a compound microscope uses transmitted light, a scale cast can be used to view the external or surface features of a hair. A scale cast is an impression or semi-permanent mold made from the scale pattern of the hair (see Experiment 2C). Scale patterns, along with other microscopic characteristics, are used primarily with animal hair for species identification. Semi-permanent and permanent mounts are used to visualize other microscopic characteristics of both animal and human hair. To properly observe these characteristics, a hair must be mounted in a medium of refractive index similar to that of the hair itself. The average refractive index for hair is 1.55. A synthetic, semi-permanent, or permanent mounting medium with a refractive index in the range of 1.5–1.6 is generally recommended.

Equipment and Supplies

Stereomicroscope

Compound light microscope with objectives of various magnifications (e.g., 4X, 10X, 20X, and 40X) and calibrated focusing ocular with micrometer scale

Micro kit

Microscope slides and cover slips

Mounting mediums

Nail polish and/or Polaroid film coating

Animal hair

Human hair

Unknown hair samples

Safety

Use standard laboratory safety procedures as described in guidelines set by your instructor. Be cautious of microscope light levels to avoid eye damage. Know the hazards associated with the mounting mediums, and use them with appropriate precautions as set by your instructor. Dispose of glass in an appropriate container.

Part I: Macroscopic Examination of Hair

Procedure

A worksheet for examination notes may be found at the end of the experiment.

1. Examine the hair with the stereomicroscope.
2. Measure the length of the hair. Record the value in centimeters.
3. Note the color and any banding patterns that may be present.
4. Note the form of the hair.
5. Note the diameter of the hair.
6. Repeat steps 1–5 for four additional animal samples and one human hair sample.

Part II: Scale Casts

Procedure

1. Use the hair samples examined in Part 1.
2. Label a microscope slide with identifying marks (analyst initials and sample).
3. Apply a thin coating of clear nail polish (Polaroid film coating may also be used).
4. While still wet, position an animal hair in the nail polish. Make sure the entire length of the hair is included.
5. Let the nail polish dry completely.
6. Gently remove the hair to obtain the scale cast.
7. Observe the scale pattern using the compound light microscope. Remember to check the microscope to ensure that samples will be viewed using Köhler illumination.
8. Be sure to observe the entire length of the hair, as scale patterns may change from the proximal to distal ends. Draw what you see.
9. Repeat steps 1–8 for additional hair samples.

Part III: Animal Hair and Human Hair Characteristics

Procedure

1. Make liquid mounts of the five animal hair samples previously examined.
2. Make liquid mounts of the human hair previously examined and four additional samples.
3. Examine the hairs using the compound light microscope.
4. Document the characteristics of each hair: color, form, and diameter.
5. Examine the hairs for any additional microscopic characteristics that would aid in the identification of the hair type. Document the additional characteristics of each hair: cuticle, cortex and medulla widths, medulla form, root shape, pigmentation, orientation, and so on.
6. Measure the diameter of each hair and its medulla to calculate the medullary index for all hairs. Calculate the medullary index using Equation (17-1).
7. Draw one identifying characteristic for each hair. Make sure to include information such as sample, magnification, and so on.
8. Obtain an unknown hair. Determine if the hair is animal or human. Refer to Table 17-1 as needed. List the macroscopic and microscopic characteristics for the hair on the Hair Worksheet.

Report Requirements

Include all drawings, calculations, and other information obtained during the laboratory procedure. Notes and/or drawings should include the sample identification, magnification, and a complete description.

Report Questions

1. For the following terms, first describe the term and then give at least two examples of differences that might be observed during a hair exam. For instance, describe root, then give examples of different root characteristics.
   a. Root
   b. Cuticle
   c. Cortex
   d. Medulla
   e. Tip
2. List three characteristics that are used to distinguish human hair and animal hair. Give examples of each of the differences found between human and animal hair.
3. Describe your examination procedure for the samples you obtained.
4. What did a scale cast help determine?
5. What did the liquid hair mount help determine?
6. Describe the medullary index, and give the formula for calculating it. If a hair has a medullary index of 0.25, what species would you expect it to be? If a hair has a medullary index of 0.65, what species would you expect it to be?

7. Can a medullary index be used to give an indication as to whether or not an animal hair is from a cat or dog?

8. Provide your documentation and drawings from Parts I, II, and III. Make sure your documentation includes the appropriate labeling (name, sample numbers, and lab).

9. Provide the unknown hair number and your conclusion (animal or human). State reasons to defend your conclusion.

HAIR WORKSHEET

Sample _____

Color _____

Length _____

Shaft Form _____

Diameter _____

Cuticle _____

Cortex _____

Medulla _____

Root Shape _____

Pigmentation _____

Medullary Index _____

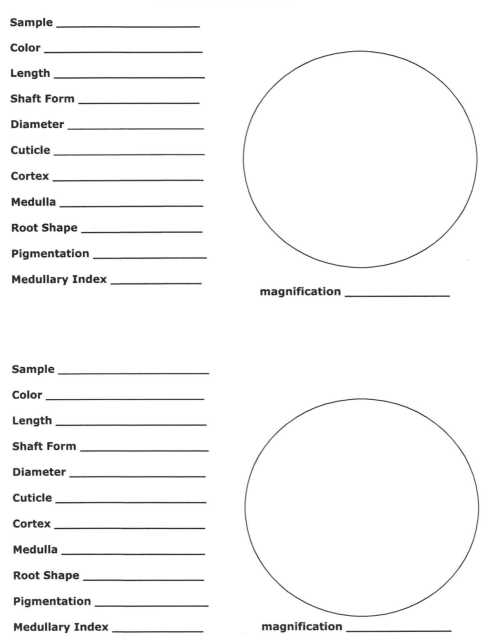

magnification _____

Sample _____

Color _____

Length _____

Shaft Form _____

Diameter _____

Cuticle _____

Cortex _____

Medulla _____

Root Shape _____

Pigmentation _____

Medullary Index _____

magnification _____

Chapter 17

Experiment 17A: Animal Hair Examinations

Recommended pre-lab reading assignments:

Brunner H. *The Identification of Mammalian Hair.* Melbourne, Australia: Inkata Press, 1974; 1–18.

Spence LE. *Study of Identifying Characteristics of Mammal Hair.* Cheyenne, WY: Wyoming Game and Fish Commission, Wildlife Disease Research Laboratory, 1963.

Objective

Upon completion of this practical exercise, the student will have developed a basic understanding of:

1. general characteristics of animal hair
2. use of the stereomicroscope to visualize the characteristics of hair
3. use of the compound or comparison light microscope to identify and visualize the characteristics of hair
4. preparation and observation of scale casts

Introduction

The Locard Exchange Principle states that whenever two objects come in contact, an exchange of matter occurs. This theory applies to hair evidence. Hair is easily shed and transferred whenever there is contact between two objects, two individuals, or an individual and another object. Pets often shed animal hairs, and these may be easily transferred to clothing or other objects. Animal hair may also be present from clothing or textile products made from animal hair (e.g., wool sweaters and blankets). These hairs may also be transferred to individuals, clothing, or other

---

Practical Forensic Microscopy: A Laboratory Manual, Second Edition. Barbara P. Wheeler.
© 2021 John Wiley & Sons Ltd. Published 2021 by John Wiley & Sons Ltd.
Companion website: www.wiley.com/go/Wheeler/Forensic

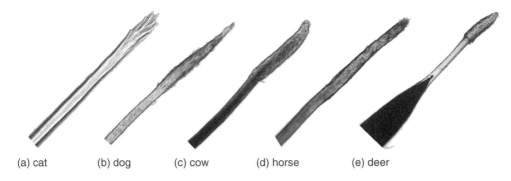

(a) cat   (b) dog   (c) cow   (d) horse   (e) deer

Figure 17A-1 Root shapes are distinctive characteristics for some animals. (a) Cat hair has a "paintbrush"-shaped root, (b) dog hair has a spade-shaped root, (c) cow hair has an elongated root with the medulla present into the root portion, (d) horse hair has an elongated root, and (e) animals included in the deer family and antelope have a wineglass-shaped root.

objects. Because of this fact, animal hair is often used to associate people with items or scenes. This makes animal hair an important source of information in forensic investigations.

The forensic scientist uses various characteristics to identify animal hair. Animal hair possesses various macroscopic and microscopic characteristics that make identifications and further association with a particular species possible at times. Because of this fact, animal hair is routinely examined in forensic situations. There are three types of animal hair that may be encountered in casework: fur, tactile, and guard. Fur hair is a fine inner coat of hair that provides the animal with warmth and insulation. Tactile hair is found on the head of the animal and provides sensory functions for the animal. Guard hair is the outer coat of hair and provides protection for the animal. These hairs are generally characteristic of the family or species and may be used for identification.

Dividing animal hair into three "families" provides easier classification of the macroscopic and microscopic characteristics of animal hair. While the term "families" has very specific meanings in some science fields, it is used as a broad classifying term when associated with animal hair. Numerous characteristics are used to identify animal hair and classify it into one of three groups: deer family and antelope, the fur-bearing family, and the domestic family. Characteristics of a hair such as its color, pigment distribution, cuticle patterns, cortex and medulla widths, medulla form, root shape (see Figure 17A-1), and overall diameter are taken into consideration when classifying a hair to a particular "family" or species.

Deer Family and Antelope

This group of animal hair can be easily distinguished by its very coarse diameter that generally has a slight wave or crimp. The "wineglass root" (see Figure 17A-1e) is also a major characteristic of this group. The medulla is composed of spherical cells that occupy the entire hair. Scale cast patterns, in addition to other microscopic characteristics and color banding patterns, can be used to distinguish hair within the deer family and/or antelope. Distinct scale patterns for animals within the deer family and antelope are shown in Figure 17A-2.

Each of these animals also displays specific color banding patterns on their hair. The color banding pattern of deer hair begins with an area of white or light gray at the root end. It then proceeds from this color to a gray-brown, then an area of yellow followed by a black tip end.

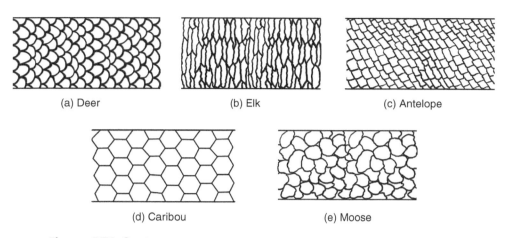

(a) Deer   (b) Elk   (c) Antelope

(d) Caribou   (e) Moose

Figure 17A-2 Cuticle scale patterns for animals in the deer family and antelope.

For elk hair, the color banding pattern begins with an area of brown-gray at the root end, then turning yellow and a black tip end. The color banding pattern for antelope hair starts with an area of brown-gray, followed by an area of brown-yellow and a dark brown tip end. For caribou hair, the color banding pattern begins with a white root end, followed by a light tan area and a black tip end. The color banding pattern of moose hair begins with a white root area, then proceeds to a brown-gray color. It then has areas of black, followed by light gray, brown-gray, and a black tip end.

Fur-Bearing Family

This group of animal hair can be distinguished by the fine overall diameter. There is also a wide variation in diameter within the hair. Characteristic medullary patterns can be used to distinguish hair within this group. Scale cast patterns, in addition to other microscopic characteristics, can be used to distinguish some fur-bearing family animals. Some fur-bearing family animals also show distinct color banding patterns. Some specific identifying characteristics for members of the fur-bearing family group are listed in Table 17A-1.

Domestic Family

This group of animal hair can be easily distinguished by the medium overall diameter with only moderate variation along the hair. Medullary patterns are generally amorphous. Characteristic root shapes may also be used to distinguish between some domestic family animal hairs. Scale cast patterns and other microscopic characteristics can be used to distinguish hairs within the domestic family animal group. Most hair in this group generally does not have color banding patterns. Some specific identifying characteristics for domestic family animals are listed in Table 17A-2.

An understanding of the macroscopic and microscopic characteristics found in animal hair allows the forensic scientist to perform animal hair examinations. Animal hair examinations involve the use of a variety of microscopes, techniques, and instruments. Initially a stereomicroscope is used to examine the hair for macroscopic characteristics. Further testing can be performed using a compound or comparison light microscope to determine the microscopic

Table 17A-1   Important identifying characteristics for the fur-bearing group.

Animal	Characteristics
Rabbit	Scale cast pattern: irregular-waved mosaic-chevron/irregular-waved mosaic
	Medulla pattern: multiserial ladder, MI > 0.9
Mink	Color banding: dark shades/lighter shades
	Scale cast pattern: diamond petal/irregular-waved mosaic
	Medulla pattern: amorphous/lattice
	Shaft shape: prominent shield
Muskrat	Color banding: reddish-brown/dark brown
	Scale cast pattern: irregular-waved mosaic, single chevron
	Medulla pattern: multiserial ladder/lattice, ½ width
	Shaft shape: prominent shield
Chinchilla	Medulla pattern: uniserial ladder
	Shaft shape: very fine diameter and usually clumped
Raccoon	Color banding: white/dark brown/yellow/black
	Scale cast pattern: diamond petal/irregular-waved mosaic
	Medulla pattern: amorphous, cellular, ½ to ¾ width
Fox	Scale cast pattern: mosaic/diamond petal
	Medulla pattern: unbroken, amorphous or vacuolated, ¾ width
	Color banding (red fox): dark brown/yellow/red-brown
	Color banding (gray fox): white/dark brown-black/light tan/black
Beaver	Medulla pattern: fur hair is continuous cellular with a beaded look, thin
Seal	Scale pattern: petal
	Medulla pattern: absent
Otter	Scale pattern: petal
	Medulla pattern: lattice, wide
Sheep	Scale cast pattern: mosaic
	Medulla pattern: absent
	Shaft shape: usually crimped, fur hair curly
Camel	Scale cast pattern: mosaic
	Medulla pattern: amorphous
Sable	Scale pattern: petal
	Medulla pattern: lattice, fine, MI > 0.5
Bear	Scale cast pattern: very large irregular-waved
	Medulla pattern: amorphous, vacuolated, and thin, MI < 0.5
	Shaft shape: very wide

Table 17A-1 (*Continued*)

Animal	Characteristics
Ermine	Color banding: brown-gray/light brown
	Scale cast pattern: irregular petal/irregular-waved mosaic
	Medulla pattern: multiserial ladder
	Shaft shape: prominent shield area
Lynx	Color banding: gray/dark brown/white/black *or* light brown/dark brown/yellow/black
	Scale cast pattern: petal
	Medulla pattern: unbroken cellular

MI: Medullary index.

Table 17A-2 Important identifying characteristics of domestic animal hair.

Animal	Characteristics
Dog	Medulla pattern: vacuolated or amorphous, ½ diameter of overall hair
	Root shape: spade-like (see Figure 17A-1b)
	Shaft shape: may have barrel shape
Cat	Scale cast pattern: petal, usually prominent
	Medulla pattern: uniserial ladder, wide
	Root shape: elongated and fibrils frayed at base (see Figure 17A-1a)
	Shaft shape: fine
Cow	Medulla pattern: amorphous and thin
	Root shape: elongated with pigment into root area (see Figure 17A-1c)
	Shaft shape: coarse diameter
	Special characteristics: ovoid bodies prominent with coarse streaky pigment
Horse	Medulla pattern: amorphous, cellular, MI > 0.5
	Root shape: elongated bulb-like shape (see Figure 17A-1d)
	Shaft shape: coarse diameter
	Special characteristics: even, fine pigment
Ferret	Scale cast pattern: mosaic/petal/diamond
	Medulla pattern: uniserial and lattice
	Shaft shape: shield
Hog	Shaft shape: very coarse, stiff, even diameter
	Special characteristics: split tips
Goat	Scale cast pattern: irregular-waved mosaic
	Medulla pattern: lattice ½ to ¾ diameter of overall hair
	Root shape: wineglass
	Shaft shape: coarse
	Special characteristics: cortex visible

Table 17A-2 (*Continued*)

Animal	Characteristics
Opossum	Color banding: white/black
	Scale cast pattern: mosaic/irregular-waved mosaic
	Medulla pattern: vacuolated and amorphous, ½ diameter of overall hair
	Shaft shape: fine diameter
Skunk	Scale cast pattern: irregular-waved mosaic
	Medulla pattern: amorphous
Squirrel	Scale cast pattern: irregular waved
	Medulla pattern: vacuolated, fine
Coyote	Color banding: white/dark gray-brown/white/black
	Scale cast pattern: mosaic/diamond petal/irregular-waved
	Medulla pattern: vacuolated, ½ to ¾ diameter of overall hair
Otter	Color banding: light brown-gray/dark brown
	Scale cast pattern: diamond petal/irregular-waved mosaic
	Shaft shape: prominent shield
Mountain lion	Color banding: gray-brown/black/light brown/black
	Scale cast pattern: mosaic/irregular-waved mosaic
	Medulla pattern: vacuolated, very wide
Wolf	Medulla pattern: thick amorphous or vacuolated
	Special characteristics: little to no pigment in the cortex
Groundhog	Color banding: dark/white/black
	Scale cast pattern: irregular-waved mosaic
	Medulla pattern: vacuolated
	Special characteristics: red pigment near medulla

MI: Medullary index.

characteristics of the hair sample. To do this, a scale cast and either a semi-permanent or permanent mount is utilized. When a conclusion is reached as to a possible species origin of the hairs, it should be pointed out that the animal hairs do not possess enough individual characteristics to be identified to a particular animal to the exclusion of other animals of the same species.

Equipment and Supplies

Stereomicroscope

Compound light microscope with objectives of various magnifications (e.g., 4X, 10X, 20X, and 40X) and focusing ocular with micrometer scale

Micro kit

Microscope slides and cover slips

Mounting medium (a colorless mounting medium in the refractive index range of 1.5–1.60)

Clear nail polish and/or Polaroid film coating

Animal hair

Unknown hair samples

Safety

Use standard laboratory safety procedures as described in guidelines set by your instructor. Be cautious of microscope light levels to avoid eye damage. Know the hazards associated with the mounting mediums, and use them with appropriate precautions as set by your instructor. Dispose of glass in an appropriate container.

Part I: Animal Hair Examination

Procedure

A worksheet for examination notes may be found at the end of the experiment.

1. Obtain an animal hair from each group (deer and antelope, fur bearing, and domestic).
2. Examine the first hair with the stereomicroscope.
3. Measure the length of the hair. Record the value in centimeters.
4. Note the color and any banding patterns that may be present.
5. Note the form of the hair.
6. Note the diameter of the hair.
7. Label a microscope slide with identifying marks (analyst initials and sample).
8. Make a scale cast by applying a thin coating of clear nail polish to the microscope slide. Polaroid film coating may also be used instead of clear nail polish.
9. While still wet, position the hair in the nail polish. Make sure the entire length of the hair is included.
10. Let the nail polish dry completely.
11. Gently remove the hair to obtain the scale cast. This hair will be used for the liquid mount.
12. Using the scale cast, observe the scale pattern using the compound light microscope. Remember to check the microscope to ensure that samples will be viewed using Köhler illumination.
13. Be sure to observe the entire length of the hair, as scale patterns may change from the proximal to distal ends. Draw what you see.
14. Make a liquid mount of the hair.
15. Examine the hair using the compound light microscope.
16. Document the microscopic characteristics of the hair: color, form, and diameter.
17. Examine the hair for any additional microscopic characteristics that would aid in the identification of the hair type. Document the additional characteristics of each hair: cuticle, cortex and medulla widths, medulla form, root shape, pigmentation, orientation, and so on.
18. Measure the diameter of the hair and the medulla for all hairs to calculate the medullary index of each hair using Equation 17-1.
19. Draw one identifying characteristic for each hair, including information such as: sample identification, magnification, and so on.

20. Do your results agree with the known characteristics for the animal? List the identifying macroscopic and microscopic characteristics for the hair.
21. Repeat steps 1–20 for hairs from the other groups.
22. Obtain an unknown hair.
23. Repeat steps 1–20 to identify the hair.
24. Describe your examination procedure for the unknown sample.
25. Include the unknown hair number and the species that you identified the hair to be. State your reasons to defend your conclusion.

Report Requirements

Include all drawings, calculations, and other information obtained during the laboratory procedure. Notes and/or drawings should include the sample identification, magnification, and a complete description.

Report Questions

1. Describe each term as it relates to animal hair: root, cuticle, cortex, medulla, and tip. Include drawings and/or examples with your description for each term.
2. What are the main divisions for animal hair? Pick a species from each division, and describe the microscopic characteristics that are used for its identification.
3. Why are scale casts used for animal hair identifications?
4. Can animal hair be identified without a scale cast?
5. An animal hair was found with a medulla that looks like corn on the cob. What species could it be?
6. Dog and cat hair are the most commonly identified animal hairs in forensic cases. What are the identifying characteristics for dog hair?
7. What are the identifying characteristics for cat hair?
8. Can dog and cat hairs be compared?
9. Some animal hairs are used for fibers. How can you determine if it is a hair or an animal hair used as a fiber?

HAIR WORKSHEET

Sample _____

Color _____

Length _____

Shaft Form _____

Diameter _____

Cuticle _____

Cortex _____

Medulla _____

Root Shape _____

Pigmentation _____

Medullary Index _____

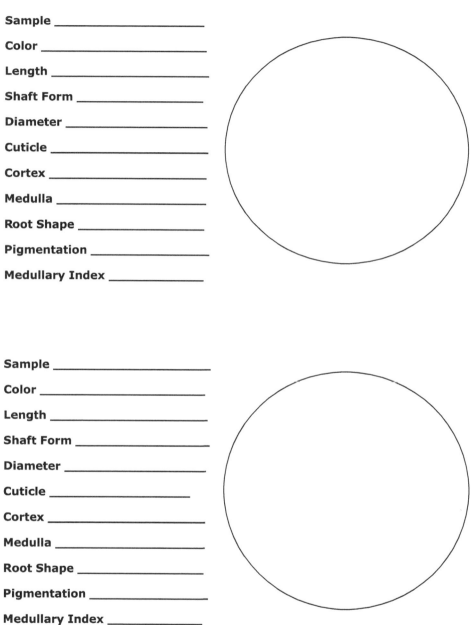

Sample _____

Color _____

Length _____

Shaft Form _____

Diameter _____

Cuticle _____

Cortex _____

Medulla _____

Root Shape _____

Pigmentation _____

Medullary Index _____

Chapter 17

Experiment 17B: Determination of Racial and Somatic Origin Characteristics of Human Hair

> **Recommended pre-lab reading assignments:**
>
> Ogle RR. *Atlas of Human Hair Microscopic Characteristics*. Boca Raton, FL: CRC Press, 1998.
>
> Robertson J. Forensic and Microscopic Examination of Human Hair. In: Robertson J, ed. *Forensic Examination of Hair*. London: Taylor & Francis, 1999; 79–153.

Objective

Upon completion of this practical exercise, the student will have developed a basic understanding of:

1. general racial characteristics of human hair
2. general somatic region characteristics of human hair
3. use of the stereomicroscope to visualize the characteristics of hair
4. use of the compound or comparison light microscope to visualize the characteristics of hair
5. preparation and observations of hair cross sections
6. identification of human hair

Introduction

Like animal hair, human hair is also easily shed and transferred whenever there is contact between two objects, two individuals, or an individual and another object. Many factors can

Practical Forensic Microscopy: A Laboratory Manual, Second Edition. Barbara P. Wheeler.
© 2021 John Wiley & Sons Ltd. Published 2021 by John Wiley & Sons Ltd.
Companion website: www.wiley.com/go/Wheeler/Forensic

affect whether or not a hair is shed or transferred. The growth stage of the hair is one determining factor. More importantly, any activity of the individual and/or other individuals and objects involved will affect the shedding or transfer of hair. The average person loses approximately 100 hairs each day. These can be shed or transferred through contact. This contact can occur through daily activities, such as combing hair, or by violent contact, such as an assault or rape. Human hair may be easily transferred to clothing or other objects. Because of this fact, human hair is often used to associate people with items or scenes. This makes human hair an important source of information in forensic investigations.

Like animal hair, the forensic scientist uses several hair characteristics to identify human hair. Human hair possesses many macroscopic and microscopic characteristics, which make identifications and comparisons sometimes possible. These characteristics were discussed in Experiment 17. Because of this fact, human hair is routinely examined and compared in forensic casework.

In some instances, microscopic characteristics for a head hair can be associated with one of the three generally accepted anthropological groups: people of European, African, and Asian origin. European is an anthropological term designating the peoples originating from Europe and the Indian subcontinent. African is an anthropological term designating most of the peoples originating from Africa. Asian is an anthropological term designating peoples originating from Asia excluding the Indian subcontinent but including the Native American Indians.

Hairs that are characterized as European exhibit an overall shaft diameter that is generally moderate with little variation. Pigment granules are fairly evenly distributed, light to heavy in density, and the cross-sectional shape is oval (see Figure 17B-1a). Hairs that are characterized as African exhibit an overall shaft diameter that is fine to moderate with considerable variation. Pigment granules are densely distributed and somewhat clumpy. The cross-sectional shape is flattened with areas of buckling, curling, and twisting (see Figure 17B-1b). And finally, for hairs that are characterized as Asian, the overall shaft diameter is coarse with little to no variation. Pigment granules are densely distributed and streaky. A prominent medulla is generally present with a well-defined thick cuticle. The cross-sectional shape is round (see Figure 17B-1c). Racial group microscopic characteristics are summarized in Table 17B-1. At times a possible racial group cannot be determined. This may be due to racial characteristic mixing. It is important to

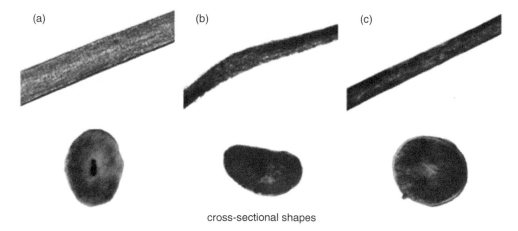

cross-sectional shapes

Figure 17B-1   Some hair characteristics are associated with anthropological groups: (a) European, (b) African, and (c) Asian.

Table 17B-1 Racial group microscopic characteristics.

Racial group	Diameter	Cross-sectional shape	Pigment	Cuticle	Undulation
African	60–90 μm	Flattened	Dense and clumped	Varies	Prevalent
European	70–100 μm	Oval	Even	Varies	Varies
Asian	90–120 μm	Round	Dense and streaky	Thick	None

note that when characteristics within the sample may be inconsistent or poorly defined, or have only a limited number within the sample, a determination of association with one specific racial group may not be possible.

The somatic region from which a hair was shed can also be determined at times. Head hairs are generally long in length with moderate shaft diameter and variation. A thin medulla may be present or absent. For head hair the distal ends can be cut, worn, or split. Pubic hairs are generally coarse with wide variations in diameter and somewhat prominent buckling. The medulla is usually thick, present, and continuous. Large root ends generally have follicular tags. Pubic hair distal ends are tapered, cut, or worn and sometimes bleached from urine. Limb hairs are generally fine with little variation. Their overall shape is short and arc-like. The medulla is usually broad and discontinuous. Limb hair distal ends are usually worn. Facial hairs are generally coarse and irregular with a triangular cross section. The medulla is usually broad and continuous. Some facial hair may exhibit multiple medullas. Facial hair distal ends are generally cut, sometimes angular. Chest hairs are generally moderate in diameter. The overall shape is long and arc-like. Chest hair distal ends are usually worn or tapered. Axillary hairs are generally moderate and resemble pubic hair with less buckling. Their distal ends are usually long and fine, being frequently bleached from deodorant. Eyebrow and eyelash hairs are generally short and stubby, with little shaft diameter variation. The overall shape of these hairs is saber-like. Hairs that are generally a mix of characteristics from two body areas are transitional hairs. An example of transitional hair is sideburn hair that may possess a combination of head and facial characteristics. Somatic region microscopic characteristics are summarized in Table 17B-2.

An understanding of the macroscopic and microscopic characteristics found in human hair allows the forensic scientist to perform human hair examinations. Human hair examinations involve the use of a variety of microscopes, techniques, and instruments. Initially a stereomicroscope is used to examine the hair for macroscopic characteristics. Further testing can be performed using a compound or comparison light microscope to determine the microscopic characteristics of the hair sample. To do this, a cross section and either a semi-permanent or permanent mount are utilized.

A cross section is a perpendicular sampling of a hair. The cross section is then mounted in either a semi-permanent or permanent mount to observe its shape. Cross sections of a hair sample provide information about characteristics that are associated with determining racial and somatic origins. At times, the cross-sectional shape may also be determined by viewing the hair sample longitudinally. However, more detail can be obtained by preparing an actual cross section of the sample. Semi-permanent and permanent mounts are used to visualize other microscopic characteristics of a hair. Once a hair has been identified as human, further characterization of the hair can be done.

When human hair examinations are performed, the forensic examiner may reach several conclusions. These may include information concerning the characteristics associated with either

Table 17B-2 Somatic region microscopic characteristics.

Hair	Length	Diameter	Texture	Tip end	Medulla	Other
Head	Long, varies	Moderate; shaft varies	Soft	Cut or split	Narrow	
Pubic	Short	Coarse; wide variation with buckling	Stiff	Tapered, cut, or rounded	Thick	
Facial	Varies	Coarse with variation	Stiff	Cut or rounded	Broad, doubled	Triangular cross-sectional shape
Limb	Varies	Fine with variation	Soft	Tapered, rounded, or cut	Discontinuous	Arc-like shaft form
Chest	Varies	Moderate with variation	Stiff	Tapered, rounded, or abraded; long and fine	Granular	Arc-like shaft form
Axillary	Varies	Moderate with variation	Stiff	Tapered, rounded, cut, or abraded; long and fine	Discontinuous	Bleached ends
Eyebrow/ eyelash	Short	Slight fluctuation	Stiff	Tapered		Saber-like shaft form

racial groups and/or somatic origin. The examiner may state that a hair contains microscopic characteristics consistent with a particular racial group: European, African, or Asian. Likewise, the examiner may state that a hair contains microscopic characteristics consistent with a particular somatic origin (e.g., head, pubic, or limb).

Equipment and Supplies

Stereomicroscope

Compound light microscope with objectives of various magnifications (e.g., 4X, 10X, 20X, and 40X) and focusing ocular with micrometer scale

Micro kit

Microscope slides and cover slips

Mounting medium (a colorless mounting medium in the refractive index range of 1.5–1.60)

Polyethylene or plastic sheets

Hot plate

Pipette tips

Microtome

Thread

Nail polish

Human hair

Unknown hair samples

Safety

Use standard laboratory safety procedures as described in guidelines set by your instructor. Be cautious of microscope light levels to avoid eye damage. Know the hazards associated with the mounting mediums, and use them with appropriate precautions as set by your instructor. Dispose of glass in an appropriate container.

Part I: Human Hair Examination

A worksheet for examination notes may be found at the end of the experiment.

Procedure

Complete the human hair worksheet for each hair sample.

1. Obtain samples of human hair from each group (European, African, Asian, head, pubic, facial, chest, axillary, eyebrow, and eyelash).
2. Examine the first hair with the stereomicroscope for macroscopic characteristics.
3. Measure the length of the hair. Record the value in centimeters.
4. Record the color that may be present. It is important to note if the color changes along the length of the hair.
5. Record the shaft form of the hair. Examples are: straight, waved, curled, kinked, or curved.
6. Set up Köhler illumination on a compound light microscope.
7. Using a calibrated ocular micrometer, measure the diameter of the hair.
8. Determine the cross-sectional shape of the hair (round, oval, flattened, or triangular). Choose one of the cross-sectioning methods described below, or determine the cross section by a longitudinal examination once the liquid mount has been made. Draw what you see.
   A. Cross-sectioning by sandwiching the sample:
      1. Using either microscope slides or sheets of plastic film, "sandwich" the sample. Some laboratories use thick polyethylene sheets that can be melted to enclose the sample.
      2. Align the blade of a scalpel or razor perpendicular to the sample.
      3. Cut a thin cross section.
      4. Mount the sample in a suitable mounting medium for viewing on the microscope.
   B. Cross-sectioning by imbedding the sample:
      1. Fill a pipette tip with a small amount of mounting medium that will harden (Flo-texx^{TM} or Norland 65^{TM}).
      2. Insert sample into tip.
      3. Allow the mounting medium to cure until hardened. This may involve heating in the oven, drying at room temperature, or the use of UV light.
      4. Align the blade of a scalpel or razor perpendicular to the sample.

    5. Cut a thin cross section.

    6. Mount the sample in a suitable mounting medium for viewing on the microscope.

Or:

    1. Using several layers of tape, create a small form on a microscope slide.

    2. Fill the area with a mounting medium that will harden (Flo-texx™ or Norland 65™).

    3. Insert the sample.

    4. Allow the mounting medium to cure until hardened. This may involve heating in the oven, drying at room temperature, or the use of UV light.

    5. Align the blade of a scalpel or razor perpendicular to the sample.

    6. Cut a thin cross section.

    7. Mount the sample in a suitable mounting medium for viewing on the microscope.

C. Cross-sectioning using a microtome:

    1. Facing the microtome, turn the dial counterclockwise to lower the plunger.

    2. Loosen the small right screw on the top moveable plate, and push plate toward the back.

    3. Unscrew and remove the two larger screws, and remove plate.

    4. Place 1 drop of microtome oil between the base plate and the top moveable plate.

    5. Take approximately 12 inches of thread (white or black for contrast with the sample) and double the thread until it forms a small bundle.

    6. Place the sample in the center of the bundle.

    7. Place the bundle in the larger hole in the moveable plate, and slide the bundle back into the small plunger hole.

    8. Push the plunger up against the bundle, and tighten the right screw.

    9. Using a razor, evenly slice the top of the sample protruding from the plunger hole.

    10. Set the moveable plate back on the microtome, and secure using the large screws.

    11. Slightly loosen the small right screw, and push back to tighten the packing on the bundle. Tighten screw.

    12. Turn the microtome dial clockwise, watching carefully, until the bundle begins to move upward.

    13. Cut the protruding sample off smoothly and evenly with a razor blade.

    14. Dial the microtome up one or two additional notches.

    15. Brush a thin film of nail polish over the sample. Allow to dry.

    16. Carefully remove the sample and nail polish using a razor blade and a gentle sawing motion.

    17. Repeat steps 14–16 as necessary.

    18. Mount the sample in a suitable mounting medium for viewing on the microscope.

9. Make a liquid mount of the hair sample. If a cross section was not made, examine the hair to determine the variation of the diameter along the shaft, so that a cross-sectional assessment can be made of the longitudinal view.

10. Examine the hair using the compound light microscope.

11. Document the microscopic characteristics of the hair: color, form, and diameter.

12. Examine the hair for any additional microscopic characteristics that would aid in the identification of the hair type. Document the additional characteristics of each hair: pigmentation distribution and density, root shape, cuticle, medulla width and distribution, and distal end condition.

13. Draw one identifying characteristic for each hair, including sample information and magnification.
14. Do your results agree with the known characteristics for the racial group or somatic region for your hair sample? List the identifying macroscopic and microscopic characteristics for the hair that agree.
15. Repeat steps 1–13 for hairs from the other groups.
16. Obtain an unknown hair.
17. Repeat steps 1–12 to identify the unknown hair. Complete the Human Hair Characteristics Worksheet for an unknown sample. In addition to the worksheet, include your unknown hair number and what you identified the hair to be. State your reasons for your decision, and defend your conclusion.

Report Requirements

Include all drawings, calculations, and other information obtained during the laboratory procedure. Notes and/or drawings should include the sample identification, magnification, and a complete description.

Report Questions

1. Describe each term as it relates to human hair: root, cuticle, cortex, medulla, and distal tip. Include drawings and/or examples with your description for each term.
2. Describe your examination procedure for the unknown sample.
3. List all of the macroscopic characteristics of human hair. Give an example of each.
4. List all of the microscopic characteristics of human hair. Give an example of each.
5. What is a cross section of human hair? How is it prepared?
6. List the macroscopic and microscopic characteristics of hair that are used to classify hair into the three racial groups. Give an example of why a racial group might not be able to be determined from a single questioned hair.
7. Does hair have enough identifying characteristics that allow it to be individualized to a person?
8. A hair examiner has examined an unknown hair and a set of known head hairs in a case. If all of the characteristics examined have been similar, write a statement that the examiner can use in reporting the results of the comparison.

Human Hair Characteristics Worksheet

SAMPLE _____

Macroscopic:
    Color   _____
    Length   _____
    Shaft form _____
    Diameter   _____

Microscopic:
    Cuticle appearance: _____
    Cortex:
        Pigmentation color _____
        Pigmentation distribution _____
        Pigmentation density _____
        Other characteristics _____
    Medulla:
        Appearance _____
        Distribution _____
    Root appearance: _____
    Tip appearance: _____
    Special characteristics: _____

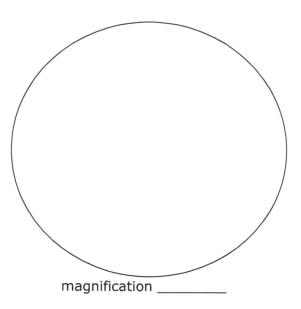

magnification _____

Chapter 17

Experiment 17C: Human Hair Examinations and Comparisons

Recommended pre-lab reading assignments:

Barnett PD, Ogle RR. Probabilities and Human Hair Comparisons. *Journal of Forensic Science.* 1982; 27(2): 272–278.

Deadman HA. Human Hair Comparisons Based on Microscopic Characteristics. *Proceedings of the International Symposium on Forensic Hair Comparisons.* 1985: 45–49.

Gaudette BD. Forensic Hair Comparison. *Crime Laboratory Digest.* 1985; 12: 44–59.

Objective

Upon completion of this practical exercise, the student will have developed a basic understanding of:

1. general characteristics of human hair
2. use of the stereomicroscope to visualize the characteristics of hair
3. use of the compound or comparison light microscope to visualize the characteristics of hair
4. cross sections of human hair
5. comparison of human hair

Introduction

Human hair comparisons are performed to determine possible associations between people, places, and objects. This association is accomplished through the comparison of macroscopic and microscopic characteristics. Learning to recognize the characteristics and the range found within an individual's known hair sample allows the forensic scientist to identify and compare human hair. Careful examination of known samples and unknown hair samples can provide information as to similarities or dissimilarities for an investigation.

Since such a variety of macroscopic and microscopic characteristics are found among hairs within a single source, it is important to obtain a suitable sample when performing comparisons. Known samples should be collected from each somatic region that hair comparisons might be performed. So, if the unknowns to be compared are both head and pubic hairs, a known sample should be collected from each region. It is also necessary to have a known sample that contains the range of characteristics found within a particular source. This should include hairs from all growth phases and from several locations from that particular body area. For example, head hair should be collected by combing and pulling to obtain all growth phases and from several

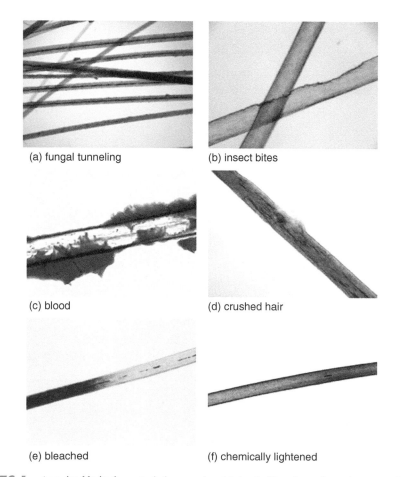

(a) fungal tunneling   (b) insect bites

(c) blood   (d) crushed hair

(e) bleached   (f) chemically lightened

Figure 17C-1   Acquired hair characteristics may be obtained either through environmental conditions or by artificial treatments. (a) Fungal tunneling (viewed as dark irregular spaces) are air pockets that are caused by fungal growth. (b) Insect bites are found on hair that has been discarded for a time period (dustballs, etc.). (c) Blood can leave colored material along the hair shaft. (d) The type of damage to a hair can also be determined at times; this hair has a crushed portion. The color of hair can be chemically changed by (e) bleaching or (f) dyeing.

different areas of the head: center, back, front, and sides. This typically provides samples that contain the range of characteristics that might be found from that source. In most instances, suitable known samples are found if the quantity of the known sample is sufficient. 50–100 hairs for head hair and 25–50 hairs for pubic hair are usually considered sufficient quantity. However, in some instances more or less can be used. Once a suitable known sample has been obtained, the macroscopic and microscopic characteristics are determined.

Unknown hairs are examined next to identify the range of macroscopic and microscopic characteristics displayed by that particular sample. Comparison of these characteristics to the range found within the known sample can then be performed.

A large number of macroscopic and microscopic characteristics should be considered when performing human hair examinations and comparisons. Many of these have been discussed in Experiments 17 and 17B. Environmental characteristics, acquired traits, artificial treatments, and diseases provide additional characteristics that can individualize a hair sample. Environmental traits are characteristics that the hair acquires, such as fungal growth or insect bites (Figure 17C-1a and 17C-1b). Acquired traits usually involve changes or damage to the hair. In many situations, hair care products such as hair spray or gel may be visible along the hair shaft. Blood may also be visible on the hair shaft (Figure 17C-1c). Various types of damage can also be seen on the hair. Most of the time, this involves the tip end of the hair; however, some characteristics, like singeing and crushed areas (Figure 17C-1d), may be found along the entire hair shaft. Artificial treatments are chemical actions that are done to the hair. These may be semi-permanent or permanent (Figure 17C-1e and 17C-1f).

Characteristics caused by disease are more rarely viewed; however, they can be important abnormalities when identified. Some abnormalities produce defects in the hair shaft (e.g., areas of swellings, twisting), while others may damage the hair shaft (e.g., splits and breaks) or change the appearance of the root (see Figures 17C-2 and 17C-3).

Table 17C-1 contains a summary of human hair characteristics and possible descriptions for each.

An understanding of the macroscopic and microscopic characteristics found in human hair allows the forensic scientist to perform human hair comparisons. Human hair comparisons

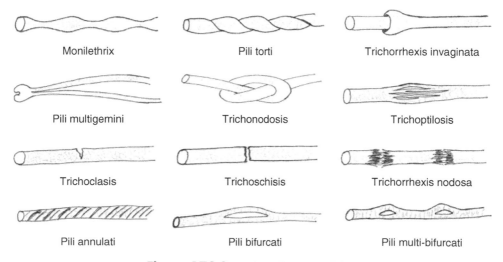

Figure 17C-2 Hair shaft abnormalities.

Alopecia areata   Alopecia difusa

Alopecia pityrodes   Alopecia seborrhoicum

Figure 17C-3 Hair root abnormalities.

Table 17C-1 Human hair characteristics and possible descriptions for each.

Macroscopic characteristics	Descriptions
Color	White/gray, blonde, red, brown, black, other
Length	Usually measured in centimeters or inches
Shaft form	Straight, waved, curled, kinked, curved
Diameter	Fine, medium, coarse, variations
Microscopic characteristics	
Color	Colorless, yellow, red, brown, black, opaque, other
Secondary color	Gray, yellow, red
Intensifier	Light, dark
Pigmentation distribution	Uniform, peripheral, one-sided
Pigmentation granule color	Red, brown
Pigmentation granule size	Small, medium, large
Pigmentation granule density	Light, medium, heavy
Pigmentation granule aggregation size	Small, medium, large
Pigmentation aggregation shape	Streaked, clumped, patchy
Pigmentation aggregation density	Light, medium, heavy
Shaft shape	Buckled, shouldered, convoluted, undulated, twisted, uniform
Cross-sectional shape	Round, oval, flattened, triangular
Root characteristics	
Root present	Anagen, catagen, telogen, sheathed, follicular tag, postmortem changes
Root absent	Square cut, angular cut, angular cut with tail, crushed, broken, singed, postmortem changes
Cuticle characteristics	
Cuticle thickness	Thin, moderate, thick
Cuticle color	Transparent, translucent, yellow

Table 17C-1 (*Continued*)

Macroscopic characteristics	Descriptions
Cuticle outer margin	Smooth, flattened, serrated, looped, ragged, cracked
Cuticle inner margin	Distinct, pigment gapping
Cortex characteristics	
Cellular texture	Apparent, not apparent, extreme
Ovoid bodies	Size, distribution, abundance
Cortical fusi	Size, shape, location, distribution, abundance
Medulla characteristics	
Medulla continuity	Absent, continuous, discontinuous
Medulla appearance	Opaque, translucent, absent
Medulla width	Fine, moderate, coarse, double
Tip characteristics	Tapered, rounded, square cut, angular cut, angular cut with tail, frayed, split, crushed, broken, singed, abraded
Artificial treatments	Bleaching, dyeing (permanent, semi-permanent, color rinses), permanent waves, relaxers, hair sprays and gels, crème rinses
Environmental or acquired characteristics	Lice, mold, fungal tunneling, insect bite marks, debris, blood
Diseases	Pili annulati, trichoschisis, monilethix, trichorrhexis nodosa, trichorrhexis invaginata, pili torti, trichonodosis, cartilage hair hypoplasis, trichoptilosis, trichoclasis, pili multigemini, pili bifurcati, alopecia

involve the use of a variety of microscopes, techniques, and instruments. Initially a stereomicroscope is used to examine the hair for macroscopic characteristics. Further testing can be performed using a compound or comparison light microscope to determine the microscopic characteristics of the hair sample. To do this, a cross section and either a semi-permanent or permanent mount are utilized. Whereas most head and pubic hair samples contain characteristics worthy of further comparison, hairs from other somatic regions are generally identified but not compared to known samples. Once the known sample has been examined, characteristics can then be compared for the unknown sample. This is usually performed on a comparison compound microscope (see Figure 17C-4).

A comparison compound microscope is composed of two compound microscopes that are connected by an optical bridge. The bridge contains prisms and mirrors that are used to direct the light to a common set of oculars. A set of knobs is used to adjust the field of view, so that items can be viewed from either microscope independently or combined. In the combined view, the field of view is split into side-by-side views of portions from each microscope. This allows the examiner to view two items side-by-side on a microscopic scale (see Figure 17C-5). The comparison compound microscope usually uses a mechanical stage instead of a rotating stage. This allows for precise alignment of two hairs.

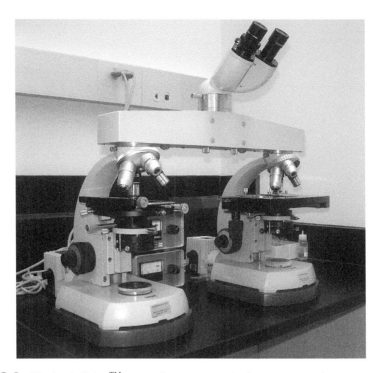

Figure 17C-4   The basic Zeiss ™ comparison compound microscope contains two compound micro-scopes connected by an optical bridge. This allows viewing and comparison of two samples within one field of view.

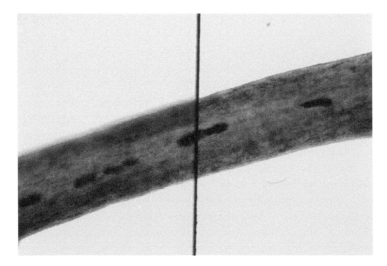

Figure 17C-5   The split field of view as seen on the comparison microscope. This allows comparison of known and unknown samples within the same viewing field.

If all the characteristics displayed by the unknown hair are found within the known sample, an association may be reached. The examiner may state that a hair containing microscopic characteristics associated with a particular somatic origin and racial group is similar to a known sample. However, when an association is reached as to a possible origin of the hair, it should be pointed out that a similarity to a known sample does not constitute a positive means of identification (i.e., exclude the possibility of another similar source).

Equipment and Supplies

Stereomicroscope

Compound light microscope with objectives of various magnifications (e.g., 4X, 10X, 20X, and 40X) and focusing ocular with micrometer scale

Comparison microscope with objectives of various magnifications (e.g., 4X, 10X, 20X, and 40X) and focusing ocular with micrometer scale

Micro kit

Microscope slides and cover slips

Mounting medium (a colorless mounting medium in the refractive index range of 1.5–1.60)

Nail polish and/or Polaroid film coating

Known human hair samples

Unknown hair samples

Safety

Use standard laboratory safety procedures as described in guidelines set by your instructor. Be cautious of microscope light levels to avoid eye damage. Know the hazards associated with the mounting mediums, and use them with appropriate precautions as set by your instructor. Dispose of glass in an appropriate container.

Part I: Human Hair Examinations

A worksheet for examination notes may be found at the end of the experiment.

Procedure

Complete a known human hair worksheet for each sample.

1. Obtain two known samples of human hair.
2. Examine the first sample with the stereomicroscope.
3. Measure the range of length of several hairs in the sample. Record the value in centimeters or inches.
4. Record the colors that may be present. It is important to note any color changes.
5. Note the shaft form of the hairs.
6. Describe the diameter of the hairs.
7. Using a compound microscope set up with Köhler illumination. Determine the cross-sectional shape. This can be done by making a cross section (refer to Experiment 17B if necessary) or from a longitudinal liquid-mounted hair.

8. Make a liquid mount of the hair sample. Remember: You want to obtain the range found within the sample, so more than one hair should be examined.
9. Examine the hairs using the compound light microscope.
10. Document the microscopic characteristics of the hair: color, shaft form, diameter, cross section, root, cuticle, cortex, medulla, and any special characteristics.
11. Draw four identifying characteristics for the hair sample, including information such as sample, magnification, and so on.
12. Examine the second known sample following steps 2–11.

Part II: Human Hair Comparisons

1. Obtain an unknown hair.
2. Repeat steps 2–11 of Part I with the unknown hair. It will be necessary to first determine if the sample is a hair, and if it is animal or human.
3. Compare the macroscopic and microscopic characteristics that you have documented to the known samples analyzed in Part I. Is the unknown hair sample similar to one of the known hair samples?
4. If possible, use a comparison microscope to examine both samples simultaneously. If you believe that the samples are similar, find areas in the known sample that have similar characteristics as those in the unknown hair. Draw what you see for the root end, tip, and sections of the shaft, showing cuticle, cortex, and medulla similarities.
5. Include the unknown hair number, and state the result of the hair comparison. Fully defend your conclusion.

Report Requirements

Include all drawings, calculations, and other information obtained during the laboratory procedure. Notes and/or drawings should include the sample identification, magnification, and a complete description.

Report Questions

1. Why is it possible to perform human hair comparisons?
2. How is a human hair comparison conducted?
3. What percentage of the population would have similar characteristics?
4. Can a hair be associated with only one person? Explain your answer.
5. How many head hairs must be taken and examined in order to determine if a questioned hair sample could have come from an individual? Why is the number so large?
6. How many pubic hairs must be taken and examined in order to determine if a questioned hair sample could have come from an individual? Why is the number so large?
7. Is it possible for an unknown hair from a murder scene to be similar to a known sample, but for that person to have no involvement in the crime? Explain your answer.
8. Is it possible for an unknown hair from a murder scene to be dissimilar to a known sample, but for that person to be involved in the crime? Explain your answer.

Human Hair Characteristics Worksheet
KNOWN SAMPLE

Macroscopic:
  Color   _____
  Length_____
  Shaft form   _____
  Diameter   _____

Microscopic: magnification _____
  Cuticle appearance: _____
  Cortex:
    Pigmentation color _____
    Pigmentation distribution _____
    Pigmentation density _____
    Other characteristics _____
  Medulla:
    Appearance _____
    Distribution _____
  Root appearance: _____
  Tip appearance: _____
  Special characteristics: _____

Magnification _____

Magnification _____

Magnification _____

Magnification _____

Human Hair Characteristics Worksheet
UNKNOWN SAMPLE

Macroscopic:
    Color _____
    Length _____
    Shaft form _____
    Diameter _____

Microscopic: magnification _____
    Cuticle appearance: _____
    Cortex:
        Pigmentation color _____
        Pigmentation distribution _____
        Pigmentation density _____
        Other characteristics _____
    Medulla:
        Appearance _____
        Distribution _____
    Root appearance: _____
    Tip appearance: _____
    Special characteristics: _____

Magnification _____

Magnification _____

Magnification _____

Magnification _____

Chapter 17

Experiment 17D: Evaluation of Human Hair for DNA

Recommended pre-lab reading assignments:

Dizinno J, Wilson M, Budowie B. Typing of DNA Derived from Hairs. In: Robertson J, ed. *Forensic Examination of Hair*. London: Taylor & Francis, 1999; 155–174.

Linch C, Smith S, Prahlow J. Evaluation of the Human Hair Root for DNA Typing Subsequent to Microscopic Comparison. *Journal of Forensic Sciences*. 1998; 43(2): 305–314.

Objective

Upon completion of this practical exercise, the student will have developed a basic understanding of:

1. development of the hair follicle
2. hair growth and hair growth phases
3. basic root characteristics of the hair growth phases (anagen, catagen, and telogen)
4. use of the stereomicroscope to visualize the roots of the hair
5. use of the compound light microscope to visualize the roots of the hair

Introduction

With the advent of deoxyribonucleic acid (DNA), hair examinations have taken on additional importance. While microscopic examinations provide physical, phenotype, variable, and qualitative information, DNA provides genetic, genotype, invariant, and quantifiable information. These are complementary techniques, and both should be utilized in forensic work.

To evaluate hair roots for DNA, one must understand the growth of the hair follicle and hair. The hair follicle develops through several stages. Pre-germ stage takes place approximately 8 weeks after conception. In this stage, the cells begin to cluster in the basal layer of the epidermis. This begins the development of a protrusion on the underside of the epidermis that becomes the hair germ, which is the next stage. The hair germ stage begins around 11 weeks. The epidermal basal cells begin to become columnar, with elongated nuclei, perpendicular to the skin. This produces a bulge in the external epidermis and also a downward growth in the dermis. Additional cells begin to accumulate, causing the formation of the dermal papilla.

In the hair peg stage, continued cell division causes the hair germ to elongate further into the dermis as a solid column of epithelial cells. The cells advance longitudinally in a manner that creates a concave end. The cells at the leading edge of the hair peg push further down, creating the dermal papilla. The outer layer of the elongated hair germ is continuous with the basal layer, forming the sheath. Tissue differentiation begins at the bulbous peg stage. Two epithelial swellings develop along the posterior side of the follicle. The lower swelling is the site of the bulge, where the arrector pili muscle attaches. The upper swelling contains lipids and is the site of the sebaceous gland. The advancing end of the developing follicle broadens, enclosing the dermal papilla and forming the base of the hair bulb. The central cells in the peg begin to elongate backward, forming the hair canal. Now that the follicle has been formed, the cells in the hair bulb begin to divide. The inner root sheath differentiates, forming the hair cone. The hair cone elongates, pushed upward by the dividing cells below. When the tip of the hair cone is about halfway up the follicle, it begins to harden. The new hair finally breaks through the skin around 19–21 weeks. The initial hairs developed are called lanugo hairs. These hairs are shed prior to birth and replaced by new lanugo or vellus hairs. Vellus hairs are extremely soft and fine and are replaced by terminal hairs. Terminal hairs are commonly examined in casework.

Once the hair follicle has developed, hair growth begins a continuous process of cell proliferation, cell differentiation, and cell synthesis. This continuous growth process occurs in several zones of the hair follicle. The structure and development of these zones are attributed to several regions of the hair follicle. The root is the region of active cell division. The greatest cell activity is at the widest portion of the dermal papilla. The cells in this area are undifferentiated and characterized by a high nuclear-to-cytoplasmic ratio. These cells actively divide. They are several layers thick and begin to give way to concentric layers that will form the follicle and hair shaft. Twenty percent of these cells differentiate into the hair fiber, while the remaining cells make up the sheath. Changes can be seen in the medulla cells as they begin to move upward from the dermal papilla. Differentiation begins, and amorphous granules appear. The granules vary in size and become irregular as the nuclei degenerate with the upward movement. The granules fuse, giving rise to hardened proteins. With the fusing, intercellular spaces are created, forming the central core of the hair fiber. Cortical cells are derived from further cell division around the bulb. As cells move upward surrounding the medulla cells, they elongate into filaments and align themselves with the axis of the hair fiber. Cortical cells harden and dehydrate as they reach the keratogenous zone. Cuticle cells arise from a single layer surrounding the cortex cells. The cells undergo change as they move upward from the bulb, creating an elongated flattened cell. The inner and outer root sheaths are layers surrounding the cuticle cells. Maturation and hardening of the inner root sheath form and shape the hair fiber. The outer root sheath is the outermost layer of the follicle. Once the follicle has developed a hair fiber, the follicle continues this process of ongoing hair growth in a cycle. The cycle is composed of the anagen, catagen, and telogen phases.

The anagen phase is a period of high metabolic and mitotic activity. This phase will last approximately 17 weeks to 8 years. Eighty to ninety percent of the hair on a head is in the anagen

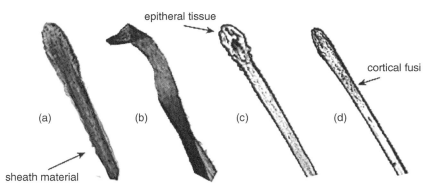

Figure 17D-1 (a) Hair root in the anagen phase. The root end is heavily pigmented, and a large amount of sheath material is present. (b) Hair root in the anagen phase. The shape of this root is distorted because of the force used to dislodge the hair; however, the root end still has heavy pigmentation and a slight amount of sheath material present. (c) A hair root in the catagen phase. Note the epithelial tissue present and the lack of pigmentation in the root area. (d) A hair root in the telogen phase. The hair contains no tissue or pigmentation in the root end; however, the formation of cortical fusi has begun.

phase. Because hair in the anagen phase is alive, it is strongly attached to the dermal papilla, so the detached root will be fleshy and sheath material may be present. Since it is actively growing, the root will be pigmented (see Figure 17D-1a and 17D-1b).

The catagen phase is a period of transition. The follicle undergoes morphological changes and stops growing. This phase will last approximately 2–3 weeks. About two percent of the hair on a head is in the catagen phase. Because hair in the catagen phase is transitional, the detached hair will display a disintegrating root sheath that will appear brush-like. Pigmentation is no longer being produced, so the root will be lacking in color. The epithelial sac may be visible, but no sheath material will be present (see Figure 17D-1c).

The telogen phase is a period of resting. This phase will last approximately 3–4 months. About eight percent of the hair on a head is in the telogen phase. Because hair in the telogen phase is resting, the root shows no pigment or coloration. The medulla, when present, is distant from the root, and no sheath material will be attached (see Figure 17D-1d). As a hair reaches the telogen phase, it rests. After a short period of time, a new hair begins an anagen phase in the hair follicle. This action helps to naturally push out the telogen hair.

DNA can be analyzed from hair using two techniques: nuclear DNA and mitochondrial DNA. For successful DNA results, the type of DNA technique utilized on human hair depends on the growth phase of the hair, thus the need for understanding the growth phases. If a hair is in the anagen stage, nuclear DNA is contained with the root and sheath material. If the hair is in the catagen or telogen stage, and if there is a good amount of follicular tag, nuclear DNA may be possible. However, if the hair does not have sheath material or a follicular tag or does not have a root, mitochondrial DNA may be possible. The length of the hair is then important, since this type of analysis generally takes approximately 1 centimeter of hair. Table 17D-1 compares the parameters utilized when determining the extraction techniques for nuclear DNA and mitochondrial DNA.

Hairs that are in the anagen phase have the root sheath attached; however, this may become dislodged as it dries. Roots appear fleshy, and at times, a portion of the dermal papilla may be attached. Pigment granules will be present in the roots of anagen-phase hairs. The hair shaft may be twisted, stretched, or broken since force is required for removal. Hairs that are in the catagen

Table 17D-1   Criteria utilized when deciding on DNA technique for extraction.

nDNA	mtDNA
• Sheath material present • Anagen-phase or early catagen-phase hair (cells in the root area are more easily extracted than differentiated cells further down the shaft) • Large root diameter • Length of hair: 2 cm	• Telogen-phase hair • Length of hair: 1 cm

phase may contain dried root sheath. The root may appear club shaped. Generally, the root sheath is dried up. Pigmentation in the root area is diminishing and, when present, is located more distally. Telogen-phase hairs have no sheath material around the root area. There is no pigmentation close to the root area and, likewise, no medulla close to the root area. Cortical fusi will be present near the root.

The average person has approximately 2 million hair follicles. Approximately 100,000 of these hair follicles are on the head. The average person will lose approximately 100 hairs per day. These are normally hairs that are in the catagen or telogen phase, since they are ready to be shed. However, in addition to these hairs, other hairs may become evidence through transfer. A microscopic evaluation of hairs should be performed prior to DNA extractions. The stereomicroscope provides low-level magnification that allows for viewing of the initial characteristics of the root of a hair. Further examination can be performed using the compound light microscope for more detail. The microscopic assessment of the hair will determine which type of DNA analysis should be utilized for the best results.

Equipment and Supplies

Stereomicroscope

Compound light microscope with objectives of various magnifications (e.g., 4X, 10X, 20X, and 40X) and calibrated focusing ocular with micrometer scale

Micro kit

Microscope slides and cover slips

Mounting medium (a colorless mounting medium in the refractive index range of 1.5–1.60)

Human hair

Unknown hair samples

Safety

Use standard laboratory safety procedures as described in guidelines set by your instructor. Be cautious of microscope light levels to avoid eye damage. Know the hazards associated with the mounting mediums, and use them with appropriate precautions as set by your instructor. Dispose of glass in an appropriate container.

Part I: Evaluation of Human Hair for DNA

Procedure

1. Mount hair samples onto microscope slides using techniques previously learned. (You can use previously mounted hair also.)
2. Examine the hair using the stereomicroscope.
3. Note the characteristics of each root, if present, and the length of the hair.
4. Next examine the same hair using the compound light microscope. Remember to check the microscope to ensure that samples will be viewed using Köhler illumination.
5. Examine the hair for the microscopic characteristics of each root/hair. Draw what you see.
6. Observe several hair samples using steps 1–5.

Report Requirements

Include all drawings, calculations, and other information obtained during the laboratory procedure. Notes and/or drawings should include the sample identification, magnification, and a complete description.

Report Questions

1. Describe each term as it relates to hair: anagen, catagen, and telogen. Include drawings and/or examples with your description for each term.
2. List three characteristics that are used to distinguish anagen hairs from telogen hairs.
3. Why is it necessary to determine the growth phase of hair prior to DNA extractions?
4. What are the criteria for nuclear DNA (nDNA) hair samples?
5. What are the criteria for mitochondrial DNA (mtDNA) hair samples?

Recommended and Further Reading

Aitken CGG, Robertson J. The Value of Microscopic Features in the Examination of Human Head Hairs – Statistical-Analysis of Questionnaire Returns. *Journal of Forensic Sciences.* 1986; 31(2): 546–562.

Barnett PD, Ogle RR. Probabilities and Human Hair Comparisons. *Journal of Forensic Sciences.* 1982; 27(2): 272–278.

Bisbing RE. Forensic Identification and Association of Human Hair. In: Saferstein R, ed. *Forensic Science Handbook*, 2nd ed. Upper Saddle River, NJ: Pearson Education, 2002; 390–428.

Bruner H, Coman B. *The Identification of Mammalian Hair*. Melbourne: Inkata Press, 1974.

Deadman HA. Human Hair Comparisons Based on Microscopic Characteristics. *Proceedings of the International Symposium on Forensic Hair Comparisons.* 1985: 45–49.

Deedrick DW, Koch SL. Microscopy of Hair: A Practical Guide and Manual for Human Hair. *Forensic Science Communications* [Online]. 2004.

Deedrick DW, Koch SL. Microscopy of Hair Part I: A Practical Guide and Manual for Human Hair. *Forensic Science Communications.* 2004; 6(1).

Deedrick DW, Koch SL. Microscopy of Hair Part II: A Practical Guide and Manual for Animal Hairs. *Forensic Science Communications.* 2004; 6(3).

Degaetano DH, Kempton JB, Rowe WF. Fungal Tunneling of Hair from a Buried Body. *Journal of Forensic Sciences.* 1992; 37(4): 1048–1054.

Dizinno J, Wilson M, Budowle B. Typing of DNA Derived from Hairs. In: Robertson J, ed. *Forensic Examination of Hair.* London: Taylor & Francis, 1999; 155–174.

Forensic Science Research and Training Center (FBI Academy). *Proceedings of the International Symposium on Forensic Hair Comparisons.* Washington, DC: Laboratory Division, Federal Bureau of Investigation, and US Government Printing Office, 1987.

Garn SM. Examination of Hair under Polarizing Microscope. *Annals of the New York Academy of Sciences.* 1951; 53: 649–652.

Gaudette BD. Forensic Hair Comparison. *Crime Laboratory Digest.* 1985; 12: 44–59.

Hicks JW. *Microscopy of Hairs: A Practical Guide and Manual.* Washington, DC: Federal Bureau of Investigation and US Government Printing Office, 1977.

Higuchi R, Vonberoldingen CH, Sensabaugh GF, Erlich HA. DNA Typing from Single Hairs. *Nature.* 1988; 332(6164): 543–546.

Houck MM, Bisbing RE. Forensic Human Hair Examination and Comparison in the 21st Century. *Journal of Forensic Sciences.* 2005; 17: 51–66.

Houck MM, Bodowle B. Correlation of Microscopic and Mitochondrial DNA Hair Comparisons. *Journal of Forensic Sciences.* 2002; 47: 964–967.

Houck MM, Siegel JA. *Fundamentals of Forensic Science*, 3rd ed. Amsterdam: Elsevier Academic Press, 2015; 291–311.

Huffman JE, Wallace JR. *Wildlife Forensics: Methods and Applications.* Chichester, UK: John Wiley & Sons, Ltd, 2012.

Kolowski JC, Petraco N, Wallace MM, De Forest PR, Prinz M. A Comparison Study of Hair Examination Methodologies. *Journal of Forensic Sciences.* 2004; 49(6): 1253–1255.

Lee HC, DeForest PR. *Forensic Hair Examination.* Newark, NJ: Matthew Bender, 1984.

Linch CA, Smith SL, Prahlow JA. Evaluation of the Human Hair Root for DNA Typing Subsequent to Microscopic Comparison. *Journal of Forensic Sciences.* 1998; 43: 305–314.

McCrone WC. Characterization of Human Hair by Light Microscopy. *Microscope.* 1998: 15–30.

Moeller MR, Fey P, Sachs H. Hair Analysis as Evidence in Forensic Cases. *Forensic Science International.* 1993; 63(43–53).

Moore JE. A Key for the Identification of Animal Hairs. *Journal of the Forensic Science Society.* 1988; 28(5–6): 335–339.

Moore TD, Spence LE, Dubnolle CE. *Identification of the Dorsal Guard Hairs of Some Mammals of Wyoming.* Cheyenne, WY: Wyoming Game and Fish Department, 1974.

Niyogi SK. Abnormality of Hair Shaft Due to Disease: Its Forensic Importance. *Journal of Forensic Medicine.* 1968; 15: 148–150.

Ogle RR. *Atlas of Human Hair Microscopic Characteristics.* Boca Raton, FL: CRC Press, 1998.

Ogle RR, Fox MJ. *Atlas of Human Hair.* Boca Raton, FL: CRC, 1999.

Ogle RR, Mitosinka GT. A Rapid Technique for Preparing Hair Cuticle Scale Casts. *Journal of Forensic Sciences.* 1973; 18: 82.

Petraco N. Microscopical Method to Aid in the Identification of Animal Hair. *Microscope.* 1987: 83–91.

Petraco N. Modified Technique for the Cross-Sectioning of Hair and Fibers. *Journal of Police Science Administration.* 1981; 9: 448.

Petraco N, Fraas C, X CF, R DP. Morphological and Evidential Significance of Human Hair Roots. *Journal of Forensic Sciences.* 1988; 33: 68–76.

Quadros J, Monteiro ELD. Collecting and Preparing Mammal Hairs for Identification with Optical Microscopy. *Revista Brasileira De Zoologia.* 2006; 23(1): 274–278.

Robertson J. *Forensic Examination of Hair.* London: Taylor & Francis, 1999.

Roe GM, Cook R, North C. An Evaluation of Mountants for Use in Forensic Hair Examinations. *Journal of Forensic Sciences Society.* 1991; 31: 59–65.

Scientific Working Group on Materials Analysis (SWGMAT). Position on Hair Evidence. *Journal of Forensic Sciences.* 2009; 54(5).

Smith SL, Linch CA. A Review of Major Factors Contributing to Errors in Human Hair Association by Microscopy. *American Journal of Forensic Medicine and Pathology.* 1999; 20(3): 269–273.

Spence LE. *Study of Identifying Characteristics of Mammal Hair.* Cheyenne, WY: Wildlife Disease Research Laboratory, Wyoming Game and Fish Commission, 1963.

Strauss MAT. Forensic Characterization of Human Hair. *Microscope.* 1983: 15–29.

Zhou Y-W, Wang Z-W. Identification of Animal Hair by Examination under Polarizing Microscope. *Sichuan Journal of Zoology.* 2006; 25(3): 614.

Chapter 18

Experiment 18: Feather Examinations

Recommended pre-lab reading assignment:

Dove CJ, Koch SL. Microscopy of Feathers: A Practical Guide for Forensic Feather Identification. *Journal of the American Society of Trace Evidence Examiners.* 2010; (1)1: 15–61.

Objective

Upon completion of this practical exercise, the student will have developed a basic understanding of:

1. general characteristics of a feather
2. use of the stereomicroscope to visualize the macroscopic characteristics of a feather
3. use of the compound light microscope to visualize the microscopic characteristics of a feather

Introduction

Feathers are one of the epidermal growths that form an outer covering on birds. Just like hair on humans, feathers are composed of the protein beta-keratin and develop from follicles. Also, each feather grows from a small outgrowth of the skin called a papilla. As the feather matures, the tip gets pushed away from the papilla, forming the quill or calamus. The feather's structure develops as proteins are laid down around the surface of this outward growth. This begins to form the central shaft of the feather that is called the rachis. As the growth continues, barbs are formed and also secondary branches called barbules. The color of a feather is determined by the presence of pigments. Melanins such as pheomelanin and eumelanin provide beige and brown shades and also gray and black colors. Carotenoids provide yellow, orange, and red shades, while porphyrins produce red and green coloration. Blue shades are generally a product of light reflecting from different layers of structures within the feather. White feathers lack pigmentation. As the feather continues to grow, a protective sheath covers the feather and helps it maintain the cylindrical shape until it matures. Once mature, the sheath falls off and the feather unfurls.

Feathers are classified into several categories according to the structure and location on a bird's body: wing, tail, contour, semiplume, down, filoplume, and bristle. The wing feathers, also called regimes, are characterized by a uniform surface that is created by an interlocking microstructure. The wing feathers are asymmetrical, which prevents midair twisting. Tail feathers, or rectrices, have an interlocking microstructure similar to wing feathers; however, they are typically arranged in a fan shape and display levels of asymmetry toward the outer pairs, blending into the contour feathers. These feathers help support steering while in flight. Contour feathers, also called coverts, cover the bird's body and help streamline its shape. The tip end of a contour feather is smooth, creating a waterproof surface, which covers the fluffy area of the feather close to the bird's body. These feathers provide lift and drag as the bird flies. Semiplumes have no interlocking barbules, so the fluffy structure provides insulating warmth to the bird. Down feathers are similar to semiplumes but with even looser branching barbs. They are relatively short, providing another insulating layer to trap the bird's body heat. Filoplumes are very short feathers with very few barbs. Filoplumes sense the position of the contour feathers. Bristles are the simplest feather and lack barb branching. They are commonly found on the head, protecting the eyes and face.

Although feathers come in a variety of forms, they are all made up of the same basic parts that allow identification of a feather: calamus, rachis, barbs, and barbules. The calamus is the hollow base of the feather. The calamus narrows, forming the center shaft of the feather that is called the rachis. Barbs are the main branches off the rachis. These basic parts are shown in Figure 18-1a. Barbules are secondary branches that fuse off the barb (see Figure 18-1b). Barbules can be either smooth (plumulaceous) or interlocked into nearby barbules (pennaceous). Plumulaceous

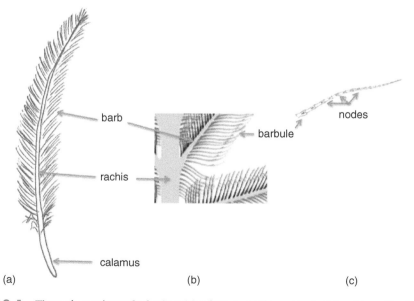

Figure 18-1 The main portions of a feather: (a) calamus, rachis, and barb; (b) rachis and barb enlarged to show smaller barbules; and (c) barbule microscopic view to show node features.

barbules have a loose feather structure that creates a flexible, fluffy surface. These barbules are relatively long and help trap air close to a bird's body, providing warmth. The pennaceous barbules may have hooklets, which interlock to create a smooth, flat surface. These barbules form a windproof and waterproof barrier that allows the bird to fly and stay dry.

When conducting a feather examination, several characteristics help in identification. The overall morphology and pigmentation of the feather are important, but when paired with microscopic features of the barbules, identifications of family or species can be determined in many instances. Initial examinations involve noting the type of feather. While all feather types might be obtained in forensic casework, typically it is the contour feather that provides the most information for identification. This feather contains areas of both plumulaceous and pennaceous barbules. While characteristics are examined from both regions, it is the plumulaceous region that has less variation of characteristics from the same bird and same order or family.

Once the feather type has been determined, the color and patterns of the feather should also be documented so that these characteristics can be compared to a reference collection. The "Feather Atlas: Flight Feathers of North American Birds"[1] contains information on many wing and tail feathers. Colors are generally described as the most characteristic or striking color; brown, gray, black, white, black and white, blue/purple, green, yellow/orange, red/rufous, or pink. Patterns may be designated as unpatterned, two-toned, mottled, barred, spotted, colorful iridescence, dark tip, and pale tip.

Next, a closer examination is done of the barb and barbules. Once again, barbules are the secondary branches that fuse off the barbs. A barbule consists of a base and a segmented pennulum. Each segment of the pennulum is a separate cell. The main portion of the cell is the internode that thickens or swells at the distal end, creating a node. Each node holds the proximal end of the next internode. Segments connect in a tapering manner (see Figure 18-1c).

Characteristics such as node structure, node distribution and density, and pigmentation distribution help to further classify the feather. Nodes can be enlarged areas or can take on a specific shape. Because of this, nodes may be characteristic to a particular order of bird. Several structural shapes of nodes are shown in Figure 18-2. Enlarged nodes include ring and vase shapes. Ring nodes are common to the Galliformes order that includes chickens, pheasants, and turkeys. Ring nodes surround the barbule and at times may become detached, sliding loosely

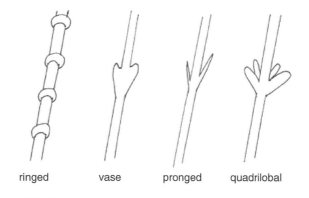

ringed   vase   pronged   quadrilobal

Figure 18-2 Node structure shapes commonly found on barbules.

---

[1] Published by the US Fish and Wildlife Service, Forensics Laboratory. Available from: http://www.fws.gov/lab/featheratlas/index.php.

along the barbule. The Passeriformes order includes more than half of all bird species. This order consists of perching birds or songbirds, such as sparrows, robins, bluejays, and chickadees, and commonly displays a vase-shaped node. Some nodes show a pronged or lobed shape, either triangular or quadrilobed. Triangular nodes are common to the Anseriformes and Psittaciformes orders. Anseriformes are waterfowl, among them the geese, ducks, and swans. Parakeets, parrots, macaws, and cockatoos are common Psittaciformes. The shape of the triangular node can distinguish Anseriformes and Psittaciformes. Smooth triangular nodes belong to Anseriformes, while sharper, pointed triangular nodes belong to Psittaciformes. Columbiformes display quadrilobed nodes. Common Columbiformes are pigeons and doves. Barbules may also show pointed prongs of varying lengths: short cilia-like, long asymmetrical, or a combination. They may also be flared or close.

The distribution and density of nodes are also important features. There are three arrangement classifications for node distribution: proximal orientation, distal orientation, and uniform. Node distribution that is classified as proximal orientation displays a prominence of nodes toward the base of the barbule. Likewise, distal orientation is more heavily shown toward the tip of the barbule. For both proximal and distal orientations, a size difference between nodes should be apparent. Uniform distribution is evenly spaced along the length of the barbule. Uniform node distribution may show a gradual size reduction toward the tip of the barbule. Density of nodes is usually determined by an examination of a 1 mm length. This can be described as: less than 10 nodes per millimeter, between 10 and 20 nodes per millimeter, between 20 and 30 nodes per millimeter, or more than 30 nodes per millimeter.

Node pigment distribution is another feature used in feather examinations. While pigmentation is usually either brown or black, it does not contribute directly to the overall plumage color. The pigmentation can be concentrated in the node structure or stippled. Pigment location within a node can be described as nodal, prenodal, or postnodal, as shown in Figure 18-3. Pigmentation can be found in three arrangements: uniform, internode, or distal (see Figure 18-4).

nodal   prenodal   postnodal

Figure 18-3 Location of node pigment: contained within the node, beginning before and into node, or in the node and extending beyond.

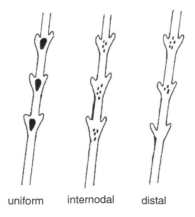

uniform   internodal   distal

Figure 18-4 Pigment distribution of nodes may be complete and uniform, intermittently spaced within the node, or distally spaced.

Some feathers display a unique feature called villi. When present, villi are tiny transparent structures usually at the base of the barb. They may be sickle-shaped as found in the order Piciformes, or knob-shaped as found in birds of the order Passeriformes.

Feathers as evidence can possess characteristics that make identifications possible at times. Because of this fact, microscopic examination of a feather presents itself as indirect or circumstantial evidence in a court of law. This evidence is generally used in conjunction with other forensic evidence.

Equipment and Supplies

Stereomicroscope

Compound light microscope with objectives of various magnifications (e.g., 4X, 10X, 20X, and 40X)

Micro kit

Cover slips

Microscope slides

Xylene

Mounting medium (a colorless mounting medium in the refractive index range of 1.5–1.60)

Feather samples

Safety

Use standard laboratory safety procedures as described in rules set by your instructor. Be cautious of microscope light levels to avoid eye damage.

Part I: Feather Examination

A worksheet for examination notes may be found at the end of the experiment.

Procedure

1. Obtain a feather sample.
2. Examine the feather using the stereomicroscope to determine the type of feather (wing, down, tail, contour, semiplume, bristle, or filoplume). Remember: It is the contour feather that provides the most information since it has both pennaceous and plumulaceous regions.
3. Note various characteristics, such as color, texture, and patterns. Draw/photograph the feather to support your findings.
4. Remove one barb for further examination.
5. Place a small drop of xylene on a microscope slide. Carefully lay the feather barb on the xylene. This will allow the feather barb to "float."
6. Next, tilt the slide slightly over a kimwipe to drain off the xylene. This will leave the barb with the barbules spread apart, allowing better viewing.
7. Apply a few drops of mounting medium and then cover the feather barb with a coverslip.

8. Using the compound light microscope, view the sample under low power (40X or 100X power). Note the details of the barb, barbule, and any pigment patterns. Draw/photograph what you see.
9. Increase your magnification to a higher power (200X or 400X). Once again, note the finer details about the barbule, particularly the nodes. Identify the type of node present, and describe the node distribution. Determine the node density for 1 mm. Draw/photograph the node.
10. Using the ocular micrometer, measure the distance between nodes and the width of a node.
11. If pigmented, describe the distribution of the pigment.
12. Repeat steps 2–11 with a second feather sample.

Report Requirements

Include all drawings/photos, calculations, and other information obtained during the laboratory procedure. Notes and/or drawings should include the sample identification, magnification, and a complete description.

Report Questions

1. From your examination of the first feather, what type of node is present? Provide as much information about the feather and node characteristics as possible.
2. Identify a possible order or species of bird. Explain the justification behind your conclusion.
3. From your examination of the second feather, what type of node is present? Provide as much information about the feather and node characteristics as possible.
4. Identify a possible order or species of bird. Explain the justification behind your conclusion.
5. Find a criminal case that used feathers as part of the forensic evidence. Write a short summary of the case and what importance the feathers played in the case result. Include: bird identification, what type of feather, and what characteristics are used to identify that bird (you may have to research beyond the criminal case).

Recommended and Further Reading

Chandler AC. A Study of the Structure of Feathers, with Reference to Their Taxonomic Significance. *University of California Publications in Zoology.* 1916; 13: 243–466.

Davies A. Micromorphology of Feathers Using the Scanning Electron Microscope. *Journal of the Forensic Science Society.* 1970; 10: 165–174.

Deedrick DW, Mullery JP. Feathers Are Not Lightweight Evidence. *FBI Law Enforcement Bulletin.* 1985; 50(9): 22–23.

Dove CJ, Koch SL. Microscopy of Feathers: A Practical Guide for Forensic Feather Identification. *The Microscope.* 2011; 59(2): 51–71.

Robertson J, Harkin C, Govan J. The Identification of Bird Feathers: Scheme for Feather Examination. *Journal of the Forensic Science Society.* 1984; 24(2): 85–98.

Scott SD, McFarland C. *Bird Feathers: A Guide to North American Species.* Mechanicsburg, PA: Stackpole Books, 2010.

Feather Characteristics Worksheet

Sample: _____

Macroscopic:

       Feather type _____

       Color _____

       Pattern _____

       Feather length _____

       Calamus length _____

       Feather width: overall _____

                asymmetrical _____

                non-asymmetrical _____

Microscopic Barb Morphology:

       Color _____

       Length _____

       Width: asymmetrical _____

              non-asymmetrical _____

Microscopic Barbule Morphology:

       Color _____

       Length _____

       Hooklets _____

       Node shape _____

       Node size: width _____ length _____

       Node distribution _____

       Node density _____

       Node pigmentation _____

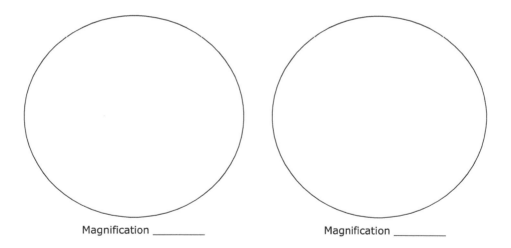

Magnification _____   Magnification _____

Chapter 19

Experiment 19: Glass Breakage Determinations

Recommended pre-lab reading assignments:

Koons RD, Buscaglia J, Bottrell M, Miller ET. Forensic Glass Comparisons. In: Saferstein R, ed. *Forensic Science Handbook*, 2nd ed. Upper Saddle River, NJ: Pearson Education, 2002; 188–189.

McJunkins SP, Thornton JI. Glass Fracture Analysis: A Review. *Forensic Science*. 1973; 2(1): 1–27.

Objective

Upon completion of this practical exercise, the student will have developed a basic understanding of:

1. float glass manufacturing method
2. identification of float glass
3. glass breakage and determination of impact points
4. determination of order of impact points
5. determination of direction of force for impact points

Introduction

Glass is one of the most common types of evidence examined with a microscope. The main components of synthetic glass are formers, fluxers, and stabilizers. Formers are compounds that, when cooled quickly after melting, will solidify without crystallizing. Common formers are silicon oxide or boric oxide. Fluxers are compounds that are added to the former to lower the melting temperature. Common fluxers are soda ash, salt cake, or potash. While the fluxers will lower the melting point of the formers, they can also create silicates that are unstable, so

Practical Forensic Microscopy: A Laboratory Manual, Second Edition. Barbara P. Wheeler.
© 2021 John Wiley & Sons Ltd. Published 2021 by John Wiley & Sons Ltd.
Companion website: www.wiley.com/go/Wheeler/Forensic

stabilizers containing elements such as calcium or magnesium are added to the glass mixture. When silicon oxide is combined with sodium carbonate and calcium oxide, soda lime glass is produced. However, if boric oxide is also added, borosilicate glass is produced. Other ingredients can also be added to provide various characteristics to the glass. Oxides are sometimes added to increase durability—specifically, hardness and refractive index (lead), chemical corrosion resistance (alumina), and temperature change resistance (boron). The color of the glass is controlled by additional elements such as copper (blue), chromium (green), manganese (violet), Fe^{3+} (yellow-brown), and Fe^{2+} (bluish-green). It is easy to see that glass has great variability in its composition.

Glass can be divided into three main manufacturing categories: flat glass, bottle or container glass, and specialty glass. Most forensic glass examinations involve flat glass. Flat glass is typically used in windows and any glass products that contain sheet glass (e.g., mirrors, windshields, and doors). Most flat glass is now produced by the float method. This process begins by feeding the ingredients into a mixer that feeds into the furnace. Full melting is achieved in the furnace at approximately 1600°C. Once the now-molten glass reaches the end of the furnace, it is fed onto a bath of heated liquid, usually molten tin. Since the liquid is so hot, irregularities in the molten glass are melted out, ensuring a flat surface. The molten glass next enters the spreader area, which stretches the glass to the desired width. The thickness of the glass is dictated by the speed of the float and spreader process. Toward the end of the spreader area, the molten glass enters an annealing phase. Annealing is the controlled heating and/or cooling during glass production that reduces the residual strain within the glass. This phase cools the glass to 200°C. Once cooled, the glass finally enters a cutting, stacking, and offloading area. Float glass will exhibit a white fluorescence when illuminated with short-wave UV light (254 nm) on a non-fluorescent background because minute amounts of molten tin become mixed with the molten glass.

Some glass goes through additional processes to meet special needs. Two examples of this are tempered glass and laminated glass.

Tempering is a process that quickly heats the glass to a softening point (700°C) and then quickly cools it with a blast of compressed air. When tempered glass shatters, it breaks into small pebble-like pieces, without sharp edges. Tempered glass has bending and impact strengths that are three to five times higher than those of annealed glass of the same thickness. It is used for glass doors, side and rear windows of automobiles, and other applications where safety is an issue. When two or more layers of glass are held together with a plastic interlayer, the glass is called laminated glass. Usually polyvinyl butyral (PVB) is utilized. The PVB is sandwiched between the glass panes that are then passed through rollers to expel any air pockets. The initial bond is formed by the rollers, but ensured when heated to around 70°C in a pressurized oil bath. Laminated glass is often referred to as safety glass because it holds together when shattered. It is commonly used when there is a possibility of human impact or where glass could fall if shattered. The tint at the top of some cars' windshields is actually in the PVB.

When glass is struck, it will tend to bend on the side opposite from the impact. When stretched too far, it finally breaks, causing radial fractures in the glass. Radial fractures start at the impact point and propagate outward like the spokes on a bicycle (see Figure 19-1). As the radial fractures break, ridges are formed on the broken edge of the fracture. These ridges are called Wallner lines or rib markings (see Figure 19-2). Wallner lines (rib markings) form perpendicular to the side opposite the impact and parallel to the side of impact. As the radial fractures bend away from the force applied, additional fractures will then begin. These are called concentric fractures. Concentric fractures are fractures forming after the radial fractures in a circular pattern around the point of impact, and can be compared to the wheel of the bicycle (see Figure 19-3). Since radial fractures always develop prior to concentric fractures, the order of impact points

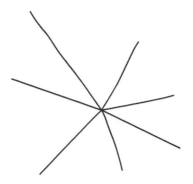

Figure 19-1 Radial fractures are the first fractures to begin after an impact has occurred. They begin at the impact point and propagate outward.

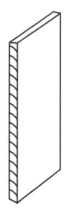

Figure 19-2 Wallner lines (rib markings) are formed on the broken edge of glass as it breaks. Force causing the impact in this example is applied from the right.

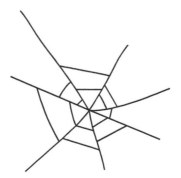

Figure 19-3 An impact point with both radial and concentric fractures.

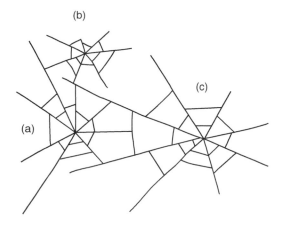

Figure 19-4   Order of impact determination. The order of impact shown here from first to last is (c) first, (a) second, and (b) third.

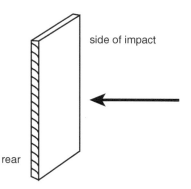

Figure 19-5   Wallner lines on a radial fracture showing force was applied from the right side.

can sometimes be determined. Figure 19-4 shows three impact points for which order may be determined.

At times, it may also be important to determine from which side the force causing the breakage was applied. This can be determined by two methods. An examination of the rib markings on fractures can determine the direction of the force breaking the glass. To accomplish this, you must first determine the point of impact. Portions of the broken glass must be put back together enough to determine the point of impact. This allows you to distinguish a radial fracture from a concentric fracture. Once the point of impact is determined, the 4R rule can be applied. The 4R rule is: **R**idges on **R**adial fractures are at **R**ight angles to the **R**ear (side opposite the impact). This is shown in Figure 19-5.

The direction of force can at times also be determined by examining the impact point. When glass breaks, some glass will continue to move with the force that was applied. With

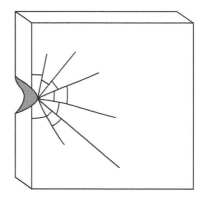

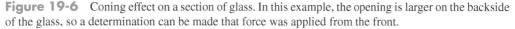

Figure 19-6   Coning effect on a section of glass. In this example, the opening is larger on the backside of the glass, so a determination can be made that force was applied from the front.

high-velocity impacts such as gunshots, a coning or cratering effect is seen in the glass fracture. This is visualized by a wider hole being created on the exit side than the side from which the force was applied (see Figure 19-6).

Exceptions to this directional examination include tempered glass that shatters, small windows held tightly so that they cannot bend, and windows that are broken by heat or explosion where there is no point of impact.

Equipment and Supplies

> UV light box
>
> Broken float glass samples
>
> Broken molded glass samples
>
> Unknown glass samples

Safety

Use standard laboratory safety procedures as described in rules set by your instructor. Broken glass samples have sharp edges; use caution when handling. The UV light box can damage the eyes and skin. View samples through the viewer only. Do not turn the box over and look directly at the bulb. Do not keep your hand under the light while the UV light is on.

Part I: Fluorescence of Float Glass

The fluorescence test for float glass requires short-wave UV light to excite the tin that is present in the glass. Observations should be made in a dark room if possible.

Procedure

1. Place a section of known float glass under the UV light box. Illuminate the glass with short-wave light. Observe the first side of the glass sample. Turn the glass over and observe the other side. Did one or both sides fluoresce?
2. Now observe both sides under long-wave UV light. Is there any difference? Alternate between short-wave and long-wave UV light. Different colors of fluorescence have sometimes been observed when switching between the two lights. Record your observations in your report.
3. Next, repeat steps 1 and 2 with a known sample of molded glass. Record your observations in your report.

Part II: Reconstruction of Glass Fragments

Procedure

A. Direction of Force
   1. Obtain a plastic bag with broken glass fragments.
   2. Examine and carefully piece together the broken windowpane made of float glass. (Hint: Use the fluorescence test to determine the tin side of the glass.) Draw the reconstructed windowpane.
   3. Next, determine the point of impact. Label this on your drawing.
   4. Identify the radial and concentric fractures. Label a radial and concentric fracture on your drawing. Using the 4R rule, determine from which side the force was applied. Draw the radial fractures and the Wallner lines used for your determination.
   5. Using the "coning effect," determine from which side the force was applied. Does this conclusion agree with your conclusion from step 4?
B. Order of Breakage
   1. Obtain a plastic bag with broken glass fragments.
   2. Examine and carefully piece together the broken windowpane made of float glass. (Hint: Use the fluorescence test to determine the tin side of the glass.) Draw the reconstructed windowpane.
   3. Next, determine the points of impact. Label these as "A" and "B" on your drawing.
   4. Determine the order in which the impacts occurred. Identify the radial or concentric fractures used in your determination. Label these on your drawing.

Report Requirements

Include all drawings, calculations, and other information obtained during the laboratory procedure. Notes and/or drawings should include the sample identification, magnification, and a complete description.

Report Questions

1. Describe the portion of glass manufacturing that allows float glass to be easily identified.
2. Which side of a piece of float glass is found to exhibit fluorescence when using short-wave UV light? What component of the glass is being excited?
3. What is a radial fracture? How is it formed?
4. What is a concentric fracture?
5. What are Wallner lines? Why are they important?
6. Given Figure 19-7 below:
   a. Label a radial fracture.
   b. Label a concentric fracture.
   c. Place the impacts in order:

      1 _____ 2 _____ 3 _____ 4 _____

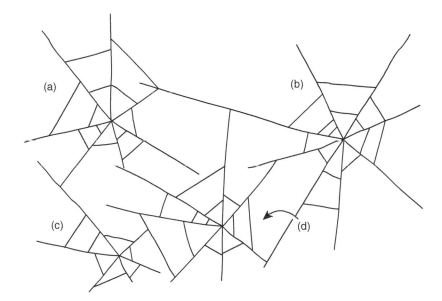

Figure 19-7

Chapter 19

Experiment 19A: Glass Examinations

Recommended pre-lab reading assignments:

Koons RD, Buscaglia J, Bottrell M, Miller ET. Forensic Glass Comparisons. In: Saferstein R, ed. *Forensic Science Handbook*, 2nd ed. Upper Saddle River, NJ: Pearson Education, 2002; 162–213.

McCrone WC. Microscopical Characterization of Glass Fragments. *Journal of the Association of Official Analytical Chemists*. 1972; 55: 834–839.

McCrone WC. Microscopical Characterization of Glass Fragments. *Journal of the Association of Official Analytical Chemists*. 1974; 57: 668–670.

Objective

Upon completion of this practical exercise, the student will have developed a basic understanding of:

1. examination of glass fragments using the immersion method
   a. Becke line method
   b. oblique illumination method
2. density comparisons of glass fragments

Introduction

One optical characteristic of glass that can be used to compare and distinguish glass fragments is refractive index. Glass types can easily be distinguished by measurement of their refractive index using a compound or phase contrast microscope. Table 19A-1 contains a list of five common types of glass and their average refractive index at 25°C.

Practical Forensic Microscopy: A Laboratory Manual, Second Edition. Barbara P. Wheeler.
© 2021 John Wiley & Sons Ltd. Published 2021 by John Wiley & Sons Ltd.
Companion website: www.wiley.com/go/Wheeler/Forensic

Table 19A-1 Refractive indices for some common types of glass.

Glass type	n_D^{25}
Fused silica quartz	1.459
Borosilicate	1.479
Soda lime	1.512
Alumina silicate	1.530
High-lead glass	1.693

Determining the refractive index of glass using the Becke line method was discussed in Experiment 2D. When using this method, the glass fragment is immersed in an oil and the Becke line is observed when increasing the stage to objective distance, often called "raising the focus." The Becke line moves to the medium with the higher refractive index when the focus is raised. Refractive index is known to vary with wavelength and temperature. The variation with wavelength is known as dispersion. Refractive index measurements of glass are typically recorded at sodium's D line (589 nm, yellow-orange). For dispersion measurements, refractive index is also commonly measured at hydrogen's C (656 nm, red) and F lines (486 nm, blue). The dispersion of refractive index is then determined either graphically, by plotting refractive index versus wavelength, or by Equation 2D-3. Since refractive index also varies with temperature, it is important that temperature control be maintained. If temperature control is not possible, a temperature correction must be applied. This is done by taking into consideration the temperature coefficient of the immersion oil. The change per degree centigrade, $-dn/dT$, is called the temperature coefficient. Commercially available Cargille^{TM} refractive index liquids have a $-dn/dT$ marked on each bottle. Refractive index is commonly reported at 25°C, while the immersion bottles often contain refractive index measured at 23°C. To perform a temperature correction, the following formula is applied:

$$n^{25} = n^{23} - (25 - 23)\frac{dn}{dT} \tag{19A-1}$$

where n^{25} is the index of refraction at 25°C, n^{23} is the index of refraction obtained at the measurement temperature of 23°C, and dn/dT is the temperature coefficient of refractive index for the liquid, which is found on the immersion oil bottle.

Since temperature and refractive index are inversely related, it is important to check your answer using the rule that states: As temperature increases, refractive index decreases, and vice versa. A similar relationship exists for dispersion of refractive index. Normal dispersion is exhibited when an increase in refractive index occurs at shorter wavelengths.

An older method of refractive index determination that still has some value in forensic examinations is the oblique illumination method. Oblique illumination is obtained by creating a shade: covering one side of a fully opened substage aperture with an opaque material such as a business card. When the condenser and "shade" are properly positioned, about half of the field appears dark while the other is light. It is also possible to mimic this effect by partially inserting an accessory plate. A glass particle that has a higher refractive index than the mounting liquid will be shaded on the dark side of the field of view. The color fringes that appear on the edges of the glass particles provide additional information summarized in Table 19A-2.

Table 19A-2 Information provided by color fringes in oblique illumination method.

Fringes	Information to be gained
Blue, green, violet	Ignore these colors. They are difficult to interpret.
Yellow	The glass particle has a higher refractive index than the oil.
Brown	The glass particle has a lower refractive index than the oil.
Orange-red	The glass particle has the same refractive index as the oil.
Bright fringes	The glass particle has a lower refractive index than the oil.
Dim fringes	The glass particle has a higher refractive index than the oil.

A physical property of glass that is sometimes used to compare and identify glass fragments is density. Density is defined as mass per unit volume:

$$D = \frac{mass}{volume} \qquad (19A-2)$$

For example, lead has a density of 11.3 grams per cubic centimeter, while table salt (sodium chloride) has a density of 2.2 grams per cubic centimeter. Hence a given volume of lead weighs 5.1 times as much as the same volume of salt. Different types of glasses also have distinctly different densities in the range of 2.2–2.6 grams per cubic centimeter. Density can be used as a screening technique where large numbers of fragments are encountered. The density of glass fragments varies with the chemical composition and the thermal history of glass. Thermal history must be considered when measuring density of glass from an arson case. Absolute measurements of density report a numerical value for the density of the glass fragment, while comparative measurements of density are used to determine if two glass fragments have the same or different densities. Absolute measurement of density can be accomplished by several techniques, such as (1) the sink-float method, (2) density gradient tubes, or (3) use of a density meter. The sink-float method requires placing a glass fragment in a liquid whose density is adjusted to obtain a "glass suspension point." It can then be concluded that the glass particle has the same density as the liquid. For absolute density measurements, the density of the liquid that suspends the sample should then be accurately determined using a calibrated plummet. Density gradient tubes require that specific liquids be layered so that various density levels can be determined, and the density of the position at which the glass is suspended can then be identified. Both of these methods can be used for absolute or comparative density determinations. For comparative examinations, fragments are easily distinguished by their relative position in the liquid.

Density is temperature dependent. As the temperature increases, generally the density of a substance decreases. However, there are exceptions to this generalization. For example, the density of water increases between its melting point at 0°C and 4°C, and similar behavior is observed in silicon at low temperatures. Comparison of densities can be made at the same room temperature without temperature control. However, if the absolute density of a glass fragment is being measured, it is important to control the temperature and also record the temperature.

An understanding of the physical and optical properties of glass allows the forensic scientist to perform complete glass examinations. Since glass manufacturing has stringent quality control guidelines, the refractive index and density of glass samples are becoming less variable and therefore less of a probative factor for comparison of unknown and known samples.

However, many glass manufacturers now utilize a variety of chemical components to develop specific properties for their glass products. This variety of components yields a diversified elemental composition for each glass produced. With enhanced instrumental techniques, elemental compositions are now becoming the most discriminating method for glass examinations.

Equipment and Supplies

Compound light microscope with objectives of various magnifications (e.g., 4X, 10X, 20X, and 40X)

Accessory plates

Cargille™ Refractive Index Liquids

Density liquids

    Bromoform

    Bromobenzene

    Methanol

    PolyGee™ (sodium polytungstate saturated solution)

    Distilled water

Micro kit

Cover slips

Microscope slides

Glass fragments of known refractive index

Glass fragments of known density

Glass fragment unknowns

Disposable beakers

Safety

Use standard laboratory safety procedures as described in rules set by your instructor. Be cautious of microscope light levels to avoid eye damage. Bromobenzene and bromoform are **extremely toxic and suspected carcinogens**. Use these chemicals in a hood, and wear protective eyewear and gloves for this procedure.

Part I: Refractive Index by Immersion Method

Becke Line Method

Procedure

1. Choose a glass particle of known refractive index (RI) and immerse it in:
   a. a Cargille oil of **higher** RI and
   b. a Cargille oil of **lower** RI
      Example: Glass with RI of 1.52 in oil of 1.500 and 1.540.

2. With the microscope set up and adjusted for Köhler illumination, focus on the edges of a representative particle using the 10X objective. Use the orange filter to obtain monochromatic light. This will give you refractive index values for the sodium D line.

3. Close the substage condenser to the minimum setting. Using the glass particle that has been mounted in the lower RI oil, observe the Becke line. Focus "upward" and "downward" to determine whether the glass fragment or the solution has the higher refractive index. Remember that as you focus up (raise the microscope lens away from the specimen), the Becke line will move toward the substance with the higher index. When the refractive index of the glass and the immersion oil are the same, the chip will become almost invisible, and it may be difficult to find and bring the edges of the chip into focus. Draw what you observe. What is your conclusion?

4. Repeat the steps above with a glass particle mounted in a higher RI oil. What did you observe? What are your conclusions?

5. Repeat the steps above with another known glass particle. What did you observe? What are your conclusions?

6. Choose one of the unknown glass samples.

7. Select an oil in the middle of the range of the unknowns provided by the instructor. Prepare a liquid mount.

8. Focus on the glass particle using the 10X objective. Be careful not to get any oil on the objective. If oil does get on the objective, your instructor will show you how to clean it with lens paper.

9. Using the coarse focus adjustment, raise the focus (increase the distance between the stage and the objective). Watch the Becke line movement. The Becke line moves to the medium with the higher refractive index.

10. Repeat the previous step with an oil of a higher or lower refractive index.

11. Continue to try new oils until you obtain minimum relief. If you cannot obtain a good match with a single oil, mix two oils by adding a drop of each to the glass particles and dropping a cover slip on top.

12. Draw what you observe once you have determined the RI.

13. Using a thermometer, measure the room temperature. If necessary, correct the refractive index determined for the glass by using Equation (19A-1) to determine the refractive index at 25°C. The temperature coefficient of refractive index can be found on the Cargille oil that was found to be a match to your glass fragment's refractive index.

14. Report the RI of the matching oil and unknown number on a circle template.

Oblique Illumination Method

Procedure

1. Choose glass particles of known RI. Immerse the particles in an oil of higher RI. With the accessory plate inserted into its slot, darken half of the field of view and examine how the bright and dark shadows appear on the glass particles. Are they toward the bright or dark sides of the field? Remember: A glass particle that has a refractive index that is higher than the oil will be shaded on the dark side of the field of view. Color fringes may also provide additional information about the refractive index; see Table 19A-2. Draw what you observe.

2. Repeat with an oil of lower RI than the glass particles. Draw what you observe.

3. Obtain an unknown glass sample. Using the oblique illumination method, determine the refractive index of the sample by utilizing different oils until you obtain minimum relief. Remember that you are looking for an orange-red fringe for the match point. Use the brown and yellow fringe colors to enable you to choose your oils according to Table 19A-2. Draw what you observe when you find the match point.

4. Check the value by the Becke line method.

5. Using a thermometer, measure the room temperature. Correct the determined refractive index by using Equation (19A-1). The temperature coefficient of refractive index can be found on the Cargille oil that was found to be a match to your glass fragment's refractive index.

Part II: Density by the Sink-Float Method

This method relies on a determination that a glass particle will either float, sink, or be suspended in a liquid. Before making a determination of floating, make sure the glass fragment has broken the surface tension of the liquid. A fragment that never breaks the surface tension of the liquid may appear to float when it is actually the same density and would be suspended. A suspended particle may be near the top or near the bottom. As long as it does not sink all the way to the bottom or float on the surface, it can be determined to be suspended. These experiments are performed at room temperature, so it is important not to heat up the test tubes unnecessarily. Slight warming can cause a glass fragment to sink, whereas slight cooling can cause it to float. Holding the test tube at the top will prevent unnecessary warming. While not practical in most educational settings, but required in a forensic laboratory, the use of temperature-controlled equipment should be utilized to determine accurate measurements of absolute density.

Comparative Density Determination of Glass Fragments by the Sink-Float Method

Additional Note: This procedure must be performed in the hood, since bromoform is **extremely toxic and a suspected carcinogen**. Wear protective eyewear and gloves for this procedure.
   The instructor may choose to substitute sodium polytungstate and water for this procedure.

Procedure

1. Obtain a clean dry piece of a known glass density standard. Examine it carefully under the microscope, and note any identifying features. Make a sketch of the piece of glass. Repeat this for each density standard.

2. Obtain your unknown glass fragment. Examine it carefully under the microscope, note any identifying features, and make a sketch of the piece of glass. It is important to be able to recognize each piece of glass separately, as they will at times be placed together in the same test tube. Discrimination of the glass samples will be possible using the sketches and the stereomicroscope. The unknown and density standards should be approximately the same size.

3. Place the first density standard into a test tube containing a small amount of bromoform (tribromomethane). If the glass is less dense than the solution, it will float on the surface of the liquid. If this occurs, slowly add a drop of the less dense methanol. (HINT: To ensure

that the solution is uniform, mix thoroughly.) Observe the position of the glass fragment. Continue to add bromoform or methanol until the particle is suspended. Remember: Between additions of liquids, it is important to observe the sample after thoroughly mixing the solution.

4. Add a similar-sized, clean, dry fragment of unknown glass that has been microscopically examined and for which an identifying sketch has been made. If the two fragments are the same density, they will both remain suspended in the liquid. If not, one will float or sink relative to the other. Record your observations.

5. If the known and unknown densities are different, remove your known glass particle and clean it with acetone. Repeat steps 3 and 4 for the remaining known density standards until a match is found.

6. The standard that matches the unknown should react in exactly the same manner as the unknown. It is possible to have an unknown that does not match any of the standards.

7. Report the density of the unknown if it is found to match one of the standards. If the unknown does not match any of the standards, report the density range (i.e., higher than standard 3, in between standard 2 and 3, or lower than standard 1). Write a paragraph defending your conclusions. Be sure to include your identifying sketches.

Absolute Density Determination of Glass Fragments by the Sink-Float Method

Additional Note: This procedure uses PolyGee™ (sodium polytungstate solution) and water.

The instructor may choose to substitute bromoform and methanol for this procedure. Bromoform is an **extremely toxic and suspected carcinogen**, so it should be used in a hood, with protective eyewear and gloves.

Procedure

1. Obtain a clean dry piece of glass of known density. Examine it carefully under the stereomicroscope, and note any identifying features.

2. Next, place the glass sample into a test tube containing a small amount of PolyGee (sodium polytungstate solution). The glass will most likely float on the surface of the liquid. Slowly add water, which is less dense, dropwise with stirring, until the particle is suspended in the middle of the liquid. (HINT: To ensure that the solution is uniform, mix thoroughly.) If too much water is added so that the glass fragment sinks, slowly add more of the denser PolyGee liquid.

3. Once suspended, determine the density of the glass fragment. Since the glass fragment is suspended, it has the same density as the liquid. To determine the density of the liquid, accurately pipette a known volume of liquid into a small plastic beaker that has been weighed on an analytical balance. Next weigh the beaker and liquid on the same balance. Subtracting the weight of the beaker, use the density equation (Equation (19A-2)) to determine the density of the liquid. Report the density of the known glass sample to the appropriate number of significant figures. Record the room temperature at the time of this measurement.

4. Next, examine the unknown glass sample using the same procedure as performed with the known glass. Recheck the room temperature.

5. Report the density of each piece of glass to the appropriate number of significant figures. You will be provided the density of the known sample. Calculate the percent error in the density you obtained according to Equation (19A-3):

$$\%error = \left| \frac{known - measured}{known} \right| \times 100 \qquad (19A\text{-}3)$$

As part of your lab report, discuss the accuracy of this method using the percent error for the known glass sample. Discuss possible sources of error with the procedure.

Report Requirements

Include all drawings, calculations, and other information obtained during the laboratory procedure. Notes and/or drawings should include the sample identification, magnification, and a complete description.

Report Questions

1. What are the main ingredients used to produce glass?
2. How would changes in the amount of these ingredients affect the refractive index of various glass types? Give at least one example.
3. How would changes in the amount of these ingredients affect the density of various glass types? Give at least one example.
4. Why does leaded glass sparkle? Explain why leaded glass has a high refractive index.
5. Give the density range for glass samples in the following categories: borosilicate glass, leaded glass, soda lime glass.
6. Include the calculations made to determine the density of your known glass sample. What type of glass do you suspect that it might be?
7. Include the calculations made to determine the density of your unknown glass sample. What type of glass do you suspect your unknown glass to be?
8. If your known and unknown glass samples have similar densities, how would you examine the samples further to determine if they have a common origin?
9. Why is it important to use temperature control in absolute density measurements? How could you have controlled temperature in this experiment?

Recommended and Further Reading

Almirall J. Elemental Analysis of Glass Fragments. In: Caddy B, ed. *Trace Evidence Analysis and Interpretation*. London: Taylor & Francis, 2001; 65–83.

Almirall JR, Cole MD, Gettinby G, Furton KG. Discrimination of Glass Sources Using Elemental Composition and Refractive Index: Development of Predictive Models. *Science & Justice*. 1998; 38(2): 93–100.

Bennett RL, Kim ND, Curran JM, Coulson SA, Newton AWN. Spatial Variation of Refractive Index in a Pane of Float Glass. *Science & Justice*. 2003; 43(2): 71–76.

Bottrell MC, Webb JB. Review of Forensic Interpretation of Glass Evidence. *Journal of Forensic Sciences*. 2002; 47(4).

Brown GA. Factors Affecting the Refractive Index Distribution of Window Glass. *Journal of Forensic Sciences*. 1985; 30(3).

Caddy B. *Forensic Examination of Glass and Paint: Analysis and Interpretation*. London: Taylor & Francis, 2001.

Cassista AR, Sandercock PML. Precision of Glass Refractive Index Measurements: Temperature Variation and Double Variation Methods and the Value of Dispersion. *Canadian Society of Forensic Science Journal.* 1994; 27(3): 203–208.

Curran JM. The Statistical Interpretation of Forensic Glass Evidence. *International Statistical Review.* 2003; 71(3): 497–520.

Curran JM, Buckleton JS, Triggs CM. Commentary on Koons RD, Buscaglia J. The Forensic Significance of Glass Composition and Refractive Index Measurements. *Journal of Forensic Sciences.* 1999; 44(3): 496–503. *Journal of Forensic Sciences.* 1999; 44(6): 1324–1325.

Dabbs MDG, Pearson EF. The Variation in Refractive Index and Density across Two Sheets of Window Glass. *Journal of Forensic Sciences Society.* 1970; 10: 139–148.

Heideman DH. Glass Comparisons Using a Computerized Refractive Index Data Base. *Journal of Forensic Sciences.* 1975; 20(1).

Houck MM, Siegel JA. *Fundamentals of Forensic Science*, 3rd ed. Amsterdam: Elsevier Academic Press, 2015; 436–449.

Koons RD, Buscaglia JA. The Forensic Significance of Glass Composition and Refractive Index Measurements. *Journal of Forensic Sciences.* 1999; 44(3): 496–503.

Koons RD, Buscaglia J, Bottrell M, Miller ET. Forensic Glass Comparisons. In: Saferstein R, ed. *Forensic Science Handbook*, 2nd ed. Upper Saddle River, NJ: Pearson Education, 2002; 161–213.

Lambert JA, Satterthwaite MJ, Harrison PH. A Survey of Glass Fragments Recovered from Clothing of Persons Suspected of Involvement in Crime. *Science & Justice.* 1995; 35(4): 273–281.

Locke J. Improvements in the Use of Silicone Oils for the Determination of Glass Refractive Indices. *Journal of the Forensic Science Society.* 1982; 22: 257–262.

Locke J, Scranage JK. Breaking of Flat Glass. Part 3: Surface Particles from Windows. *Forensic Science International.* 1992; 57: 73–80.

Locke J, Unikowski JA. Breaking of Flat Glass. Part 1: Size and Distribution of Particles from Plain Glass Windows. *Forensic Science International.* 1991; 51: 251–262.

Locke J, Unikowski JA. Breaking of Flat Glass. Part 2: Effect of Pane Parameters on Particle Distribution. *Forensic Science International.* 1992; 56: 95–106.

Luce RJ, Buckel JL, McInnis I. A Study on the Backward Fragmentation of Window Glass and Transfer of Glass Fragments to Individual's Clothing. *Canadian Society of Forensic Science Journal.* 1991; 1991(2): 79–89.

McCrone WC. Microscopical Characterization of Glass Fragments. *Journal of the Association of Official Analytical Chemists.* 1972; 55: 834–839.

McCrone WC. Microscopical Characterization of Glass Fragments. *Journal of the Association of Official Analytical Chemists.* 1974; 57: 668–670.

McJunkins SP, Thornton JI. Glass Fracture Analysis: A Review. *Forensic Science.* 1973; 2(1): 1–27.

Michalske TA, Bunker BC. The Fracturing of Glass. *Scientific American.* 1987; 12: 122–129.

Miller ET. Forensic Glass Comparisons. In: Saferstein R, ed. *Forensic Science Handbook*, vol. 1. Englewood Cliffs, NJ: Prentice-Hall, 1982.

Newton AWN, Curran JM, Triggs CM, Buckleton JS. The Consequences of Potentially Differing Distributions of the Refractive Indices of Glass Fragments from Control and Recovered Sources. *Forensic Science International.* 2004; 140(2–3): 185–193.

Newton AWN, Kitto L, Buckleton JS. A Study of the Performance and Utility of Annealing in Forensic Glass Analysis. *Forensic Science International.* 2005; 155(2–3): 119–125.

Pounds CA, Smalldon KW. The Distribution of Glass Fragments in Front of a Broken Window and the Transfer of Fragments to Individuals Standing Nearby. *Journal of Forensic Science Society.* 1978; 20: 274–282.

Rhodes EF, Thornton JI. The Interpretation of Impact Fractures in Glassy Polymers. *Journal of Forensic Sciences.* 1975; 29: 274–282.

Springer E, Zeichner A. The Breaking of Tempered Glass Vehicle Windows Using Broken Spark Plug Insulators. *Journal of Forensic Sciences.* 1986; 31: 691–694.

Suzuki Y, Sugita R, Suzuki S, Marumo Y. Forensic Discrimination of Bottle Glass by Refractive Index Measurement and Analysis of Trace Elements with ICP-MS. *Analytical Sciences.* 2000; 16(11): 1195–1198.

Thornton JI, Cashman PJ. Glass Fracture Mechanism: A Rethinking. *Journal of Forensic Sciences.* 1986; 24: 101–108.

Zadora G. Glass Analysis for Forensic Purposes – a Comparison of Classification Methods. *Journal of Chemometrics.* 2007; 21: 174–186.

Chapter 20

Experiment 20: Fiber Examinations

Recommended pre-lab reading assignments:

Carroll GR. *Forensic Examination of Fibres*. London: Ellis Horwood, Ltd, 1992; 99–105.

Eyring MB, Gaudette BD. An Introduction to the Forensic Aspects of Textile Fiber Examination. In: Saferstein R, ed. *Forensic Science Handbook*, 2nd ed. Upper Saddle River, NJ: Pearson Education, 2002; 245–261.

Objective

Upon completion of this practical exercise, the student will have developed a basic understanding of:

1. general characteristics of textile fibers
2. use of the stereomicroscope to visualize the characteristics of textile fibers
3. use of the polarizing light microscope to visualize the characteristics of textile fibers
4. preparing and observing cross sections of fibers
5. refractive indices for fibers
6. sign of elongation
7. dyed and pigmented fibers

Introduction

Items manufactured from natural and man-made fibers surround us. Therefore, people find themselves in constant contact with fabrics and the fibers of which they are composed. Natural fibers are typically limited in characteristics to determine color and general fiber type. However, man-made fibers possess characteristics that make identifications and further comparisons possible at times. Because of this fact, microscopic examination of fibers presents itself as indirect

Practical Forensic Microscopy: A Laboratory Manual, Second Edition. Barbara P. Wheeler.
© 2021 John Wiley & Sons Ltd. Published 2021 by John Wiley & Sons Ltd.
Companion website: www.wiley.com/go/Wheeler/Forensic

or circumstantial evidence in a court of law. This evidence is generally used in conjunction with other forensic evidence. Fiber examinations are performed to determine possible associations between people, places, and objects.

Fibers are divided into two main types, natural and man-made. Natural and man-made fibers can easily be differentiated by macroscopic and microscopic characteristics. Natural fibers are created from plant, animal, or mineral sources. Due to their cellular structures, natural fibers are easily recognized when using the microscope. Man-made fibers are created from raw materials, either natural or chemical based. Natural-based man-made fibers are called natural polymers. They may be composed of regenerated cellulose or regenerated protein. Chemical-based man-made fibers are referred to as synthetic fibers. Man-made fibers are also easily recognized due to their unique microscopic characteristics.

As already stated, natural fibers are derived from plant, animal, or mineral sources. Plant fibers originate from any part of a plant: the stem or bast, leaf, fruit, or seed. Therefore, plant fibers are easily recognized by the presence of cellular walls, features of the cell walls, and the lumen. During microscopic examinations, it is also important to note the appearance or lack of the following: pits and spiral thickenings, convolutions, wall thickness, transverse markings, crystals, bundles, and length. Animal fibers generally originate from the "fur hair" of animals. Because of this, they are also easily recognized by their microscopic characteristics. Scale margin appearance, scale margin distance, and scale patterns, along with morphological features, can be used to identify animal fibers. Mineral fibers are inorganic fibers and are either asbestos or mineral wool. Extinction characteristics make these fibers easy to identify.

Since man-made fibers are generated by mechanical means, certain microscopic characteristics remain consistent. During microscopic examinations of man-made fibers, it is important to note the appearance or lack of the following characteristics: color, luster, thickness, inclusions, cross section, variations in characteristics within the fiber, birefringence, pleochroism, and sign of elongation.

Fiber examinations involve the use of a variety of microscopes, techniques, and instruments. Examinations are usually performed to identify a fiber and then, when necessary, to compare a fiber back to a known fiber source. Initially a stereomicroscope is used to examine the fiber for color and possibly determine whether it is a natural or man-made fiber. The length and diameter are determined, as well as crimp if present.

Further testing can be performed using a polarized light microscope to determine optical properties such as extinction, refractive index, birefringence, and sign of elongation. Some fibers will exhibit extinction when light emerging from the fiber is vibrating at right angles to the preferred direction of the analyzer. Because of their chemical orientation, some fibers never go to extinction (see Experiment 3A). The refractive indices of a fiber are a measurement of how much light is slowed as it passes through the fiber. For fibers, there are two refractive indices: parallel and perpendicular to the long axis. The refractive indices are determined by examining the fiber with orientation of its long axis parallel and perpendicular to the plane of polarization. The Becke line method, discussed in Experiment 3B, is commonly used to determine the refractive index of fibers. The Becke line is a bright halo appearing at the boundary of a particle. This halo will move as the focus is adjusted up and down. As the working distance of a microscope is increased, the Becke line will travel toward the medium of higher refractive index. With natural fibers, refractive indices are not the most distinguishing characteristic; however, it is still an identifying feature. Refractive indices for common plant and animal fibers are found in Appendix A. Depending on the variety, mineral fibers may have three refractive indices. Data for mineral fibers are also contained in Appendix A. With man-made fibers, the refractive index is even more important in that it can be used to distinguish between fibers and, at times, manufacturers. Refractive indices for common man-made fibers are found in Appendix B.

The birefringence of fibers can also be used to aid in the identification of a fiber (see Experiment 3C). Birefringence is an optical property of a material having a refractive index that depends on the polarization and vibrational direction of light.

The thickness of the fiber can be measured using a calibrated ocular micrometer. Using these two characteristics and the Michel-Lévy birefringence chart or tabular data such as that found in Appendices A and B, the identification of the fiber can be determined.

Another identifying characteristic is the sign of elongation (see Experiment 3C). If n-parallel is greater than n-perpendicular, the sign of elongation is said to be positive. If the reverse is true, the sign of elongation of the fiber is negative. Sign of elongation can be determined by two methods: (1) When using immersion oils, the sign can be determined by mathematical subtraction: n-parallel minus n-perpendicular; or (2) by inserting a compensator into the optical path. When inserting a compensator, the light path will either be "added" or "subtracted." This can be determined by using the Michel-Lévy birefringence chart as a reference to determine if the retardation adds (increases to a higher order) or subtracts (decreases in order). Sign of elongation for common fibers is found in Appendices A and B.

In addition to the overall color of the fiber, microscopic color assessments should also be made. The color of the fiber may be uniform along its length, or it may vary. There may also be variation in colors between fibers within the same sample. A microscopic examination of the fiber will show differences when the fiber is dyed, surface-dyed, or pigmented. Dyed and surface-dyed fibers are chemically colored after the fiber has been manufactured. Since pigmented fibers are colored during the manufacturing process, only man-made fibers can be pigmented. The size, shape, and distribution of pigment granules should be taken into consideration. Some fibers may also contain delustering agents. Delustering agents are pigment granules that are used to dull the luster of a manufactured fiber. The size, shape, and concentration of the particles provide varying degrees of light diffraction, which in turn creates differing degrees of luster. A dull fiber will have many delustering agents, while a bright fiber will have none present. Titanium dioxide is commonly used as a delustering agent.

Other microscopic characteristics, including solubility of the fiber and cross-sectional shape, may also be determined during fiber examinations. Solubility testing of fibers may be a useful technique in the identification of natural and man-made fibers. Solubility testing involves a possible reaction of the fiber with a variety of solvents from an identification scheme. Although this method is destructive, valuable information can be obtained from solubility testing. The cross-sectional shape of a fiber is one characteristic that may be used to help establish a fiber type and usage. Natural fibers have very distinct cellular shapes. Man-made fibers have various shapes produced by the manufacturing process. These cross sections come in a wide variety of shapes: round, bilobal, trilobal, multilobal, bell, dogbone, triangular, hollow, and irregular (see Figure 20-1).

Fiber examinations involve the use of a variety of microscopes, techniques, and instruments. Initially a stereomicroscope is used to examine the fiber for macroscopic characteristics. Further testing can be performed using a compound or comparison light microscope to determine optical properties. Other analytical techniques may also be utilized to further identify specific fiber characteristics. Thermal microscopy (Experiment 31), infrared microscopy (Experiment 29), fluorescence microscopy (Experiment 4A), microspectrophotometry (Experiment 30), and thin-layer chromatography are techniques that may also be performed on fibers.

Natural and man-made fibers can easily be differentiated by macroscopic and microscopic characteristics. Most natural fibers (plant and animal) contain various cellular features that

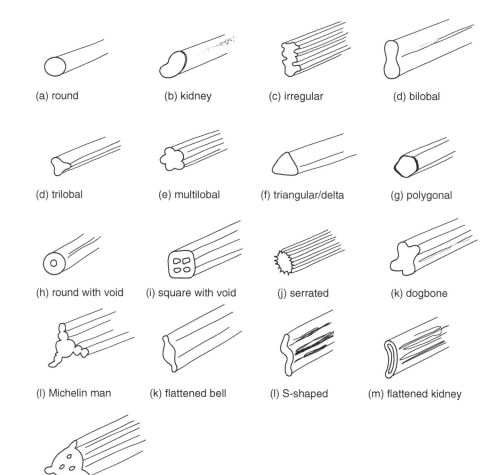

(a) round   (b) kidney   (c) irregular   (d) bilobal

(d) trilobal   (e) multilobal   (f) triangular/delta   (g) polygonal

(h) round with void   (i) square with void   (j) serrated   (k) dogbone

(l) Michelin man   (k) flattened bell   (l) S-shaped   (m) flattened kidney

(n) puffed trilobal with voids

Figure 20-1   Common cross-sectional and longitudinal views for fibers.

make their microscopic differentiation easy. Mineral wool and asbestos fibers show extinction characteristics that make their microscopic characterization possible. Man-made fibers have many documented microscopic characteristics that also make their identification possible.

Equipment and Supplies

Stereomicroscope

Polarizing light microscope with objectives of various magnifications (e.g., 4X, 10X, 20X, and 40X) and focusing ocular with micrometer scale

Micro kit

Microscope slides and cover slips

Mounting medium (a colorless mounting medium in the refractive index range of 1.50–1.70)

Vegetable fibers (flax, ramie, jute, hemp, sisal, coir, kapok, cotton, akund, abaca, sunn)

Animal fibers (wool, mohair, alpaca, angora, cashmere, camel, llama, silk)

Mineral fibers (asbestos and mineral wool)

Natural-based man-made fibers (acetate, triacetate, rayon, lyocell)

Synthetic fibers (nylon, polyester, acrylic, modacrylic, olefin)

Safety

Use standard laboratory safety procedures as described in guidelines set by your instructor. Be cautious of microscope light levels to avoid eye damage. Know the hazards associated with the mounting mediums, and use them with appropriate precautions as set by your instructor. Dispose of glass in an appropriate container.

Special precautions: Ventilation is required when working with asbestos, a human carcinogen. Disposal of asbestos-containing materials should follow EPA Guidelines.

Part I: Examination of Fibers

A worksheet for examination notes may be found at the end of the experiment.

Procedure

1. Examine the fiber with the stereomicroscope. Note the color, length, and longitudinal form of the fiber.
2. Set up a polarized light microscope for Köhler illumination. Determine the cross-sectional shape. This can be done by making a cross section (procedures for making cross sections are outlined in Experiment 17B) or from a liquid-mounted fiber.
3. Using the liquid-mounted fiber, examine the fiber under non-polarized light. Determine the diameter and longitudinal shape. Draw what you see. Note any other morphological or microscopic features of the fiber. Rotate the fiber 90°, making note of any changes to the fiber as you rotate it. Return it to the original position.
4. Examine the fiber under crossed polars. Draw what you see.
5. Rotate the fiber 90°, making note of any changes to the fiber as you rotate it. Document any further characteristics viewed.
6. Repeat steps 1–5 while using a higher magnification.
7. Repeat steps 1–6 for all fibers assigned.
8. Make a chart of the features you examined for each fiber. Required features are cross-sectional shape, longitudinal shape, diameter, birefringence, and extinction characteristics. Additional characteristics should also be noted, such as color, striations, cellular structures, and so on.

Report Requirements

Include all drawings, calculations, and other information obtained during the laboratory procedure. Notes and/or drawings should include the sample identification, magnification, and a complete description.

Report Questions

1. What are the two classifications of fibers?
2. What are the three types of natural fibers? Name one example of each type. What are these fibers composed of?
3. How are man-made fibers different from natural fibers?
4. What are the types of man-made fibers? Name an example of each type, and provide the chemical makeup.
5. What feature is always present in natural fibers?
6. Is asbestos isotropic or anisotropic?
7. What are two microscopic characteristics that could be used to distinguish acrylic fibers from polyester fibers?

Fiber Characteristics Worksheet

Sample: _____

Macroscopic:
      Color __ _____
      Length _____
      Longitudinal form _____

Microscopic Morphology:
      Color _____
      Diameter _____
      Longitudinal shape _____
      Cross-sectional shape _____
      Other _____

Microscopic Optical Properties:
      Refractive Index: n-parallel _____
                      n-perpendicular _____
      Birefringence _____
      Extinction _____
      Sign of elongation _____
      Pleochroism _____
      UV fluorescence _____
      Melting point _____
      Solubilities _____
                  _____
                  _____
      Fluorescence _____
      Other _____

Instrumental Properties:
      FTIR _____
      Microspec _____

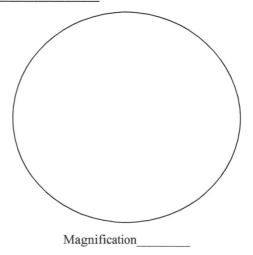

Magnification_____

Chapter 20

Experiment 20A: Natural Fiber Examinations

Recommended pre-lab reading assignments:

Eyring MB, Gaudette BD. An Introduction to the Forensic Aspects of Textile Fiber Examination. In: Saferstein R, ed. *Forensic Science Handbook*, 2nd ed. Upper Saddle River, NJ: Pearson Education, 2002; 263–265.

Palenik SJ. Microscopic Examination of Fibres. In: Robertson J, Grieve M, eds. *Forensic Examination of Fibres*. London: Taylor and Francis, 1999; 153–176.

Textile Institute. *Identification of Textile Materials*, 7th ed. Manchester, England: Textile Institute, 1975.

Objective

Upon completion of this practical exercise, the student will have developed a basic understanding of:

1. general characteristics of natural fibers: plant, animal, and mineral
2. use of the stereomicroscope to visualize and identify the characteristics of natural fibers
3. use of the polarizing light microscope to visualize and identify the characteristics of natural fibers
4. determination of cross-sectional shape for natural fibers
5. measurement of refractive indices of natural fibers
6. use of the fluorescence microscope to visualize characteristics of man-made fibers
7. use of complementary tests for identification of natural fibers
    a. twist test
    b. Billinghame test
    c. Herzog test
    d. burn test
    e. solubility tests

Practical Forensic Microscopy: A Laboratory Manual, Second Edition. Barbara P. Wheeler.
© 2021 John Wiley & Sons Ltd. Published 2021 by John Wiley & Sons Ltd.
Companion website: www.wiley.com/go/Wheeler/Forensic

Introduction

The Locard Exchange Principle states that whenever two objects come in contact, an exchange of matter occurs. This theory applies to fiber evidence. Fibers are easily shed and transferred whenever there is contact between two objects, two individuals, or an individual and another object. Therefore, fiber examinations are often used to associate people with items or scenes. This makes fibers an important source of information in forensic investigations.

Natural fibers are derived from either plant, animal, or mineral sources and possess various macroscopic and microscopic characteristics that make identifications and further association with a particular source possible at times. Because of this fact, natural fibers are routinely examined in forensic casework. A discussion of microscopic characteristics for common plant, animal, and mineral fibers follows.

Plant Fibers

Examinations of natural plant fibers include viewing the microscopic features of the fiber cells. Observing the longitudinal and cross-sectional properties of the fiber allows a forensic scientist to determine the microscopic features. Characteristics such as the shape of the cells; the relative thickness of the cell wall; the cell length; the size, shape, and thickness of the lumen; the shape of fiber bundles; and the presence of crystals should be noted.

Plant fibers are categorized according to the area of the plant from which the fibers are collected.

Seed Fibers (seed or seed-casing fibers)
- *Cotton*: The cotton fiber is obtained from the herbaceous shrubs *Gossypium hirsutum*, *barbadense, arboretum, and herbaceum*. Cotton fibers are essentially 95% cellulose. They are tapered at each end and twisted or convoluted along the length of their shaft, reversing occasionally, resembling flattened, twisted ribbons. There is generally a central canal, although both the lumen and the convolutions are absent at the tip ends. Cotton is easily distinguished from other natural fibers in that, under crossed polars, they do not go to extinction upon stage rotation but remain bright in all orientations (see Figure 20A-1a). Some cotton fibers undergo a process called mercerization. This helps improve the luster and dying qualities of the fiber. Mercerized cotton fibers appear slightly "swollen" and straighter.
- *Kapok*: The kapok fiber is obtained from the seed pod of a tree of the Bombaceae family, *Ceiba pentranda* or *Bombax malabaricum*. The kapok fiber resembles a smooth, cylindrical, hollow, thin-walled fiber that at times is flattened. The fiber tapers to a point at one end, with the other end having a bulbous base with annular reticular markings.
- *Akund*: The akund fiber is obtained from the seed hair of *Calotropis procera*. These fibers resemble the kapok fiber but do not show the net-like thickenings.

Bast Fibers (stem skin or bast fibers)
- *Flax*: Flax fibers are obtained from *Linum usitatissimum* L. Flax fibers are straight with distinct lengthwise striations. The shape is rounded-polygonal. The fibers have a thin, indistinct lumen. Flax is easily distinguished by the slight thickenings at the nodes, which give an identifiable "X, Y, V, or I" marking when observed under crossed polars (see Figure 20A-1b).
- *Hemp*: Hemp fibers are obtained from the plant *Cannabis sativa*. Hemp fibers are colorless cylinders with surface irregularities such as joints and fractures, similar to that

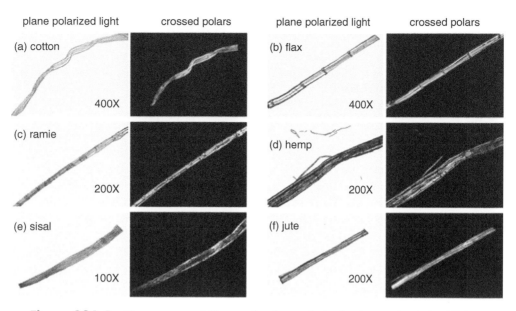

plane polarized light   crossed polars   plane polarized light   crossed polars

(a) cotton   400X

(b) flax   400X

(c) ramie   200X

(d) hemp   200X

(e) sisal   100X

(f) jute   200X

Figure 20A-1   Common natural fibers under plane-polarized and crossed polarized light.

of the flax fiber. At times crystals may appear on the surface of untreated bundles. The fibers have a polygonal cross section with rounded edges. The lumen is generally broad and flattened. The twist test further differentiates flax and hemp (see Figure 20A-1d).

- *Sunn*: Sunn fibers are obtained from the stem of the legume *Crotolaria juncea* L. The sunn fiber resembles hemp microscopically, with the exception of the presence of crystals found in hemp fibers.
- *Jute*: Jute fibers are obtained from annual herbaceous plants of the genus *Corchorus*, *C. capsularis or Corchorus C. olitorius*. Jute fibers taper at both ends and are generally smooth, straight cylinders with occasional markings. The cell walls are thick, and the lumen is well defined with irregular constrictions (see Figure 20A-1f). Cross-sectional shape is polygonal with sharp edges.
- *Ramie*: Ramie fibers are obtained from the stem of *Boehmeria nivea*. Ramie fibers are cylindrical and have node-like ridges and longitudinal striations. The cell wall is thick, with a well-defined lumen (see Figure 20A-1c). Cross-sectional shape is elliptical.

Leaf Fibers (leaf or leaf stalk fibers)

- *Sisal*: Sisal fibers are obtained from the plant *Agave sisalana*. Sisal fibers are cylindrical with broadening toward the middle. Ends are blunt and thick. Cell walls are thick, with a rounded polygonal lumen that is large but not prominent. Rod-like crystals may also be present (see Figure 20A-1e). Cross-sectional shape is oval to rounded polygonal.
- *Abaca* (manila): Abaca fibers are obtained from the plant *Musa textilis*. The abaca fiber is identified by the characteristic stegmata (small silica cells) that are present in the longitudinal files adjacent to the fibers. Cross-sectional shapes are an oval outline.

Other:

- *Coir*: Coir fibers are obtained from the fruit or husk of the *Cocos nucifera* L. plant. Coir fibers are short with well-defined and broad lumen. The cells have a distinct wavy outline.

Animal Fibers

Morphological features that should be noted for animal fibers include the root, medulla, and cuticle. Shield size and shape may also be helpful characteristics. Scale casts can be useful in distinguishing some animal fibers.

- *Wool*: Wool fibers are obtained from several species of sheep. Wool fibers are colorless cylinders with visible, prominent, overlapping scale structure. The fiber edges appear serrated and wavy (see Figure 20A-2b).
- *Mohair*: Mohair fibers are obtained from the Angora goat. The scale structure found on mohair fibers is a faint, irregular-wave mosaic pattern (see Figure 20A-2d).
- *Cashmere*: Cashmere fibers are obtained from the Cashmere goat. Cashmere fibers are generally longer and more uniform than the mohair fiber. The scale structure is a wavy, irregular pattern.
- *Camel*: Camel fibers are obtained from two areas of the camel: the outer coarse hair and the fine fur hair. Camel fibers have faint scales that project slightly from the edge of the fiber. Camel fibers are generally round to slightly oval in cross section.
- *Llama*: Llama fibers are obtained from several animals within the same family: alpaca, llama, guanaco, and vicuna. Llama fibers are generally smooth and have fine diameters.
- *Silk*: Silk fibers are obtained from the cocoon of *Bombyx mori*. Silk fibers are generally continuous ribbons with small wedge-shaped or polygonal cross sections. The fibers may exhibit oblique depressions at intervals (see Figure 20A-2a).
- *Rabbit*: Rabbit fibers are obtained from two portions of the rabbit: the guard and finer fur hairs. The scale pattern changes along the length of the rabbit hair. The medulla pattern is also characteristic (see Figure 20A-2c).
- *Horse*: Horse fibers are obtained from the mane and the tail hair. Horse fibers can be distinguished by the coarseness and coronal scale pattern.

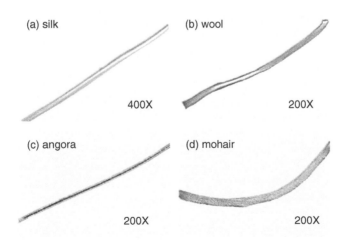

Figure 20A-2 Common animal fibers under plane-polarized light.

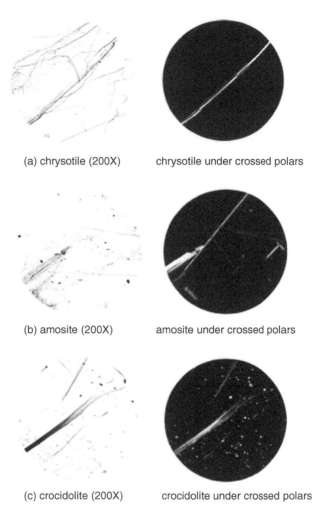

(a) chrysotile (200X)   chrysotile under crossed polars

(b) amosite (200X)   amosite under crossed polars

(c) crocidolite (200X)   crocidolite under crossed polars

Figure 20A-3   Common asbestos fibers under plane-polarized and crossed polarized light.

Mineral Fibers

Most mineral fibers or inorganic fibers are generally termed asbestos. Isotropic or low birefringent characteristics make these fibers easy to identify.

- *Asbestos*: This is a general term used for several types of natural fibers that are commonly
  occurring crystalline inorganic silicates. There are many varieties of asbestos fibers, several
  of which are shown in Figure 20A-3. Chrysotile is the most common asbestos.

Characteristics of Natural Fibers

An understanding of the macroscopic and microscopic characteristics found in natural fibers
allows the forensic scientist to perform natural fiber examinations. Fiber examinations involve
the use of a variety of microscopes, techniques, and instruments. Initially a stereomicroscope

is used to examine the fiber for macroscopic characteristics. Further testing can be performed using a compound or comparison light microscope to determine the microscopic characteristics of the fiber sample: extinction, refractive index, birefringence, and sign of elongation.

Some fibers will exhibit extinction when light emerging from the fiber is vibrating at right angles to the preferred direction of the analyzer. Because of their chemical orientation, cotton fibers never go to extinction (see Experiment 3A).

Two of the identifying characteristics of all fibers are the refractive indices and birefringence. With natural fibers, these are not the most distinguishing characteristics; however, they are still important features. The refractive index of a fiber is a measurement of how much light is slowed as it passes through the fiber. For fibers, there are two refractive indices: parallel and perpendicular. The refractive indices are determined by examining the fiber with orientation parallel and perpendicular to the plane of polarization. The refractive index is usually determined by the Becke line immersion method (see Experiment 3B). The birefringence of fibers can also be used to aid in the identification of a fiber. Birefringence is an optical property of a material having a refractive index that depends on the polarization and vibrational direction of light. Once the birefringence is determined (see Experiment 3B), the thickness of the fiber can be measured (see Experiment 2B). From the thickness and birefringence, the Michel-Lévy chart (Appendix C) and tabular data such as that found in Appendix A can be used for identification.

Another identifying characteristic is the sign of elongation. Sign of elongation is a term that refers to how a sample is elongated in relation to its refractive indices. If the refractive index for light parallel to the fiber exceeds that of the light perpendicular to the fiber, the elongation is said to be positive. If the reverse is true, the fiber is negative (see Experiment 3C).

With natural fibers, many of the other microscopic characteristics are better identifiers. Characteristics such as the shape of the cells; the relative thickness of the cell wall; the cell length; the size, shape, and thickness of the lumen; the shape of fiber bundles; and the presence of crystals for plant fibers and various morphological features for animal fibers are good identifying characteristics. Fluorescence of optical brighteners, dyes, and contaminants such as oils, fats, adhesives, pigments, toothpaste and denture cleaners, food products, cosmetics, paints, and soil may also be observed. To look for these characteristics, a cross section and either a semi-permanent or permanent longitudinal mount are utilized.

Natural Fiber Tests

Tests that may be performed during natural fiber examinations are the twist test, Billinghame test, Herzog test, burn test, and solubility test. The twist test is used to distinguish S- and Z-twist fibers. It relies on heating wet fibers quickly over a hotplate and watching them untwist. With this test, S-twist fibers (flax and ramie) will turn clockwise, while Z-twist fibers (hemp, jute, abaca, and sisal) will turn counterclockwise. Cotton and coir react irregularly.

The Billinghame test is a chemical staining test using sodium hypochlorite. It is usually used to distinguish sisal and abaca fibers. Abaca fibers will be stained orange, whereas all other leaf fibers are stained pale yellow. This test should only be performed on undyed fibers; otherwise, the results may be confusing.

Another test that can be used to determine twist is the Herzog test. This test determines addition or subtraction of retardation with a fiber oriented in the NE-SW direction under crossed polars. The S-twist fibers (flax and ramie) will display a slight additive effect, while Z-twist fibers (jute, hemp, sisal, and abaca) display a slight subtractive effect upon insertion of a compensator.

Table 20A-1 Common uses of natural fibers.

Fiber type	Common uses
Cotton fiber	Numerous types and grades of textile products and cordage
Kapok fiber	Stuffing for pillows, mattresses, lifejackets, lifebelts, buoys, and other water-related safety items
Akund fiber	Uses similar to kapok
Flax fiber	Primary use in textile products, cordage, and paper making
Hemp fiber	Twine and thin ropes, fabrics, canvas, sacking, and paper making
Sunn fiber	Cigarette papers
Jute fiber	Coarse woven fabrics (bags, backing for carpets and rugs), twines and ropes, electrical insulation, and fuses
Ramie fiber	Textile, clothing and upholstery, cordage and twine, paper making, fish nets, firehoses, canvas, industrial packing, and filter cloths
Sisal fiber	Agricultural twine, ropes, coarse fabrics for bags, hammocks, and shoe soles
Abaca fiber	Cordage, twine and cables, hat braids, woven stiffening materials, padding, and paper making
Coir fiber	Marine cordage, clothes, bristles for brushes, doormats, matting, mattress fiber and yarns, and fish nets
Animal fiber	Numerous types and grades of textile products, clothing, and other general uses
Mineral fiber	Numerous grades and types of insulating products

Burn tests may also be used to characterize a natural fiber. This test involves classifying the fiber according to its behavior when approaching a flame, when it enters the flame, and when it is removed. The ash and odor produced are also characteristic.

Finally, the solubility behavior of fibers in different solvents may also provide additional information when identifying natural fibers. The solubility behavior of fibers is examined using a variety of solvents that vary in polarity and acidity. Here the principle "like dissolves like" is used. The fibers that contain polar groups will dissolve more readily in polar solvents. The solubility behavior of most fibers can be found in the literature.[1] However, the tests are usually performed using known fibers, and the results are compared to the unknown fiber being identified.

Natural fibers have many uses. Some of the more common uses are listed in Table 20A-1.

Natural fiber examinations involve the use of a variety of microscopes. Initially a stereomicroscope is used to examine the fiber for macroscopic characteristics. Further testing can be performed using a compound or comparison light microscope to determine optical properties. Fluorescence may also be determined. At times, other techniques may be used. Twist, burn, staining, or solubility tests may also be performed during natural fiber examinations. Further testing

---

[1] *Identification of Fibers in Textile Materials*, DuPont Technical Information Bulletin X-176, December 1961.

can be performed using a variety of instruments to identify additional characteristics. Fourier transform infrared microspectrophotometry (Experiment 29), UV-VIS microspectrophotometry (Experiment 30), and scanning electron microscopy are all complementary techniques commonly performed on natural fibers. Information gained by performing each of these examinations can aid a forensic scientist in natural fiber identification.

Equipment and Supplies

Stereomicroscope

Polarizing light microscope with objectives of various magnifications (e.g., 4X, 10X, 20X, and 40X) and focusing ocular with micrometer scale and full wave plate

Fluorescence microscope with objectives of various magnifications (e.g., 4X, 10X, 20X, and 40X) and various excitation and barrier filters

Micro kit

Microscope slides and cover slips

Mounting mediums

Cargille™ oils

Plant fibers (flax, ramie, jute, hemp, sisal, coir, kapok, cotton, akund, abaca, sunn)

Animal fibers (wool, mohair, alpaca, angora, cashmere, camel, llama, silk)

Mineral fibers (asbestos)

Unbleached cotton, washed with detergent and rinsed

Polyethylene or plastic sheets

Hot plate

Pipette tips

Microtome

Thread

Nail polish

Test tubes

95% ethanol

5% nitric acid

0.25N Sodium hypochlorite

Bunsen burner

Solvent kit (40% sodium hydroxide, concentrated sulfuric acid, 75% sulfuric acid, concentrated hydrochloric acid, concentrated formic acid, dimethylformamide, glacial acetic acid, acetonitrile, chloroform, hexafluoroisopropanol, concentrated nitric acid, and cyclohexanone)

Safety

Use standard laboratory safety procedures as described in guidelines set by your instructor. Be cautious of microscope light levels to avoid eye damage. Know the hazards associated with the mounting mediums and solvents used in the procedures, and use them with appropriate precautions as set by your instructor. The solvent kit contains hazardous materials that should be handled with care. It is important that gloves and eye protection be used. Addtionally, proper ventilation is required. Refer to the safety data sheet (SDS) if necessary. Dispose of glass in an appropriate container.

Part I: Natural Fiber Examination

A worksheet for examination notes may be found at the end of Experiment 20.

Procedure

1. Obtain the assigned fibers.
2. Examine the first sample with the stereomicroscope. Note the color, length, and longitudinal form of the fiber.
3. Set up the compound or polarizing light microscope for Köhler illumination.
4. Determine the cross-sectional shape. This can be done by making a cross section (procedures for making cross sections are outlined in Experiment 17B) or from a liquid-mounted fiber. Remember to check the compound light microscope to ensure that samples will be viewed using Köhler illumination.
5. Using the liquid-mounted fiber, examine the fiber under non-polarized light. Determine the diameter and longitudinal shape. Draw what you see. Note any other morphological or microscopic features of the fiber. Rotate the fiber 90°, making note of any changes to the fiber as you rotate it. Return it to the original position.
6. Examine the fiber under crossed polars. Draw what you see.
7. Rotate the fiber 90°, making note of any changes to the fiber as you rotate it. Document any further characteristics viewed.
8. Repeat steps 1–6 while using a higher magnification.
9. Repeat steps 1–8 for all fibers assigned.

Part II: Refractive Index Determination

Procedure

1. Obtain the assigned fibers.
2. Using the polarizing light microscope, check the lighting to ensure that samples will be viewed using Köhler illumination.
3. Place the unknown fiber on a microscope slide, and add a cover slip. Place a drop of Cargille oil on the edges of the cover slip, and allow it to be drawn up under the cover slip.
4. Place the microscope slide on the stage, and focus using high magnification and plane-polarized light.
5. Rotate the fiber so that the length of the fiber is parallel to the plane of polarized light. For most microscopes, this would be E-W.
6. Close down the condenser to increase contrast and prevent the formation of a false Becke line. A false Becke line may be observed as a second bright line that moves in the opposite direction of the Becke line. This is visible when the difference in refractive index between a sample and the immersion liquid is low and the true Becke line is faint.

7. Using the focus knob, adjust the focus while observing the edges of the fiber. When the fiber is slightly out of focus, the Becke line will appear either inside or outside the fiber edge. The Becke line will move toward the higher refractive index when the focal distance is increased. Document which medium has the higher refractive index.

8. Rotate the fiber so it is oriented perpendicular to the plane of polarized light. For most microscopes, the fiber would be oriented N-S.

9. Once again, focus the edges to determine which medium has the higher refractive index. Document which medium has the higher refractive index.

10. Repeat with different Cargille oils until you are able to determine the refractive indices for your fiber. Determine which liquid to use next by depending on your previous results.

11. Report n-parallel and n-perpendicular for the room temperature.

12. Using the temperature coefficient on the bottle of Cargille oils that were a match, report the refractive index at 25°C.

13. Calculate the birefringence of the fiber at 25°C.

14. Repeat steps 2–13 for all assigned fibers.

15. Produce a chart showing your findings.

Part III: Observing Fluorescence

Procedure

1. Obtain a section of unbleached cotton.

2. Turn on the power supply for the specialized illuminator of the fluorescence microscope.Slide lamp diaphragm into the closed position while the lamp warms up.

3. Prepare a sample of unbleached cotton using non-fluorescent slides, cover slips, and mounting medium.

4. Turn on the power supply for the base light illuminator. Adjust the microscope to obtain Köhler illumination.

5. Using the lowest magnification, place the prepared sample on the microscope stage and bring it into focus. Lower the intensity of the base light and room lighting. Steps 3 and 4 are only necessary if the base light will be used to aid in the visualization of samples.

6. Open the lamp diaphragm on the specialized illuminator. Refocusing of the sample may be necessary.

7. Observe the sample using the various excitation and barrier filters available.

8. Next, prepare a sample of cotton that has been washed with detergent and rinsed and a sample of cotton that has been washed with detergent and is not rinsed.

9. Observe both samples using the various excitation and barrier filters available.

10. Compare each of the treated samples to the unbleached sample.

11. Produce a chart showing your findings.

Part IV: Twist Test

Procedure

1. Obtain the assigned fibers.

2. Soak the first fiber in water.

3. Using tweezers, hold the fiber above a hot plate, with the free end faced toward you.
4. Observe the direction of twist as the fiber is warmed.
5. Repeat steps 2–4 for all assigned fibers.
6. Produce a chart showing your findings.

Part V: Billinghame Test

Procedure

1. Obtain the assigned fibers.
2. Wash the first fiber sample with 95% ethanol to remove any oils, and allow to dry.
3. Boil the sample in 5% nitric acid for 5–10 minutes.
4. Remove the excess acid, and immerse the sample in cold 0.25N sodium hypochlorite solution for 10 minutes.
5. Remove the sample, and allow to dry. Note the color of the fiber.
6. Repeat steps 1–5 for all fibers assigned.
7. Produce a chart showing your findings.

Part VI: Herzog Test

Procedure

1. Obtain the assigned fibers.
2. Mount the first fiber in a Cargille oil.
3. Set up Köhler illumination on a polarizing light microscope.
4. Rotate the stage so the mounted fiber is in an NE-SW orientation under crossed polars.
5. Insert the first-order red compensator.
6. Observe the retardation color change.
7. Repeat steps 2–6 for all fibers assigned.
8. Produce a chart showing your findings.

Part VII: Burn Tests

Procedure

1. Obtain the assigned fibers.
2. Beginning with the first sample, hold the fiber using tweezers. Note the behavior of the fiber as it slowly approaches the Bunsen burner flame.
3. Note the behavior of the fiber as it enters the flame.
4. Note the color of the flame.
5. Note the behavior of the fiber after removal of the flame.
6. Note the type of ash.
7. Note the odor produced.
8. Repeat steps 2–7 for all fibers assigned.
9. Produce a chart showing your findings.

Part VIII: Solubility Test

Additional Safety Notice: The solvent kit contains organic solvents, concentrated acids and bases, and oxidizers. All solvents must be used with proper ventilation. Precautions should be taken to avoid inhalation and contact with the skin and eyes. Gloves and eye protection must be worn when handling these reagents.

Procedure

1. Obtain the assigned fibers.
2. Place a single fiber on a microscope, and add a small cover slip.
3. Place the microscope slide on the microscope stage.
4. Using a capillary tube, draw up a small amount of the first solvent from the solvent kit. Allow the solvent to be drawn under the cover slip.
5. Observe any changes to the fiber. Document your findings by notes and/or drawings.
6. Repeat with another fiber from the same source using a second solvent. Repeat until the fiber sample has been tested with all fiber solvents.
7. Repeat steps 2–6 for all assigned fibers.
8. Produce a chart showing your findings.

Part IX: Unknown Natural Fiber

Procedure

1. Obtain an unknown fiber.
2. Using any or all of the procedures above, examine the unknown fiber to determine its identity.
3. Describe your examination procedure for the unknown sample.
4. Include the unknown fiber number and what you identified the fiber to be. State your reasons to defend your conclusion.

Report Requirements

Include all drawings, calculations, and information obtained during the laboratory procedure. Notes and/or drawings should include sample identification, magnification, and a complete description.

Report Questions

1. What are the main divisions for natural fibers? Pick a fiber from each division, and describe the microscopic characteristics that would be used to identify it.

2. What are the differences between seed, stem, and leaf plant fibers? Pick a fiber from each category, and identify its source.
3. Describe each term as it relates to natural fibers: lumen, fiber bundles, cuticle scales, isotropic. Include drawings and/or examples with your description for each term.
4. How does a cross section assist in determining the identity of a natural fiber?
5. How does refractive index assist in determining the identity of a natural fiber?
6. How does fluorescence assist in fiber examinations?

Chapter 20

Experiment 20B: Man-made Fiber Examinations

Recommended pre-lab reading assignments:

Eyring MB, Gaudette BD. An Introduction to the Forensic Aspects of Textile Fiber Examination. In: Saferstein R, ed. *Forensic Science Handbook*, 2nd ed. Upper Saddle River, NJ: Pearson Education, 2002; 245–281.

Palenik SJ. Microscopic Examination of Fibres. In: Robertson J, Grieve M, eds. *Forensic Examination of Fibres*. London: Taylor and Francis, 1999; 153–176.

Textile Institute. *Identification of Textile Materials*, 7th ed. Manchester, England: Textile Institute, 1975; 95–133.

Objective

Upon completion of this practical exercise, the student will have developed a basic understanding of:

1. general characteristics of man-made fibers
2. use of the stereomicroscope to identify and visualize the characteristics of man-made fibers
3. use of the polarizing light microscope to identify and visualize the characteristics of man-made fibers
4. determination of cross-sectional shape of man-made fibers
5. measurement of refractive indices of man-made fibers
6. determination of the sign of elongation
7. use of the fluorescence microscope to visualize characteristics of man-made fibers
8. use of complementary testing such as burn and solubility tests

Introduction

The Locard Exchange Principle states that whenever two objects come in contact, an exchange of matter occurs. This theory applies to fiber evidence. Fibers are easily shed and transferred

---

Practical Forensic Microscopy: A Laboratory Manual, Second Edition. Barbara P. Wheeler.
© 2021 John Wiley & Sons Ltd. Published 2021 by John Wiley & Sons Ltd.
Companion website: www.wiley.com/go/Wheeler/Forensic

plane polarized light   crossed polars

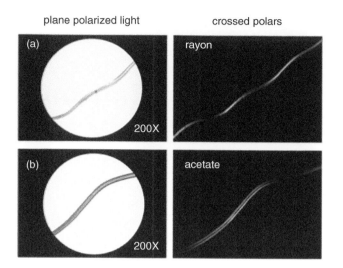

Figure 20B-1   Common cellulose-based polymer fibers under plane-polarized and crossed polarized light.

whenever there is contact between two objects, two individuals, or an individual and another object. Therefore, fiber examinations are often used to associate people with items or scenes. This makes fibers an important source of information in forensic investigations.

Man-made fibers are created from raw materials, either natural or chemical based, and possess various macroscopic and microscopic characteristics that make identifications and further association with a particular source possible at times. Because of this fact, man-made fibers are routinely examined in forensic casework. Common man-made fibers are discussed here.[1]

Cellulose-based polymers

  Acetate: Acetate is a manufactured fiber in which the fiber-forming substance is cellulose acetate (see Figure 20B-1b).

  Triacetate: The production of triacetate is similar to that of acetate, only differing in that the initial reaction product is hydrolyzed to a product in which not less than 92% of the hydroxyl groups are acetylated.

  Rayon: Rayon is a manufactured fiber composed of regenerated cellulose, as well as manufactured fiber composed of regenerated cellulose in which substituents have replaced not more than 15% of the hydrogens in the hydroxyl groups (see Figure 20B-1a).

  Lyocell: The production of lyocell is similar to that of rayon, differing only in that the fiber is composed of cellulose precipitated from an organic solution, and in which no substitution of the hydroxyl groups takes place and no chemical intermediates are formed.

  Bamboo: Bamboo fiber is manufactured by chemically treating the pulp of the *Bambusoideae* plant.

Regenerated protein polymers

  Azlon: Azlon is a manufactured fiber in which the fiber-forming substance is composed of any regenerated, naturally occurring protein.

---

[1] From Federal Trade Commission, Textile Products Identification Act, 1954.

Chemical-based (synthetic) polymers

Polyamide fibers

- *Nylon*: Nylon is a manufactured fiber in which the fiber-forming substance is a long-chain synthetic polyamide with less than 85% of the amide linkages being attached directly to the two aromatic rings (see Figure 20B-2b).
- *Nylon-6,6*: Nylon-6,6 is designed using adipic acid and diamine from which a polymer is synthesized containing six carbons. Coal tar intermediates or other derivatives are used as the starting materials.
- *Nylon-6*: Nylon-6 is produced through the use of caprolactam, the internal cyclic amide of aminocaproic acid, derived petrochemically. Caprolactam is polymerized by ring opening, followed by repetitive addition, until the desired molecular weight is achieved.
- *Qiana*: Qiana, a nylon fiber, is a condensation polymer containing alicyclic rings.

Aramid: Aramid is a manufactured fiber in which the fiber-forming substance is a long-chain synthetic polyamide with at least 85% of the amide linkages being attached directly to two aromatic rings.

Polyester: Polyester is a manufactured fiber in which the fiber-forming substance is a long-chain synthetic polymer composed of at least 85% by weight of an ester of a substituted aromatic carboxylic acid, including, but not restricted to, substituted terephthalate units and para-substituted hydroxl-benzoate units (see Figure 20B-2c).

Acrylic: Acrylic is a manufactured fiber in which the fiber-forming substance is any long-chain synthetic polymer composed of at least 85% (by weight) acrylonitrile units (see Figure 20B-2a).

Modacrylic: Modacrylic fibers are also based on acrylonitrile; however, lower unit content is utilized (less than 85% but at least 35% [by weight] acrylonitrile units).

Vinyon: Vinyon is a manufactured fiber in which the fiber-forming substance is any long-chain synthetic polymer composed of at least 85% (by weight) vinyl chloride units.

Saran: Saran is a manufactured fiber in which the fiber-forming substance is any long-chain synthetic polymer composed of at least 80% (by weight) vinylidene chloride units.

Vinal: Vinal is a manufactured fiber in which the fiber-forming substance is any long-chain synthetic polymer composed of at least 50% (by weight) vinyl alcohol units, and in which the total of the vinyl alcohol units and any one or more of the various acetal units is at least 85% (by weight) of the fiber.

Spandex: Spandex is a manufactured fiber in which the fiber-forming substance is any long-chain synthetic polymer composed of at least 85% segmented polyurethane.

Olefin: Olefin is a manufactured fiber in which the fiber-forming substance is any long-chain synthetic polymer composed of at least 85% (by weight) ethylene, propylene, or other olefin units except amorphous polyolefins qualifying under rubber or vinal.

Fluorocarbon: Fluorocarbon fibers are manufactured containing at least 95% of a long-chain polymer synthesized from aliphatic fluorocarbon monomers.

Nytril: Nytril is a manufactured fiber in which the fiber-forming substance is a long-chain polymer of vinylidene dinitrile, with the vinylidene content being no less than every other unit in the polymer chain.

Novoloid: Novoloid is a manufactured fiber in which the fiber contains at least 85% (by weight) of cross-linked nonolac.

Anidex: Anidex is a manufactured fiber in which the fiber-forming substance is any long-chain synthetic polymer composed of at least 50% (by weight) of one or more esters of a monohydric alcohol and acrylic acid.

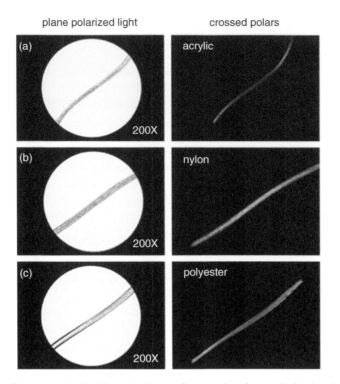

Figure 20B-2   Common chemical-based polymer fibers under plane-polarized and crossed polarized light.

Metallic: Metallic fibers are manufactured fibers composed of metal, plastic-coated metal, metal-coated plastic, or a core completely covered by metal.

Sulfar: Sulfar is a manufactured fiber in which the fiber-forming substance is a long-chain synthetic polysulfide with at least 85% of the sulfide linkages being attached directly to two aromatic rings.

PBI: PBI is a manufactured fiber in which the fiber-forming substance is a long-chain aromatic polymer containing reoccurring imidazole groups as an integral part of the polymer chain.

Elastoester: Elastoester fibers are manufactured fibers in which the fiber-forming substance is a long-chain synthetic polymer composed of at least 50% (by weight) of an aliphatic polyether, and at least 35% (by weight) polyester.

Melamine: Melamine fibers are manufactured fibers in which the fiber-forming substance is a synthetic polymer composed of at least 50% (by weight) of a cross-linked melamine polymer.

Glass: Glass fibers are a manufactured fiber in which the fiber-forming substance is glass.

PLA: A manufactured fiber in which the fiber-forming substance is composed of at least 85% (by weight) lactic acid ester units derived from naturally occurring sugars.

An understanding of the macroscopic and microscopic characteristics found in man-made fibers allows the forensic scientist to perform man-made fiber examinations. Man-made fiber examinations involve the use of a variety of microscopes, techniques, and instruments. Initially a stereomicroscope is used to examine the fiber for macroscopic characteristics. Further testing can be performed using a compound or comparison light microscope to determine the microscopic characteristics of the fiber sample: extinction, refractive index, birefringence, and sign of elongation.

Some fibers will exhibit extinction when light emerging from the fiber is vibrating at right angles to the preferred direction of the analyzer.

Two of the identifying characteristics of all fibers are their refractive indices and birefringence. With man-made fibers, these properties can be used to distinguish between fibers and manufacturers. The refractive index of a fiber is a measurement of how much light is slowed as it passes through the fiber. For fibers, there are two refractive indices: parallel and perpendicular. The refractive indices are determined by examining the fiber with orientation parallel and perpendicular to the plane of polarization. The Becke line method is used to determine the refractive index of fibers (see Experiment 3B). The birefringence of fibers can also be used to aid in the identification of a fiber. Birefringence is an optical property of a material having a refractive index that depends on the polarization and vibrational direction of light. Once the birefringence is determined (see Experiment 3B), the thickness of the fiber can be measured. Using these two characteristics and the Michel-Lévy birefringence chart (Appendix C), the fiber identification can be determined. Appendix B contains a table of refractive indices and birefringence for many common man-made fibers.

Another identifying characteristic is the sign of elongation. Sign of elongation is a term that refers to how a sample is elongated in relation to its refractive indices. With the use of a compensator, addition of retardation results in a positive sign of elongation (+). Subtraction of retardation results in a negative sign of elongation (−). When using the values for refractive index, if the refractive index for light parallel to the fiber exceeds that of the light perpendicular to the fiber, the elongation of the fiber is said to be positive. If the reverse is true, the fiber has a negative sign of elongation (see Experiment 3C).

Although size and shape are utilized in natural fiber identification, the man-made fiber manufacturing process lends itself to an endless variety of size and shape possibilities for most man-made fibers. However, this manufacturing process also produces characteristics that remain constant and uniform. Therefore, the appearance, or lack, of the following characteristics is noted and used for identification during a microscopic examination of man-made fibers: color, luster, thickness, inclusions, cross-sectional shape, and variations in characteristics within the fiber. Fluorescence of optical brighteners, dyes, and contaminants such as oils, fats, adhesives, pigments, toothpaste and denture cleaners, food products, cosmetics, paints, and soil may also be observed.

Burn and solubility tests may also be performed during man-made fiber examinations. Burn tests may also be used to characterize a man-made fiber. This test involves classifying the fiber according to its behavior when approaching a flame, when it enters a flame, and when it is removed. The ash and odor produced are also characteristic. Solubility tests may also provide additional information when identifying man-made fibers. The solubility behavior of fibers is examined using a variety of solvents that vary in polarity and acidity. Here the principle "like dissolves like" is used. The fibers that contain polar groups will dissolve more readily in polar solvents. The solubility behavior of most fibers can be found in the literature.[2] However, the tests are usually performed using known fibers, and the results are compared to the unknown fiber being identified.

---

[2] *Identification of Fibers in Textile Materials*, DuPont Technical Information Bulletin X-156, December 1961.

With the wide variety of manufactured fibers available, numerous uses for these fibers have also been employed. See further scientific literature for more details on the microscopic characteristics and uses of the various manufactured fibers.

Man-made fiber examinations involve the use of a variety of microscopes, techniques and instruments. Initially a stereomicroscope is used to examine the fiber for macroscopic characteristics. Further man-made fiber examinations can be performed using a compound or comparison light microscope to determine optical properties. Fluorescence may also be determined. At times, other techniques may be used. Burn or solubility tests may also be performed during man-made fiber examinations. Further testing can be performed using a variety of instruments to identify additional characteristics. Fourier transform infrared microspectrophotometry (Experiment 29), UV-VIS microspectrophotometry (Experiment 30), and scanning electron microscopy are all complementary techniques commonly performed on man-made fibers. Information gained by performing each of these examinations can aid a forensic scientist in man-made fiber identification.

Equipment and Supplies

Stereomicroscope

Polarizing light microscope with objectives of various magnifications (e.g., 4X, 10X, 20X, and 40X), focusing ocular with micrometer scale, and 530 nm gypsum plate

Fluorescence microscope with objectives of various magnifications (e.g., 4X, 10X, and 20X, and 40X) and various excitation and barrier filters

Micro kit

Microscope slides and cover slips

Mounting mediums

Cargille™ oils

Man-made fibers (acetate, acrylic, aramid, azlon, glass, fluorocarbon, lyocell, modacrylic, novoloid, nylon, nytril, olefin, polyester, rayon, saran, spandex, sulfar, triacetate, vinal, vinyon)

Man-made fabrics that have been stained with a variety of fluorescent contaminants (oil, fats, toothpaste, creamer, paint, etc.)

Polyethylene or plastic sheets

Hot plate

Pipette tips

Microtome

Thread

Nail polish

Bunsen burner

Solvent kit (40% sodium hydroxide, concentrated sulfuric acid, 75% sulfuric acid, concentrated hydrochloric acid, concentrated formic acid, dimethylformamide, glacial acetic acid, acetonitrile, chloroform, hexafluoroisopropanol, concentrated nitric acid, and cyclohexanone)

Safety

Use standard laboratory safety procedures as described in guidelines set by your instructor. Be cautious of microscope light levels to avoid eye damage. Know the hazards associated with the mounting mediums and solvents used in the procedures, and use them with appropriate precautions as set by your instructor. The solvent kit contains hazardous materials that should be handled with care. It is important that gloves and eye protection be used. Addtionally, proper ventilation is required. Refer to the safety data sheet (SDS) if necessary. Dispose of glass in an appropriate container.

Part I: Man-Made Fiber Examination

A worksheet for examination notes may be found in Experiment 20.

Procedure

1. Obtain the assigned fibers.
2. Examine the first sample with the stereomicroscope. Note the color, length, and longitudinal form of the fiber.
3. Set up the compound or polarizing light microscope for Köhler illumination.
4. Determine the cross-sectional shape. This can be done by making a cross section (procedures for making cross sections are outlined in Experiment 15B) or from a liquid-mounted fiber. Remember to check the compound light microscope to ensure that samples will be viewed using Köhler illumination.
5. Using the liquid-mounted fiber, examine the fiber under non-polarized light. Determine the diameter and longitudinal shape. Draw what you see. Note any other morphological or microscopic features of the fiber. Rotate the fiber 90°, making note of any changes to the fiber as you rotate it. Return it to the original position.
6. Examine the fiber under crossed polars. Draw what you see.
7. Rotate the fiber 90°, making note of any changes to the fiber as you rotate it. Document any further characteristics viewed.
8. Repeat steps 1–6 while using a higher magnification.
9. Repeat steps 2–8 for all fibers assigned.

Part II: Refractive Index Determination

Procedure

1. Obtain the assigned fibers.
2. Using the polarizing light microscope, check the lighting to ensure that samples will be viewed using Köhler illumination.
3. Place the unknown fiber on a microscope slide, and add a cover slip. Place a drop of Cargille oil on the edges of the cover slip, and allow it to be drawn up under the cover slip.
4. Place the microscope slide on the stage, and focus using high magnification and plane-polarized light.

5. Rotate the fiber so that the length of the fiber is parallel to the plane of polarized light. For most microscopes, this would be E-W.

6. Close down the condenser to increase contrast and prevent the formation of a false Becke line. A false Becke line may be observed as a second bright line, which moves in the opposite direction of the Becke line. This is visible when the difference between the refractive index of a sample and the immersion liquid is low and the true Becke line is faint.

7. Using the focus knob, adjust the focus while observing the edges of the fiber. When the fiber is slightly out of focus, the Becke line will appear either inside or outside the fiber edge. The Becke line will move toward the higher refractive index when the focal distance is increased. Document which medium has the higher refractive index.

8. Rotate the fiber so it is oriented perpendicular to the plane of polarized light. For most microscopes, the fiber would be oriented N-S.

9. Once again focus the edges to determine which medium has the higher refractive index. Document which medium has the higher refractive index.

10. Repeat with different Cargille oils until you are able to determine the refractive indices for your fiber. Determine which liquid to use next by referring to your previous results.

11. Report n-parallel and n-perpendicular for the room temperature.

12. Using the temperature coefficient on the bottle of Cargille oils that were a match, report the refractive index at 25°C.

13. Calculate the birefringence of the fiber at 25°C.

14. Repeat steps 2–13 for all assigned fibers.

15. Produce a chart showing your findings.

Part III: Sign of Elongation

Procedure

1. Using the polarizing light microscope, check the lighting to ensure that samples will be viewed using Köhler illumination.

2. Obtain a prepared slide of Dynel^{TM} (modacrylic).

3. Observe the Dynel fiber under crossed polars. Rotate this fiber into an upper right–lower left position (NE-SW). Draw what you see. Remember: If interference colors other than gray are observed, the fiber should have a + sign of elongation.

4. Insert the first-order red compensator, and draw the colors.

5. Rotate the stage 90°, and redraw the colors.

6. Consult the Michel-Lévy interference color chart (Appendix C), and determine if addition or subtraction of interference colors is occurring. Is this a positive or negative fiber?

7. Next, obtain a prepared slide with acrylic fibers.

8. Observe the fiber under crossed polars. Rotate the fiber into the upper right–lower left position (NE-SW), and draw.

9. Insert the first-order red compensator plate, and draw the colors.

10. Consult the Michel-Lévy interference color chart, and determine if addition or subtraction of interference colors is occurring. Is this a positive or negative fiber?

11. Report your findings, including your notes, explaining how you reached your conclusion.

Part IV: Observing Fluorescence

Procedure

1. Obtain a section of stained fabric.
2. Turn on the power supply for the specialized illuminator of the fluorescence microscope. Slide lamp diaphragm into the closed position while the lamp warms up.
3. Prepare a sample from an unstained portion of the fabric using non-fluorescent slides, cover slips, and mounting medium.
4. Turn on the power supply for the base light illuminator. Adjust the microscope to obtain Köhler illumination.
5. Using the lowest magnification, place the prepared sample on the microscope stage, and bring it into focus. Lower the intensity of the base light and room lighting. Steps 3 and 4 are only necessary if the base light will be used to aid in the visualization of samples.
6. Open the lamp diaphragm on the specialized illuminator. Refocusing of the sample may be necessary.
7. Observe the sample using the various excitation and barrier filters available.
8. Next, prepare a sample from the stained portion of the fabric.
9. Observe this sample using the various excitation and barrier filters available.
10. Compare your results for the unstained and stained samples.
11. Repeat steps 1–10 for all assigned fibers.
12. Produce a chart showing your findings.

Part V: Burn Tests

Procedure

1. Obtain the assigned fibers.
2. Beginning with the first sample, hold the fiber using tweezers. Note the behavior of the fiber as it slowly approaches the Bunsen burner flame.
3. Note the behavior of the fiber as it enters the flame.
4. Note the color of the flame.
5. Note the behavior of the fiber after removal from the flame.
6. Note the type of ash.
7. Note the odor produced.
8. Repeat steps 2–7 for all fibers assigned.
9. Produce a chart showing your findings.

Part VI: Solubility Test

Additional Safety Note: The solvent kit contains organic solvents, concentrated acids and bases, and oxidizers. All solvents must be used with proper ventilation. Precautions should be taken to avoid inhalation and contact with the skin and eyes. Gloves and eye protection must be worn when handling these reagents.

Procedure

1. Obtain the assigned fibers.
2. Place a single fiber on a microscope, and add a small cover slip.
3. Place the microscope slide on the microscope stage.
4. Using a capillary tube, draw up a small amount of the first solvent from the solvent kit. Allow the solvent to be drawn under the cover slip.
5. Observe any changes to the fiber. Document your findings by notes and/or drawings.
6. Repeat with another fiber from the same source using a second solvent. Repeat until the fiber sample has been tested with all fiber solvents.
7. Repeat steps 2–6 for all assigned fibers.
8. Produce a chart showing your findings.

Part VII: Unknown Man-Made Fiber

Procedure

1. Obtain an unknown fiber.
2. Using any or all of the procedures above, examine the unknown fiber to determine its identity.
3. Describe your examination procedure for the unknown sample.
4. Include the unknown fiber number and what you identified the fiber to be. State your reasons to defend your conclusion.

Report Requirements

Include all drawings, calculations, and other information obtained during the laboratory procedure. Notes and/or drawings should include sample identification, magnification, and a complete description.

Report Questions

1. What are the main divisions for man-made fibers? Pick a fiber from each division, and describe the microscopic characteristics that would be used to identify it.
2. What is refractive index? How can it be determined?
3. What is sign of elongation? How can it be determined?
4. Describe each term as it relates to man-made fibers: n-parallel, n-perpendicular, birefringence. Include examples with your description for each term.
5. How does a cross section assist in determining the identity of a man-made fiber?
6. How does refractive index assist in determining the identity of a man-made fiber?
7. How does sign of elongation assist in determining the identity of a man-made fiber?
8. How does fluorescence assist in fiber examinations?
9. What are the advantages and disadvantages of using refractive index and birefringence for identification of fibers?
10. Explain the logic behind the burn test and solubility test. Were these useful in determining the identification of your unknown fiber?

Chapter 20

Experiment 20C: Fiber Comparisons

Recommended pre-lab reading assignment:

Eyring MB, Gaudette BD. An Introduction to the Forensic Aspects of Textile Fiber Examination. In: Saferstein R, ed. *Forensic Science Handbook*, 2nd ed. Upper Saddle River, NJ: Pearson Education, 2002; 280–284.

Objective

Upon completion of this practical exercise, the student will have developed a basic understanding of:

1. techniques used for comparison of fibers

Introduction

Fiber comparisons are performed to determine possible associations between people, places, and objects. This association is accomplished through the comparison of macroscopic and microscopic characteristics. Learning to recognize the characteristics and the range found within a sample allows the forensic scientist to identify and compare fibers. Careful examination of known samples and unknown samples can provide information as to similarities or dissimilarities for an investigation.

Like hair comparisons, a suitable known fiber sample is extremely important when doing comparison examinations. Because there is such a variety of macroscopic and microscopic characteristics among fibers, known samples should be collected from each possible fiber source. So, if the unknowns to be compared are both blue cotton and red polyester, a known sample should be collected from all possible blue cotton and red polyester sources. It is also necessary to have a known sample that contains the range of characteristics found within a particular source. For instance, if the known source is a pair of blue jeans, it may be necessary

---

Practical Forensic Microscopy: A Laboratory Manual, Second Edition. Barbara P. Wheeler.
© 2021 John Wiley & Sons Ltd. Published 2021 by John Wiley & Sons Ltd.
Companion website: www.wiley.com/go/Wheeler/Forensic

for samples to be taken from all sections of fabric making up the jeans: right leg front, right leg back, left leg front, left leg back, pockets, and so on. This would provide a sample of the fibers that contains the range of characteristics that might be found from that source. Usually fabric sections for a garment are cut from the same piece of cloth; however, this may or may not always be the case. Minor dye differences between sections may not be visually identifiable; however, under the microscope small differences could be detected, preventing an association if suitable knowns had not been collected. Because of this fact, it is usually easier for the analyst to collect his or her known samples when possible. When handled this way, if more than one section needs to be tested, it is possible for the analyst to obtain another sample, but at the same time if the sample shows similarities, duplicate samples wouldn't have to be received and examined.

An understanding of the macroscopic and microscopic characteristics found in fibers allows the forensic scientist to perform fiber examinations and comparisons. Generally, unknown fibers are examined macroscopically first. If they appear different than the known samples, no further analysis is required. However, if they appear similar, analysis to identify both the known and unknown will begin. Initially a stereomicroscope is used to examine the fiber for all macroscopic characteristics. Further examination is performed using a compound or comparison light microscope and a fluorescence microscope to determine the microscopic characteristics of the fiber sample. To do this, a cross section is prepared, and either a semi-permanent or permanent mount is utilized. Known fiber samples are first identified. Unknown samples are then examined to determine their identity. If there is the possibility of a match, comparisons are then performed. This is usually performed on a comparison compound microscope.

The comparison microscope is composed of two similar microscopes, which are connected by an optical bridge (see Figure 17C-4). The bridge contains prisms and mirrors that are used to direct the light to a common set of oculars. A set of knobs is used to adjust the field of view, so that items can be viewed from either microscope independently or combined. In the combined view, the field of view is split into side-by-side views of the field of view from each microscope. This allows the examiner to view two items side-by-side on a microscopic scale. These comparison microscopes may also use one translational stage instead of a rotating stage. This allows for precise alignment of two fibers.

Comparison compound microscopes may be used for comparison of many of the fiber characteristics; however, a comparison polarizing light microscope should also be used to view some optical properties that are found in fibers. Extinction, refractive index, birefringence, sign of elongation, and pleochroism (see Experiments 3A, 3B, and 3C) may be compared using the comparison polarized light microscope. It is also necessary to use the comparison fluorescence microscope when determinations are made concerning the similarity of fiber dyes, whiteners, and brighteners. If all the characteristics displayed by the unknown fiber are found within the known sample, an association may be reached. However, when an association is reached as to a possible origin of the fiber, it should be pointed out that a similarity to a known sample does not exclude the possibility of another similar source.

Equipment and Supplies

Stereomicroscope

Comparison compound light microscope with objectives of various magnifications (e.g., 4X, 10X, 20X, and 40X) and focusing ocular with micrometer scale

Comparison polarized light microscope with objectives of various magnifications (e.g., 4X, 10X, 20X, and 40X) and focusing ocular with micrometer scale

Comparison fluorescence microscope with objectives of various magnifications (e.g., 4X, 10X, 20X, and 40X) and various excitation and barrier filters

Micro kit

Microscope slides and cover slips

Mounting medium

Cargille™ oils

Polyethylene or plastic sheets

Hot plate

Pipette tips

Microtome

Thread

Nail polish

Test tubes

95% ethanol

5% nitric acid

0.25N sodium hypochlorite

Bunsen burner

Solvent kit (40% sodium hydroxide, concentrated sulfuric acid, 75% sulfuric acid, concentrated hydrochloric acid, concentrated formic acid, dimethylformamide, glacial acetic acid, acetonitrile, chloroform, hexafluoroisopropanol, concentrated nitric acid, and cyclohexanone)

Known fiber samples

Unknown fiber samples

Safety

Use standard laboratory safety procedures as described in guidelines set by your instructor. Be cautious of microscope light levels to avoid eye damage. Know the hazards associated with the mounting mediums and solvents used in the procedures, and use them with appropriate precautions as set by your instructor. The solvent kit contains hazardous materials that should be handled with care. It is important that gloves and eye protection be used. Additionally, proper ventilation is required. Refer to the safety data sheet (SDS) if necessary. Dispose of glass in an appropriate container.

Part I: Fiber Comparisons

A worksheet for examination notes may be found in Experiment 20.

Procedure

1. Obtain both a known and an unknown fiber sample.
2. Examine the known sample with the stereomicroscope.

3. If the fiber can be determined to be natural, proceed with testing as outlined in Experiment 20A. If the fiber is determined to be man-made, proceed with testing as outlined in Experiment 20B.

Additional Safety Note: The solvent kit contains organic solvents, concentrated acids and bases, and oxidizers. The organic solvents must be used with proper ventilation. Precautions should be taken to avoid inhalation and contact with the skin and eyes. Gloves and eye protection must be worn when handling these reagents.

4. Repeat step 3 with the unknown fiber sample.
5. Compare the macroscopic and microscopic characteristics that you have documented for the unknown sample and the known sample.
6. If possible, use the various comparison microscopes to examine both samples simultaneously. If you believe that the samples are similar, find areas in the known sample that have similar characteristics as that in the unknown fiber. Draw what you see.
7. Include your documentation and drawings. Make sure your documentation includes the appropriate labeling (name, sample numbers, and lab).
8. Include the unknown fiber number, and state the result of your fiber comparison. State your reasons to defend your conclusion.

Report Requirements

Include all drawings, calculations, or other information obtained during the laboratory procedure. Notes and/or drawings should include the sample identification, magnification, and a complete description.

Report Questions

1. Why is it possible to perform fiber comparisons?
2. How is a fiber comparison conducted?
3. Can a fiber be associated with only one source? Explain your answer.
4. Is it possible for an unknown fiber from a murder scene to be similar to a known sample, but for that source to have no involvement in the crime? Explain your answer.
5. Is it possible for an unknown hair from a murder scene to be dissimilar to a known sample, but for that source to be involved in the crime? Explain your answer.

EXTRA CREDIT: Why is it important to use another method of testing (other than a visual microscopic examination) to assess the colors of a fiber association?

Recommended and Further Reading

American Association of Textile Chemists and Colorants (AATCC). *AATCC Technical Manual*. Research Triangle Park, NC: AATCC, 1996.
ASTM. *Standard Test Materials for Identification of Fibers in Textiles (ASTM D 276-87)*. Philadelphia: ASTM, 1996.

Carroll GR. Forensic Fiber Microscopy. In: Robertson J, ed. *Forensic Examination of Fibres*. New York: Ellis Horwood, 1992.

Carroll GR, Demers J. Technical Note: A New Methods for Determining the Refractive Indices and Birefringence of Textile Fibers. *Canadian Society of Forensic Science Journal*. 1993; 26: 15–117.

Causin V, Marega C, Schiavone S, Marigo A. A Quantitative Differentiation Method for Acrylic Fibers by Infrared Spectroscopy. *Forensic Science International*. 2005; 151(2–3): 125–131.

Cho LL, Reffner JA, Gatewood BM, Wetzel DL. A New Method for Fiber Comparison Using Polarized Infrared Microspectroscopy. *Journal of Forensic Sciences*. 1999; 44(2): 275–282.

Cwiklik C. An Evaluation of the Significance of Transfers of Debris: Criteria for Association and Exclusion. *Journal of Forensic Sciences*. 1999; 44(6): 1136–1150.

Eyring MB, Gaudette BD. An Introduction to the Forensic Aspects of Textile Fiber Examination. In: Saferstein R, ed. *Forensic Science Handbook*. Upper Saddle River, NJ: Pearson Education, 2002; 245–281.

Fong W. Analytical Methods for Developing Fibers as Forensic-Science Proof – a Review with Comments. *Journal of Forensic Sciences*. 1989; 34(2): 295–311.

Fong W, Inami SH. Simple, Rapid, and Unique Hand Techniques for Cross-Sectioning Fibers and Hair. *Journal of Forensic Sciences*. 1988; 33(2).

Gaudette B. The Forensic Aspects of Textile Fiber Examination. In: *Forensic Science Handbook*. Englewood Cliffs, NJ: Prentice Hall, 1988; 209–272.

Grieve M. The Evidential Value of Black Cotton Fibers. *Science and Justice*. 2001; 41: 245–260.

Grieve MC. The Role of Fibers in Forensic Science Examinations. *Journal of Forensic Sciences*. 1983; 28(4).

Grieve MC, Deck S. A New Mounting Medium for the Forensic Microscopy of Textile Fibers. *Science and Justice*. 1995; 35(2): 109–112.

Grieve MC, Wiggins KG. Fibers under Fire: Suggestions for Improving Their Use to Provide Forensic Evidence. *Journal of Forensic Sciences*. 2001; 46(4): 835–843.

Hall D. *Practical Fiber Identification*. Auburn, AL: Auburn University, 1982.

Hartshoene AW, Wild FM. The Discrimination of Cellulose Di- and Tri- Acetate Fibers by Solvent Tests and Melting Point Determination. *Journal of Forensic Sciences Society*. 1991; 31(4): 457–461.

Hemmings J. Fiber Microscopy In: Siegel J, Saukko P, eds. *Encyclopedia of Forensic Sciences*, 2nd ed. Amsterdam: Elsevier, 2013; 143–147.

Houck MM, Siegel JA. *Fundamentals of Forensic Science*, 3rd ed. Amsterdam: Elsevier Academic Press, 2015; 383–403.

Identification of Fibers in Textile Materials. DuPont Technical Information Bulletin, December 1961.

Laing DK, Locke J, Richard RA, Wilkerson JM. The Examination of Paint Films and Fibers as Thin-Sections. *Microscope*. 1987; 35: 233–248.

Martin P. Color Analysis. In: Siegel J, Saukko P, eds. *Encyclopedia of Forensic Sciences*, 2nd ed. Amsterdam: Elsevier, 2013; 148–154.

Mauersberger H. *Matthews' Textile Fibers*, 6th ed. New York: John Wiley & Sons, Inc., 1975.

McCrone W. Refractive Indices and Birefringence of Fibers. *The Microscope*. 1991; 39: 57–58.

Moncrief RW. *Man Made Fibers*, 6th ed. London: Newnes-Butterworth, 1975.

Palenik S, Fitzsimons C. Fiber Cross-Sections: Part I. *The Microscope*. 1990; 38: 187–195.

Palenik S, Fitzsimons C. Fiber Cross-Sections: Part II. *The Microscope*. 1990; 38: 313–320.

Paulsson N, Stocklassa B. A Real-Time Color Image Processing System for Forensic Fiber Investigations. *Forensic Science International*. 1999; 103(1): 37–59.

Pelton WR. Distinguishing the Cause of Textile Fiber Damage Using the Scanning Electron-Microscope (Sem). *Journal of Forensic Sciences*. 1995; 40(5): 874–882.

Petraco N. Modified Technique for the Cross-Sectioning of Hair and Fibers. *Journal of Police Science Administration*. 1981; 9: 448.

Roberston J, Roux C. Fiber: Protocols for Examination. In: Siegel J, Saukko P, eds. *Encyclopedia of Forensic Sciences*, 2nd ed. Amsterdam: Elsevier, 2013; 124–128.

Robertson J, Roux C, Wiggins K. *Forensic Fibre Examinations*, 3rd ed. London: Taylor & Francis, 2013.

Shahin MM. Optical Microscopy Study on Poly(P-Phenylene Terephthalamide) Fibers. *Journal of Applied Polymer Science*. 2003; 90(2): 360–369.

Sokkar TZN, Ramadan WA. Optical Anisotropy in Dyed Polyester Fibers. *Journal of Applied Physics*. 1991; 70(7): 3815–3820.

Stoeffler SF. A Flowchart System for the Identification of Common Synthetic Fibers by Polarized Light Microscopy. *Journal of Forensic Sciences*. 1996; 41(2): 297–299.

Tungol MW, Bartick EG, Montaser A. Forensic Analysis of Acrylic Copolymer Fibers by Infrared Microscopy. *Applied Spectroscopy*. 1993; 47(10): 1655–1658.

Wildman AB. Identification of Animal Fibers. *Journal of the Forensic Science Society*. 1961; 1: 79–154.

Chapter 21

Experiment 21: Soil Examinations

Recommended pre-lab reading assignments:

McCrone WC, McCrone LB, Delly JG. *Polarized Light Microscopy.* Ann Arbor, MI: Ann Arbor Science, 1978; 125–168.

Murray RC, Solebello LP. Forensic Examination of Soil. In: Saferstein R, ed. *Forensic Science Handbook*, 2nd ed. Upper Saddle River, NJ: Pearson Education, 2002; 615–625.

Petraco N. *Color Atlas and Manual of Microscopy for Criminalists, Chemists and Conservators.* Boca Raton, FL: CRC Press, 2004; 135–149.

Objective

Upon completion of this practical exercise, the student will have developed a basic understanding of:

1. general characteristics of soil samples
2. color of soil samples
3. particle size distributions of soil samples
4. density of soil samples

Introduction

Soil is a common form of physical evidence found at most crime scenes. Soil may be picked up by a vehicle, thus providing a valuable link between the car and a scene. Similarly, soil found adhering to clothing or shoes might provide an association that can link a suspect to

Practical Forensic Microscopy: A Laboratory Manual, Second Edition. Barbara P. Wheeler.
© 2021 John Wiley & Sons Ltd. Published 2021 by John Wiley & Sons Ltd.
Companion website: www.wiley.com/go/Wheeler/Forensic

a particular crime scene. Since there is the possibility of soil associations, soil examinations have become a valuable portion of an investigation. There are two types of soil examinations encountered in the forensic laboratory. The majority of soil examinations involve comparisons between soil samples collected from known locations and unknown soil samples. However, some soil examinations may be performed to identify and compare additives or contaminants to the soil samples themselves. This evidence is generally used in conjunction with other forensic evidence.

Soil is a mixture of decaying vegetable matter and rock that has weathered and decayed by erosion, oxidation, hydration, and the actions of acids such as carbonic acid on the rock. As it decays, water, wind, gravity, plants, and animals move it, causing a mixture of the minerals present. Through this constant mixing, soils form in a variety of manners and different locations, yielding characteristics that allow an examiner to look for unique properties in a soil identification and comparison.

Common soil mineral constituents are clay, silica, calcite, numerous silicoaluminates, and smaller quantities of mica, hornblends, and iron oxides. A variety of quartz and feldspars, halite, garnet, tourmaline, rutile, epidote, pyrite, pumice, obsidian, augite, gypsum, talc, limonite, serpentine, magnetite, dolomite, and hematite may also be found in soil samples. In addition to the mineral constituents, the organic and miscellaneous constituents (coal, cinders, diatoms, pollen, seeds, peat, etc.) also contribute to the variety of characteristics found in soils.

Since soil is a complex mixture, the examination is a detailed procedure, utilizing several techniques. The method for collecting appropriate soil samples relies on the reliability of the source. Soil samples can vary greatly within short geographical distances. They can change vertically as well as horizontally. Therefore, soil samples should be taken from the area and to the depth that is believed to be the actual source. It is essential that further samples be taken near the source, so that the variability of the soil may be established. Each should be packaged separately and in a container to allow drying. A handful is usually an appropriate size sample.

Once the size and collection of a soil sample have been determined to be sufficient, analysis can begin. Soil color is one of the most obvious features of a soil sample. However, soil color is very dependent on soil moisture. Since unknown soil samples and soil samples collected from scenes may vary in moisture content, samples must be dried before color comparisons can be performed. The color of the soil is compared to a set of standard colors, usually the Munsell Soil Color Chart^{TM}. In this classification system, colors are expressed on a numerical basis in terms of their hue, value, and chroma. Hue is the base color of the soil. The system uses five primary hues (blue, green, purple, red, and yellow) and five intermediate hues for a total of 10 hue names. The intermediate hues are green-yellow (GY), yellow-red (YR), blue-green (BG), red-purple (RP), and purple-blue (PB). Each of these 10 hues is divided into colors that are equally spaced. These are given numerical values before the hue name. For example, 10Y marks a limit of yellow hue. Four equally spaced steps of the adjacent yellow-red (YR) hue are identified as 2.5YR, 5YR, 7.5YR, and 10YR, respectively. The standard chart for soil has separate hue cards from 10R through 5Y.

Value is a measure of the lightness or darkness of this color. It increases vertically from bottom to top. Since value is a measure of how much light reaches the eye, value increases as it gets further from black (total absence of light). Neutral gray is used to show levels of light and dark on an achromatic scale. Value extends from pure black (0/) to pure white (10/). The value notation is a measure of the amount of light that reaches the eye under daylight conditions. Gray is perceived as about halfway between black and white, and has a value notation of 5/.

Chroma is the degree of saturation of the color or the strength of the color. For soils, the scales of chroma extend from /0 for neutral colors to a chroma of /8 as the strongest saturation.

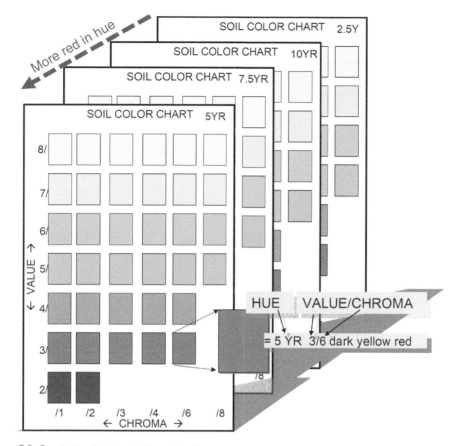

Figure 21-1 Soil color description using the *Munsell Soil Book of Color*. Source: Weil RR. *Laboratory Manual for Introductory Soils*, 9th ed. Dubuque, IA, © 2014 Kendall/Hunt Publishing Company.

Figure 21-1 shows the arrangement of color chips in the *Munsell*^TM *Soil Book of Color*. Each page is a different hue. Value increases vertically from bottom to top. Since value is a measure of how much light reaches the eye, the value increases as it goes further from black (a total absence of light). Chroma increases horizontally from left to right on the color page. Chroma increases as the color saturation reaches pure color hues (this is the furthest from black). For example, a dark reddish-brown soil would have Munsell color notation of 5YR 3/6, where 5YR is the hue corresponding to the page containing the matching color, 3 is the value corresponding to the matching row, and 6 is the chroma corresponding to the matching column. The Munsell^TM system allows analysts to speak the same color language and normalizes color descriptions. Munsell^TM is not the only color system used in forensic science; however, it is the most common system used for soils.

Next, a stereomicroscopic examination is performed. Any contaminants, such as paint chips, glass, brick, glass, cement, and so on, are noted. For some contaminants, further analysis and comparison may be possible. The dried soil samples are then sieved into sections, and the colors compared again. The soil samples are passed through a set of wire sieves with the size of the openings decreasing from top to bottom. Sieve sizes should range from 40 to 280 mesh. After sieving, the relative amount of each particle size is determined. The particle size distribution in soil can be used to distinguish and compare samples and to determine its texture class. The three primary texture classes are sand (diameters between 0.05 and 2.0 mm), silt (diameters between 0.002 and 0.05 mm), and clay (diameters less than 0.002 mm). Variations in the particle sizes are distinctive and can be used to distinguish different samples. Because some of these particles are smaller than the smallest sieve, they can only be determined using the so-called "settling methods." These methods are based on the idea that larger particles fall more quickly through water than smaller ones. Equal-volume aliquots of the soil suspension are taken from the same depth in a measuring vessel at different time intervals and allowed to evaporate. In both the sieving and settling methods, the dried particles from each fraction are weighed and the weight of each is plotted in a graph as a function of sampling interval for comparison purposes.

Usually the 40 and 60 mesh sieved fractions are used for density comparisons and mineral content identifications. Density comparisons are usually performed through the use of density gradient tubes. Each gradient tube is composed of numerous layers starting with an undiluted heavy-density liquid, followed by various dilutions of the heavy-density liquid and water to provide a range of densities, with the final layer being unmixed water. For instance, if using Poly-Gee™ (which is sodium polytungstate) and water, ratios of 10:0, 9:1, 8:2, 7:3, 6:4, 5:5, 4:6, 3:7, 2:8, 1:9, and 0:10 might be used. The density of the liquid for each layer may be determined by using Equation (21-1):

$$D_T = \frac{D_{PG,T}V_{PG} + D_{DW,T}V_{DW}}{V_{PG} + V_{DW}} \qquad (21\text{-}1)$$

where $D_{PG,T}$ is the density of Poly-Gee™ in g/mL at temperature T, V_{PG} is the volume of Poly-Gee™ in mL, $D_{DW,T}$ is the density of distilled water at temperature T, and V_{DW} is the volume of distilled water. Since density is temperature dependent, it is important to record density at the specific temperature, T. (Note: Temperature does not have to be as carefully controlled when comparisons are made using the density gradient method. However, if it is necessary to report a numerical value for density, the temperature should be kept constant using a circulating water bath or other method.)

Color, particle size, and texture class are used to compare different soils. However, they have limited discriminating value in forensic cases. If it is necessary to further differentiate soil samples, the analyst would identify the mineral content of the soil by analyzing the optical properties of the sieved portions, as discussed in Experiment 21A.

Equipment and Supplies

Stereomicroscope

Compound light microscope with objectives of various magnifications (e.g., 4X, 10X, 20X, and 40X) and focusing ocular with micrometer scale and 530 nm gypsum plate

Micro kit

Microscope slides and cover slips

Known soil samples (or mineral combinations)

Unknown soil samples (or mineral combinations)

Munsell™ soil color chart

Sieve set (20, 40, 60, 80, and 100 mesh sizes and trap)

Density tubes

Poly-Gee™

One 250 mL or 400 mL beaker

Plastic weigh boats

20% hydrogen peroxide solution

Hot plate

Stirring rod

Mortar and pestle

Balance for weighing at least +/− 0.1 g

Disposable glass or plastic pipettes and bulbs

Safety

Use standard laboratory safety procedures as described in guidelines set by your instructor. Be cautious of microscope light levels to avoid eye damage. Know the hazards associated with the solvents used in the procedures, and use them with appropriate precautions as set by your instructor. It is important to wear safety glasses and gloves when handling hydrogen peroxide solutions. Contact with the eyes can cause serious long-term damage. The hydrogen peroxide solution is corrosive and can cause skin burns. Slow decomposition of the solution in storage may lead to a buildup of pressure in sealed containers. Hydrogen peroxide can form potentially explosive compounds with a wide variety of materials. Refer to the safety data sheet (SDS) if necessary.

Important Safety Reminder: ALWAYS wear safety glasses and gloves when handling hydrogen peroxide solutions. Hydrogen peroxide solutions should be diluted with lots of water before they are poured into the sink.

Part I: Color and Overall Composition

Procedure

Source: Procedure adapted from Quarino L. *Soil Identification – Particle Size Distribution.* Trace Evidence and Microscopy. Allentown, PA: Cedar Crest College, 2006.

Students will work in pairs for Part I. One student will examine the known, and one will examine the unknown.

1. Weigh a clean evaporation dish to at least 0.1 gm.
2. Next, weight the evaporation dish with the soil sample. Use the same balance for all weighing in this procedure.
3. Dry the soil samples in an oven overnight at about 65°C in the evaporation dish.
4. Reweigh the evaporation dish with the soil sample. Subtracting the weight of the evaporation, dish determine the mass of the soil sample. Calculate the percent weight of the dry content in the original sample using Equation (21-2).

$$\text{Percent Dried Content} = \frac{\text{mass of dried sample (gm)}}{\text{mass of wet sample (gm)}} \times 100 \qquad (21\text{-}2)$$

5. Break up any large clumps, and determine the color using the Munsell soil color chart. For comparison to the color charts, use daylight if possible since the type of illumination will affect your results.

6. Examine each sample with the stereomicroscope to identify any foreign contaminants that might be present in the samples.

7. Sieve the soil samples into the designated portions.

8. Weigh the portion that cannot pass through the largest sieve. This is generally referred to as the gravel portion of the sample. Calculate the percent weight of the gravel portion using Equation (21-3).

$$\text{Percent Weight} = \frac{\text{weight of fraction (gm)}}{\text{weight of moisture free sample (gm)}} \times 100 \qquad (21\text{-}3)$$

This formula can also be used to calculate the percent weight for the other fractions.

9. Classify the color of this portion using the Munsell soil color chart.

10. Organic matter in the remaining portions needs to be oxidized before an accurate weight can be determined. Weigh a 250 or 400 mL beaker. Transfer the unsieved fraction to the beaker, and reweigh. Calculate the mass of this unsieved fraction.

11. Add 100 mL of 20% hydrogen peroxide. Add in increments, stirring well between increments. Allow to stand overnight in the hood with a watch glass covering the beaker. Make sure your name and a description of the contents of the beaker are written on the beaker.

12. Place the beaker in an oven for two hours to destroy the remaining organics and to decompose the remaining peroxide. Look at the beaker periodically to make sure the liquid does not froth. If frothing occurs, wash the sides of the beaker with distilled water using a wash bottle.

13. Add enough distilled water to bring the volume to 150 mL, and stir well. Cool and allow to stand overnight – any remaining large organic particles will float to the surface.

14. Carefully decant off as much of the clear fluid as possible with a disposable glass or plastic pipette without disturbing the solid matter. Boil the remaining liquid on a hot plate to remove as much water as possible. Place the remainder in an oven for as long as it takes to dry. Cool in a desiccator for 30 minutes and then weigh, subtracting the weight of the beaker to give the weight of the mineral soil free of organic matter. Calculate the percentage of organic matter using the mass of the unsieved fraction determined in step 10, according to Equation (21-4):

$$\text{Percent organic matter} = \frac{\text{mass after digestion (gm)}}{\text{mass before digestion (gm)}} \times 100 \qquad (21\text{-}4)$$

15. Transfer the completely dry material to a mortar and pestle, and break apart any clumps in the sample. Minerals should not adhere to each other.

16. Pour the sample into the set of remaining sieves, retaining the fine particles beneath the sieve in a collecting tray. As best you can, make sure all the soil is transferred from the mortar and pestle. Shake the sieve set, making sure that particles get trapped on the proper sieve.

17. Transfer the particles from each sieve to a plastic weigh boat. Record the weight of each fraction by subtracting the weight of each weigh boat.

18. Determine the color of each fraction using the Munsell color charts.

19. Calculate the percent weight of each fraction using the original dry weight of the soil sample and Equation (21-3).

20. For both the known and the unknown soil samples, prepare a histogram of percent weight of each fraction (including the gravel fraction) versus fraction name by mesh size. Sum the cumulative weight of each fraction, and compare to the original weight of the soil sample. Account for any differences in these masses in your report. Tabulate the color of each fraction and any additional observations about the fraction. Report the percent moisture content and organic matter for your sample.

21. Pooling data with your partner, compare the known and unknown samples using all the data collected. Are the two samples from a probable common source? Why or why not?

22. Keep either the 40 or 60 mesh fraction for density testing in Part II.

Part II: Density Distribution of Mineral Content

Procedure

Additional Note: This procedure uses Poly-Gee and water. The instructor may choose to substitute bromoform and bromobenzene for this procedure to have a wider range of density possibilities. **Both bromoform and bromobenzene are extremely toxic and suspected carcinogens**, and should be used in a hood with protective eyewear.

1. Obtain two dry tubes. Position the tubes on a stand so that you will be able to add liquids evenly to create two comparable density gradient tubes.

2. Using water (s.g. of 1.00) and Poly-Gee (s.g. of 2.89), you need to prepare five mixtures to get a density distribution that could be used to separate minerals ranging in densities from 1.68 to 2.89. (100% water and 100% Poly-Gee will be your sixth and seventh portions.) Select five density values, and calculate the amounts of water and Poly-Gee needed to prepare about 10 mL of each density mixture. You can prepare this in small beakers. Be sure the beakers are CLEAN and DRY before you begin.

3. When preparing the mixtures, add water to the beaker FIRST, and then add the Poly-Gee. This will make it easier to form the solutions. Stir very well.

4. Starting with the most dense mixture, 100% Poly-Gee, slowly add about 5 mL to each tube. Remember, you will be comparing the mineral samples in the two tubes, so you want the liquid levels to be identical.

5. Next, slowly add about 5 mL of the next densest mixture into each tube. Add the liquids carefully so that minimal mixing occurs.

6. Proceed with each additional liquid mixture (in the order of 3–5), slowly adding portions until the final mixture is added. Add 5 mL of 100% water to each tube.

7. Cover each density gradient tube with a small section of Parafilm™.

8. Allow the density gradient tubes to equalize at least 24 hours prior to use.

9. Obtain your known mineral mixture and unknown sample. If continuing from Part I, use the 40 or 60 mesh portion of the sieved samples.

10. Examine a small portion of the known sample under a stereoscope. Make sure you don't contaminate this, because you will return it to the known vial.

11. Examine your unknown sample under the stereomicroscope. Make sure you don't contaminate this, because you will return it to the unknown vial.

12. Slowly add 0.1 gm of the sample for comparison into each density gradient tube. (Known sample into one tube and unknown sample into the other.)

13. Allow the samples to separate and equilibrate for approximately 48 hours.
14. Compare levels of separation for the samples.
15. If possible, take a photograph of the two tubes. Count the number of different types of mineral grains found in each sample. If possible, count the number of grains within each mineral type, and tabulate the data. Note color differences between different mineral types. Write a concise statement about the two samples. Are they from a probable common source? Why or why not? Explain your choice. Comment on the accuracy and precision of the method, and give sources of error with the procedure.
16. Record room temperature. Are the results here accurate without temperature control?

Report Requirements

Include all drawings, calculations, and other information obtained during the laboratory procedure. Notes and/or drawings should include the sample identification, magnification, and a complete description.

Report Questions

1. How are soil samples collected?
2. What information can be gained in an investigation with a soil comparison?
3. How is color determined for soil samples? Name three things that affect the color of soil samples.
4. Why were the Munsell color determinations done using daylight?
5. Estimate the color of an object that has a Munsell color notation of (a) 5Y/6/1 and (b) 10R/4/2.
6. Describe how the density distribution of a mineral portion is determined.
7. If two samples are being compared for possible differences, which do you think would be the most discriminating: (a) density distribution of mineral content, (b) percent organic matter, (c) particle distribution, or (d) color? Fully explain your choice.
8. What are the three texture classes for soil? How would the texture class be determined?
9. What determined the amount of organic matter in soil? Would the amount of organic matter affect the color of soil?
10. What was the purpose of the hydrogen peroxide?
11. A trace examiner compares two soils samples by determining the color and percent weight of the sieved fractions. They were found to be similar in all characteristics. If this is all that was done, could the examiner state that the two were of a probable common source? Why or why not?
12. A trace examiner compares two soil samples by determining the density distribution of the minerals found in the soil. They were found to be similar in all characteristics. If this is all that was done, could the examiner state that the two samples were of a probable common source? Why or why not?
13. Could the density determinations of mineral content be determined for the known sample on one day and compared to the density determination of minerals for the unknown sample on the next day? Could different laboratories work on the known and unknown and compare the results? Why or why not?

Chapter 21

Experiment 21A: Identification of Minerals in Soil

Recommended pre-lab reading assignments:

McCrone WC, McCrone LB, Delly JG. *Polarized Light Microscopy*. Ann Arbor, MI: Ann Arbor Science, 1978.

Murray RC, Solebello LP. Forensic Examination of Soil. In: Saferstein R, ed. *Forensic Science Handbook*, 2nd ed. Upper Saddle River, NJ: Pearson Education, 2002; 615–625.

Petraco N, Kubic T. *Color Atlas and Manual of Microscopy for Criminalists, Chemists, and Conservators*. Boca Raton, FL: CRC Press, 2004; 135–149.

Objective

Upon completion of this practical exercise, the student will have developed a basic understanding of:

1. conoscopic observations of minerals
2. determining the orientation of a uniaxial mineral to determine which refractive index is being observed
3. use of conoscopic illumination to determine if a mineral is + or −
4. distinction of uniaxial and biaxial minerals using interference figures
5. use of the compound or comparison light microscope to visualize soil characteristics

Introduction

It has been said, "Soil is merely a rock on its way to the sea."[1] Because soil is a product of rock decay, it is possible to discriminate soil samples by identification of the many microscopic

---

[1] Weil RR. *Laboratory Manual for Introductory Soils*, 6th ed. Dubuque, IA: Kendall/Hunt Publishing Company, 1998; 1.

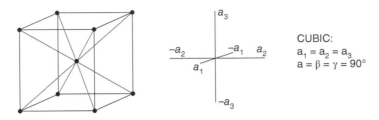

Figure 21A-1   Cubic crystals have one refractive index and are isotropic.

mineral particles found in the soil. Minerals are naturally occurring inorganic materials with a definite chemical composition. Minerals are composed of atoms that are arranged in a regular pattern to produce a crystalline form. The ordered nature of minerals makes them anisotropic, with the notable exception of minerals belonging to the cubic crystal system. Optical properties covered in earlier chapters such as birefringence, refractive index, and relief can be used in mineral identifications. In addition to these properties, mineral identification is aided by the use of color, optic sign, optic angle, and interference figures. Crystal form and cleavage also offer insight to mineral identification.

Since crystals possess an orderly arrangement, if a beam of white light enters a crystal, several things can happen depending on the crystal structure. The reaction to a beam of white light is shown by the use of an optical indicatrix. An indicatrix is the geometric figure that shows the refractive index and vibrational direction for light passing through a material in any direction. Each vector of the figure is drawn proportional in length to the material's refractive index for light vibrating parallel to that vector direction. The geometric figure is a surface that connects all the tips of these vectors.

Minerals, like other crystals and particles, can be isotropic and have one refractive index, or anisotropic and have more than one refractive indices. In isotropic materials, the chemical bonding is the same in all directions, so the velocity of light passing through is the same in all directions. The refractive index remains constant regardless of the direction in which the light is vibrating; therefore, the indicatrix shape is a sphere. The same can be said for all isometric (cubic) crystals (see Figure 21A-1). Common isotropic crystals and their refractive indices are listed in Table 21A-1.

Anisotropic minerals, however, react differently. Anisotropic minerals are those in the remaining six crystal systems: hexagonal, rhombohedral, tetragonal, orthorhombic, monoclinic, and triclinic. In these anisotropic materials, the chemical bonding is different in parallel and perpendicular directions, so the velocity of light passing through is different in parallel and perpendicular directions. The refractive index is different depending on the direction in which the light is vibrating. Therefore, the indicatrix shape is an ellipse.

Anisotropic minerals may be further divided into uniaxial (having a single unique optic axis and two refractive indices) or biaxial (having two optic axes and three refractive indices).

Uniaxial minerals belong to the hexagonal, rhombohedral, and tetragonal crystal systems and have directions that are alike (multiple a-axes) and one distinct (c-axis) (see Figure 21A-2). The name uniaxial is used because only one axis is unique to the other directions and is commonly referred to as the optic axis. A uniaxial mineral under crossed polars produces two rays of light, known as the e-ray (with refractive index n_ϵ or epsilon) and the o-ray (with refractive index n_ω or omega). These rays vibrate perpendicular to each other. Depending on the orientation of the crystal when viewed under the microscope, n_ϵ and n_ω are visible, or some combination of the two known as $n_{\epsilon'}$. For a review of determining refractive indices of anisotropic materials, see

Table 21A-1 Refractive index for common isotropic crystals.

Mineral	n
Opal	1.43
Fluorite	1.433
KCl	1.490
Pumice	1.450
Halite	1.544
NH_4Cl	1.640
Sphalerite	2.37
Magnetite	2.42
Diamond	2.42
Cuprite	2.85

Source: Barthelmy D. Minerals by Physical and Optical Properties Tables [cited 2020]. Available from: http://www.webmineral.com.

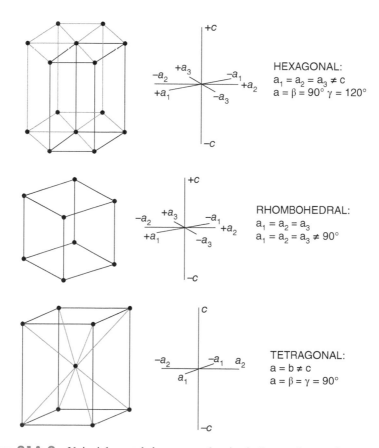

HEXAGONAL:
$a_1 = a_2 = a_3 \neq c$
$a = \beta = 90°$ $\gamma = 120°$

RHOMBOHEDRAL:
$a_1 = a_2 = a_3$
$a_1 = a_2 = a_3 \neq 90°$

TETRAGONAL:
$a = b \neq c$
$a = \beta = \gamma = 90°$

Figure 21A-2 Uniaxial crystals have two refractive indices and one unique optic axis.

Table 21A-2 Refractive index for common uniaxial crystals.

Mineral	n_ω	n_ε
Quartz	1.544	1.553
Beryl	1.581	1.564
Apatite	1.630	1.632
Tourmaline	1.650	1.621
Calcite	1.658	1.486
Dolomite	1.682	1.503
Corundum	1.7681	1.759
Zircon	1.91	1.968
Rutile	2.616	2.903
Carborundum	2.654	2.697
Hematite	3.15	2.87

Source: Barthelmy D. Minerals by Physical and Optical Properties Tables [cited 2020]. Available from: http://www.webmineral.com.

Experiment 3B. Table 21A-2 lists a number of common uniaxial minerals and their refractive indices. An analyst must determine the orientation of the uniaxial mineral in order to know which refractive index they are observing. When minerals are first mounted and viewed, they will be in random orientations. It is possible to perform a random search of each mineral in the preparation to find one with the proper orientation. Another technique used to align minerals is to roll the mineral on a spindle stage or, after mounting it, in a very viscous medium. In both the random search and rolling methods, interference figures are used to confirm orientation of the c-axis. Interference figures are light patterns that emerge from a crystal when viewed under high magnification with conoscopic illumination and under crossed polars.

Depending on the orientation of the mineral particle with respect to the optic axis, there are three possible views that can be seen: (1) When the mineral particle is oriented so that one is looking "down the c-axis," only the ω refractive index will be seen. This orientation aligns the c-axis parallel to the optic axis of the microscope. (2) A mineral particle perpendicular to the optical axis of the microscope shows two refractive indices, ω and ε_{max}. (3) Orientations in between parallel and perpendicular will show ω and some ε value ranging from zero to ε_{max}. Therefore, ω is common to every view of the uniaxial crystal, and ε will range from zero to ε_{max}.

By mounting the mineral in a refractive index oil equal to ω and viewing the mineral grain with polarized light and the analyzer removed, these orientations can be observed. What is actually seen varies depending upon the three orientations previously described. (1) The first orientation describes a situation where only ω is visible. Therefore, the mineral will appear isotropic upon stage rotation, and mineral particles with this orientation will exhibit minimum birefringence under cross polars. Mounting the mineral in a refractive index oil equal to ω, if known, will cause the mineral to remain invisible at all locations of stage rotation when the analyzer is removed. (2) Observations in plane-polarized light (analyzer removed) with the mineral oriented with its c-axis perpendicular to the optic axis of the microscope will result in disappearance when only ω is observed. Only ω is seen when the e-ray's vibration direction is N-S and blocking the E-W polarized light allowed by the polarizer. Because the mineral is mounted in a liquid matching the o-ray and the e-ray is blocked, the mineral appears to disappear at two locations 180° apart during a 360° stage rotation. At two other locations, maximum relief is observed when ε_{max} is the only visible refractive index. At these locations, the o-ray is vibrating N-S and blocking the E-W polarized light, allowing only ε_{max} to be seen. (3) At locations in between parallel and perpendicular, the mineral will always show ω and some ε in between zero and ε_{max}. The relief of the particle will then vary between a minimum and a maximum value upon stage rotation.

A biaxial mineral under crossed polars produces three rays of light—X, Y, and Z—which vibrate in different directions and are always mutually perpendicular. In contrast, the three crystallographic directions (a, b, and c) are not perpendicular in monoclinic and triclinic crystals (see Figure 21A-3). The refractive indices corresponding to the three orientations are referred to as n_α (alpha), n_β (beta), and n_γ (gamma). Table 21A-3 contains a list of common biaxial minerals and their refractive indices. The slowest vibrational direction is Z, which is the n_γ refractive index; n_α, which is always the highest refractive index, is the X vibrational direction. The intermediate refractive index is n_β, corresponding to the Y direction. The X and Z directions are always in the optical axis plane, making Y the optical normal.

It is possible to classify minerals using a microscope by viewing their interaction with polarized light. Isotropic minerals, which belong to the isotropic cubic system, can immediately

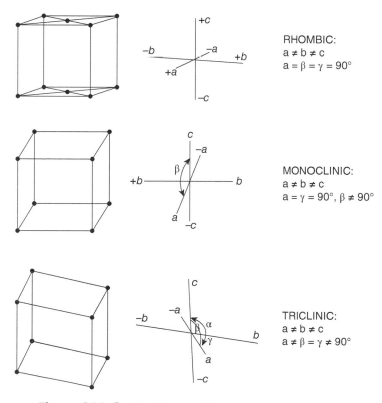

Figure 21A-3 Biaxial crystals have three refractive indices.

Table 21A-3 Refractive index for common biaxial crystals.

Mineral	n_α	n_β	n_γ
Gypsum	1.521	1.523	1.530
Orthoclase	1.518	1.524	1.526
Albite	1.528	1.529	1.536
Biotite	1.565	1.605	1.605
Talc	1.539	1.589	1.589
Microcline	1.520	1.523	1.530
Vermiculite	1.525	1.545	1.545
Muscovite	1.552	1.582	1.584
Topaz	1.619	1.620	1.627
Olivine	1.635	1.665	1.670
Barite	1.636	1.637	1.648
Hornblende	1.646	1.656	1.661
Olivine	1.662	1.680	1.699
Malachite	1.655	1.875	1.909
Augite	1.680	1.684	1.706
Epidote	1.723	1.730	1.736
Azurite	1.73	1.758	1.838
Carnotite	1.75	1.90	1.95
Monazite	1.79	1.795	1.842

Source: Barthelmy D. Minerals by Physical and Optical Properties Tables [cited 2020]. Available from: http://www
.webmineral.com.

be identified since they remain dark under crossed polars. Uniaxial and biaxial minerals require the use of conoscopic illumination for identification.

Conoscopic illumination refers to the observation of the back focal plane of the objective. It is obtained by removal of the ocular or insertion of the Bertrand lens to obtain a magnified image of this area (see Figure 21A-4). With conoscopic illumination, the focal planes are now at five locations along the optical path: (1) the lamp filament, (2) the substage aperture diaphragm, (3) the objective back focal plane, (4) the intermediate image, and (5) the retina of the eye.

At the objective back focal plane, an anisotropic mineral gives an "interference figure." Interference figures are light patterns that emerge from a crystal when viewed at high magnification and under crossed polars with conoscopic illumination. This light pattern provides information about the mineral's orientation and can also be used to determine if the mineral is uniaxial or biaxial. It is also possible to determine the optic sign for a mineral (i.e., whether or not the mineral is positive or negative). A more advanced topic, which is beyond the scope of this book, is determination of the optic axial angle, or "optic angle," for biaxial minerals. The optic angle is the acute angle between the two optic axes.

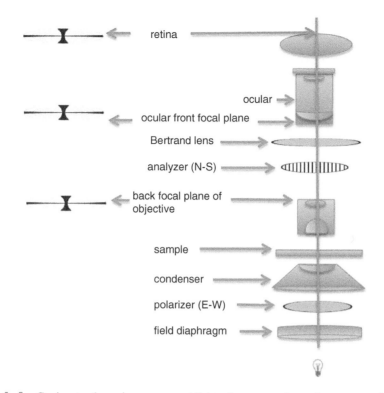

retina

ocular

ocular front focal plane

Bertrand lens

analyzer (N-S)

back focal plane of objective

sample

condenser

polarizer (E-W)

field diaphragm

Figure 21A-4 Conjugate planes in a compound light microscope when using conoscopic viewing for observation of interference figures. The image-forming planes occur at the lamp, the front focal plane of the condenser, the back focal plane of the objective, the ocular front focal plane, and the retina of the eye. While this shows the placement of the analyzer, it is not inserted for viewing of sample interference figures.

Interference figures result when the many rays passing though the mineral under crossed polarized light converge as a cone of light. The light rays always converge evenly with ortho-scopic illumination; however, they are considered less convergent, and the term "orthoscopic" suggests an almost parallel illumination. For conoscopic illumination, it is sometimes necessary to increase the numerical aperture (NA) of the condenser by insertion of an auxiliary condens-ing lens in the light path. This causes the illumination rays to be highly convergent so that they focus within a mineral on the stage. This produces conoscopic illumination where a cone of light emerges from the mineral, diverging rapidly. Removal of the ocular or insertion of the Bertrand lens allows an analyst to interpret the emergent cone of light.

A typical interference figure observed when the optic axis (c-axis) is vertical on a uniaxial crystal resembles a cross (see Figure 21A-5a).

The figures arms intersect at the center, or melatope. The arms or isogyres remain N-S and E-W during 360° stage rotation as long as the mineral is oriented with its c-axis parallel to the optical axis of the microscope. To obtain a vertical c-axis, a mineral is selected that exhibits minimum birefringence under crossed polars with orthoscopic illumination. The optic sign of the mineral is determined by insertion of a first-order red plate, which adds or subtracts 530 nm of retardation (see Figure 21A-6). In the northeast quadrant of the interference figure, upon insertion of the first-order red plate, the overall retardation will become blue due to addition for a

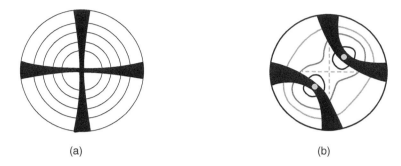

Figure 21A-5   Interference figures for (a) uniaxial crystal and (b) biaxial crystal.

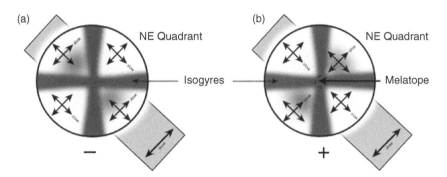

Figure 21A-6   A typical interference figure for a uniaxial mineral. The isogyres appear first-order red upon insertion of the first-order red plate. (a) A negative mineral will appear yellow in the NE quadrant because subtraction has occurred (slow rays of mineral and accessory plate are perpendicular). (b) A positive mineral will appear blue in the NE quadrant because addition has occurred (slow rays of the mineral and accessory plate are parallel).

positive (+) mineral and yellow due to subtraction for a negative (−) mineral. This classification refers to $n_\varepsilon > n_\omega$ for a + mineral and $n_\omega > n_\varepsilon$ for a − mineral. If there is any inclination of the optic axis, then an off-centered figure is obtained. Rotation of the stage and isogyres allows the analyst to identify the northeast quadrant and repeat the test to view the retardation color.

As with uniaxial minerals, interference figures can be used to determine the optic sign of biaxial minerals as well as distinguish uniaxial minerals from biaxial minerals. The biaxial mineral has two optic axes due to the three vibrational directions, creating a different interference figure. In a centered acute bisectrix figure (see Figure 21A-5b), the isogyres appear as a black cross that changes into a pair of hyperbolic isogyres with interference colors, four times with each complete rotation of the stage (see Figure 21A-7a and 21A-7b). Distinction of positive and negative optic signs for biaxial crystals is determined by orienting the optic plane NE-SW and observing addition or subtraction of light upon insertion of the first-order red plate at the center of the cross-hairs. The optic sign of a biaxial mineral is negative if $n_\gamma - n_\beta > n_\beta - n_\alpha$ and retardation adds at the center position, yielding blue upon insertion of the first-order red plate

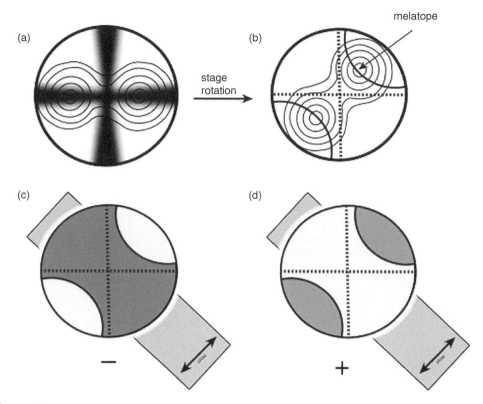

Figure 21A-7   A biaxial interference figure. With stage rotation, the interference figure changes from (a) a black cross above interference rings with melatopes to (b) two hyperbolic isogyres above each melatope. Upon insertion of the first-order red plate, the center of the cross hairs in (b) turn blue (c) for a negative mineral and yellow (d) for a positive mineral.

(Figure 21A-7c). Likewise, the optic sign of a biaxial mineral is positive when all vibration components parallel to the optic plane are fast. Since the Z direction (slow ray or γ) is along the acute bisectrix, and $n_\gamma - n_\beta > n_\beta - n_\alpha$, retardation will always subtract between the isogyres for positive crystals, which will yield yellow at the center upon insertion of the first-order red plate (Figure 21A-7d).

Equipment and Supplies

Stereomicroscope

Polarized light microscope with objectives of various magnifications (e.g., 4X, 10X, 20X, and 40X), focusing ocular with micrometer scale, and first-order red compensator (530–550 nm)

Micro kit

Microscope slides and cover slips

Cargille™ Refractive Index Liquids

Flo-texx™

Calcite (from 100 to 200 mesh sieves)

Sodium nitrate (ACS grade)

Sodium sulfite (from 100 to 200 mesh sieves)

Quartz or apatite

Muscovite plates

Unknown minerals

Safety

Use standard laboratory safety procedures as described in guidelines set by your instructor. Be cautious of microscope light levels to avoid eye damage. Know the hazards associated with the solvents used in the procedures, and use them with appropriate precautions as set by your instructor. Refer to the safety data sheet (SDS) if necessary.

Part I: Observing the Two Refractive Indices in a Uniaxial Crystal

Procedure

1. Examine a prepared slide of calcite. Draw a few representative particles in both uncrossed and crossed polars.
2. Now, view the particles while rotating the stage under both uncrossed and crossed polars. What do you see? (Include these comments under each of the previous drawings.)
3. Next, mount a few particles of crushed calcite in an immersion oil with a refractive index of 1.658 (this matches the refractive index of ω). Using the lowest magnification, observe the particles with both uncrossed and crossed polars. Slowly rotate the stage 360°, and observe the relief of some of the particles. What happens to the particles as the stage is rotated? (Remember that the particles are in random orientations.) With the analyzer out, find a grain that disappears or shows minimum relief twice at two positions 180° apart during each complete rotation of the stage. Which refractive index are you observing?

Part II: Determining ω Refractive Index for a Uniaxial Crystal

1. Using the Becke line immersion method discussed in Experiment 2C, determine the ω refractive index for sodium sulfite.
2. Find an immersion oil where the mineral disappears twice upon 360° stage rotation at locations 180° apart.
3. Record the room temperature for this measurement, and correct the temperature according to Equation 2C-1.
4. Report the ω refractive index of sodium sulfite at 25°C.

Part III: Observing a Typical Uniaxial Interference Figure: Determining the Optic Sign of a Uniaxial Crystal

Procedure

1. Place several particles (totaling about the size of a pencil eraser) of sodium nitrate on a microscope slide. Since sodium nitrate has a high melting point (>300°C), place the particles near one end of the slide to decrease the chance of breaking the slide by uneven heating.
2. Cover the particles with a cover slip. Make a melt mount by fusing the particles of sodium nitrate between the slide and cover slip (this is done by heating the microscope slide on a hot plate). When the sodium nitrate melts, push the cover slip down to obtain a thin, even crystal. **Remember: The slide will be very hot!** Remove the microscope slide from the hot plate, and allow it to cool.
3. Place the microscope slide containing the recrystallized sample on the microscope. Sodium nitrate typically recrystallizes so that the c-axis is parallel to the optic axis of the microscope, making an interference figure easily visible.
4. Focus on the sample using low magnification. Search for a portion that shows the lowest retardation throughout stage rotation under crossed polars. Switch to the 40X objective, and check your focus. Now observe the sample with the Bertrand lens inserted. A good interference figure will have a black cross (isogyres) with concentric circles of interference colors. Remember: You may need to refocus slightly since you've switched objectives. If you cannot obtain a black cross, rotate the stage to see if the isogyres move across the field of view. If this happens, you have selected a mineral whose c-axis orientation is off-centered. To proceed, you can either choose another mineral or try to locate the NE quadrant as discussed in the next step.
5. Observe the colors in each quadrant. Draw what you see. To determine the optic sign for the crystal, insert the first-order red plate. Observe, and draw the color change in the NE (upper-right) quadrant. If you are using an off-centered interference figure, determine the NE quadrant by rotating the stage until the east isogyre just passes by. The NE quadrant is after the east isogyre but before the north isogyre passes by.
6. Determine if sodium nitrate is a + or − uniaxial crystal by observing either addition or subtraction in the NE quadrant. Compare the colors seen upon insertion of the first-order accessory plate to the Michel-Lévy chart, using Figure 21A-5a as a guide. If the colors move up the chart (blue), they are said to add and the crystal is positive. If they move down the chart (yellow), the colors are said to subtract and the mineral is negative.

Part IV: Determining Crystal Orientation

Procedure

1. Observe a typical uniaxial crystal by mounting a few grains of quartz or apatite on a slide using Flo-texx.
2. Find a grain showing the lowest retardation throughout stage rotation, and observe its interference figure. Leave that grain in the center of the field of view, switch to the 40X objective, and insert the Bertrand lens.

3. If necessary, focus the interference figure to the largest circle by adjusting the focus very slightly using the fine focus knob. You should see a black cross with concentric circles of interference colors, a typical uniaxial interference figure. Remember: It may be off-center, so you may only see the arms of the cross. Rotating the stage will be necessary to determine if you are indeed seeing a cross.
4. Repeat this process until at least one centered interference figure is obtained. (a) Draw the crystal under conoscopic illumination. (b) Draw the crystal under orthoscopic illumination.
5. Explain the orientation of the c-axis for the crystal grain that gave you the centered interference figure on the circle template. On the orthoscopic drawing made in the previous step, indicate the location and direction of the c-axis.

Part V: Observing a Typical Biaxial Interference Figure: Determining the Optic Sign of a Biaxial Crystal

Procedure

1. To observe a biaxial crystal interference figure, place a thin section of muscovite on a slide without a cover slip. This mineral has the acute bisectrix parallel to the optical axis of the microscope.
2. Focus on the muscovite using low magnification. Switch to the 40X objective and refocus if necessary, cross the polars, and insert the Bertrand lens to obtain an interference figure. With biaxial minerals, the black cross will change into a pair of hyperbolic isogyres with interference colors upon rotation of the stage. This should happen four times during one complete rotation of the stage. Remember: You may need to refocus slightly since you've switched objectives. If you cannot find an interference figure initially, move the slide around to obtain the mineral's preferred orientation. Draw what you see.
3. To determine the optic sign for the mineral, rotate the stage until the interference figure resembles Figure 21A-5b. Insert the first-order red plate. Compare the colors seen upon insertion of the first-order accessory plate to the Michel-Lévy chart to determine if muscovite is a + or − biaxial crystal. Check for the color change at the center of the two melatopes. If the color changes to yellow, the optic sign is positive. If the color changes to blue, the mineral is negative.
4. Draw the interference figure with the first-order red plate inserted. Make sure the stage is rotated to show the two hyperbolic isogyres above each melatope. Record the optic sign under the drawing.

Part VI: Unknown Crystal Type and Optic Sign

Procedure

As you've observed from Parts III and V, biaxial crystals have a different interference pattern than uniaxial crystals. Obtain an unknown sample. Mount it on a microscope slide using Flo-texx. Using conoscopic illumination, determine if the sample is biaxial or uniaxial by its interference figure. Also, report if the crystals are positive or negative.

Report Requirements

Include all drawings, calculations, and other information obtained during the laboratory procedure. Notes and/or drawings should include the sample identification, magnification, and a complete description.

Report Questions

1. What are the four foci obtained with conoscopic illumination?
2. What is a uniaxial crystal? Define e-ray, o-ray, n_ε, and n_ω.
3. Why is the mineral called uniaxial, given that it has three axes?
4. Which refractive index are you observing for the calcite particles in Part I when they disappear at the two locations 180° apart? Explain your answer.
5. Which refractive index are you observing 90° from those two positions? Note the particles that have the most contrast or highest relief. Explain your answer.
6. Which refractive index are you observing in the other grains showing intermediate relief? Explain your answer.
7. What would you expect to see if the mineral was isotropic? Explain your answer. What is a biaxial mineral? Define acute bisectrix. Define + biaxial mineral and how the optic sign is determined using an interference figure.
8. Why is a mineral called biaxial when it has three axes?
9. Draw an off-centered interference figure for a uniaxial mineral, and label the isogyres, melatope, and NE quadrant.
10. Explain why the black isogyres turn into red isogyres upon insertion of the first-order red plate.
11. Explain how you could find a mineral grain whose c-axis was oriented parallel to the optical axis of the microscope using an interference figure. Which refractive index is being observed with this orientation? Explain.

Recommended and Further Reading

Antoci PR, Petraco N. A Technique for Comparing Soil Colors in the Forensic Laboratory. *Journal of Forensic Sciences.* 1993; 38(2): 437.

Bonetti J, Quarino L. Comparative Forensic Soil Analysis of New Jersey State Parks Using a Combination of Simple Techniques with Multivariate Statistics. *Journal of Forensic Sciences.* 2014; 59(3): 627–636.

Bull PA, Parker A, Morgan RM. The Forensic Analysis of Soils and Sediment Taken from the Cast of a Footprint. *Forensic Science International.* 2006; 162(1–3): 6–12.

Craig JR, Vaughan DJ. *Ore Microscopy and Ore Petrography*, 2nd ed. New York: Wiley, 1994.

Curtil L, Gielly J, Murat M. The Polarizing Microscope – a Tool of Interest for Investigation on Concrete – Application to Carbonation. *Cement and Concrete Research.* 1993; 23(2): 329–334.

Graves WJ. A Mineralogical Soil Classification Technique for the Forensic Scientist. *Journal of Forensic Sciences.* 1978; 24(2).

Houck MM, Siegel JA. *Fundamentals of Forensic Science*, 3rd ed. Amsterdam: Elsevier Academic Press, 2015; 427–436.

Jansses DW, Ruhf WA, Prichard WW. The Use of Soil Color Comparisons. *Journal of Forensic Sciences.* 1983; 28(3): 773–776.

Murray RC, Solebello LP. Forensic Examination of Soil. In: Saferstein R, ed. *Forensic Science Handbook.* Upper Saddle River, NJ: Pearson Education, 2002; 615–625.

Petraco N. Microscopic Examination of Mineral Grains in Forensic Soil Analysis. 1. *American Laboratory.* 1994; 26(6): 35.

Petraco N, Kubic T. A Density Gradient Technique for Use in Forensic Soil Analysis. *Journal of Forensic Sciences.* 2002; 45(4).

Quarino L. Soil Identification – Particle Size Distribution. In: *Trace Evidence and Microscopy.* Allentown, PA: Cedar Crest College, 2006.

Rawlins BG, Kemp SJ, Hodgkinson EH, Riding JB, Vane CH, Poulton C, et al. Potential and Pitfalls in Establishing the Provenance of Earth-Related Samples in Forensic Investigations. *Journal of Forensic Sciences.* 2006; 51(4): 832–845.

Ruffell A, McKinley J. Forensic Geoscience: Applications of Geology, Geomorphology and Geophysics to Criminal Investigations. *Earth-Science Reviews.* 2005; 69(3–4): 235–247.

Saferstein R. *Forensic Science Handbook.* Upper Saddle River, NJ: Prentice Hall, 1982; 653–671.

Stoermer EF, Smol JP. *The Diatoms: Applications for the Environmental and Earth Sciences.* Cambridge: Cambridge University Press, 1999.

Stoiber RE. *Crystal Identification with the Petrographic Microscope.* Hanover, NH: n.p., 1962.

Wanogho S, Gettinby G, Caddy B, Robertson J. Determination of Particle-Size Distribution of Soils in Forensic-Science Using Classical and Modern Instrumental Methods. *Journal of Forensic Sciences.* 1989; 34(4): 823–835.

Weil RR. *Laboratory Manual for Introductory Soils*, 7th ed. Dubuque, IA: Kendall/Hunt, 2005.

Woods B, Lennard C, Kirkbride K, Robertson J. Soil Examination for a Forensic Trace Evidence Laboratory – Parts I and II. *Forensic Science International.* 2014.

Chapter 22

Experiment 22: Microchemical Testing – Inorganic Ions

Recommended pre-lab reading assignment:
Chamot EM, Mason CW. *Handbook of Chemical Microscopy*. New York: John Wiley and Sons, 1938.

Objective

Upon completion of this practical exercise, the student will have developed a basic understanding of:

1. microchemical testing
2. techniques for performing microchemical tests
3. several tests for determination of ions/anions
4. use of the compound light microscope to visualize test results

Introduction

With current analytical instrumental methods for the identification of unknown materials, one might think that microchemical testing is outdated. However, the techniques utilized are widely accepted and easily obtainable. Because microchemical testing is simple, very inexpensive, sensitive, reliable, and quick, its popularity in forensic science remains. It is commonly used as a screening technique, with other instrumental confirmatory tests to follow. In a few forensic disciplines, such as drug analysis and trace evidence, microchemical testing is widely used. The principles behind microchemical testing follow the qualitative analysis scheme commonly used to separate and detect cations and anions in a sample substance. The "semi-micro" level of qualitative analysis employs methods used to detect 1–2 mg of an ion in 5 mL of solution, and

Practical Forensic Microscopy: A Laboratory Manual, Second Edition. Barbara P. Wheeler.
© 2021 John Wiley & Sons Ltd. Published 2021 by John Wiley & Sons Ltd.
Companion website: www.wiley.com/go/Wheeler/Forensic

detection is visually observed. Using a microscope allows analysts to identify single grains of the sample substance.

Almost any chemical test performed in a qualitative analysis scheme can be carried out on a microscope slide. There are six main procedures used in microchemical testing: reagent mixing, solubility, evaporation, decantation, sublimation, and fusion. A short summary of the many variations of these types of procedures resulting in a wide variety of microchemical tests follows. Reagent mixing involves the combining of two or more chemical compounds.

Solubility testing involves placing a single crystal or grain in a drop of water or other solvent. For many of the reactions performed on the microscopic level, water turns out to be the best solvent; however, certain reactions work better when the solution is slightly acidic or basic. The analyst should note if the test sample is soluble, slightly soluble, or insoluble in the solvent. The initial test of solubility tells the analysts something about the polarity of the sample substance and illustrates what is meant by the comment "like dissolves like." Polar compounds dissolve in polar solvents, and nonpolar compounds dissolve in nonpolar solvents.

Evaporation entails heat being applied to a solvent that contains the test sample. Sources of heat used for evaporation include an alcohol flame, a warm lamp bulb, or a hot plate if spark-free heating is needed. The microscope slide is held over the heat source. When it is warm, it is common to blow gently across the drop so that a uniform film of the substance is produced. After evaporation has occurred, characteristic crystals often remain that can be used in identification.

Decantation involves separating a precipitate from the solvent. The solvent is drawn away from the precipitate with a microspatula, and then allowed to dry. Back flow can be avoided by making a channel between the excess solvent and precipitate using a small piece of filter paper and slight warming of the channel area.

Sublimation is the transformation of the solid phase to the gaseous phase without passing through the liquid phase. This can occur on the microscopic scale. Crystal formation after sublimation can be used in identification. A reagent drop is suspended over the solid test sample by use of a hanging drop on a cover slip over a glass ring, as shown in Figure 22-1c. Upon heating, sublimation occurs, and crystals form on the underside of a cover glass.

In fusion methods the test sample is mixed with a flux agent such as borax and heated on a platinum wire. A glassy bead is formed, which may then be studied for its unique interference colors, crystal habit, or other unusual properties. Fusion methods are particularly useful for identifying insoluble compounds, although tabulated information about the fusion properties is not readily available. This is just a short summary of the many variations of these types of procedures, resulting in a wide variety of microchemical tests.

Microchemical testing involves the application of known reagents to small amounts of unknown material to form identifiable crystalline products. These reactions are typically carried out on a microscope slide using a test drop (drop containing unknown substance) and a reagent drop (reagent dissolved in appropriate solvent). Mixing can be achieved using one of the three methods shown so that a reaction between the two substances occurs (see Figure 22-1). The result of the reaction can vary from a color change to gas bubble formation or characteristic crystals of the resulting compound. Crystals can be observed with a compound microscope and polarized light. 100X–400X magnification is typically used to view formed crystals.

Describing the crystalline color and shapes can be a difficult process when performing microchemical crystal testing. However, several terms are commonly used when describing crystal shapes: bars, blades, needles, plates, prisms, rod, tablets, and grains. Bars are crystals

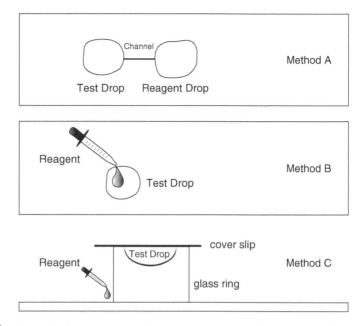

Figure 22-1 Inorganic ion microcrystalline test methods. (a) The reagent and test sample are dissolved. The reaction occurs when connected by a channel formed with a toothpick; (b) reagent is dissolved, then dropped onto the dissolved or solid test sample; and (c) reagent is suspended over the test sample, which is dissolved in a glass ring.

that have three unequal dimensions. Thin flat crystals that have greater length than width are termed blades. Needles are formed when the width and thickness are very fine compared to the length of the crystal. Plates are thin flat crystals that have similar width and length. Crystals that are termed prisms have similar width and thickness with greater length. Rods are crystals that have greater length than width or thickness, and in such a way that the width and thickness are equal. Tablets are usually short and stubby with similar length and width that are greater than its thickness. Some crystal reactions are described as grains, meaning the precipitate is granular without a distinct shape, having length, width, and thickness approximately the same. Arrangement of these shapes may be singly, or multiples in the form of burrs, bundles, clusters, crosses, dendrites, fans, rosettes, sheaf, stars, and tufts. Figure 22-2 shows various microcrystal morphologies.

Sample concentration, impurities, and reagent problems may cause difficulties when performing microchemical testing. Because of these problems, a control test must be performed at the same time that an unknown is tested. It is important to note that a positive result must be determined by a comparison to a control test and not to published literature that uses different reagents and techniques. Positive controls of all samples in question should also be run to become familiar with the microchemical technique, the procedures used, and the appearance of crystals prior to attempting work with unknown samples. It is also important to run negative controls using all reagents without analyte to ensure that the reagent itself does not cause formation of the observed crystals. While the positive and negative controls are often run as

Figure 22-2   Common microcrystalline shapes that can be formed when doing microchemical testing.

preliminary procedures, it is important that they be run at the same time as the unknown in a side-by-side manner.

Because of the sensitivity of these tests, special precautions should be taken to guard against contamination. All equipment (slides, micropipettes, microspatulas) that comes in contact with the unknown or reagents should be scrupulously clean. Microscope slides must be cleaned prior to use. Flat wooden toothpicks serve nicely as disposable microspatulas. It is very important that your work area be kept well organized and neat to minimize confusion and the opportunity for contamination.

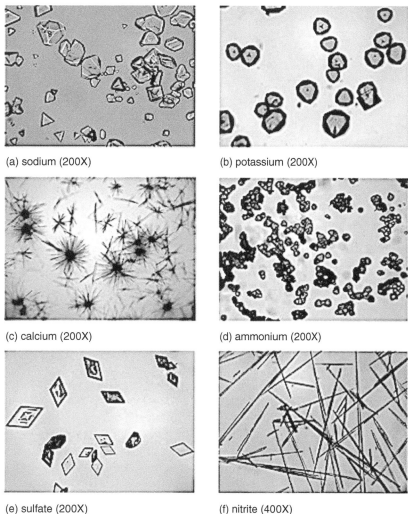

(a) sodium (200X)

(b) potassium (200X)

(c) calcium (200X)

(d) ammonium (200X)

(e) sulfate (200X)

(f) nitrite (400X)

Figure 22-3 Characteristic crystal morphology for common microchemical tests for inorganic ions: (a) sodium with zinc uranyl acetate dissolved in acetic acid, (b) potassium with chloroplatinic acid, (c) calcium with sulfuric acid, (d) ammonium with chloroplatinic acid forms crystals with exactly the same habit as potassium in (b), (e) sulfate with silver nitrate, and (f) nitrite with silver nitrate.

This experiment will focus on commonly used microchemical crystal testing. Figure 22-3 shows the characteristic crystal for common microchemical tests for inorganic ions.

Several subsequent experiments will focus on using microchemical testing for specific evidence types: building materials (Experiment 23), explosives residues (Experiment 24), and drug residues (Experiment 27).

Equipment and Supplies

Compound light microscope with objectives of various magnifications (e.g., 4X, 10X, 20X, and 40X)

Micro kit

Microscope slides (specialized spot well slides may be used)

Cover slips

Toothpicks (or closed-end capillary tubes)

Chemicals as listed with each test

Known samples containing anions and cations to be tested

Unknown samples

Safety

Use standard laboratory safety procedures as described in rules set by your instructor. Be cautious of microscope light levels to avoid eye damage. Students should know the hazards associated with the solvents used in the procedures, and use them with appropriate precautions as set by your instructor. Refer to the safety data sheet (SDS) as needed. Students should wear personal protective equipment such as goggles and nitrile gloves for all parts of this lab. Several of the reagents contain concentrated acid solutions and should be handled with caution.

Standard Methods for Microcrystalline Tests

Scan areas on the microscope slide where the test sample and reagent meet. Since the crystal formation occurs when the test sample and reagents are at a specific ratio, crystals may not be immediately obtained. If this is the case, continue to scan the slide after a short time expires. This will allow for the solutions to evaporate, creating the correct concentrations and causing crystal formation. However, it is also important to note that crystal formation cannot be viewed if the slide has gone to complete dryness.

Method A: Place a small amount of the reagent and test substance in separate drops of water. After they are dissolved, join the two drops by a thin "channel" using a toothpick. Characteristic crystals will form as the reaction occurs between the two sample drops. See Figure 22-1a.

Method B: Dissolve the test substance in a drop of water. Add a small amount of reagent directly to the test drop. Characteristic crystals will form as the reaction occurs between the samples. At times, higher concentrations of the test sample quicken the crystal formation. In these situations, the test sample can be added directly into the reagent. See Figure 22-1b.

Method C: A hanging drop is subjected to the gases of a reaction between the sample test drop and a reagent. A spacer (made of cut ¼-inch [6 mm] glass tubing) is used to hold the cover slip holding the reagent over the dissolved sample. Once crystals have formed, invert the cover slip and place it on a microscope slide for viewing. See Figure 22-1c.

Cations

Na⁺ The best reaction for sodium is obtained with zinc uranyl acetate using method A. First dissolve the sodium containing solid in distilled water. Next dissolve the zinc uranyl acetate in acetic acid. Excess acetate ions are necessary for crystal formation. Characteristic crystals will appear as monoclinic polysynthethic twins possessing octahedral aspects. Photos of crystals are shown in Figure 22-3a.

K⁺ Dissolve potassium salts in dilute hydrochloric acid. React this solution with chloroplatinic acid using method A. Characteristic well-formed colorless highly bire-fringent octahedrons and cubes will appear. Elongated and distorted shapes may also appear. Elongated octahedral crystals appear as orthorhombic crystals. Because of their birefringence, the crystals are best observed using crossed polars. It is help-ful if the test drop is cold and relatively dilute. Photos of crystals are shown in Figure 22-3d.

Ca²⁺ Using method A, add a drop of dilute sulfuric acid to the dissolved calcium sam-ple. Colorless birefringent needles will form, appearing as starbursts. These thin crystals are hard to view. Because of their birefringence, the crystals are best observed using crossed polars. Photos of crystals are shown in Figure 22-3c. An alternate procedure is to add a drop of sulfuric acid to the solid calcium salt. This produces larger needle crystals.

NH₄⁺ Using the hanging drop method (method C), add dilute sodium hydroxide to the test sample. Quickly cover this sample with a cover slip that holds a hanging drop of chloroplatinic acid. Highly refractive octahedra are produced (Figure 22-3a), which have exactly the same habit as the potassium crystals obtained with chloroplatinic acid (shown in Figure 22-3b).

Anions

Cl⁻ Characteristic finely grained octahedra are formed when a chlorine compound has been exposed to silver nitrate using method A. This appears as an amorphous white precipitate unless viewed at high magnification (>500X). Because many anions form a white precipitate with silver nitrate, further testing is required.

SO₄²⁻ Place a drop of sulfuric acid on a microscope slide. Neutralize this with dilute sodium hydroxide. Place a few drops of silver nitrate on the slide next to the drop. Add a drop of distilled water to dissolve the solid. Allow the two to react using method A. Characteristic colorless, highly refractive rhombic shaped tablets and prisms with angular ends are formed (see Figure 22-3e).

NO₂⁻ A mass of fine needles with long acicular prisms form (see Figure 22-3f) when nitrites are exposed to solutions of silver nitrate using method A. Upon standing, short stout prisms with imperfect ends are formed.

CO₃²⁻ When dilute hydrochloric acid is added using method A or B to a carbonate-containing compound, effervescence occurs as carbon dioxide forms.

Part I: Microchemical Testing of Known Samples

Procedure

Remember: Crystal formation occurs when the test sample and reagents are at a specific ratio. Since the actual concentration and amount used (of samples and reagents) can vary, crystals may not be immediately obtained. If this is the case, continue to scan the slide after a short time expires. This will allow for the solutions to evaporate, creating the correct concentrations and causing crystal formation.

1. Samples containing known cations and anions will be provided.
2. Perform positive controls. Using the procedures listed above, perform microchemical testing of the known samples.
3. Place the slide on a polarizing compound microscope, and observe crystal formation under 100X–200X magnification using plane-polarized light. Be careful not to get any reagent on the objective. If this does occur, ask the instructor how to clean the objective. Use the search-and-find technique to locate any crystals that may have formed. It is especially important to look at the junction of the two drops and near the edges of the liquid.
4. Fully describe your observations in Table 22-1 for each of the known samples. Draw the characteristic crystals obtained, and note any special distinguishing features observed.
5. Perform negative controls. For each test, mix the reagents with a drop of water side-by-side to the positive control. Observe the negative control to ensure the reagent itself does not result in the observed reaction. Report the results in Table 22-2.
6. Once you have learned the methods used to perform the reactions and observe the results, move to Part II.

Part II: Microchemical Unknowns

1. Samples containing unknown cations and anions will be provided. Repeat the tests performed for the positive controls, and report the results in Table 22-3.
2. In identifying the ions in your unknown, only one positive crystal test for each ion should be obtained.
3. As part of your lab report, write a paragraph that justifies your answer.

Microchemical Tests Worksheet

Table 22-1 Positive Control Using Knowns

Ion	Reagent Used	Result (+ or −)	Draw Crystals on Circle Template. Summarize Results Here.

Table 22-2 Negative Control

Ion	Reagent Used	Result (+ or −)	Draw Crystals on Circle Template. Summarize Results Here.

Unknown Number _____

Table 22-3 Tests on Unknown Samples

Ion	Reagent Used	Result (+ or −)	Draw Crystals on Circle Template. Summarize Results Here.

Ions present in unknown: _____

Report Requirements

Include all drawings, calculations, and other information obtained during the laboratory procedure. Notes and/or drawings should include the sample identification, magnification, and a complete description.

Report Questions

1. What are microchemical tests? Give the purpose and value of the tests.
2. List three reactions that are used for microchemical testing. Give an example of each.
3. If you were given a sample that was thought to be gypsum, how would you use microchemical testing to prove or disprove this?
4. If you were given an acid, how would you determine which acid it was?
5. What are positive and negative controls? Why are they required?
6. You have a white sample particle that is about 40 µm × 50 µm × 3 µm that you believe to be lead paint. Find a microchemical test for lead. Write the procedure, and properly reference the literature source. A website is not an appropriate source for this question.

Recommended and Further Reading

Benedetti-Pichler AA. *Identification of Materials via Physical Properties, Chemical Tests, and Microscopy*. New York: Springer, 1964.

Chamot EM, Mason CW. *Handbook of Chemical Microscopy*. New York: John Wiley and Sons, 1938.

Cooke PM. Chemical Microscopy. *Analytical Chemistry*. 1994; 66(12): R558–R94.

Cooke PM. Chemical Microscopy. *Analytical Chemistry*. 1996; 68(12): R333–R78.

Cooke PM. Chemical Microscopy. *Analytical Chemistry*. 2000; 72(12): 169R–88R.

El-Hinnawi EE. *Methods in Chemical and Mineral Microscopy*. Amsterdam: Elsevier, 1966.

Fiegel F, Anger V. *Spot Tests in Inorganic Analysis*, 6th ed. Amsterdam: Elsevier, 1972.

McCrone WC, McCrone LB, Delly JG. *Polarized Light Microscopy*. Ann Arbor, MI: Ann Arbor Science, 1978.

Novoseisky Y, Glattstein B, Volvok N, Zeichner A. Microchemical Spot Tests in Toolmark Examinations. *Journal of Forensic Sciences*. 1995; 40(5).

Palenik S. The Overlooked Clue – the Practical Use of Chemical Microscopy in the Forensic Examination of Microtraces. *Abstracts of Papers of the American Chemical Society*. 1995; 210: 274-CHED.

Schaeffer HF. *Microscopy for Chemists*. New York: Dover, 1966.

Chapter 23

Experiment 23: Building Material Examinations

Recommended pre-lab reading assignment:

Petraco N. *Trace Evidence (Inside Forensic Science)*. Langhorne, PA: Chelsea House, 2007.

Recommended website:

Insulation Materials and Their Thermal Properties [cited 2018]. Available from: http://www.greenspec.co.uk/building-design/insulation-materials-thermal-properties/.

Objective

Upon completion of this practical exercise, the student will have developed a basic understanding of:

1. general characteristics of common building material samples
2. techniques used for Portland cement and concrete examinations
3. techniques used for insulation examinations
4. techniques used for drywall and plaster examinations
5. use of the polarized light microscope to identify building material samples

Introduction

A building material is any product that can be used for construction purposes. These products may be used for construction of an item or a structure. Generally, when building materials are

Practical Forensic Microscopy: A Laboratory Manual, Second Edition. Barbara P. Wheeler.
© 2021 John Wiley & Sons Ltd. Published 2021 by John Wiley & Sons Ltd.
Companion website: www.wiley.com/go/Wheeler/Forensic

considered for forensic examination, it involves contact by a person or object with a structure. The Locard Exchange Principle states that whenever two objects come in contact, an exchange of matter occurs. This theory applies to building materials. Building materials can easily be transferred whenever there is contact between two objects, or an individual and another object. For example, small particles of concrete may be transferred to a vehicle that has hit a concrete barrier during a traffic accident. Likewise, a person may use a tool to pry open a doorway during the act of "breaking and entering." Wood, insulation, and paint may be easily transferred to the tool used or the perpetrator's clothing. Because of this fact, microscopic examinations of common building materials are presented as indirect or circumstantial evidence in a court of law. This evidence is generally used in conjunction with other forensic evidence. These examinations are performed to determine possible associations between people, places, and objects.

Building materials may be either naturally occurring or man-made products. Wood (see Experiment 13), clay, and sand (see Experiment 21A) are a few examples of common naturally occurring products. There are also many man-made products that are used as building materials. Common man-made products encountered in forensic examinations are brick, cement, concrete, plastics, engineered wood products, roofing materials, insulation, drywall, and plaster. This experiment will concentrate on cement and concrete, insulation, and common materials used for interior walls (e.g., drywall and plaster samples).

Cement and Concrete

Portland cement is the most common type of cement, and therefore is commonly examined as evidence. To produce Portland cement, raw materials containing calcium oxide, silica, alumina, and iron oxide (i.e., limestone, chalk, shells, shale, sand, clay, iron ore, and marl) are ground, blended, and heated to approximately 1480°C. This calcinates the limestone (calcium carbonate) into carbon dioxide and lime (calcium oxide), and bonds the calcium oxide to silicates that are present. The product, called "clinker," is then ground to a fine powder and mixed with a small amount of gypsum (calcium sulfate). The proportions of ingredients present in the "cement mill" determine the Portland cement classification (see Table 23-1). The mixture contains a broad range of particle sizes. Hydration with water creates a hard substance. The rate of hydration is proportional to the particle size in that higher surface area mixtures hydrate and harden quicker. If the substance is mixed with gravel or sand prior to hardening, concrete is formed. Macroscopic appearance and microchemical tests for various anions and cations can be used to identify cement and concrete. At times, further mineral identification can also be performed on concrete samples.

Insulation

Thermal insulation materials are used to reduce unwanted heat loss or gain and to allow heating and cooling systems to run more efficiently. Insulation materials accomplish this by preventing heat flow. Since solid materials pass heat by means of conduction, various materials can be used that lessen heat loss (or gain) depending on their conductivity. Metals have a very high conductivity, whereas materials used for insulating have lower conductivity (see Table 23-2). The thermal conductivity value for insulating materials can range from 0.035 to 0.16 W/mK, depending on the material. W/mK stands for Watts per meter-Kelvin, which specifies the rate of heat transfer in any homogeneous material. This variance is caused by "voids" in the structure of the material, which in turn prevents the exchange of heat.

Table 23-1 Portland cement classifications. The oxide proportions of tricalcium silicate (C_3S), tricalcium aluminate (C_3A), and tetracalcium aluminoferrite (C_4AF) present in a sample determine the classification of Portland cement.

	Classification	Characteristics	Applications
Type I	General purpose	Fairly high C_3S content for good early strength development	General construction (most buildings, bridges, pavements, precast units, etc.)
Type II	Moderate sulfate resistance or moderate-heat cement	Low C_3A content (<8%)	Structures exposed to soil or water containing sulfate ions
Type III	High early strength, rapid-hardening cement	Ground more finely, may have slightly more C_3S	Rapid construction, cold weather concreting
Type IV	Low heat of hydration (slow reacting)	Low content of C_3S (<50%) and C_3A	Massive structures (such as dams, levees)
Type V	High sulfate resistance	Very low C_3A content (<5%)	Structures exposed to high levels of sulfate ions
White	White color	No C_4AF, low MgO	Decorative (otherwise has properties similar to Type I)

A wide variety of products can be used for insulation: cellulose fibers, animal fibers, vermiculite, perlite, and numerous polymers and polymer foams such as polystyrene, polyisocyanurate, polyurethane, rock wool, and fiberglass. Most cellulose insulation is made from recycled paper materials, usually newspaper. It is treated with inorganic salts for added resistance to fire, mold, and insects. Hemp and straw fibers are also used as insulators. Procedures used for paper fiber identifications (see Experiment 16) can be performed on cellulose insulation samples. Wool insulation is made from the hair of sheep and either mechanically held together or bonded using recycled polyester adhesive foam. Microscopic characteristics for hair can be used to help identify this type of insulation (see Experiment 17A). Vermiculite is a common insulator used in older buildings. Vermiculite insulation may be pure vermiculite or combined with asbestos, biotite, or phlogopite. Vermiculite appears as green or yellow-brown thin, shiny flakes. It is a biaxial mineral that exhibits pleochroism and can be identified by its microscopic characteristics (see Experiment 21A). Perlite is a type of hydrated obsidian characterized by small spheroidal masses of volcanic glass. It will appear as an isotropic substance under crossed polars. Numerous polymers and polymer foams are also used as insulation. These chemical compounds can be identified through the use of various instruments, including Fourier transform infrared microspectrometry. Rock wool and fiberglass both resemble fibrous materials. Rock or mineral wool is formed by spinning or drawing molten minerals (i.e., basalt or diabase) or furnace slag. Fiberglass, or glass wool, is one of the most ubiquitous forms of insulating materials. It consists of fine molten glass fibers that are held together by a binder. Both of these types of insulation can be identified by their microscopic morphology and optical characteristics.

Table 23-2   Thermal conductivity values for common insulating materials.

Material	Thermal conductivity; W/m K
Cellulose, blown	0.03–0.04
Fiberglass	0.035
Hemp	0.039–0.04
Perlite	0.031
Phenolic foam	0.02
Polyisocyanurate foam	0.023
Polystyrene	0.034–0.038
Polyurethane	0.039
Rock wool	0.032–0.044
Straw	0.05–0.07
Urea–formaldehyde foam	0.035
Vermiculite	0.065
Wool	0.038
Wood fiberboard	0.038

Plaster and Drywall

Most walls within structures are covered with either plaster or drywall. Early plaster walls are lime-based plasters. These plasters contain lime, sand, hair, and water. A series of layers of the thick substance is applied to wood laths, covering the section of wall. By the 1950s, gypsum-based plasters became more popular since the drying time was much faster. Flattening the viscous gypsum-based plaster between two layers of paper creates drywall (sheetrock). Many walls are now covered with drywall. Macroscopic appearance, including an examination to identify hair, and microchemical tests for various anions and cations can be used to identify plaster samples. Since plaster is held in place by a wooden lath, at times wood may also be adhering to the sample. Drywall samples can also be identified by a macroscopic and microscopic examination. Paper surrounding the gypsum-based plaster may also be present for examination.

The examination of building materials can aid in many types of investigations. Macroscopic and microscopic characteristic determinations can be made to identify the building material. When necessary, further analytical testing can be performed to detect significant similarities or differences between samples.

Equipment and Supplies

Stereomicroscope

Polarized light microscope with objectives of various magnifications (e.g., 4X, 10X, 20X, and 40X)

Micro kit

Microscope slides and cover slips

Toothpicks (or closed-end capillary tubes)

Mounting mediums

Cement and concrete samples

Fiberglass samples

Rock wool samples

Plaster samples

Drywall samples

Chemicals from Experiment 22

Safety

Use standard laboratory safety procedures, as described in rules set by your instructor. Be cautious of microscope light levels to avoid eye damage. Students should know the hazards associated with the solvents used in the procedures, and use them with appropriate precautions as set by your instructor. Refer to the safety data sheet (SDS) as needed. Students should wear personal protective equipment such as goggles and nitrile gloves for all parts of this lab. Several of the reagents contain concentrated acid solutions and should be handled with caution.

Part I: Cement and Concrete

Procedure

1. Obtain a sample.
2. Using the stereomicroscope, examine the surface and describe any features: color, porosity, fractures, grain size, and texture. If the sample is concrete, describe the aggregate composition. Using the circle template in Appendix E, draw the structure.
3. Next, refer back to Experiment 22 to test for the presence of calcium in the sample.
4. Make a chart with your results.

Part II: Fiberglass versus Rock Wool Samples

Procedure

1. Obtain a fiberglass sample.
2. Using the stereomicroscope, examine the sample and describe any overall features: color, size, and texture.
3. Describe the length and shape of the fibers.
4. Describe the color and density of the resin binder.
5. Next, place a few fibers from the sample on a microscope slide. Add mounting medium and a cover slip.
6. Examine the sample using plane-polarized light.

7. Describe and draw what you see in your field of view.
8. Examine the sample under crossed polars. Describe what you see.
9. Repeat steps 2–8 with the rock wool sample.

Part III: Plaster and Drywall Samples

1. Obtain a plaster sample.
2. Using the stereomicroscope, examine the sample and describe any overall features: color, size, and texture.
3. Remove a sample of any hair particles.
4. Examine the hair according to the procedures in Experiment 17A.
5. Next, refer back to Experiment 22 to test for the presence of calcium and sulfate in the sample.
6. Repeat steps 2–5 with a drywall sample.
7. Make a chart of your findings.

Report Requirements

Include all drawings, calculations, and other information obtained during the laboratory procedure. Notes and/or drawings should include the sample identification, magnification, and a complete description.

Report Questions

1. What are the main components of concrete?
2. What physical differences would you expect when viewing a sample of Portland cement type I and type III?
3. How would you perform an examination to identify perlite?
4. Describe the steps that you would take to examine an insulation sample that contained hemp.
5. What are the differences between fiberglass and rock wool?
6. Why is a fiberglass sample slightly visible under crossed polars?
7. Is it possible to determine the refractive index of fiberglass? Explain your answer.
8. Would you expect plaster walls from a 1910s building and a 1940s building to be similar? Explain your answer.
9. When testing drywall samples from different companies, would you expect the same results?

Recommended and Further Reading

ASTM. *Standard Guide for Mineral Fiber Blanket Insulation and Blanket-Type Pipe Insulation (ASTM C592-16)*. Philadelphia: ASTM.
ASTM. *Standard Practice for Petrographic Examination of Hardened Concrete (ASTM C 856-96)*. Philadelphia: ASTM.
ASTM. *Standard Specification for Portland Cement (ASTM C 150)*. Philadelphia: ASTM.
Bisbing RE, Schneck WM. Particle Analysis in Forensic Science. *Forensic Science Review*. 2006; 18(2).

Bogue RH. *Chemistry of Portland Cement*. New York: Van Nostrand Reinhold, 1955.

Brown RS, Boltin WR, Bandli BR, Millette JR. Light and Electron Microscopy of Mineral Wool Fibers, *Microscope*. 2007; 55(1): 37–44.

Campbell DH. *Microscopical Examination and Interpretation of Portland Cement and Clinker*, 2nd ed. Portland Cement Association. Skokie, IL: Construction Technologies Laboratories, 2000.

Double DD, Hellawell A. The Solidification of Concrete. *Scientific American*. 1977; July: 82–90.

Palenik S, Palenik C. *Microscopy and Microanalysis*. 2016; 22: 2024–2025.

Powers TC. Structure and Physical Properties of Hardened Cement Paste. *Journal American Ceramic Society*. 1958; 41(1): 1–6.

Schneck WM. Forensic Microanalysis: Hardened Concrete, Bricks and Engineered Wood. *Global Forensic Science Today*. 2007; May.

Taupin JM, Cwiklik C. *Scientific Protocols for Forensic Examination of Clothing*. Boca Raton, FL: Taylor & Francis Group, 2011.

Chapter 24

Experiment 24: Explosive Residue Examinations

Recommended pre-lab reading assignments:

Hoffman CM, Byall EB. Identification of Explosive Residues in Bomb Scene Investigations. *Journal of Forensic Sciences*. 1974; 19(1): 54–63.
Parker RG, Stephenson MO, McOwen JM, Cherolis JA. Analysis of Explosives and Explosive Residues, Part 1: Chemical Tests. *Journal of Forensic Sciences*. 1975; 20(1): 133–140.

Objective

Upon completion of this practical exercise, the student will have developed a basic understanding of:

1. general characteristics of explosives
2. classifications used for explosives
3. spot test examinations of explosive residue
4. microchemical test for explosive residue
5. use of the polarized light microscope to identify explosive residue samples

Introduction

A detailed investigation of a blast site can reveal information after an explosion. Fragments found at a scene from the exploded device (either container fragments, concealing container fragments, and/or any detonating device fragments) can provide clues about the explosive device. Residues found on these pieces can be examined to help determine the explosive that was present.

Practical Forensic Microscopy: A Laboratory Manual, Second Edition. Barbara P. Wheeler.
© 2021 John Wiley & Sons Ltd. Published 2021 by John Wiley & Sons Ltd.
Companion website: www.wiley.com/go/Wheeler/Forensic

An explosive is a chemical substance or mixture that is capable of producing an explosion. Most explosive materials require a stimulus (e.g., blow or spark) to start the liberation of energy. It is the manner in which the explosive material responds to the stimuli that provides a classification system for explosives. Explosives are classified as either low or high explosives, according to their rate of combustion and brisance. Combustion is an exothermic oxidation reaction that may include burning, deflagration, and detonation. The shock or shattering power produced when the material explodes is called brisance.

Low explosives burn rapidly. They deflagrate, which means that they undergo decomposition by exothermic reaction that propagates a flame front that occurs particle to particle at subsonic speed (i.e., less than 3280 ft/sec). To be effective, they require confinement. Because of that fact, some of the common primary explosives are used as propellants in ammunition: black powder, smokeless powder, flash powder. Black powder or gunpowder is composed of potassium nitrate, charcoal, and sulfur. It is one of the oldest explosives known, and produces lots of residue. Black powder substitutes such as pyrodex, golden powder, and black canyon powder are also potassium nitrate based. Smokeless powder leaves fewer residues than black powder. It also produces less smoke, but provides greater heating power and approximately six times the gas generation of black powder. There are three types of smokeless powder: single based (nitrocellulose), double based (nitrocellulose and nitroglycerine), and triple based (nitrocellulose, nitroglycerine, and nitroguanidine). Flash powder is a mixture of oxidizer and metallic fuel that burns quickly and, if confined, produces a loud report. Metallic salts and powdered metals are also added to produce color and flash to the "display."

High explosives detonate. Their decomposition is by exothermic reaction that propagates a shockwave at supersonic speed (i.e., greater than 3300 ft/sec). Because of this fact, they are commonly used for mining, demolition, and military applications. High explosives are very sensitive to heat or shock, so they are categorized by their sensitivity: either primary or secondary. Primary high explosives are materials that can be initiated by a relatively small amount of heat or pressure. These explosives (see Table 24-1) are commonly used in detonators or to trigger larger charges of less sensitive secondary high explosives. Secondary explosives are materials that are relatively insensitive and require initiation. These explosives (see Table 24-2) are commonly used in larger quantities in an explosive train and are usually initiated by a smaller amount of a primary high explosive. A wide variety of chemical compounds can also be used as secondary high explosives: ammonium nitrate, nitroaromatics, nitroamines, nitrate esters, and even some mixed compositions.

When performing a microscopic examination of samples collected from a blast site, it is important to identify any unexploded materials first. Unexploded fragments may provide information about the components of the device and any concealing containers (pipe, pressure cooker,

Table 24-1   Common examples of primary high explosives.

Primary high explosives	Chemical formula
Mercury fulminate	$Hg(CNO)_2$
Lead styphnate	$C_6HN_3O_8Pb$
Lead azide	$Pb(N_3)_2$
Diazodinitrophenol (DDNP)	$C_6H_2N_4O_5$

Table 24-2 Common examples of secondary high explosives.

Secondary high explosives	Chemical formula
Ammonium nitrate	NH_4NO_3
Trinitrotoluene (TNT)	$C_6H_2(NO_2)_3CH_3$
2,4,6-Trinitrophenylmethylnitramine (tetryl)	$C_7H_5N_5O_8$
1,3,5-Trinitrobenzene (TNB)	$C_6H_3N_3O_6$
2,4,6-Trinitrophenol (picric acid)	$C_6H_3N_3O_7$
Cyclomethylenetrinitramine (RDX)	$C_3H_6N_6O_6$
Cyclotetramethylene–tetranitramine (HMX)	$C_4H_8N_8O_8$
Nitroglycerine (NG)	$C_3H_5N_3O_9$
Pentaerythrite tetranitrate (PETN)	$C_5H_8N_4O_{12}$
Propylene glycol dinitrate (PGDN)	$C_3H_6N_2O_6$
Ethylene glycol dinitrate (EGDN)	$C_2H_4N_2O_6$
Mixed compositions	
ANFO	Ammonium nitrate and fuel oil
C4	91% RDX and additives
Composition B	60% RDX, 40% TNT and wax
Detasheet	63% PETN, 8% nitrocellulose, and 29% ATBC
Dynamite	3 parts NG and 1 part diatomaceous earth and sodium carbonate
Gelignite	Nitrocellulose dissolved in either NG or nitroglycol and mixed with wood pulp and saltpetre
Pentolite	50% PETN and 50% TNT
Semtex	RDX and PETN
Tovex	Ammonium nitrate and methylammonium nitrate

blasting cap, leg wires, wrappers, fuses, timing devices, batteries, fabric, zippers, etc.). The morphology of residue can provide valuable information about the explosive. Physical properties such as the color, size, and shape of the residue should be noted. This is especially important for propellant particles. The Smokeless Powders Database[1] uses physical characteristics to identify a propellant. Shapes of propellants (see Figure 24-1) may be described as ball, flattened ball,

---

[1] Smokeless Powders Database, National Center for Forensic Science, University of Central Florida. Available from: http://www.ilrc.ucf.edu/powders/.

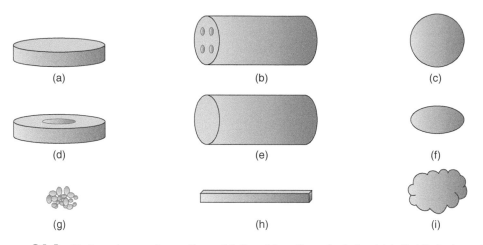

Figure 24-1   Various shapes of propellants: (a) disc, (b) perforated tubular, (c) ball, (d) single perforated disc, (e) tubular, (f) flattened ball, (g) agglomerate, (h) lamel, and (i) irregular.

irregular ball, lamel, disk, cylinder, irregular, agglomerate, flattened ball and irregular flattened ball, flattened ball and irregular, ball and irregular flattened ball, or flattened ball and ball. At times the particle may be perforated or have more distinguishing features such as being teardrop, dumbbell, or oblong shaped. They may also be bias cut or striated. Black, gray, green, brown, gold, orange, red, pink/brown, pink/green, and green/brown are terms used to describe the color of propellant particles. They may also be shiny, dull, or a mixture of both. Finally, the diameter, length, and thickness should also be noted.

Residues found on fragments can also be analyzed to determine the possible explosive that was present. Both microscopic spot tests and microchemical tests can be used to aid in this identification. Spot tests can be used on explosive residues as a presumptive test based on the chemical reaction between the sample and indicator reagents. The indicator reagent will react with the sample to cause a color change. There are a variety of spot tests that can be used on explosive residues. The following spot tests are some of the more commonly used ones in forensic investigations. The formation of a blue color is given with the presence of oxidizing ions such as nitrates, nitrites, chlorates, and ferric ions when diphenylamine (DPA) is added. Nessler's reagent can be used to indicate the presence of ammonium ions. When present, an orange-brown color is formed. A blue-green test reaction with anthrone reagent is given when sugars and starches are present. Alcoholic potassium hydroxide can also be used as a color test for explosives. This reagent gives a red or red-violet color for organic explosives. The Griess and modified Griess test can be used on samples that contain nitrates and nitrites (see Experiment 11A). Some expected results for explosive color tests are shown in Table 24-3.

A wide variety of microchemical tests can also be performed. When specific reagents are added to a sample, unique crystals will be formed. The Cropen test is used to identify explosives that contain perchlorates and chlorates. When perchlorates are present, blue needles grow both singly and in bundles. Chlorates develop into blue rosettes. The needles are generally thinner and develop at a slower rate than the perchlorates. Squaric acid can also be used to identify various elements.

The examination and identification of explosive residues can aid in many types of investigations. Macroscopic and microscopic characteristic determinations can be performed to

Table 24-3 Expected results of common explosives using various color tests.

Reagent	Reacts with	Expected positive result for some common explosives
DPA	Oxidizing ions: chlorates, nitrites, and nitrates	Nitrocellulose (blue-black)
		Nitroglycerine (blue)
		PETN (blue)
		RDX (blue)
		Tetryl (blue)
		TATP (blue)
Nessler's	Ammonium ions	ANFO (orange-brown)
		Nitroglycerine (black)
		TNT (red)
Anthrone	Carbohydrates	Sugars and starches (blue-green precipitate)
Alcoholic KOH	Organic explosives	TNT (blue to purple-brown)
		2,3-DNT (yellow)
		Tetryl (violet)
Griess	Nitrate and nitrite ions	Nitrocellulose (pink)
		Nitroglycerine (pink to red)
		PETN (pink to red)
		RDX (pink to red)
		Tetryl (pink to red)

help identify the material. When necessary, further analytical instrumental testing (i.e., FTIR, SEM/EDX, XRD, GCMS, or CE) can be performed to identify explosive samples.

Equipment and Supplies

Stereomicroscope

Polarized light microscope with objectives of various magnifications (e.g., 4X, 10X, 20X, and 40X)

Micro kit

Spot plates

Microscope slides

Toothpicks (or closed-end capillary tubes)

Propellant samples

DPA reagent: Place 5 gm diphenylamine in 20 mL distilled water. Slowly add 100 mL of concentrated sulfuric acid. Store in a brown bottle, and label.

Nessler's reagent: Dissolve 50 gm of KI in the smallest possible quantity of cold water (50 mL). Add a saturated solution of mercuric chloride (about 22 gm in 350 mL of water will be needed) until an excess is indicated by the formation of a precipitate. Then add 200 mL of 5 N NaOH and dilute to 1 L. Let settle, and draw off the clear liquid. Store in a dropper bottle, and label.

Anthrone reagent: Dissolve 200 mg of Anthrone in 100 mL concentrated sulfuric acid. Place into a dropper bottle, and label.

Alcoholic potassium hydroxide: Dissolve 10 gm of KOH in 100 mL ethanol. Place into a dropper bottle, and label.

Cropen reagent:

  Solution A: 5 gm of zinc sulfate and 4 gm of potassium nitrate in 40 mL of water

  Solution B: 0.015% methylene blue

Black powder

Ammonia fertilizer

Sugar

TNT residue

Perchlorate or chlorate sample

Safety

Use standard laboratory safety procedures as described in rules set by your instructor. Be cautious of microscope light levels to avoid eye damage. Students should know the hazards associated with the solvents used in the procedures, and use them with appropriate precautions as set by your instructor. Refer to the safety data sheet (SDS) as needed. Students should wear personal protective equipment such as goggles and nitrile gloves for all parts of this lab. Several of the reagents contain concentrated acid solutions and should be handled with caution.

Part I: Propellant Examination

Procedure

1. Examine the propellant using the stereomicroscope to determine the various physical features of the sample. Document your determinations. Draw your sample.
   a. shape
   b. distinguishing features
   c. color
   d. luster
   e. other (perforations, marker colors)
   f. diameter
   g. length and thickness

Part II: Spot Tests

A. Diphenylamine (DPA)
   1. Obtain a small volume of nitrate residue (use black powder), and place it in the well of a spot plate.

2. Add a drop of DPA. Stir to make sure the entire surface of the black powder is exposed to the DPA.
   3. Observe and record the color produced.
B. Nessler's
   1. Obtain a small volume of ammonium residue (fertilizer or dynamite residue), and place it in a well of a spot plate.
   2. Add a drop of Nessler's reagent.
   3. Observe and record the color produced.
C. Anthrone
   1. Obtain a small amount of sugar (this is a component in some explosive devices), and place it in a well of a spot plate.
   2. Add a drop of Anthrone reagent.
   3. Observe and record the color produced.
D. Alcoholic Potassium Hydroxide
   1. Obtain a small amount of TNT residue, and place it in a well of a spot plate.
   2. Add a drop of ethyl alcohol–saturated potassium hydroxide.
   3. Observe and record the color produced.

Part III: Microchemical Test

Procedure

A. Cropen Test
   1. Obtain a small amount of known perchlorate or chlorate sample.
   2. On a microscope slide, place one drop of Solution A. On the same slide, a short distance away, place a drop of solution B.
   3. Add your sample to the drop of solution A.
   4. Draw the two drops together.
   5. Observe and record the crystals formed.

Report Requirements

Include all drawings, calculations, and other information obtained during the laboratory procedure. Notes and/or drawings should include the sample identification, magnification, and a complete description.

Report Questions

1. What are the classifications used for explosives? Explain what determines how explosives are classified.
2. Go to the Smokeless Powder Database at www.ilrc.ucf.edu/powders. Click on "Search Database" so that you can enter the information that you determined from your examination of the sample. Search the database to determine the possible sources. Review these to make a possible identification.
3. Make a chart with your results from the spot tests run on your samples.

4. Research another spot test that could be used on explosive residues. Explain the procedure and expected results for a positive reaction.
5. Show the chemical reaction/equation that takes place when a positive reaction is obtained for a spot test that can be used on explosive residue.
6. Why are spot tests considered presumptive tests?
7. Research another microchemical test that can be used on explosive residues. Explain the procedure and expected results for a positive reaction.

Recommended and Further Reading

Beveridge A. *Forensic Investigation of Explosions*. Bristol, PA: Taylor & Francis, 1998.

Crippin JB. *Explosives and Chemical Weapons Identification*. New York: CRC Press, Taylor & Francis, 2006.

Davis TL. *The Chemistry of Powder and Explosives*. California: Angriff Press, 1975.

Feigl F. *Spot Tests in Inorganic Analysis*, 6th ed. New York: Elsevier Publishing Co., 1972.

Heramb R, McCord B. Manufacture of Smokeless Powders and their Forensic Analysis – A Brief Review. *FBI-Forensic Science Communications*. 2002; 4(2).

Hoffman CM, Byall EM. Identification of Explosive Residues in Bomb Scene Investigations. *Journal of Forensic Sciences* 1974; 19(1): 54–63.

Hollifiend J. Characterization of Squaric Acid Precipitates. *Microscope*. 2003; 51: 81–103.

Hopen TJ, Crippin JB. Methylene Blue Microchemical Test for the Detection and Identification of Perchlorates and Chlorates. *Microscope*. 2001; 49(1); 41–45.

Houck MM, Siegel JA. *Fundamentals of Forensic Science*, 3rd ed. Amsterdam: Elsevier Academic Press, 2015; 479–487.

Jungries, E. *Spot Test Analysis – Clinical, Environmental, Forensic and Geochemical Applications*. New York: John Wiley and Sons, Inc., 1985.

Kilbourne JH, McCrone WC. Fusion Methods: Identification of Inorganic Explosives. *Microscope*. 1985; 33(2); 73–90.

Lange NA. *Handbook of Chemistry*, 10th ed. New York: McGraw-Hill, 1971.

Meyer RE. A Systematic Approach to the Forensic Examination of Flash Powders. *Journal of Forensic Sciences* 1978; 23(1): 66–73.

Saferstein R, ed. *Forensic Science Handbook, Vol. 1*, 2nd ed. Upper Saddle River, NJ: Prentice Hall, 2002, 479–524.

Urbanski T. *Chemistry and Technology of Explosives*, Vols. 1–3. Oxford: Pergamon Press, 1964.

Whitman VL, Wills WF Jr. Extended Use of Squaric Acid as a Reagent in Chemical Microscopy. *Microscope*. 1977; 25(1); 1–13.

Yinon J., Zitrin S. *The Analysis of Explosives*. Oxford: Pergamon Press, 1981.

Chapter 25

Experiment 25: Food Condiment Examinations

Recommended pre-lab reading assignments:

Hollifield JM, Kellsay I. Dispersion Staining of Sugars. *The Microscope*. 2009; *57*(2): 75–81.

Jackson BP, Snowdon DW. *Powdered Vegetable Drugs*. London: J&A Churchill, 1968.

Recommended website:

MicrolabNW. Photomicrograph Gallery [cited 2018]. Available from: http://www.microlabnw.com .

Objective

Upon completion of this practical exercise, the student will have developed a basic understanding of:

1. general characteristics of condiments used as drug-cutting agents
2. techniques used for sugar examinations
3. techniques used for starch examinations
4. use of the stereomicroscope to identify some common drug-cutting agents
5. use of the polarized light microscope to identify some common drug-cutting agents

Introduction

Most drugs are adulterated with a cutting agent to some degree. A cutting agent is a material that is used to add bulk to a drug. In most instances, the cutting agent is used to create more profit for the drug dealer or manufacturer by adulterating the original substance. For instance,

Practical Forensic Microscopy: A Laboratory Manual, Second Edition. Barbara P. Wheeler.
© 2021 John Wiley & Sons Ltd. Published 2021 by John Wiley & Sons Ltd.
Companion website: www.wiley.com/go/Wheeler/Forensic

if a drug dealer purchases several thousand dollars' worth of pure cocaine, he can increase his profit by adding a cutting agent. With such as addition, what was once one kilogram of cocaine may become two kilograms. The manufacturer or drug dealer chooses a cutting agent (e.g., filler chemical) that is inexpensive, easy to obtain, relatively nontoxic, and mimics the physical attributes of the drug. For example, a water-soluble cutting agent would be used if the drug were water-soluble.

Many chemical compounds can be used as cutting agents. A wide variety of powders such as phenacetin, lidocaine, benzocaine, phenobarbital, levamisole, diltiazem, hydroxyzine, quinine, scopolamine, methylsulfonylmethane, dextromethorphan, or acetaminophen can be used, but even particles such as lead, glass, and aluminum have been identified in plant material. While many of these cutting agents require analysis by instrumentation for identification, sugars and starches, which are frequently used, can be easily identified with a polarized light microscope.

Sugar

Sugar is a soluble carbohydrate. There are various types of sugars, but generally monosaccharides, disaccharides, and sugar alcohols are used as cutting agents. Monosaccharides are the most basic unit of carbohydrates with a general formula of $C_nH2_{1n}O_n$, where n is 3 to 8. They cannot be hydrolyzed to a simpler compound. Glucose, commonly in d-dextrose form, and fructose are common monosaccharides. They are also the building blocks of disaccharides. Disaccharides are sugars formed by glycosidic links between two monosaccharides with the general formula of $C_{12}H_{22}O_{11}$. Common disaccharides are sucrose (glucose and fructose), maltose (two glucose units), and lactose (galactose and glucose). Sugar alcohols are technically not classified as a sugars, but, like sugars, they do provide sweetness. These polyol compounds are derived from sugars and contain multiple hydroxyl groups. Mannitol and inositol are examples of sugar alcohols used as cutting agents. Sugars and sugar alcohols can be crystalline in nature. Because of that fact, a microscopic examination of the sample can be a good indication as to the cutting agent's identity. Since the refractive indices of cutting agents are known, immersion techniques can be used to identify the optical properties of the sample (see Table 25-1). When using the dispersion staining objective (see Experiment 2D), portions of the light cone can be examined separately. The color observed when using the annular stop is the color of the wavelength of light at which the particle and the mounting medium have the same refractive index. When using the central stop, the complementary color of the wavelength at which the particle and the mounting medium have the same refractive index is observed. Table 25-2 contains dispersion colors for common cutting agents. Observations made using Cargille™ oil 1.560 can differentiate all of these cutting agents except for two: maltose and inositol. However, these two samples can be confirmed by using one additional Cargille™ oil, 1.540.

Starch

Starch is a complex carbohydrate found in most green plant tissues. It consists of two types of molecules, amylose and amylopectin, joined by α-1,4 glycosidic linkages. The relative proportions of amylose to amylopectin differ depending on the plant source. For instance, corn starch is approximately 30% amylose and 70% amylopectin, while rice starch has a ratio of about 20% amylose to 80% amylopectin. This varying ratio affects the shape of the particle, as those high in amylose tend to be more irregular and elongated. Because of this, the size, shape, and structure of starch particles are very distinct and can be used to identify the type of starch when doing microscopic examinations.

Table 25-1 Optical properties of common drug-cutting agents.

Sugar	Crystal shape for white powder	α	β	γ	Birefringence	Optic sign
Glucose	Biaxial; orthorhombic bisphenoidal	1.528	1.556	1.565	Moderate	−
Fructose	Irregular block-like, displays pleochroism	1.558	1.558	1.561	Low	+
Sucrose	Biaxial; monoclinic	1.540	1.567	1.572	Moderate	−
Maltose	Uniaxial; orthorhombic, grainy	1.540 (ε)		1.550 (ω)	Low	−
Lactose	Biaxial; monoclinic sphenoidal, crystals have a distinct tomahawk appearance	1.517	1.553	1.555	Moderate	−
Mannitol	Biaxial; rough irregular rectangular rods	1.532	1.545	1.550	Moderate	−
Inositol	Biaxial; rectangular rods with distinct twinning	1.553	1.562	1.566	Moderate	−

Source: Based on Hollifield JM, Kelsay I. Dispersion Staining of Sugars. *The Microscope*. 2009; 57(2): 76.

Pure starch is a white, tasteless, and odorless powder. Since starch particles vary in their structure, size, and shape, these differences can be used to differentiate the plant source. The center or core of a starch particle is called the hilum. Molecules are arranged radially in the particle so that as the radius increases, the number of branches required to fill the space also increases. This forms concentric regions or growth layers within the particle called lamellae. This high degree of internal organization causes starch particles to be almost crystalline in structure, having both amorphous and semi-crystalline portions. These features are shown in Figure 25-1. Some starch particles contain fissures or open hila (i.e., vacuoles). The size of particles can vary from 1 to 100 μm, but all starches are basically spherulitic. Identifications can be made by viewing the particles under plane-polarized and crossed polarized light. The morphology of the particle can be viewed using plane-polarized light. Microscopic characteristics for common starches are listed in Table 25-3. When using crossed polarized light, the particles will exhibit a very distinctive characteristic called a Maltese cross. A Maltese cross is a cross with arms of equal length that broaden from the center. For starch particles, the hilum is the crossing point of the Maltese cross.

The distinguishing morphology and microscopic characteristics of a cutting agent particle allow an analyst to identify the sample. Sugars and sugar alcohols can be crystalline in nature. Because of that fact, optical properties can be used to identify that sample. A microscopic examination of the sample with a dispersion staining objective provides a rapid method to obtain information so that a preliminary indication as to the cutting agent's identity can be made. The morphology and microscopic characteristics of starch particles are very distinctive and can be used to differentiate various plant sources. Further analysis of these samples using instrumentation should be performed when necessary for confirmation.

Table 25-2 Dispersion staining colors of common drug-cutting agents.

		1.530	1.540	1.550	1.560	1.570	1.580	1.590
Glucose								
MP 146–150°C	n_1		Green-yellow	Green-yellow	Orange	Red-brown		
Annular	n_2		Violet	Blue-green	Green	Orange		
Central	n_1		Purple	Purple	Blue-green	Pale blue-green		
	n_2		Yellow	Orange	Red-purple	Blue-green		
Fructose								
MP 103°C	n_1		Blue	Green-yellow	Orange	Red-brown		
Annular	n_2		Blue	Green	Yellow	Orange		
Central	n_1		Golden yellow-orange	Purple	Blue-green	Pale blue-green		
	n_2		Golden yellow	Red-purple	Blue	Light blue-green		
Sucrose								
Decomposes 186°C	n_1		Green-yellow	Green-yellow	Green-yellow	Red-brown	Red-brown	
Annular	n_2		Blue	Blue	Green	Yellow	Orange	
Central	n_1		Purple	Purple	Purple	Purple	Blue-green	
	n_2		Yellow	Pale-yellow	Red-purple	Blue	Pale blue-green	
Maltose								
MP 160–165°C	n_1	Green-yellow	Green-yellow	Red-brown				
Annular	n_2	Blue	Blue-green	Yellow				
Central	n_1	Purple	Purple	Pale blue-green				
	n_2	Golden yellow	Red	Blue-green				

Table 25-2 (Continued)

		1.530	1.540	1.550	1.560	1.570	1.580	1.590
Lactose								
MP 202–252°C	n_1			Yellow	Yellow	Orange	Red-brown	Red-brown
Annular	n_2			Blue-green	Blue-green	Blue-green	Green	Orange
Central	n_1			Blue	Blue	Blue-green	Light blue-green	Pale blue-green
	n_2			Orange	Orange	Orange-red	Red-purple	Blue-green
Mannitol								
MP 165°C	n_1 ↕		Green-yellow	Yellow	Red-brown	Dark brown		
	n_2 ↕		Blue	Green	Yellow	Red-brown		
	n_1 ↕		Purple	Blue	Light blue-green	Pale blue-green		
	n_2 ↕		Golden yellow	Red-purple	Blue	Light blue-green		
Inositol								
MP 225–227°Cx	n_1		Yellow	Green-yellow	Orange	Dark brown		
Annular	n_2		Blue	Blue-green	Green	Orange		
Central	n_1		Blue	Purple	Light blue-green	Pale blue-green		
	n_2		Yellow	Orange	Red-purple	Blue-green		

Source: Based on Hollifield JM, Kelsay I. Dispersion Staining of Sugars. *The Microscope*. 2009; 57(2): 79–81.

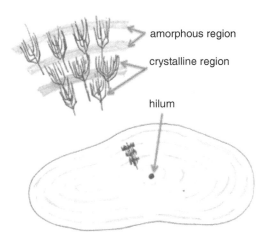

amorphous region

crystalline region

hilum

Figure 25-1   Structure of a starch particle.

Table 25-3   Microscopic characteristics of common starches.

Starch	Diameter	Microscopic characteristics
Corn (*Zea mays* L.)	2–30 μm	Simple granules, polyhedral to subspherical with a central hilum occurring as an irregular split or star; lamellae are not visible.
Arrowroot (*Maranta arundinacea* L.)	7–50 μm	Simple granules, irregularly ovoid to ellipsoidal with a slit-shaped hilum located near the broader end; lamellae are visible.
Rice (*Oryza sativa* L.)	2–10 μm	Simple granules and aggregates, polyhedral or subspherical with a visible hilum in some granules; lamellae are not visible.
Potato (*Solanum tuberosum* L.)	5–100 μm	Simple with occasional compound granules, ovoid to subspherical with great variation in size; hilum is located near the narrow end of the granule; lamellae are well marked.
Tapioca (*Manihot esculenta* Crantz.)	4–35 μm	Single granules with one or more truncated sides, indicating they were part of a compound granule, rounded or subspherical; large central hilum; some granules show lamellae.
Wheat (*Triticum aestivum* L.)	1–40 μm	Simple granules of two size ranges: 25–45 μm or 3–15 μm. Granules are oval and appear lenticular or circular, depending on their orientation; hilum appears as a line; faint lamellae on larger granules.

Equipment and Supplies

Stereomicroscope

Polarized light microscope with objectives of various magnifications (e.g., 4X, 10X, 20X, and 40X)

Micro kit

Microscope slides and cover slips

Mounting mediums

Cargille™ oils

Sugar samples

Starch samples

Safety

Use standard laboratory safety procedures as described in guidelines set by your instructor. Be cautious of microscope light levels to avoid eye damage. Know the hazards associated with the mounting mediums, and use them with appropriate precautions as set by your instructor. Dispose of glass in an appropriate container.

Part I: Sugar and Sugar Alcohol Examination

Procedure

1. Using the stereomicroscope, examine the known samples, taking note of color, size, shape, texture, and any other characteristics that can be used to help identify that sample. Describe/draw each sample.
2. Next, turn on the light source for the polarized light microscope, and rotate the objective turret until the dispersion staining objective is in place.
3. Prepare a microscope slide using a known sugar and a Cargille oil with a refractive index value of 1.560.
4. Place the sample on the microscope stage, and focus using the full aperture position. Adjust the microscope to obtain Köhler illumination.
5. Insert the Bertrand lens (or remove one eyepiece). Adjust the dispersion staining objective by rotating the selector disk until the central stop is selected (position marked by a dark center).
6. Close down the substage diaphragm until the field of view is just inside the central stop (background is dark).
7. Remove the Bertrand lens (or replace the eyepiece).
8. Insert the analyzer to establish a point of extinction for the sugar particle (the point at which the particle disappears).
9. Remove the analyzer. Observe the colors visible in focus and slightly out of focus (Becke line) around the edges of the sample.
10. Insert the analyzer, and rotate the sample to the next point of extinction. Remove the analyzer. Observe the colors visible in focus and slightly out of focus around the edges of the sample.

11. Insert the analyzer, and return the sample to its original position (the first extinction point viewed). Remove the analyzer.
12. Insert the Bertrand lens (or remove one eyepiece). Adjust the dispersion staining objective by rotating the selector disc until the annular stop is selected (position marked by a bright center).
13. Close down the substage diaphragm until the field of view is just inside the annular stop (background is bright).
14. Remove the Bertrand lens (or replace the eyepiece).
15. Insert the analyzer to establish a point of extinction for the sugar particle (the point at which the particle disappears).
16. Remove the analyzer. Observe the colors visible in and slightly out of focus (Becke line) around the edges of the sample.
17. Repeat this procedure (steps 3–17) with all other assigned samples.
18. Repeat this procedure (steps 3–17) with a Cargille oil with a refractive index of 1.540 to differentiate any similar results. Compare the color observations to the dispersion staining colors in Table 25-2.
19. Make a chart with your results.
20. Repeat this procedure to determine the identity of your unknown sample.
21. Verify your result by using the appropriate additional Cargille oils so that you can plot a dispersion curve for the unknown.

Part II: Starch Examination

Procedure

1. Examine a known sample using the stereomicroscope, making note of color, size, shape, texture, and any other characteristics that can be used to help identify that sample. Describe/draw each sample.
2. Next, prepare a slide with the known starch sample.
3. Examine the sample using various magnification powers, and select a magnification that is appropriate for the sample.
4. Record the range observed of the size of the particles. Also note the shape of the particle.
5. Describe the visibility and position of the hilum. Also note any fissures or open hila.
6. Draw your sample.
7. Next, observe the sample under crossed polars.
8. Draw the sample.
9. Repeat steps 1–8 with any other assigned samples.
10. Repeat steps 1–8 to determine the type of starch present in your unknown.

Report Requirements

Include all drawings, calculations, and other information obtained during the laboratory procedure. Notes and/or drawings should include the sample identification, magnification, and a complete description.

Report Questions

1. Why are cutting agents added to drugs? Give an example of why a sugar might be added to heroin.
2. At times, other chemical compounds (phenacetin, lidocaine, benzocaine, phenobarbital, levamisole, diltiazem, hydroxyzine, quinine, scopolamine, methylsulfonylmethane, dextromethorphan, or acetaminophen) may also be used. Pick one of these compounds, and explain why the physical or chemical properties of the sample make it a choice of cutting agent for a particular drug. For example, why is phenacitin used as a cutting agent with cocaine?
3. Plot your data for the unknown sugar on the Dispersion Staining Graph found in Appendix D. Compare the data obtained for your unknown sample to Table 25-1. The refractive index is usually given as n_D.
4. Explain why a microscopic examination of a starch particle can be used to differentiate samples.
5. Why do starch particles display a Maltese cross under crossed polars?
6. What other test could be performed on starch particles to aid in the identification of the sample?

Recommended and Further Reading

Cortella AR, Pochettino ML. Starch Grain Analysis as a Microscopic Diagnostic Feature in the Identification of Plant Material. *Economic Botany*. 1994; 48: 171.

Fitt LE, Snyder EM. Photomicrographs of Starches. In Whistler RL, Bemiller JN, Paschall EF, eds. *Starch: Chemistry and Technology*, 2nd ed. Orlando, FL: Academic Press, 1984.

MacMasters MM, Wolf M, Seckinger HL. Starch Identification, Microscopic Characteristics of Starches in the Identification of Ground Cereal Grains. *Journal of Agricultural and Food Chemistry*. 1957; 5(6): 455–458.

Moss GE. The Microscopy of Starch. In: Radley JA, ed. *Examination and Analysis of Starch and Starch Products*. Dordrecht: Springer, 1976.

Schneider F. *Qualitative Organic Microanalysis*. New York: John Wiley and Sons, Inc., 1946.

Seckinger HL, Wolf M. Polarization Color of Maize Starches Varying in Amylose Content and Genetic Background. *Die Starke*. 1966; 18(1): 2–5.

Snyder EM. Industrial Microscopy of Starches. In: Whistler RL, BeMiller JN, Paschall EF, eds. *Starch: Chemistry and Technology*, 2nd ed. New York: Academic Press, 1984.

Sterling C. The Structure of the Starch Grain. In: Radley J, ed. *Starch and Its Derivatives*, 4th ed. London: Chapman and Hall, 1968.

Torrence R, Barton H, eds. *Ancient Starch Research*. Walnut Creek, CA: Left Coast Press, 2006.

Wallis TE. Some Characteristics of Wheat Starch. *Pharmacy Journal*. 1922; 55: 82– 83.

Winchell AN. *The Optical Properties of Organic Compounds*, 2nd ed. New York: Academic Press, 1954.

Chapter 26

Experiment 26: Plastic Film Examinations

Recommended pre-lab reading assignments:

Castle DA, Gibbins B, Hamer PS. Physical Methods for Examining and Comparing Transparent Plastic Bags and Cling Films. *Journal of Forensic Science Society.* 1994; 34: 61–68.

Smith J. The Forensic Value of Duct Tape Comparisons. *Midwestern Association of Forensic Scientists Newsletter.* 1998; 27(1): 28–33.

Objective

Upon completion of this practical exercise, the student will have developed a basic understanding of:

1. general characteristics of plastic films and bags
2. macroscopic and microscopic techniques for examination of plastic films and bags
3. macroscopic and microscopic techniques for examination of tape
4. use of the stereomicroscope and polarizing light microscope to perform plastic film, bag, and tape examination.

Introduction

A wide variety of everyday items are made from plastic films. Some of these items are used for containing or transferring objects (e.g., saran wrap, plastic baggies, and garbage bags), while others are used for holding items together (e.g., pressure-sensitive tape). Because of the ubiquitous nature of these products, they are commonly encountered at crime scenes and can be used to associate evidence items with possible sources.

Practical Forensic Microscopy: A Laboratory Manual, Second Edition. Barbara P. Wheeler.
© 2021 John Wiley & Sons Ltd. Published 2021 by John Wiley & Sons Ltd.
Companion website: www.wiley.com/go/Wheeler/Forensic

Plastic Films and Bags

Most plastic films are made of polyethylene. Color and chemical additives are adjusted to improve the mechanical, physical, and chemical properties of the film. Clarity, strength, stretch-ability, sealability, and surface appearance are a few of the product concerns that can be altered with changes in the film ingredients. Plastic films are manufactured by either slit-die or blown film extrusion. Both of these methods begin with an extruder section that heats and mixes the ingredients, compresses the mixture to produce a liquid polymer, and finally filters and meters the liquid polymer so that it can be pumped through a die. The shape of the die is determined by the manufacturing method and end product use. Solid profiles such as small bags and items that require post-application additions (e.g., drawstrings or zippers) are produced by the slit-die method, while hollow profiles such as shopping and garbage bags are usually produced by the blown film method.

Plastic film examinations are performed to determine possible associations between people, places, and objects. This association is accomplished through the comparison of macroscopic, microscopic, and at times instrumental characteristics. While similar examination techniques and characteristics can be performed for the thin polymer samples, pressure-sensitive tapes also have adhesive and possible fiber reinforcement portions that can be examined, so the two topics will be discussed separately.

Physical properties of plastic bags and films can be determined macroscopically. Plastic bags and films are initially classified by four general characteristics: (1) use and type; (2) color, scent, and size; (3) closure type; and (4) seams and perforations. Examples of item use and/or type include choices for either disposal or storage. Trash bags, waste bags, and hazardous bags are examples of the disposal classification. Freezer, daily food, or vacuum seal bags are classified as storage. When describing the color of the sample, notations concerning the color, finish (gloss or matte), and opacity of the plastic film should be made. The width, length, and thickness of the film should also be used to describe the size or capacity of the item. The scent of the sample, if any, should also be noted. If the sample has a closure, further details of the closure location and type should be made. Re-closable, flap, handle, slider, drawstring, fold-top, bar-seal, heat-seal, and other are all types of bag closures used when describing samples. Details concerning the seams and perforations should also be described for samples. Heat sealers may be used to cut and seal seams, so the width and any pattern impressions produced by the heated metal strips can be characterized. If a cutting device is used to cut the bags or to add perforations, snag marks and shape of the perforation can be determined. The number and spacing of perforations are also important to note.

Once the initial characteristics are determined, further examination for finer manufacturing features can be done. Hairline marks are striations left in the plastic from the die and mandrel, and rollers used to extrude the heated plastic. Die lines are a type of hairline mark and are caused by damage to the die. If the die and mandrel are rotated during production, these hairline marks can appear to spiral. When the die and mandrel are not rotated, weld lines may be formed. Weld lines are hairline marks created from impurities caught in the die. Pigment bands are created by the inadequate mixing of the dye or pigment with the polymer resin during production. Tiger stripes are streaks in the plastic that are formed by the stretching of the plastic during production. Arrowheads and fisheyes are terms used for impurities in the plastic caused by undissolved resin or pigment that gets trapped during the film production. Surface features can also be imparted on the plastic by printing defects, scratches to the rollers, and pinching marks from stretching.

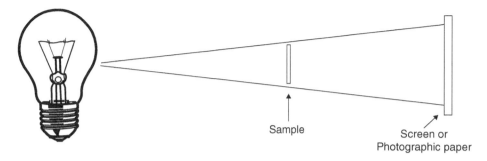

Figure 26-1 Shadowgraph photography takes advantage of light being refracted when passing through a transparent sample.

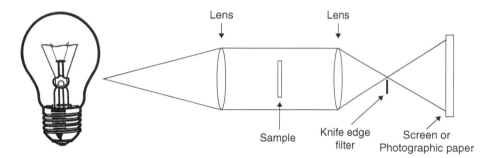

Figure 26-2 Schlieren photography utilizes lenses or filters to visualize the light being refracted when passing through a transparent sample.

Some of these features are easily determined using transmitted, reflected, or oblique lighting; however, others may require specialized techniques. Shadowgraph or Schlieren photography can be used to enhance some features. Shadowgraph photography is a technique that is used to help visualize extrusion marks and edge marks, whether cut or heat-sealed. This technique takes advantage of the fact that light is refracted when passing through transparent materials. As the light passes through a film, it is scattered or deflected by the inhomogeneities of the plastic, leaving a shadow (see Figure 26-1). The shadow image can be photographed for documentation.

Schlieren photography takes advantage of the same principle; however, the resulting image is formed by placing lenses and/or filters before and after the plastic sample (see Figure 26-2). This image can also be photographed.

During plastic film production, the heating, stretching, and cooling of the liquid polymer cause the plastic to become more orderly. As it becomes more orderly, it acts like a crystal and exhibits characteristics similar to a crystal. Because of that fact, several optical properties can also be determined for plastic films by performing examinations on a polarized light microscope.

Light passing through a transparent sample, like plastic, will be altered depending on the atomic structure and atomic spacing of the sample. This change in direction of light is referred to as the refractive index of the sample. Polymer films that have been stretched in one direction will be stretched equally normal to the plane and along the length of the machine direction, and as a result, they will exhibit two refractive indices. These films are termed monoaxially oriented (MO). A polymer that is stretched in two directions will exhibit three refractive indices: normal to the plane, along the length of the machine direction, and crosswise to the machine direction. These films are termed biaxially oriented (BO). While the refractive indices can be determined, this information is more commonly used as a discrimination tool when comparing samples. To determine whether the plastic is MO or BO oriented, samples are examined slightly off extinction under crossed polarized light. A MO film will exhibit birefringent colors in one direction, while a BO film will exhibit a bi-directional stretch. If the sample is BO, the stretching angles can also be determined. Weakly oriented polymers will show no linear interference color orientation. Under crossed polars, a plastic film will also create a visible interference figure in the back focal plane of the objective when using conoscopic illumination and high magnification (see Experiment 21A).

The extinction angle relative to the machine edge can also be determined for plastic film samples. Extinction points are the orientations when light emerging from the sample is vibrating at right angles to the preferred direction of the analyzer. The extinction angle can be determined by initially orienting the machine edge of the sample in a north-south direction. The sample is then rotated under crossed polars until extinction is achieved. The angle can be determined by noting the difference between the initial stage position and the extinction position. Some films may not go to complete extinction. Theses films are considered non-uniform or exhibiting undulose extinction.

Measurement of a sample's optical anisotropy can be another characteristic of the sample. This is accomplished by the addition of a compensator into the light path. Normally a first-order wave plate that adds between 530 and 560 nanometers (depending on the manufacturer) is used to determine the relative retardation of a sample. When aligned, this compensator introduces a relative retardation between the slow and fast ray of a sample. For fiber samples, this can be used to determine the birefringence, sign of elongation, and thickness (see Experiments 3B and 3C). However, with plastic film samples, it is typically used for comparison information.

While most plastic film examinations involve comparison to a known sample, there is also a plastic bag database that can be utilized: Polyethylene Repository and Information Database for Evidence (PRIDE). The database can be used when a particular source is not known. By entering the characteristics associated with a sample, possible matches can be obtained and compared to "known" bag descriptions, details, and images.

Tapes

Since pressure-sensitive tapes are constructed of a polymer backing with an adhesive, the polymer layer can be examined with many of the same techniques as a plastic film. The adhesive layer can also be examined microscopically. The color should initially be compared to the Munsell™ color charts. The adhesive may also contain air bubbles. These are created through the drying process and may vary in size and density.

Some pressure-sensitive tapes also have fiber reinforcements, which require additional examinations. Fiber reinforcements are added to a tape to strengthen the tape. Reinforcements can be added as filaments, cloth, or scrim. Loose filaments of nylon, polyester, or glass are commonly added to strapping tape. Medical tape commonly has cloth reinforcements. Cloth reinforcements are woven using warp and weft yarns. Warp yarns are the lengthwise or longitudinal yarns, while weft yarns are the crosswise yarns. Weft yarns can also be called fill yarns. Scrim is used in duct tape. Various weave patterns (see Figure 7-3) composed of filament bundles and spun yarns are used for scrim. Filament bundles are composed of single- or multiple-filament fibers. Spun yarns are composed of staple fibers that are held together by a binding mechanism, usually either a "Z" or "S" twist. Warp and weft are also used to describe yarns used in woven scrim. Plain weave scrim is an open mesh that has successive spun yarns interlaced in both directions varied over and under. Plain weave can also be produced with fiber bundles in the weft orientation. Another scrim weave involves open mesh that has two or more spun yarns crossing over each other that interlace with one or more weft spun yarns. This type of scrim is called warp knit with inserted weft thread. Warp knit with inserted weft bundles reinforcement is an open mesh composed of a warp spun-yarn knit chain stitch that has weft inserted fiber bundles. In addition to noting the weave of the reinforcement, details concerning the thread count, number of filaments, direction of twist, and fiber composition should also be determined (see Experiments 20, 20A, and 20B).

Various instruments can also provide additional chemical property information for plastic film and tape samples. Careful microscopic and instrumental examination of known samples and unknown samples can provide information as to similarities or dissimilarities for an investigation.

Equipment and Supplies

Stereomicroscope

Polarized light microscope with objectives of various magnifications (e.g., 4X, 10X, 20X, and 40X)

First-order compensator

Micro kit

Microscope slides and cover slips

Mounting mediums

Cargille™ oils

Shadowgraph and/or Schlieren photography setup

Physical separation method: hair dryer, freezer, or liquid nitrogen

Chemical separation method: hexane or methanol

Plastic bag samples

Plastic film samples

Pressure-sensitive tape samples

Safety

Use standard laboratory safety procedures as described in guidelines set by your instructor. Be cautious of microscope light levels to avoid eye damage. Know the hazards associated with the mounting mediums, and use them with appropriate precautions as set by your instructor. Dispose of glass in an appropriate container.

Part I: Physical Examination of Plastic Film Samples

Procedure

1. Obtain an assigned plastic bag or film sample.
2. Record the overall color, size, shape, and condition of the sample.
3. Determine the use/type of the sample.

4. Characterize the closure type and location.

5. Describe the seams and any edges.

6. Determine if there are any marks that may have been induced during the manufacturing process, using the stereomicroscope if necessary. Describe/draw these characteristics. If available, use either Shadowgraph or Schlieren photography to document these characteristics.

7. Prepare a small portion of the sample, including the machine edge, on a microscope slide.

8. Using the polarized light microscope, determine if the sample is monoaxially or biaxially oriented:

   a. by observing the birefringence under crossed polars, slightly off extinction. Draw or photograph the image.

   b. by observing the sample using conoscopic illumination. Focus on the sample using low magnification. Search for a portion that shows the lowest retardation throughout stage rotation under crossed polars. Switch to the 40X objective, and check your focus. Now observe the interference figure of the sample with the Bertrand lens inserted. Draw or photograph the image.

9. If biaxially oriented, determine the stretching angle. This is done by using a protractor to measure the angle on an image that was captured.

10. Orient the machine edge of the sample in the N-S direction. Note the location of the stage. Next, rotate the sample until extinction is observed. Note the location of the stage. Determine the extinction angle relative to the machine edge.

11. Next, orient the machine edge of the sample in a NE-SW direction. Observe the interference colors under crossed polars.

12. Insert the first-order compensator. Record the retardation of the sample.

13. Obtain your unknown sample, and repeat steps 2–12.

Part II: Tape Examination

Procedure

1. Obtain an assigned tape sample.

2. Record the overall color, size (width and length), shape, and condition of the sample. When necessary, use a physical (heating or cooling) or chemical (hexane or methanol) method to separate sections that are folded onto the tape itself.

3. Determine the type of tape.

4. Characterize the overall construction of the tape sample: backing, adhesive, and any fiber reinforcements.

5. Next, with the aid of the stereomicroscope, document the characteristics of the backing: color and texture, surface features (calendaring marks, striation, dimples, inclusions, etc.), and thickness.

6. Document the characteristics of the adhesive: color and texture, size, and density of any bubbles present.

7. Determine the weave type if a fiber reinforcement is present.

8. Now, perform further examinations on the polarizing light microscope to characterize the backing.

9. Prepare a small portion of the sample, including the machine edge, on a microscope slide.

10. Using the polarized light microscope, determine if the sample is monoaxially or biaxially oriented:
    a. by observing the birefringence under crossed polars, slightly off extinction. Draw or photograph the image.
    b. by observing the sample using conoscopic illumination. Focus on the sample using low magnification. Search for a portion that shows the lowest retardation throughout stage rotation under crossed polars. Switch to the 40X objective, and check your focus. Now observe the interference figure of the sample with the Bertrand lens inserted. Draw or photograph the image.
11. If biaxially oriented, determine the stretching angle. This is done by using a protractor to measure the angle on an image that was captured.
12. Orient the machine edge of the sample in the N-S direction. Note the location of the stage. Next, rotate the sample until extinction is observed. Note the location of the stage. Determine the extinction angle relative to the machine edge.
13. Next, orient the machine edge of the sample in a NE-SW direction. Observe the interference colors under crossed polars.
14. Insert the first-order compensator. Observe the interference colors and record the retardation of the sample.
15. The fiber reinforcement can now be examined. Determine the general weave type. Record the thread count for both warp and weft directions. The number of filaments in bundles and the direction of twist for spun yarns should also be determined.
16. Fiber composition should also be determined for both warp and weft directions (see Experiments 20, 20A, and 20B).
17. Obtain your unknown sample, and repeat steps 2–16.

Report Requirements

Include all drawings, calculations, and other information obtained during the laboratory procedure. Notes and/or drawings should include the sample identification, magnification, and a complete description.

Report Questions

1. Explain the two main manufacturing methods for plastic films.
2. Using a manufacturing method as an example, how are two of the common manufacturing features created in plastic films?
3. Why can microscopy be used to characterize a plastic film?
4. When considering MO and BO, which film do you suspect could be torn by hand? Explain your answer.
5. This experiment deals with pressure-sensitive tapes. How would you analyze a water-activated tape?
6. Would examination with UV light provide additional information when performing a tape examination? Explain your answer.
7. What characteristics would you look for when trying to obtain a physical match on two tape sections?
8. What characteristics would you look for to determine if a tape sample has been crushed or slit cut?

Recommended and Further Reading

Baldwin D, Birkett J, Facey O, Rabey G. Plastic Film Examinations. In: *The Forensic Examination and Interpretation of Tool Marks*. Chichester, UK: John Wiley & Sons, 2013.

Benson JD. Forensic Examination of Duct Tape. *Proceedings of the International Symposium on the Analysis and Identification of Polymers*. 1984: 145–146.

Campbell BM. Separation of Adhesive Tapes. *Journal of Forensic Identification*. 1991; 41(2): 102–106.

Denton S. Extrusion Marks in Polythene Film. *Journal of Forensic Science Society*. 1981; 21: 259–262.

Ford KN. The Physical Comparison of Polythene Film. *Journal of Forensic Science Society*. 1975; 15: 107–113.

Goodpaste JV, Sturdevant AB, Andrews KL, Brun-Conti L. Identification and Comparison of Electrical Tapes Using Instrumental and Statistical Techniques: I. Microscopic Surface Texture and Elemental Composition. *Journal of Forensic Sciences*. 2007; 52(3): 610–629.

Griffin RME, Lewis R, Bennett J, Hamill J, Kee TG. Analysis of Cling Films and Coloured Cellophanes and the Application to Casework. *Science and Justice*. 1996; 36: 219–227.

Hobbs AL, Gauntt J, Keagy R, Lowe PC, Ward D. A New Approach for the Analysis of Duct Tape Backings. *Forensic Science Communications*. 2007; 9(1).

Keto RO. Forensic Characterization of Black Polyvinylchloride Electrical Tape. *Crime Laboratory Digest*. 1984; 11(4): 71–74.

Maynard P, Gates K, Roux C, Lennard C. Adhesive Tape Analysis: Establishing the Evidential Value of Specific Techniques. *Journal of Forensic Sciences*. 2001; 46(2): 280–287.

Mehltretter AH, Bradley MJ, Wright DM. Analysis and Discrimination of Electrical Tapes: Part I. Adhesives. *Journal of Forensic Sciences*. 2011; 56(1): 82–94.

Nir-El Y. Forensic Characteristics of Coloured Polyethylene Bags. *Journal of Forensic Sciences*. 1994; 39(3): 758–768.

Rappe RJ. Microscopical Examination of Polymer Films. *Microscope*. 1992; 40: 93–101.

Satnko RF, Attenberger DW. The Evidentiary Value of Plastic Bags. *FBI Law Enforcement Bulletin*. 1993; 11–13.

Scientific Working Group for Materials Analysis (SWGMAT). Guideline for Forensic Examination of Pressure Sensitive Tapes. *Journal of the American Society of Trace Evidence Examiners*. 2011; 2(1): 88–89, 98–99.

Scientific Working Group for Materials Analysis (SWGMAT). Guideline for Forensic Examination of Pressure Sensitive Tapes. *Journal of the American Society of Trace Evidence Examiners*. 2012; 3(1): 2–20.

Scientific Working Group for Materials Analysis (SWGMAT). Guideline for Using Light Microscopy in Forensic Examinations of Tapes. *Journal of the American Society of Trace Evidence Examiners*. 2011; 2(1): 106–111.

Smith, J. Forensic Examinations of Pressure Sensitive Tape. In: Blackledge RD, ed. *Forensic Analysis on the Cutting Edge – New Methods for Trace Evidence Analysis*. Hoboken, NJ: John Wiley and Sons, Inc., 2007; 291–332.

Smith J, Weaver R. PLM Examinations of Clear Polymer Films. *Microscope*. 2004; 53(3–4): 112–118.

Snodgrass H. Duct Tape Analysis as Trace Evidence. *Proceedings of the International Symposium on the Forensic Aspects of Trace Evidence*. 1991; 69–73.

Teetsov AS, Stellmack ML. Hand-Sectioning and Identification of Pressure-Sensitive Tapes. *Modern Microscopy Journal*. 2004; 30.

Vanderkolk JR, Identifying Consecutively Made Garbage Bags through Manufactured Characteristics. *Journal of Forensic Identification*. 1995; 45(1): 38–50.

Chapter 27

Experiment 27: Microscopic Examination of Controlled Substances

Recommended pre-lab reading assignments:

Brinsko KM, Golemis D, King MB, Laughlin GJ, Sparenga SB. *A Modern Compendium of Microcrystal Tests for Illicit Drugs and Diverted Pharmaceuticals.* Chicago: McCrone Research Institute, 2016.

Johns SH, Wist AA, Najam AR. Spot Tests: A Color Chart Reference for Forensic Chemists. *Journal of Forensic Sciences.* 1979; 24(3): 631–641.

Moffat AC. *Clarke's Isolation and Identification of Drugs.* London: The Pharmaceutical Press, 1986; 128–147.

Objective

Upon completion of this practical exercise, the student will have developed a basic understanding of:

1. the difference between presumptive and confirmatory tests
2. color tests and microcrystalline tests
3. color tests used for drug testing
4. microcrystalline tests used for drug testing

Introduction

The microscope can be used to perform presumptive tests for forensic drug analysis. Presumptive tests are used to tentatively identify possible components of a sample. They are similar to field screening tests performed by police officers. These tests provide the analyst with an initial idea of what drug might be present so that other tests can be performed to conclusively identify the substance. These additional tests are called confirmatory tests. Confirmatory tests (i.e., infrared [IR] and gas chromatography–mass spectrometry [GC-MS]) identify the presence of a specific drug or drug metabolite. The two main types of presumptive tests used for drug analysis are color tests and microcrystalline tests, both of which are sometimes called spot testing.

Color tests are the most common form of spot testing. Color tests use reagents that react with a particular compound or a functional group. Color tests for drug analysis target three primary functional groups: phenols, aromatic rings, and amines. Since many drugs have more than one active group, understanding the mechanism for color tests can be quite complicated. In general, the most commonly used color tests are Duquenois-Levine for marijuana; cobalt thiocyanate for cocaine; Marquis for opiates, hallucinogens, and amphetamines; and p-DMAB (p-dimethylaminobenzaldehyde) for LSD.[1]

Most color tests work by adding a reagent to a drug compound that shifts the optical absorption into the visible spectrum so that a color is observed. Color tests are performed using a spot plate or in some instances a test tube. To perform the test in a spot plate, a small amount of the unknown sample is placed in a well of the spot plate. A drop or two of the reagent(s) is added to the sample, and the change in color is observed under a stereomicroscope. An important component of color testing is the use of control samples. If possible, a known sample should be analyzed at the same time to ensure that the reagents are working properly. A color change can occur even when the drug is not present due to contamination, side reactions, or oxidation. Therefore, a blank or negative control is also tested using only reagent in the neighboring well of the spot plate. If a color change is observed with a negative control, the test is said to give a false positive. If there is no color change when the reagent is tested on a known sample with a target analyte, the test is said to give a false negative. If a questioned sample contains only a small amount of the target analyte, it is possible to obtain a negative result because the concentration of the analyte is below the detection limit of the test. Generally, presumptive tests have a detection limit of 1 to 50 µg.[2] The expected results for color tests for common drug substances are given in Table 27-1. When a test gives a positive result with very small amounts of analyte, it is said to be a sensitive test. However, this does not mean it can differentiate different drugs. In general, color tests react with certain classes of drugs or chemical compounds and are not necessarily selective for an individual analyte.

Officers and laboratory analysts use color tests extensively for screening purposes because of their ease of use and robustness. Trained microscopists in the laboratory, however, usually perform microcrystalline tests. These tests are also robust and have been used for more than 100 years. As shown in Experiment 22, microcrystalline testing involves the application of known reagents to small amounts of unknown material to form identifiable crystalline products. For drug samples, these reactions are carried out on a microscope slide commonly using a test drop (drop containing unknown substance) and a reagent drop (reagent dissolved in appropriate solvent). When the reagent drop is placed in contact with the unknown, a reaction between the two substances occurs. Crystal formation requires a supersaturated solution, which is a solution whose concentration exceeds the normal solubility of the solute. The solubility concentration is the concentration of the analyte in equilibrium with solid at a given temperature. Very high supersaturation will lead to precipitation or the formation of amorphous (disordered) solid.

---

[1] Bell S. *Forensic Chemistry*. Upper Saddle River, NJ: Pearson Education, 2006; 270.

[2] O'Neal CL, Crouch DJ, Fatah AA. Validation of Twelve Chemical Spot Tests for the Detection of Drugs of Abuse. *Forensic Science International*. 2000; 109: 189–201.

Table 27-1 Expected results for common color tests.

Reagent	Reacts with	Expected positive result for some common drugs
Duquenois-Levine	Marijuana and hashish	Marijuana and hashish (blue-violet color transfers to the organic layer)
Cobalt thiocyanate	Secondary and tertiary amines, alkaloids	Cocaine HCl (blue precipitate)
		Cocaine (blue)
		Codeine (blue)
		Procaine (blue)
		PCP (blue)
		Quinine sulfate (blue)
		Amitriptyline HCl (blue)
		Nortriptyline HCl (blue)
		Cathinone (pink-blue)
Mandelin	Amphetamines and opiates	Amphetamine sulfate (green) acetaminophen (olive green)
		Methamphetamine (light green)
		Quinine sulfate (light green)
		Methadone (deep blue)
		Cathinone (orange-red)
		3,4-MDPV (green-brown)
Marquis	Opiates and amphetamines	Amphetamine sulfate (orange-brown)
		Methamphetamine HCl (orange-brown)
		Benzphetamine HCl (orange-brown)
		Aspirin (dark cherry red)
		MDA/MDMA (purple-black)
		d-propxyphene HCl (purple)
		Opium (brown-purple)
		Morphine base (purple)
		Morphine HCl (red-purple)
		Codeine phosphate (brown-purple)
		Heroin HCl (red-purple)
		Oxycodone HCl (yellow-purple)
		Hydrocodone bitartrate (red-purple)
		Fentanyl citrate (orange-brown)
		Methadone (red)
		MDMA (dark blue)
		3,4-MDPV (bright yellow)

Table 27-1   (*Continued*)

Reagent	Reacts with	Expected positive result for some common drugs
Mecke	Aromatic compounds	Bufotenine (brown to black-purple)
		Diphenhydramine HCl (yellow)
		Hydrocodone bitartrate (dark blue)
		Oxycodone HCl (yellow to olive green)
		Methadone (green-brown)
		MDMA (green to dark blue)
		Opium (green)
		Morphine base (blue green)
		Morphine HCl (green)
		Heroin HCl (green-blue)
		Mescaline HCl (olive)
		3,4-MDPV (bright yellow)
Nitric acid	Differentiate heroin from morphine	Heroin (yellow)
		Morphine (orange-brown)
		Opium (dark orange-yellow)
		LSD (brown)
		Oxycodone (yellow)
Dille-Koppanyi	Barbiturates	Barbiturates (red-violet)
		Oxymorphone HCl (violet)
		Pseudoephedrine HCl (light green)
		Theophylline (violet)
Zwikker	Barbiturates	Barbiturates (purple to light green that transfers to organic layer)
Ferric chloride	phenols, enols, and GHB	Acetaminophen (violet-purple)
		GHB (red-brown)
		Morphine (dark green)
Froehde	Aromatic compounds	Oxycodone HCl (yellow-brown)
		Opium (brown)
		MDA (green to olive to blue)
		Acetaminophen (blue)
		Bufotenine (yellow-brown)
		Heroin HCl (purple)
		MDMA (yellow/green to dark blue)
		Morphine (purple)
		3,4-MDPV (bright yellow)

Table 27-1 (*Continued*)

Reagent	Reacts with	Expected positive result for some common drugs
p-DMAB	Indoles, primary aromatic amines, and carbamates	Procaine (yellow-orange)
		Benzocaine (orange-yellow)
		LSD (purple)
		Psilocin (dark purple)
		Carbamate (yellow)
Liebermann's	Methcathinone and most synthetic cannabinoids	Cathinone (bright yellow)
		Methcathinone (bright yellow)
		3,4-MDMC (bright orange)
		MDMA (brown)
		3,4-MDPV (yellow-green)
		Butylone (green-brown)
		Morphine (black)
		Naphthoylindoles (yellow-brown)
Simon's	Primary and secondary amines	Methamphetamine (blue-violet)
		Amphetamine (pink to cherry red)
		Butylone (faint blue)

Concentrations below the solubility concentration will not produce any solid. Crystals form in the metastable region of the solubility diagram. During microcrystalline testing, it is important to realize that the concentration of the reagents varies throughout the drop on the slide. A search-and-find technique is used to locate crystals that often form near the edges of the drop, where concentrations are higher due to evaporation, or near the junction where the sample and the reagent are mixed. Crossed polars can be used in the search for crystals, since this enhances the ability to see small crystals as long as the crystals formed are not cubic.

Microcrystalline testing can be much more selective than color tests if the analyst can learn to distinguish different crystal forms. Several terms are commonly used when describing crystal shapes: bars, blades, needles, plates, prisms, rod, tablets, and grains. Arrangement of these shapes may be singly, or multiples in the form of burrs, bundles, clusters, crosses, dendrites, fans, rosettes, sheaf, stars, and tufts (see Figure 22-2).

When using a polarized light microscope and microcrystalline testing, many illicit drugs can be quickly identified. The expected crystalline shape for common drug substances is given in Table 27-2. Figure 27-1 shows the crystals formed for several drugs using a single reagent. At times, the tests can be very specific. For example, microcrystalline tests are useful for differentiation of optical isomers such as *d*-amphetamine from *d,l*-amphetamine and *d*-cocaine from *l*-cocaine.[3]

---

[3]Allen AC, Cooper DA, Kiser WO, Cottrell RC. The Cocaine Diastereoisomers. *Journal of Forensic Sciences*. 1981; 26(1): 12–26.

Table 27-2 Expected results for common microcrystalline tests.

Reagent	Reacts with	Expected crystalline result for some common drugs
Gold bromide	Amphetamine	Trapezoidal blades or small red "cigars"
Gold chloride	Cocaine	Serrated needles, long thin combs, feathery crosses, or ladders with branches
	Amphetamine	Thin, flat, feathery, leaf-shaped crystals
Gold chloride in diluted phosphoric acid	Methamphetamine	Long blades and jointed crystals
	Phentermine	Long serrated blades/plates, often spearheaded
Silver nitrate	GHB	Rectangular crystals
Wagenaar's reagent	Phenobarbital	Small rectangular prisms
	Amobarbital	Needles in clusters
	Secobarbital	Large rosettes of fine needles
Mercuric chloride	Heroin	Fine dendrites
	Propoxyphene	*d* or *l* will form shingled "H"-shaped plates, and *dl* will not form any crystals

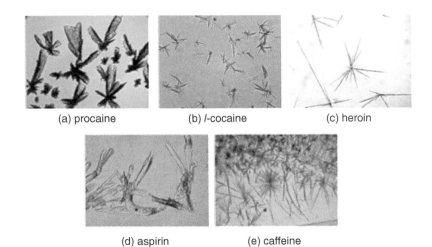

(a) procaine   (b) *l*-cocaine   (c) heroin

(d) aspirin   (e) caffeine

Figure 27-1 Crystal forms obtained from (a) procaine (s), (b) *l*-cocaine (1 mg/mL standard solution), (c) heroin (1 mg/mL standard solution), and (d) aspirin (s) and caffeine (s).

Color tests and microcrystalline tests are commonly conducted as preliminary drug tests. This gives the analyst helpful information so that subsequent and appropriate confirmatory testing can be performed. Although more advanced instrumentation has at times diminished the use of these tests, they still provide a valuable tool to the forensic scientist.

Equipment and Supplies

Stereomicroscope with magnifications of 10X–40X

Polarizing light microscope with objectives of various magnifications (e.g., 4X, 10X, 20X, and 40X)

Micro kit

Spot plate

Microscope slides

Toothpicks

Test tubes

Pipette and tips

Munsell™ Book of Color: Matte Collection

Reagents and samples as listed with each test

Safety

Use standard laboratory safety procedures as described in rules set by your instructor. Be cautious of microscope light levels to avoid eye damage. Students should know the hazards associated with the solvents used in the procedures, and use them with appropriate precautions as set by your instructor. Refer to the safety data sheet (SDS) as needed. Students should wear personal protective equipment such as goggles and nitrile gloves for all parts of this lab. All work done with chloroform and organic solvents should be completed in a hood or with adequate ventilation. Several of the reagents contain concentrated acid solutions and should be handled with caution.

Part I: Color Test

Duquenois-Levine Color Test for Marijuana

This spot test will identify the presence or absence of a 1,3-resorcinol structure in a suspected marijuana sample. A color change from gray to green through blue to violet-blue suggests the presence of cannabis. Roasted coffee and patchouli oil also produce a positive result. Fresh marijuana leaves give the best results.

1. Reagents:
   a. Duquenois reagent: Mix 0.63 mL acetaldehyde, 0.5 gm vanillin, and 25 mL of 95% ethanol.
   b. Concentrated hydrochloric acid
   c. Chloroform

2. Known samples: Known samples include coffee beans and plant samples including marijuana.
3. Unknown sample: Obtain an unknown sample extract from your instructor, and record its number in your notes.

Procedure

1. Observe the plant sample under the stereomicroscope. Pick a few leaves that have some obvious resin glands, and place in a labeled test tube.
2. Grind a coffee bean in a mortar and pestle. Place a few coffee grinds in another labeled test tube.
3. Add 20 drops of Duquenois reagent and then 20 drops of concentrated HCl into each test tube. Cover the test tubes with a cork or Parafilm, and shake. A purple color should form.
4. Next add approximately 20 drops of chloroform to the test tubes. Cover and shake. The appearance of a blue-violet color in the organic layer (bottom layer) indicates a positive test for marijuana.
5. Fully describe your observations of each of the known samples. Assign Munsell color notation for each final color using the Munsell Book of Color. The Munsell color system is explained in Experiment 21.
6. Repeat this test using an empty test tube for a control. What are your results?
7. Repeat this test using your unknown sample.
8. Fully describe your observations of the unknown sample. Assign Munsell color notation for the final color using the Munsell Book of Color.

Liebermann's Color Test for Methcathinone and Most Synthetic Cannabinoids

When methcathinone, analogs of methcathinone, or most synthetic cannabinoids with an indole substructure are present, a bright orange to brown color develops.

1. Reagents:
   a. Liebermann's reagent: Slowly add 5 gm of sodium nitrite to 50 mL of concentrated sulfuric acid. Place in a dropper bottle, and label.
   b. Methylene chloride–acetonitrile solution: Place equal amounts of methylene chloride and acetonitrile in a dropper bottle, and label.
2. Known samples: Known samples include methcathinone and synthetic cannabinoids.
3. Unknown samples: Obtain an unknown sample from your instructor, and record its number in your notes.

Procedure

1. Observe the known methcathinone sample under the stereomicroscope. Place a few particles in a well of a spot plate.
2. Add Liebermann's reagent.
3. Fully describe your observation of the known sample. Assign Munsell color notation for each final color using the Munsell Book of Color.
4. Next, observe the known synthetic cannabinoid sample under the stereomicroscope. Place a few particles in a labeled test tube.

5. Cover with the methylene chloride–acetonitrile solution.
6. Shake the test tube, and immediately pipette the liquid into a new test tube.
7. Add Liebermann's reagent, and mix.
8. Fully describe your observations of the known synthetic cannabinoid sample. Assign Munsell color notation for each final color using the Munsell Book of Color.
9. Repeat this test using an empty test tube for a control. What are your results?
10. Repeat this test using your unknown sample.
11. Fully describe your observations of the unknown sample. Assign Munsell color notation for each final color using the Munsell Book of Color.

Cobalt Thiocyanate Color Test for Cocaine and Related Drugs

In this test the pink solution of cobalt thiocyanate turns blue, through an ion-pairing mechanism, if cocaine or a related substance such as procaine is present. Procaine can be distinguished from cocaine since the blue product dissolves upon addition of stannous chloride.

1. Reagents:
    a. Cobalt thiocyanate reagent: Mix 1.5 gm of $Co(SCN)_2$ in 30 mL of ethanol. Place into a dropper bottle, and label.
    b. Stannous chloride reagent: 5.0 gm of stannous chloride is added to 10 mL of concentrated HCl. Add enough distilled water to produce 100 mL. Place in a dropper bottle, and label.
2. Known samples: Known samples include solid forms of cocaine HCl, procaine HCl, and quinine sulfate. Note: Substitution of 5–10 mg/mL standard solutions can be made in methanol. These solutions can be used for color testing by placing a few drops of the drug standard in each well. Due to the sensitivity of this test, the 1 mg/mL standard solutions available commercially do not give a color change.
3. Unknown samples: Obtain an unknown sample from your instructor, and record its number in your notes.

Procedure

1. Place a clean spot plate under the stereomicroscope. Place a 25 μL drop of the appropriate knowns in separate wells of the spot plate using the pipette and tips provided. For solid samples, use only a few grains.
2. Add 1 drop of $Co(SCN)_2$ reagent to each well. Also add 1 drop of $Co(SCN)_2$ to an empty well as a control. Note the presence or absence of blue color.
3. Add 2 drops stannous chloride reagent. Note the persistence or disappearance of blue color. Also note any solid gelatinous precipitate that may form.
4. Fully describe your observations of the known samples. Assign Munsell color notation for each final color using the Munsell Book of Color.
5. Repeat this test using an empty spot well to which a drop of water has been added for a control test. What are your results?
6. Repeat this test using your unknown sample.
7. Fully describe your observations of the unknown sample. Assign Munsell color notation for each final color using the Munsell Book of Color.

Mandelin Color Test for Opium Derivatives, Amphetamines, and Other Alkaloids

A colored vanadium complex is formed with steroids, alkaloids, or aspirin. Many compounds give a color change with this reagent, so it is important to interpret this test by comparing to a positive control. For example, hydrochlorides give a red color, and compounds containing ring-bound sulfur produce a color as long as the ring does not contain more than one nitrogen atom, as do aromatic rings with saturated 5-, 6-, or 7- membered rings containing only one nitrogen atom.

1. Reagent:
   a. Mandelin reagent: Mix 0.25 gm of ammonium vanadate in 25 mL of concentrated sulfuric acid. Place into a dropper bottle, and label.
2. Known samples: Known samples include solid forms of amphetamine sulfate, acetaminophen, Excedrin™, and quinine sulfate. Note: Substitution of 1 mg/mL standard solutions can be made. These solutions can be used for color testing by placing a few drops of the drug standard in each well. *This test works best when the color reagent is added directly to the 1 mg/mL solution.*
3. Unknown samples: Obtain an unknown sample from your instructor, and record its number in your notes.

Procedure

1. Place a clean spot plate under the stereomicroscope. Place a 25 μL drop of the appropriate known in separate wells of the spot plate using the pipette and tips provided. For solid samples, use only a few grains.
2. Add 2 drops of the Mandelin reagent to each well, and observe the color change.
3. Fully describe your observations of the known samples. Assign Munsell color notation for each final color using the Munsell Book of Color.
4. Repeat this test using an empty spot well to which a drop of water has been added for a control test. What are your results?
5. Repeat this test using your unknown sample.
6. Fully describe your observations of the unknown sample. Assign Munsell color notation for each final color using the Munsell Book of Color.

Marquis Color Test for Opium Derivatives, Amphetamines, and Other Alkaloids

All colors of the visible spectrum can be obtained with this test, so it is important to conduct positive controls. However, compounds that tend to produce color in decreasing order of efficacy are: ring sulfur, aromatic ring oxygen, and aromatic compounds consisting only of C, H, and N.

1. Reagent:
   a. Marquis reagent: Mix 2 mL of 40% formaldehyde mixed with 18 mL of concentrated sulfuric acid. Place into a dropper bottle, and label.

2. Known samples: Known samples include solid samples of amphetamine sulfate, metham-phetamine, aspirin, propxyphene, benzphetamine, morphine HCl, and codeine. Note: Sub-stitution of 1 mg/mL standard solutions for controlled substances can be made, with the exception of methamphetamine that needs a higher concentration. These solutions can be used for color testing by placing a few drops of the drug standard in each well. *This test works best when the color reagent is added directly to the 1 mg/mL solution.*

3. Unknown samples: Obtain an unknown sample from your instructor, and record its number in your notes.

Procedure

1. Place a clean spot plate under the stereomicroscope. Place a 25 μL drop of the appropriate known in separate wells of the spot plate using the pipette and tips provided. For solid samples, use only a few grains.
2. Add 2 drops of the Marquis reagent to each well, and observe the color change.
3. Fully describe your observations of the known samples. Assign Munsell color notation for each final color using the Munsell Book of Color.
4. Repeat this test using an empty spot well to which a drop of water has been added for a control test. What are your results?
5. Repeat this test using your unknown sample.
6. Fully describe your observations of the unknown sample. Assign Munsell color notation for each final color using the Munsell Book of Color.

Mecke's Color Test for Opiates

Once again, all colors of the visible spectrum can be obtained with this test, so it is important to conduct positive controls. The Mecke's reagent produces a green color when in contact with opiates.

1. Reagent:
   a. Mecke's reagent: Mix 0.25 gm selenious acid added to 25 mL concentrated sulfuric acid. Place in a dropper bottle, and label.
2. Known samples: Known samples include solid samples of oxycodone HCl, nutmeg, and sugar. Note: Substitution of 1 mg/mL standard solutions for controlled substances can be made. These solutions can be used for color testing by placing a few drops of the drug standard in each well. *This test works best when the color reagent is added directly to the 1 mg/mL solution.*
3. Unknown samples: Obtain an unknown sample from your instructor, and record its number in your notes.

Procedure

1. Place a clean spot plate under the stereomicroscope. Place a 25 μL drop of the appropriate known in separate wells of the spot plate using the pipette and tips provided. For solid samples, use only a few grains.
2. Add 2 drops of the Mecke's reagent to each well, and observe the color change.
3. Fully describe your observations of the known samples. Assign Munsell color notation for each final color using the Munsell Book of Color.

4. Repeat this test using an empty spot well to which a drop of water has been added for a control test. What are your results?
5. Repeat this test using your unknown sample.
6. Fully describe your observations of the unknown sample. Assign Munsell color notation for each final color using the Munsell Book of Color.

Part II: Microcrystalline Tests

1. Reagents:
   a. Gold chloride reagent (5% $HAuCl_4$) in a dropper bottle
   b. 3M HCl in a dropper bottle
2. Known samples:
   a. Solid samples of aspirin, caffeine, and procaine
   b. Standard solutions (1 mg/mL) of heroin and cocaine in methanol
3. Unknown samples: Obtain an unknown sample from your instructor, and record its number in your notes.

Procedure for Solid Samples

1. Obtain a mortar and pestle, and grind the assigned tablets to obtain a fine grain sample.
2. Obtain a clean microscope slide, and sprinkle just a few grains of one of the known samples onto the surface. Dissolve the sample in a tiny drop of 3M HCl.
3. Next to this drop, add a tiny drop of gold chloride reagent. Mix these two drops using Method A of Figure 22-1 in Experiment 22. Using a toothpick, draw the reagent drop to the sample drop. (If a precipitate immediately forms, your analyte concentration was too high, leading to high supersaturation, and you will need to repeat steps 2 and 3 with less sample.)

Procedure for 1 mg/mL Standard Solutions

1. Add a drop of the standard solution to the inside of a glass ring that has been placed on a microscope slide (see Method C of Figure 22-1 for arrangement). The glass ring prevents the standard solution from spreading out on the microscope slide. Allow all of the solvent to evaporate.
2. Remove the glass ring. Add a drop of crystallizing reagent to a region that has the most of the dried drug solid (Method B of Figure 22-1). A second crystallizing reagent drop can be added to another region of the same slide.

Procedure for Observing Crystals

1. Place the slide on a polarizing compound microscope, and observe the reaction mixture under 100X magnification using crossed and uncrossed polars. If necessary, increase the magnification, being careful not to get any reagent on the objective. If this does occur, ask the instructor how to clean the objective. Use the search-and-find technique to locate

any crystals that may have formed. It is especially important to look at the junction of the two drops and near the edges of the liquid, where solvent evaporation may have led to crystal formation. Use Figure 27-1 as a guide to crystal forms obtained for gold chloride. It is important to note that positive identification always requires comparison to known standards and not published photographs, as reagents and conditions may alter the crystal form.

2. If no crystals are initially found, set the microscope slide to the side and work with another drug sample, checking it periodically. With additional time crystals may form, so it is important to recheck the slide.
3. Fully describe your observations in your notes for each of the known samples.
4. Test your unknown sample using the same procedure, and report your observations.

Report Requirements

Include all drawings, calculations, and information obtained during the laboratory procedure. Notes and/or drawings should include sample identification, magnification, and a complete description.

Report Questions

Part I: Color Tests

1. Write a paragraph describing how a color test is performed, including the value and purpose of the test.
2. Define "false positive." Give three examples of a false-positive color test.
3. Define "false negative." Give three examples of a false-negative color test.
4. What test can be used to detect thiamine?
5. Describe the use of blanks and controls in spot testing.
6. What effect would mixtures have on spot test results?
7. What effect does time have on color test reagents?
8. Describe the difference between "sensitivity" and "selectivity" as they relate to presumptive tests. Are color tests or microcrystalline tests more selective?
9. Describe the Munsell™ color system.
10. Estimate the color of an object that has a Munsell™ color notation of (a) 5Y/6/1 and (b) 10R/4/2.
11. What are some substances that will give a false positive for the Duquenois-Levine color test? Did you observe this with any of the samples you tested?

Part II: Microcrystalline Tests

1. Write a paragraph describing what microcrystalline tests are and how they are performed. Give the value and purpose of the test.
2. Define the following terms: precipitate, solubility, supersaturation, and crystallization.
3. If crystals are found under plane-polarized light, why is a search for crystals recommended under crossed polars?
4. Explain why a precipitate formed in some of the microcrystalline tests.

5. What are optical isomers?
6. Describe the difference between "sensitivity" and "selectivity" as they relate to presumptive tests. Are color tests or microcrystalline tests more selective?

Recommended and Further Reading

Bailey K. The Value of the Duquenois Test for Cannabis – A Survey. *Journal of Forensic Sciences*. 1979; 24(4): 817–841.

Bell S. *Forensic Chemistry*. Upper Saddle River, NJ: Pearson Education, 2006; 270–294.

Butler WP. *Methods of Analysis for Alkaloids, Opiates, Marihuana, Barbiturates, and Miscellaneous Drugs (Publication #341)*. Washington, DC: US Treasury Department, Internal Revenue Service, 1967; 80, 105–107, 136–137.

Clarke EGC, Todd RJ, eds. *Isolation and Identification of Drugs*. London: Pharmaceutical Press, 1969; 129–130, 1183.

Cassista AR, Sandercock PML. Comparison and Identification of Automotive Topcoats: Microchemical Spot Tests, Microspectrophotometry, Pyrolysis-Gas Chromatography, and Diamond Anvil Cell FTIR. *Canadian Society of Forensic Science Journal*. 1994; 27: 209–223.

Fiegl F. *Spot Test in Organic Analysis*. Amsterdam: Elsevier Scientific, 1966.

Fulton CC. *Modern Microcrystalline Tests for Drugs*. New York: John Wiley & Sons, 1969.

Hauber DJ. Marijuana Analysis with Recording Botanical Features Present and without the Environmental Pollutants of the Duquenois-Levine Test. *Journal of Forensic Sciences*. 1992; 37(6): 1656–1661.

Houck MM, Siegel JA. *Fundamentals of Forensic Science*, 3rd ed. Amsterdam: Elsevier Academic Press, 2015; 315–348.

Jeffery W. Colour Tests. In: Moffat AC, Osselton MD, Widdop B, eds. *Clarke's Analysis of Drugs and Poisons*. London: Pharmaceutical Press, 2004; 279–300.

Kebabj DE. The Differentiation of D and L Isomers of Propoxyphene by Mixed Crystal Test. *Microgram*. 1979; 12(11).

McCrone WC, McCrone LB, Delly JG. *Polarized Light Microscopy*. Ann Arbor, MI: Ann Arbor Science, 1978.

Novoseisky Y, Glattstein B, Volvok N, Zeichner A. Microchemical Spot Tests in Toolmark Examinations. *Journal of Forensic Sciences*. 1995; 40(5).

O'Neal CL, Crouch DJ, Fatah AA. Validation of Twelve Chemical Spot Tests for the Detection of Drugs of Abuse. *Forensic Science International*. 2000; 109: 189–201.

Poyner B, et al. Presumptive Color Test for Synthetic Cannabinoids Containing an Indole Substructure. *Journal of the Clandestine Laboratory Investigating Chemists Association*. 2012; 22(4): 27–31.

Ruybal R. Microcrystalline Test for MDMA. *Microgram*. 1986; 19(6): 79–80.

Schaeffer HF. *Microscopy for Chemists*. New York: Dover Publications, 1966.

Swiatko J, De Forest PR, Zedeck MS. Further Studies on Spot Tests and Microcrystal Tests for Identification of Cocaine. *Journal of Forensic Sciences*. 2003; 48(3): 581–585.

Toole KE, Fu S, Shimmon RG, Krayment N. Color Tests for the Preliminary Identification of Methcathinone and Analogues of Methcathinone. *Microgram Journal*. 1999; 9(1): 27–32.

Wielbo D, Tebbett IR. The Use of Microcrystal Tests in Conjunction with Fourier-Transform Infrared-Spectroscopy for the Rapid Identification of Street Drugs. *Journal of Forensic Sciences*. 1992; 37(4): 1134–1148.

Chapter 28

Experiment 28: Semen Examinations

Recommended pre-lab reading assignment:

Shaler R. Modern Forensic Biology. In: Saferstein R, ed. *Forensic Science Handbook*, 2nd ed. Upper Saddle River, NJ: Pearson Education, 2002; 525–613.

Objective

Upon completion of this practical exercise, the student will have developed a basic understanding of:

1. microscopic identification of sperm

Introduction

Seminal fluid is an organic liquid that is secreted by the sexual glands and organs of males. It is a mixture of secretions from the seminal vesicle, prostate, epididymis, and bulbourethral glands. It is discharged through the process of ejaculation. Each human ejaculate is approximately 2–6 mL in volume. This fluid usually contains spermatozoa (sperm), which is the cellular structure that may be found within the seminal fluid. Each mililiter can contain between 10 and 50 million sperm cells. Some disease stages, genetic disorders, excessive drug or alcohol abuse, and elective surgical procedures can result in either a low sperm count or the complete absence of sperm. For forensics examinations, once the presumptive test for acid phosphatase has been performed, it is necessary to confirm the presence of semen through microscopic identification of the sperm cell. It is the characterization of the sperm cell that is important to the forensic scientist since this can be used in corroborating the victim's statement.

Once ejected from the body, sperm will survive for a period of time depending on a variety of factors such as the receiving surface and/or environment. A sperm cell is composed of a head,

Practical Forensic Microscopy: A Laboratory Manual, Second Edition. Barbara P. Wheeler.
© 2021 John Wiley & Sons Ltd. Published 2021 by John Wiley & Sons Ltd.
Companion website: www.wiley.com/go/Wheeler/Forensic

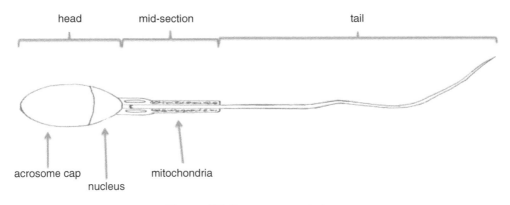

Figure 28-1   Sperm morphology.

a midsection, and a thin flagellate tail. During examinations, motile or intact sperm may be encountered by the forensic scientist. Motile sperm are active, living cells. Motile sperm may be present in samples collected from a vagina for 1–8 hours and present in samples collected from the cervix for several days. Intact sperm are cellular structures that are complete; however, they are no longer living. Intact sperm may be present in samples collected from the vagina for up to 26 hours, present in postcoital samples from the rectum for 6–65 hours, and present in samples collected from the mouth rarely more than 6 hours. The tails of the sperm are fragile and most susceptible to damage. Therefore, it is common to find sperm cells without tails in forensic casework. An analyst must be trained to visually recognize and identify differences between sperm heads and other types of cells, particularly mucosal and epithelial cells.

Sperm identification is done by differential staining. This process involves exposing the sample to various chemical solutions. Using multiple stains can distinguish between different structures or cellular components of a single organism. Depending on the sample origin and stain used to visualize the sperm, the head, midsection, and tail may stain various colors, making it easily identified (see Figure 28-1). Two stains are commonly used in forensic laboratories: Christmas tree stain and hematoxylin-eosin stain. When using Christmas tree stain, the nuclear material contained within the head of the sperm will stain red, with the anterior portion of the sperm head (acrosome) staining lighter in color than the posterior portion. Epithelial membranes and the tail portion of the sperm will stain various shades of green. When hematoxylin-eosin stain is used, nuclear material contained in the head of the sperm will stain purple, while the remaining portions of the sperm will stain pink. Once the cellular structure is visible through staining, human and animal sperm can be easily differentiated.

Most species' sperm is a similar length as human sperm; however, the head shape and head size will be different. When viewing mature human sperm from the front, the head has an oval shape with a regular contour (approximately 4–5 μm in length and 2–3 μm in width), a pale anterior part (40–70% of the head area), and a darker posterior region. The length-to-width ratio of the head is approximately 1.5–1.75. The sperm tail is symmetrically situated in a shallow depression in the broad base of the head. Only one tail should be attached, and typically it is approximately 45 μm long, not coiled, nicked, or bent. The midpiece, or area directly behind the head, is somewhat thicker (maximum width of 1 μm) and long (approximately 7–8 μm). If the sperm cell is oriented on its side, the head will appear pear-shaped.

While the overall length of animal sperm is similar to human sperm, the attachment of the head and the size and shape of the head are completely different for animal sperm. Sperm from pets (dog and cat) and farm animals (bull, horse, sheep, and pig) can be differentiated from human sperm by the evident truncation where the head neck meets the midsection. Many animal species have sperm heads that are an elongated oval (i.e., horse, cow, goat, pig), and other animal sperm heads have completely different shapes. The sperm heads of rat, turkey, and chicken are very thin and elongated, while moose, deer, and ram sperm heads have very distinctive shapes and sizes.

Complete forensic biology examinations involve the use of a variety of microscopes, techniques, and instruments. Presumptive and confirmatory tests are performed to identify semen in cases where sexual contact is suspected. The presence of sperm in a biological sample or stain is a conclusive test for semen. This usually indicates some type of sexual contact has occurred. DNA testing can be performed for additional information when necessary.

Equipment and Supplies

Compound light microscope

Biological samples

Micro kit

Reagents for staining (see specific stains below)

Immersion oil for use with oil objective

Centrifuge

Pipette tips

Test tubes

Pipettor needed for extraction

Safety

Use standard laboratory safety procedures as described in guidelines set by your instructor. Be cautious of microscope light levels to avoid eye damage. Students should know the hazards associated with the solvents used in the procedures, and use them with appropriate precautions as set by your instructor. Refer to the safety data sheet (SDS) as needed. Personal protective equipment (gloves, masks, safety glasses, etc.) should be used when working with biological materials.

Part I: Sample Slide Preparation

Procedure

If a sample slide has not been provided (as in some sexual assault kits), it is necessary to extract the biological stain and make one.

1. Extract a portion of the stain by placing a small cutting of fabric in 1 mL of distilled water. Allow it to extract for approximately 20 minutes.
2. Place the cutting and liquid in a pipette tip that is over a test tube. This allows the liquid to collect in a test tube. Centrifuge for 3 minutes at approximately 3000 rpm.
3. Draw off the majority of the extract, being careful not to disturb the sample pellet at the bottom. Leave a few drops of extract with the pellet.

4. Mix the remaining drops and the pellet by pipetting up and down. This should re-dissolve the sample pellet.
5. Pipette the sample onto a microscope slide, and allow the sample to thoroughly dry.

Part II: Sperm Slide Staining

Christmas Tree Stain

The anterior portion of human sperm heads will stain clear to pink. The posterior portion of the head will stain dark pink to red. The midsection will stain blue-green, and the tail will stain yellowish-green. Nucleated epithelial cells will also be visible as green rhomboid-like structures with a red/pink nucleus.

1. Reagents:
   a. Nuclear Fast Red (stain A): Mix 2.5 gm aluminum sulfate in 100 mL warm water. Then add in 50 mg nuclear fast red. Filter when cool.
   b. Picro Indigo Carmine (stain B): Mix 1.3 gm picric acid in 100 mL warm water. Add .33 gm indigo carmine, and stir overnight.

Procedure

1. Using a dried sample slide, place a sufficient quantity of Christmas tree stain A to cover the sample. Allow it to sit for approximately 5–10 minutes.
2. Gently rinse the slide with distilled water to remove the Christmas tree stain A.
3. Next, apply Christmas tree stain B (green stain) to the slide. Allow it to sit for 5–10 seconds.
4. Gently rinse the slide with 95% ethanol to remove the Christmas tree stain B.
5. Allow the slide to air dry.
6. Apply 1–2 drops of immersion oil to the sample slide. View the slide with the compound light microscope using a 100X oil immersion objective. Identify any sperm cells present.

Hematoxylin-Eosin Stain

Human sperm heads will stain purple, while the tail portion will stain pink.

1. Reagents:
   a. Formal alcohol (solution A): Mix 260 mL 95% ethanol, 90 mL distilled water, and 150 mL 30% formaldehyde.
   b. Hematoxylin (solution B): Mix 1 gm hematoxylin, .2 gm sodium iodate, 50 gm aluminum potassium sulfate, and 1 liter distilled water. Filter before use.
   c. Acid alcohol (solution C): Mix 350 mL of 95% ethanol, 125 mL distilled water, and 25 mL concentrated hydrochloric acid.
   d. 0.5% Disodium phosphate (solution D): Mix 2.5 gm disodium phosphate with 500 mL distilled water.
   e. 2% Eosin (solution E): Mix 10 gm eosin Y with 500 mL distilled water.

Procedure

1. Using a dried sample slide, place a sufficient quantity of solution A to cover the sample. Allow it to sit for approximately 30 seconds.
2. Gently rinse the slide with distilled water to remove solution A.
3. Next, apply solution B. Allow it to sit for approximately 10 minutes.
4. Gently rinse the slide with distilled water to remove solution B.
5. *Omit this step if using modified Mayer's Hematoxylin.* Apply solution C. Allow it to sit approximately 30 seconds. Gently rinse the slide with distilled water.
6. Next, apply solution D. Allow it to sit approximately 30 seconds.
7. Gently rinse the slide with distilled water to remove solution D.
8. Apply solution E. Allow it to sit approximately 15–20 seconds.
9. Gently rinse the slide with distilled water to remove solution E.
10. Allow the slide to air dry.
11. Apply 1–2 drops of immersion oil to the sample slide. View the slide with the compound light microscope using a 100X oil immersion objective. Identify any sperm cells present.

Report Requirements

Include all drawings, calculations, and information obtained during the laboratory procedure. Notes and/or drawings should include sample identification, magnification, and a complete description.

Report Questions

1. What is the difference between a presumptive and confirmatory test?
2. Explain differential staining as it relates to forensics.
3. Define motile and intact sperm cells. Give an example of a short case scenario where each type of sperm cell might be encountered in casework.
4. How long after a sexual assault would you expect to find identifiable sperm? Cite a reference as part of your answer.
5. How is human sperm differentiated from dog sperm?
6. Will human sperm always be identified in cases of sexual contact? Explain your answer.

Recommended and Further Reading

Aiken MM, Muram D, Keene PR, Mamelli J. Evidence Collection in Cases of Child-Abuse – the Detection of Seminal Fluid. *Adolescent and Pediatric Gynecology.* 1993; 6(2): 86–90.

Albrecht K, Schultheiss D. Seminal Stains in Legal Medicine: An Historical Review of Forensic Proof. *Urology A.* 2005; 44(5): 530.

Allery JP, Telmon, N, Mieusset R, Blanc A, Rougé D. Cytological Detection of Spermatozoa: Comparison of Three Staining Methods. *Journal of Forensic Sciences.* 2001; 46(2): 349–351.

Davies A. Evaluation of Results from Tests Performed on Vaginal, Anal and Oral Swabs Received in Casework. *Journal Forensic Science Society.* 1977; 17: 127–133.

Davies A, Wilson E. The Persistence of Seminal Constituents in the Human Vagina. *Journal of Forensic Sciences.* 1974; 3: 45–55.

Hooft P, Vandevoorde H. Evaluation of the Modified Zinc Test and the Acid-Phosphatase Test as Preliminary Screening Methods in Sexual Assault Case Material. *Forensic Science International.* 1992; 53(2): 135–141.

Houck MM, Siegel JA. *Fundamentals of Forensic Science*, 3rd ed. Amsterdam: Elsevier Academic Press, 2015; 245–250.

Inoue S, Sato H. Arrangement of DNA Molecules in the Sperm Nucleus: An Optical Approach to the Analysis of Biological Fine Structure. *Biophysical Science Series 2, Progress in Genetics III.* 1966: 151–220.

Khaldi N, Miras A, Botti K, Benali L, Gromb S. Evaluation of Three Rapid Detection Methods for the Forensic Identification of Seminal Fluid in Rape Cases. *Journal of Forensic Sciences.* 2004; 49(4): 749–753.

Martin NC, Pirie AA, Ford LV, Callaghan CL, McTurk K, Lucy D, et al. The Use of Phosphate Buffered Saline for the Recovery of Cells and Spermatozoa from Swabs. *Science & Justice.* 2006; 46(3):179–184.

Martinez P, Capilla J, Atienza I, Vallejo G, Sancho M. How Long Spermatozoa May Remain after Death; an Important Track before DNA Identification. *Forensic Science International.* 2003; 136: 44–45.

Norris JV, Manning K, Linke SJ, Ferrance JP, Landers JP. Expedited, Chemically Enhanced Sperm Cell Recovery from Cotton Swabs for Rape Kit Analysis. *Journal of Forensic Sciences.* 2007; 52(4): 800–805.

Rand S, Wiegand P, Brinkmann B. Problems Associated with the DNA Analysis of Stains. *International Journal of Legal Medicine.* 1991; 104(5): 293–297.

Schudel D. Screening for Canine Spermatozoa. *Science and Justice.* 2001; 41: 117–119.

Shaler R. Modern Forensic Biology. In: Saferstein R, ed. *Forensic Science Handbook.* Upper Saddle River, NJ: Pearson Education, 2005; 525–613.

Willott GM, Allard JE. Spermatozoa: Their Persistence after Sexual Intercourse. *Forensic Science International.* 1982; 19: 135–154.

Application Experiments, Instrumental Microscopy

Chapter 29

Experiment 29: Fourier Transform Infrared Microspectrometry Examinations

Recommended pre-lab reading assignments:

Bell S. *Forensic Chemistry*. Upper Saddle River, NJ: Pearson Education, 2006; 149–169.

Kirkbridge KP, Tungol MW. Infrared Microspectroscopy of Fibres. In: Robertson J, Grieve M, eds. *Forensic Examination of Fibres*. London: Taylor and Francis, 1999; 179–222.

Ryland SG. Infrared Microspectroscopy of Forensic Paint Evidence. In: Humecki H, ed. *Practical Guide to Infrared Microspectroscopy*. New York: Marcel Dekker, 1995; 163–243.

Steom SE, Center NMSD. Infrared Spectra. In: Linstrom PJ, Mallard WG, eds. *NIST Chemistry Web Book: NIST Standard Reference Database Number 69*. Gaithersburg, MD: National Institute of Standards and Technology; 2005. Available from: http://webbook.nist.gov.

Objective

Upon completion of this practical exercise, the student will have developed a basic understanding of:

1. general infrared spectrometry principles
2. general micro-FTIR principles
3. sample preparation for micro-FTIR analysis
4. use of the FTIR microspectrometer to identify paint characteristics
5. use of the FTIR microspectrometer to identify fiber characteristics

---

Practical Forensic Microscopy: A Laboratory Manual, Second Edition. Barbara P. Wheeler.
© 2021 John Wiley & Sons Ltd. Published 2021 by John Wiley & Sons Ltd.
Companion website: www.wiley.com/go/Wheeler/Forensic

Introduction

A Fourier transform infrared (FTIR) microspectrometer combines use of a microscope that has been adapted to a conventional instrument. Since this spectrometer measures the interaction of infrared light with matter, we must first discuss basic principles of light and matter.

Light is found all around us in the form of the electromagnetic radiation. When an electric field joins perpendicularly and in phase with a magnetic field, electromagnetic waves are formed. The electromagnetic spectrum defines the array of radiation as we know it into specific ranges. The various electromagnetic ranges are determined by the wavelength. The distance between one wave crest to the next is called the wavelength. Waves vary from very long radio waves to very short gamma rays. The area of the electromagnetic spectrum of interest in this experiment, infrared light, falls within a narrow range.

Infrared light is found within the electromagnetic spectrum from the near end of the visible spectrum to the microwaves, including radiation at wavelengths from approximately 14,000 nm to 20 nm. The spectral range of greatest use is the mid-infrared region, which covers the frequency range from $200 \, cm^{-1}$ to $4000 \, cm^{-1}$. Infrared spectroscopy involves the interaction of infrared light with matter. Twisting, bending, rotating, and vibration motions of the atoms occur within a molecule when subjected to infrared light. Upon interaction, portions of the incident radiation are absorbed at particular wavelengths. The uniqueness of the infrared spectrum arises from the multiplicity of vibrations occurring simultaneously. This is displayed by absorption, which is characteristic of the functional groups comprising the molecule and the overall configuration of the atoms as well. The absorption results in a peak in a spectrum that is a graph of wavelength versus percent transmittance, (%T), which is related to absorption (A) by $A = 2 - \log \%T$.

The FTIR microspectrometer (see Figure 29-1) is composed of an interferometer that is an instrument that divides a beam of light into two beams and then recombines the light after introducing a phase difference in one of the beams. The light beam from the source is split by a beam splitter and reflected off of two mirrors to be recombined at the beam splitter. One of the mirrors is fixed, and the other movable. It is the moving mirror that introduces the phase difference. Combining two beams of light that are "in phase" results in constructive interference and a resulting intensity enhancement. The combining of light that is "out of phase" results in destructive interference and an intensity decrease. If the intensity of the two beams of light remain the same and the phase difference is introduced incrementally, then the intensity difference will manifest itself as a cosine wave that has a frequency dependent upon the speed of the moving mirror. This resultant waveform is called an interferogram. If a sample is placed in the beam, the cosine wave will be altered according to whatever interaction the sample will have with the light itself.

In an infrared spectrometer, all wavelengths are measured at the same time. The resultant waveform is quite complex, but mathematically can be solved by use of the Fourier transform. The moving mirror increments the phase differences in small fractions of a wavelength (frequency). This means that the position of the mirror is critical to any meaningful measurement. Using mechanical measuring devices for mirror positions proved inadequate for frequency measurements. This brought about the advent of the double-beam interferometer. The double-beam interferometer uses a second mirror and laser light source. Laser light is monochromatic, and the interferogram is fairly simple and easy to track. By counting the highs and lows in the laser interferogram, it is possible to track the mirror position very precisely. Being able to track the mirror produces a reproducible spectrum and allows for the use of multiple scan averaging.

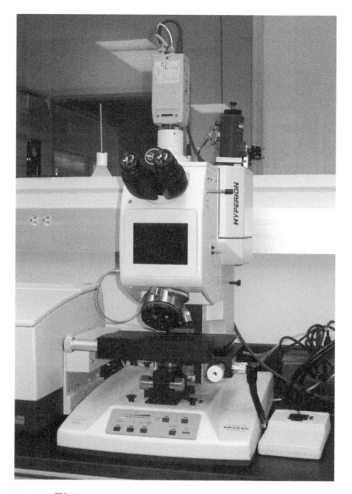

Figure 29-1 A Bruker™ FTIR microspectrometer. This instrument allows forensic scientists to acquire FTIR data from microscopic-size forensic samples. While the light beam is generated from the FTIR bench, a separate detector is utilized for the microscope.

Multiple scan averaging improves signal-to-noise ratios and results in cleaner spectra. The most common detectors for FTIR are the triglycine sulfate (TGS) and mercury-cadmium-telluride (MCT) detectors. TGS detectors operate at room temperature but the MCT detector must be cooled, usually with liquid nitrogen. These detectors respond only to the modified signal coming from the interferometer and therefore are not subject to stray light or emission from the sample. Usually the bench portion of an instrument operates with a TGS detector and the microscope attachment has a MCT detector.

The power of FTIR microspectroscopy is that it provides information about the chemical structure of the evidence being examined. Fibers and paint are composed of bonded atoms that rotate, bend, and vibrate in different modes when placed in infrared light. To determine the type of bonds and atoms in the molecule, the peaks in the spectrum must be interpreted. Table 29-1 lists the common bond types for the functional group regions.

Table 29-1 Common bond types for the functional group region.

Region (cm^{-1})	Bond type	Frequency (cm^{-1}), intensity, shape
4000–2700	OH	3600–3500, s, broad
4000–2700	NH$_2$ or NH	3500–3300, w-m, broad
4000–2700	=C–H	3100–3000, w
4000–2700	–C–H	3000–2800, s
2700–1850	C≡N	2300–2200, w
1850–1500	C=O	1780–1650, s
1850–1500	C=C	1670–1640, w-m

There are two regions assigned to the infrared spectrum: the functional group region and the fingerprint region. The functional group region runs from 4000 cm^{-1} to 2000 cm^{-1}. The functional group region has fewer peaks that remain fairly consistent. They are typically associated with stretching vibrations. In addition to the location of the peak, it is useful to interpret the intensity of the peak that is related to the path length of the sample, and the magnitude of the dipole moment change incurred during vibration. The fingerprint region is below 2000 cm^{-1} and is named after the numerous peaks that can be used to distinguish two samples. This region can be difficult to interpret due to the large number of peaks mainly due to bending-type vibrations. Because of this, it is best to start interpretation at the high wavenumbers and identify functional groups first. In addition to manual interpretation, there are numerous databases and computer library searches available that can be used to identify the exact composition of the evidence.

The shape and thickness of samples become very important when using the microscope on the FTIR spectrometer. The ideal sample is approximately 5–15 µm thick. However, even thick samples can be sufficiently prepared by cutting and flattening them prior to acquiring a spectrum. Paint and fiber samples are commonly examined using a FTIR microspectrometer.

Paint

Examinations of paint are usually performed to identify paint and then to compare a paint back to a possible paint source. Initially a stereomicroscope is used to examine the paint for layer structure and their solubilities in different solvents (Experiment 14). FTIR microspectrometry is an additional technique that may be utilized to identify and compare the many layers found in a paint sample. Original finish automotive paints will have absorption peaks at 1550 cm^{-1} and 815 cm^{-1}. Automotive repaints will not have these bands. Using functional group interpretation of paint samples, many binders, resins, pigments, and extenders can often be identified. Common binders and resins are listed in Table 29-2. Common pigments and extenders that may be identified by micro-FTIR are listed in Table 29-3.

Table 29-2 Absorption bands for some common paint binders and resins.

Binder/Resin	Identifying absorption bands (cm^{-1})
Acrylic	1450 1380 1270/1240 1150* 1070 840 750 705
Acrylic–melamine	1550* 1480 1370 1170* 1090 815* (may also have 1270/1240)
Acrylic–alkyd	1260* 1180* 1130 1070
Acrylic–urethane	1530* 1240* 1170 1070
Orthophthalic alkyd	1450 1380 1270* 1130* 1070* 740 700
Isophthalic alkyd	1475 1373 1305 1237* 1135 1074 730*
Terephthalic alkyd	1270 1250* 1120 1105 1020 730*
Alkyd–melamine	1550* 1270* 1120 1070 815* 740 700
Alkyd–urea	1650* 1540* 1270 1120 1070 770* 740 705
Polyester–melamine	1550* 1330* 1240* 815* 750 730 705
Benzoguanamine	1590 1540 825 780 710
Epoxy	1510* 1240 1180 830*
Melamine	1550 815
Nitrocellulose	1650* 1280* 840* 750
Polybutadiene	970 915
Polyurethane	1690 1530* 1470 1250 1070
epoxy modified	1730 1510
water based	1690 770
Styrene	1490 1450 760 700
Styrene–butadiene	1600 1495 1450 760* 700*
Urea	1655
Polyvinyl acetate (PVA)	1735 1370 1240* 1135-1020 945* 605*

*Main absorption peaks.

Fibers

Fiber examinations were discussed in Experiments 20, 20A, 20B, and 20C. Initially a stereomicroscope is used to examine the fiber for macroscopic characteristics. Further testing can be performed using a compound or comparison light microscope to determine optical properties such as refractive index and extinction. At times, burn or solubility tests may also be performed during man-made fiber examinations. FTIR microspectrometry is an additional technique that is frequently used in both natural and man-made fiber examinations because of the characterization potential of FTIR.

Table 29-3 Absorption bands for some common paint pigments and extenders.

Pigment/Extender	Identifying absorption bands (cm^{-1})
Calcium carbonate	
Aragonite	1445 870 857 712 317
Calcite	1445 870 712 317
Barium chromate	935 896 860
Potassium zinc chromate	950 880 805
Strontium chromate	911 887 875 844
Chromium oxide	680 634 582 446 417 400
Iron oxide	
red	560-530 480-440 350-310
yellow	899 797 606 405 278
Silicon dioxide	
Cristobalite	1090 795 621 485 387 300
Diatomaceous silica	1100 800 480
Quartz	1081 798 779 512 460 397 373
Titanium dioxide	
Rutile	600 410 340
Anatase	600 340
Zinc phosphate	1120 1080 1020 950 630
Zinc oxide	1096 888 520 501 401
Silicate	
Talc	1030 1015 670 460 450 420 390 345
Clay	1120 1030 1010 940 910 540 470 430 350 280
Mica	1065 1032 936 834 756 699 535 478 411
Barium sulfate	1175 1080 980 640 610
Lead carbonate	1412 1047 848 695 683 404
Lead sulfate	1410 1172 1078 969 687 632 600 428 363
Cobalt aluminate	1102 1035 1012 905 735 652 558 508 239
Cuprous oxide	626 425

Equipment and Supplies

Stereomicroscope
Paint samples
Fiber samples

Micro kit
Microscope slides
FTIR Microspectrometer (salt plate and salt plate holder)
Liquid nitrogen, thermos, and cryo-gloves
Methanol
Small metal roller

Safety

Use standard laboratory safety procedures as described in guidelines set by your instructor. Be cautious of microscope light levels to avoid eye damage. Use of safety glasses and cryo-gloves when handling liquid nitrogen is recommended. Refer to the safety data sheet (SDS) if necessary.

Part I: Familiarization with the FTIR

Since each instrument may be operated differently and utilize different software, please refer to the operational manual of your instrument to familiarize yourself with operating the instrument.

Part II: Paint

Procedure

1. Obtain a paint sample.
2. Using the stereomicroscope, turn the paint chip up on edge.
3. As discussed in Experiment 14, determine the layer structure of the paint chip. If necessary, immerse the paint chip in methanol to help visualize clear layers.
4. Cut a thin shaving from the top layer. Note: For most automotive paint samples, this will be a clear coat.
5. Place the shaving on a hard surface (microscope slide) and if necessary, flatten it using the roller.
6. Obtain a FTIR spectrum using the microscope attachment. Remember: The sensitivity of the microscope detector for most instruments cuts off around $650\,cm^{-1}$.
7. Identify any binders, pigments, extenders, or resins present in the top layer of the paint sample.
8. Next, cut a thin shaving from the primer layer.
9. Place it on a hard surface (microscope slide), and flatten it using the roller.
10. Obtain a FTIR spectrum using the microscope attachment. Remember: The sensitivity of the microscope detector for most instruments cuts off around $650\,cm^{-1}$.
11. Identify any binders, pigments, extenders, or resins present in the primer layer of the paint sample.
12. Repeat steps 2–10 for any assigned paints.
13. Include a copy of the FTIR spectra obtained from the paint samples. Determine any possible pigments, binders, extenders, or resins present in the paint sample. Give the chemical structures of these ingredients. Relate at least two peaks in the spectra to chemical structures present in the paint component.

Part III: Fibers

Procedure

1. Obtain a fiber sample.
2. Cut a small section of a single fiber from the fiber sample.
3. Place it on a hard surface (microscope slide) and if necessary, flatten it using the roller.
4. Obtain a FTIR spectrum using the microscope attachment. Remember: The sensitivity of the microscope detector for most instruments cuts off around $650\,cm^{-1}$.
5. Identify the fiber.
6. Repeat steps 2–5 for any assigned fibers.
7. Include a copy of the FTIR spectra obtained from the fiber samples. Draw the chemical structure of the fiber and its chemical formula. Relate at least two peaks in the spectra to chemical structure of the fiber.

Report Requirements

Include all drawings, calculations, and other information obtained during the laboratory procedure. Notes and/or drawings should include the sample identification, magnification, and a complete description.

Report Questions

1. Explain how a FTIR microspectrometer operates. Include a drawing of the mechanics of the bench portion of a FTIR. How is the instrument modified to allow collection of infrared data from the microscope?
2. Why is this a useful instrument to forensic laboratories?
3. Include a copy of the FTIR spectra obtained from the fiber samples. Determine the identity of the fiber. Give the chemical structure of the fiber, and relate at least two peaks to the chemical structure.
4. The SWGMAT Forensic Paint Analysis and Comparison Guidelines state, "Certain types of coatings, including automotive undercoats and many types of architectural coatings ··· usually contain significant amounts of inorganic pigments." Since these pigments tend to have most of their significant infrared absorptions in the lower frequency spectral regions, some well below 700 nm, how can these be identified with a FTIR?
5. The ASTM guidelines for fiber examinations state that microscopic examination is indispensable for identification of cellulose and animal fibers, while infrared and solubility relationships are essential for identifying man-made fibers. Explain why.

Recommended and Further Reading

ASTM. *Standard Guide for Forensic Paint Examination (ASTM E-1610-14)*. West Conshohocken, PA: ASTM International, 2014.

Bartick EG, Tungol MW. *Infrared Microscopy and Its Forensic Applications*. Englewood Cliffs, NJ: Prentice-Hall, 1993.

Bartick EG, Tungol MW, Reffner JA. A New Approach to Forensic Analysis with Infrared Microscopy: Internal Reflection Spectroscopy. *Analytica Chimica Acta*. 1994; 288: 35–42.

Bell SEJ, Fido LA, Speers SJ, Armstrong WJ, Spratt S. Forensic Analysis of Architectural Finishes Using Fourier Transform Infrared and Raman Spectroscopy, Part I: The Resin Bases. *Applied Spectroscopy*. 2005; 59(11): 1333–1339.

Bell SEJ, Fido LA, Speers SJ, Armstrong WJ, Spratt S. Forensic Analysis of Architectural Finishes Using Fourier Transform Infrared and Raman Spectroscopy, Part II: White Paint. *Applied Spectroscopy*. 2005; 59(11): 1340–1346.

Causin V, Marega C, Guzzini G, Marigo A. Forensic Analysis of Poly(Ethylene Terephthalate) Fibers by Infrared Spectroscopy. *Applied Spectroscopy*. 2004; 58(11): 1272–1276.

Causin V, Marega C, Guzzini G, Marigo A. The Effect of Exposure to the Elements on the Forensic Characterization by Infrared Spectroscopy of Poly(Ethylene Terephthalate) Fibers. *Journal of Forensic Sciences*. 2005; 50(4): 887–893.

Causin V, Marega C, Schiavone S, Marigo A. A Quantitative Differentiation Method for Acrylic Fibers by Infrared Spectroscopy. *Forensic Science International*. 2005; 151(2–3): 125–131.

Cho LL, Reffner JA, Gatewood BM, Wetzel DL. A New Method for Fiber Comparison Using Polarized Infrared Microspectroscopy. *Journal of Forensic Sciences*. 1999; 44(2): 275–282.

Compton S, Powell J. Forensic Applications of IR Microscopy. *American Laboratory*. 1991; 23(17): 41.

Cook R, Paterson MD. New Techniques for the Identification of Microscopic Samples of Textile Fibres by Infrared Spectroscopy. *Forensic Science International*. 1978; 12: 237–243.

Derrick MR. *Infrared Microspectroscopy in the Analysis of Cultural Artifacts*. New York: Marcel Dekker, 1995.

Ferrer N. FT-IR Spectroscopy and Microscopy with a Diamond Cell Applied to Forensic and Industrial Samples. *Mikrochimica Acta*. 1997: 329–332.

Flynn K, O'Leary R, Lennard C, Roux C, Reedy BJ. Forensic Applications of Infrared Chemical Imaging: Multi-Layered Paint Chips. *Journal of Forensic Sciences*. 2005; 50(4): 832–841.

Flynn K, O'Leary R, Roux C, Reedy BJ. Forensic Analysis of Bicomponent Fibers Using Infrared Chemical Imaging. *Journal of Forensic Sciences*. 2006; 51(3): 586–596.

Grant A, Wilkinson TJ, Holman DR, Martin MC. Identification of Recently Handled Materials by Analysis of Latent Human Fingerprints Using Infrared Spectromicroscopy. *Applied Spectroscopy*. 2005; 59(9): 1182–1187.

Grieve MC. New Man-Made Fibres under the Microscope – Lyocell Fibres and Nylon 6 Block Co-Polymers. *Science & Justice*. 1996; 36(2): 71–80.

Grieve MC, Griffin RME. Is It a Modacrylic Fibre? *Science & Justice*. 1999; 39(3): 151–162.

Harris HA, Kane T. A Method for Identification of Lysergic-Acid Diethylamide (LSD) Using a Microscope Sampling Device with Fourier-Transform Infrared (Ft/Ir) Spectroscopy. *Journal of Forensic Sciences*. 1991; 36(4): 1186–1191.

Hartshorne AW, Laing DK. The Identification of Polyolefin Fibres by Infrared Spectroscopy and Melting Point Determination. *Forensic Science International*. 1984; 26: 45–52.

Hashimoto T, Howitt DG, Land DP, Tulleners FA, Springer FA, Wang S. Morphological and Spectroscopic Measurements of Plastic Bags for the Purpose of Discrimination. *Journal of Forensic Sciences*. 2007; 52(5): 1082–1088.

Houck MM, Siegel JA. *Fundamentals of Forensic Science*, 3rd ed. Amsterdam: Elsevier Academic Press, 2015; 108–109, 390, 417–418.

Liddell CM. Field Sampling and Chemical Analysis. *Journal of Forensic Sciences*. 1997; 42(3): 398–400.

Moore DS, Hudson RO. Using the Polarizing Microscope to Complement Microscopic FT-IR Spectroscopy. *Spectroscopy*. 2001; 16(4): 20–23.

Ricci C, Chan KLA, Kazarian SG. Combining the Tape-Lift Method and Fourier Transform Infrared Spectroscopic Imaging for Forensic Applications. *Applied Spectroscopy*. 2006; 60(9): 1013–1021.

Ryland SG. *Infrared Microspectroscopy of Forensic Paint Evidence*. New York: Marcel Dekker, 1995.

Steom SE, Center NMSD. Infrared Spectra. In: Linstrom PJ, Mallard WG, eds. *NIST Chemistry Webbook: NIST Standard Reference Database Number 69*. Gaithersburg, MD: National Institute of Standards and Technology, 2005.

Suzuki EM. *Forensic Applications of Infrared Spectroscopy*. Englewood Cliffs, NJ: Regents/Prentice-Hall, 1993.

Suzuki EM. Infrared Spectra of US Automobile Original Topcoats (1974–1989). 1. Differentiation and Identification Based on Acrylonitrile and Ferrocyanide C N Stretching Absorptions. *Journal of Forensic Sciences*. 1996; 41(3): 376–392.

Thornton JI. Forensic Paint Examinations. In: Saferstein R, ed. *Forensic Science Handbook*, 2nd ed. Upper Saddle River, NJ: Pearson Education, 2002; 458–473.

Tungol MW, Bartick EG, Montaser A. The Development of a Spectral Data Base for the Identification of Fibres by Infrared Microscopy. *Applied Spectroscopy*. 1990; 44: 543–549.

Tungol MW, Bartick EG, Montaser A. Forensic Analysis of Acrylic Copolymer Fibers by Infrared Microscopy. *Applied Spectroscopy*. 1993; 47(10): 1655–1658.

Wetzel DL, LeVine SM. Microspectroscopy – Imaging Molecular Chemistry with Infrared Microscopy. *Science*. 1999; 285(5431): 1224–1225.

Wilkinson JM, Locke J, Laing DK. The Examination of Paints at Thin-Sections Using Visible Microspectrophotometry and Fourier Transform Infrared Spectroscopy. *Forensic Science International*. 1988; 38: 43–52.

Wilson JD, LaPorte GM, Cantu AA. Differentiation of Black Gel Inks Using Optical and Chemical Techniques. *Journal of Forensic Sciences*. 2004; 49(2): 364–370.

ZiebaPalus J. Application of Transmittance and Reflectance FT-IR Microscopy to Examination of Paints Transferred onto Fabrics. *Mikrochimica Acta*. 1997: 361–362.

ZiebaPalus J. The Use of Micro Fourier-Transform Infrared Spectroscopy and Scanning Electron Microscopy with X-Ray Microanalysis for the Identification of Automobile Paint Chips. *Mikrochimica Acta*. 1997: 357–359.

Chapter 30

Experiment 30: UV-Visible-NIR Microspectrophotometry Examinations

Recommended pre-lab reading assignments:

Bell S. *Forensic Chemistry*. Upper Saddle River, NJ: Pearson Education, 2006; 149–161.

Eyring MB. Visible Microscopical Spectrophotometry in Forensic Sciences. In: Saferstein R, ed. *Forensic Science Handbook*, 2nd ed. Upper Saddle River, NJ: Pearson Education, 2002; 322–387.

Objective

Upon completion of this practical exercise, the student will have developed a basic understanding of:

1. general microspectroscopy principles
2. sample preparation for analysis with the microspectrophotometer
3. use of the microspectrophotometer to analyze paint characteristics
4. use of the microspectrophotometer to analyze fiber characteristics
5. use of the microspectrophotometer to analyze ink characteristics

Introduction

Spectroscopy is the branch of science dealing with the theory and interpretation of spectra. In Experiment 29, infrared light was used to produce an infrared spectrum in order to gain structural information about a sample. The UV-visible-NIR microspectrophotometer, however, is used to gain information about the interaction of the sample with light from the ultraviolet (UV) region

Practical Forensic Microscopy: A Laboratory Manual, Second Edition. Barbara P. Wheeler.
© 2021 John Wiley & Sons Ltd. Published 2021 by John Wiley & Sons Ltd.
Companion website: www.wiley.com/go/Wheeler/Forensic

(190–400 nm), visible region (400–800 nm), and near-infrared (NIR) region (800–2500 nm) of the electromagnetic spectrum.

The visible region provides information about the color of the sample under study. The ability to determine and compare color accurately is an important skill for forensic scientists. Among other things, the analyst must rely on color changes determined in presumptive tests, and also in the comparison of colors of fibers, paints, and inks frequently encountered in casework. Presumptive tests are usually observed and compared through a visual examination. However, there are many disadvantages in determining color by visual inspection. First, each person perceives colors differently. Second, color can be difficult to describe without a common color language. Finally, the color observed depends on the source of illumination, which is often not considered when conducting a visual exam. Use of an instrument to obtain a color spectrum avoids these problems and provides additional information for regions of the spectrum outside those seen by the human eye.

In addition to color measurements within the visible spectral range, a microspectrophotometer provides measurements in the UV and NIR range (see Figure 30-1). In the UV region, only two

Figure 30-1   The SEE™ UV-visible-NIR microspectrophotometer allows forensic scientists to acquire data from microscopic-size forensic samples. Several settings and light sources are used to view microscopic samples by transmittance, absorption, reflectance, and fluorescence.

types of electronic transitions can occur. Therefore, only compounds containing π electrons will contribute peaks in this region. This will provide information about the presence or absence of double bonds and conjugation in the sample. The NIR range yields information about the vibrational and rotational transitions for molecules such as titanium oxide (found in paint evidence) and carbon dioxide.

Spectra obtained from the microspectrophotometer provide information about the interaction of the sample with light from the various regions: the UV region (190–400 nm), visible region (400–800 nm), and NIR region (800–2500 nm). There are several types of spectra that can be obtained by a microspectrophotometer: (1) transmittance, (2) absorbance, and (3) reflectance. Some microspectrophotometers are also equipped with a fluorescence mode. These will each be described briefly.

Transmission spectra can be obtained by measuring the amount of light that passes through a sample at each wavelength. Transmitted light, T, is determine by Equation (30-1):

$$T = \frac{I}{I_o} \tag{30-1}$$

where I_o is the intensity of radiant energy striking the sample, and I is the intensity of radiant energy emerging from the sample.

A more common spectrum is the absorbance spectra, which is obtained by measuring the amount of light absorbed, A, at each wavelength. A is measured by Equation (30-2):

$$A = -\log T = \log \frac{I_o}{I} \tag{30-2}$$

The Beer-Lambert Law relates transmittance, sample thickness, and concentration according to Equation (30-3):

$$A = \varepsilon bc \tag{30-3}$$

where ε is the molar absorbtivity, b is the path length, and c is the concentration of the absorbing species.

It is the relationship between absorbance and pathlength that at times requires samples to be flattened with a metal roller. This reduces the pathlength, b, and the absorbance, A, allowing consistent spectra to be obtained. These types of spectra are useful for comparing transparent evidence.

If the sample is opaque, such as with many paint samples, it is not possible to measure the amount of light that can pass through the sample. To determine the visible spectrum of these materials, the light reflected off the samples is measured with wavelength. There are two ways to obtain a reflectance spectrum. The first is known as the relative reflectance. Here the final spectrum of the sample contains some information about a reference material. Equation (30-4) determines the reflectivity, R:

$$R = \frac{I}{I_o} \tag{30-4}$$

where I_o is the intensity of energy reflected from the reference sample, and I is the intensity of energy reflected from the sample. Comparing to a reference material corrects for variations in source intensity and detector sensitivity with wavelength. However, there are times when it is not possible to obtain a suitable reference location. In this situation, absolute reflectance spectra can be measured where the final spectrum of the sample is independent of a reference material.

Finally, some samples contain chromophores, which fluoresce when excited with light of particular wavelength. Fluorescence is the emission of light as molecules return to their ground state configuration. Fluorescence, F, is measured in counts and not corrected to any standard, as is measured according to Equation (30-5):

$$F = 1 \qquad\qquad (30\text{-}5)$$

where I is the intensity of radiant energy measured by the detector. In most situations, the forensic scientist performs examinations in the reflectance, transmittance, and fluorescence modes.

In a typical spectrophotometer, white light containing all wavelengths passes through the sample. The sample absorbs certain wavelengths of light depending on the electronic structure of the molecules in the sample. Light that is not absorbed enters a monochromator, which separates the wavelengths of light, which are, in turn, detected by an array detector. The detector measures the intensity of light at each wavelength.

A microspectrophotometer combines an optical microscope with a spectrophotometer so that samples can be examined in the UV-visible-NIR ranges. This allows samples as small as 1 μm × 1 μm to be examined. A microspectrophotometer differs from a typical spectrophotometer only in that the amount of light transmitted or reflected by the sample is collected by the objective of the microscope and focused onto the mirrored aperture of the attached spectrophotometer. Since the aperture is mirrored, the majority of the light is reflected into the ocular or digital imaging system (see Figure 30-2). The spectrophotometer separates the light into its component wavelengths using a holographic grating. The separated rays of light are imaged onto a

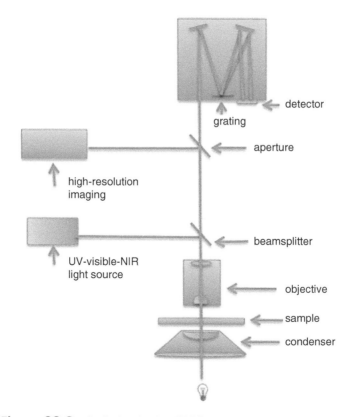

Figure 30-2   Optical path of a UV-Vis-NIR microspectrophotometer.

charged-coupled device (CCD) detector array where their intensity is measured. The intensity and wavelength are then converted to a spectrum.

Microspectrophotometers are single-beam instruments, so a standard or background spectrum is acquired prior to analyzing the sample. The resulting sample data are obtained by comparing the light reflected (transmitted, fluoresced) from the sample to the light reflected (transmitted, fluoresced) from the reference standard. This is visualized by a spectrum that is plotted with wavelength on the X-axis, while the Y-axis can be transmittance, absorbance, reflectance, or fluorescent intensity. Because of the many different types of spectra that can be acquired, it is important for the forensic scientist to pay special attention to the axes (i.e., reflectance, transmittance, fluorescence) when interpreting spectra. As with any spectral interpretation, it is the location of peaks as well as their intensities that relate to the electronic structure of the molecules in the samples.

The microspectrophotometer is a sensitive instrument that can detect small changes in wavelength and light intensity variations, which the human eye cannot. It is also able to distinguish metameric differences. Metameric differences are when two samples may appear to be the same color under one set of lighting conditions, but exhibit different colors when exposed to a different set of lighting conditions. Because of these facts, use of the microspectrophotometer is one of the first examinations done on paint, fiber, and ink evidence.

Paint

Examinations of paint are usually performed to identify paint and then to compare a paint back to a possible paint source. Initially a stereomicroscope is used to examine the paint for layer structure and their solubilities in different solvents (Experiment 14). Paints may also be examined with the FTIR microspectrophotometer (Experiment 29). Further examination of paint by the microspectrophotometer provides additional information. Paint samples are usually examined as thin sections by transmitted light. This provides information concerning the UV absorbers contained in the clear coat, and classifications of pigments. In some cases, such as metallic layers, reflectance may also be necessary.

Fibers

Fiber examinations were discussed in Experiments 20, 20A, 20B, and 20C. Initially a stereomicroscope is used to examine the fiber for macroscopic characteristics. Further testing can be performed using a compound or comparison light microscope to determine optical properties such as refractive index and extinction. At times, burn or solubility tests may also be performed during man-made fiber examinations. Fibers may also be examined with the FTIR microspectrometer (Experiment 29). Further examination of fibers by the microspectrophotometer provides additional information. Both natural and manufactured fibers may be examined with the microspectrophotometer. Because of the nature of the manufacturing process, most manufactured fibers are dyed fairly consistent. Natural fibers, however, are generally not dyed uniformly. Because of this, the heterogeneity of the dye must be taken into consideration for fiber examinations. Multiple examinations should be obtained for each fiber, whether it is natural or manufactured. It is also very important to note the orientation of the fiber while examinations are being conducted, since some fibers exhibit pleochroism. Information concerning fiber treatments such as whiteners and brighteners may be obtained by UV examination.

Ink

Ink compositions may also be examined with the microspectrophotometer, usually in reflectance mode using a clean portion of the paper as the reference. Since ink is absorbed by the paper fibers, the heterogeneity of the ink should also be taken into consideration when performing examinations. It is possible to compare ink spectra on a single sheet of paper. However, it is difficult to compare ink spectra from different sheets of paper because the resulting spectra are made up of several components, including the ink and the paper.

Equipment and Supplies

Stereomicroscope

Paint samples

Fiber samples

Ink samples

Micro kit

Quartz microscope slides

Quartz cover slips

Mounting mediums (XAM™, glycerol, Phytohistol™, FluoroMount™, Permount™, Norland 65™)

Microspectrophotometer with transmittance, reflectance, and fluorescence lamps; reference filter; Holmium Oxide filter; and Didymium filter

Small metal roller

Safety

Use standard laboratory safety procedures as described in guidelines set by your instructor. Be cautious of microscope light levels to avoid eye damage. Refer to the safety data sheet (SDS) if necessary.

Part I: Familiarization with the Microspectrophotometer

Since each instrument may be operated differently and utilize different software, please refer to the operational manual of your instrument to familiarize yourself with operating the instrument.

Part II: Paint

Procedure

1. Obtain a paint sample.
2. Using the stereomicroscope, cut a thin shaving from the top layer. This may be either a clear or colored layer.
3. Place it on a clean hard surface such as a microscope slide and flatten it, if necessary, using the roller. Mount the sample using a quartz microscope slide and cover slip and a non-fluorescing mounting medium.

4. Obtain a UV and/or visible NIR spectrum using transmitted light on the microspectropho-tometer.
5. Next, cut a thin slice from the second layer. This may be a color coat or a primer layer.
6. Place it on a clean hard surface such as a microscope slide, and flatten it using the roller. Mount the sample using a quartz microscope slide and cover slip and a non-fluorescing mounting medium.
7. Obtain a UV and/or visible NIR spectrum using the microspectrophotometer with trans-mitted light.
8. Repeat steps 5–7 for each additional layer.
9. Obtain an unknown paint sample.
10. Using steps 2–8, analyze each layer of the sample.
11. Compare your results from each sample for each layer. Include a copy of the spectra obtained from the paint samples.

Part III: Fibers

Procedure

1. Obtain a fiber sample.
2. Place it on a clean hard surface such as a microscope slide and flatten it, if necessary, using the roller. Mount the sample using a quartz microscope slide and cover slip and a non-fluorescing mounting medium.
3. Obtain a UV and/or visible NIR spectrum using the microspectrophotometer with trans-mitted light. Make sure to test several sections of the fiber to determine the degree of dye heterogeneity.
4. Obtain a visible NIR spectrum using the microspectrophotometer with transmitted light with the light source to obtain sample fluorescence.
5. Obtain an unknown fiber sample.
6. Using steps 2–4, analyze the sample.
7. Compare your results from each sample. Include a copy of the spectra obtained from the fiber samples.

Part IV: Ink

Procedure

1. Obtain an ink sample.
2. Using the stereomicroscope, separate several paper fibers with ink samples. Place one on a clean hard surface such as a microscope slide and flatten it, if necessary, using the roller. Mount the sample using a quartz microscope slide and cover slip and a non-fluorescing mounting medium.
3. Obtain a UV and/or visible NIR spectrum using the microspectrophotometer with trans-mitted light. Make sure to test several sections of the ink sample to determine the degree of dye heterogeneity.
4. Obtain a visible NIR spectrum using the microspectrophotometer with transmitted light with the light source to obtain sample fluorescence.

5. Obtain a UV and/or visible NIR spectrum using the microspectrophotometer with reflected light. Make sure to test several sections of the ink sample to determine the degree of dye heterogeneity.
6. Obtain a visible NIR spectrum using the microspectrophotometer with reflected light with the light source to obtain sample fluorescence.
7. Compare your results using transmitted light and reflected light.
8. Obtain an unknown ink sample.
9. Analyze the unknown sample using the lighting (transmitted or reflected) that you obtained the better results for your previous sample.
10. Compare your results from the unknown sample to the previously examined sample. Include a copy of the spectra obtained from the ink samples.

Report Requirements

Include all drawings, calculations, and other information obtained during the laboratory procedure. Notes and/or drawings should include the sample identification, magnification, and a complete description.

Report Questions

1. Define transmittance, absorbance, reflectance, and fluorescence.
2. Explain how the microspectrophotometer works.
3. Can you think of an example of two samples that would have different UV-visible-NIR spectra but similar colors? Explain your answer.
4. Name three samples that would use the microspectrophotometer in reflectance mode.
5. Give two examples of evidence that would use the fluorescence mode of a microspectrophotometer.
6. Why are fiber samples rolled before their spectra are obtained?

Recommended and Further Reading

Adolf FP, Dunlop J. *Microspectrophotometry/Colour Measurement*, 2nd ed. London: Taylor & Francis, 1999.

ASTM. *Standard Guide for Forensic Paint Examination (ASTM E-1610-14)*. West Conshohocken, PA: ASTM International, 2014.

Cassista AR, Sandercock PML. Comparison and Identification of Automotive Topcoats: Microchemical Spot Tests, Microspectrophotometry, Pyrolysis-Gas Chromatography, and Diamond Anvil Cell FTIR. *Canadian Society of Forensic Science Journal*. 1994; 27: 209–223.

Choudhry MY. Comparison of Minute Smears of Lipstick by Microspectrophotometry and Scanning Electron-Microscopy Energy-Dispersive Spectroscopy. *Journal of Forensic Sciences*. 1991; 36(2): 366–375.

Enoch J, Tobey F. Microspectrophotometry and Optical Phenomena: Birefringence, Dichroism and Anomalous Dispersion. *Springer Series in Optical Sciences*. 1981; 23: 337–399.

Eyring MB. Spectromicrography and Colorimetry – Sample and Instrumental Effects. *Analytica Chimica Acta*. 1994; 288(1–2): 25–34.

Eyring MB. Visible Microscopical Spectrophotometry in Forensic Sciences. In: Saferstein R, ed. *Forensic Science Handbook*, 2nd ed. Upper Saddle River, NJ: Pearson Education, 2002; 322–387.

Eyring M. *Visible Microscopial Spectrophotometry in the Forensic Sciences*, 2nd ed. Upper Saddle River, NJ: Prentice Hall, 2001.

Hartshorne AW, Laing DK. Microspectrofluroimetry of Fluorescent Dyes and Brighteners on Single Textile Fibres: Part 1 – Fluorescence Emission Spectra. *Forensic Science International*. 1991; 51: 203–220.

Hartshorne AW, Laing DK. Microspectrofluroimetry of Fluorescent Dyes and Brighteners on Single Textile Fibres: Part 2 – Colour Measurements. *Forensic Science International*. 1991; 51: 221–237.

Hartshorne AW, Laing DK. Microspectrofluroimetry of Fluorescent Dyes and Brighteners on Single Textile Fibres: Part 3 – Fluorescence Decay Phenomena. *Forensic Science International*. 1991; 51: 239–250.

Houck MM, Siegel JA. *Fundamentals of Forensic Science*, 3rd ed. Amsterdam: Elsevier Academic Press, 2015; 399, 420, 540–542.

Kopchick KA, Bommarito CR. Color Analysis of Apparently Achromatic Automotive Paints by Visible Microspectrophotometry. *Journal of Forensic Sciences*. 2006; 51(2): 40–43.

Saitoh N, Akiba N. Ultraviolet Fluorescence Imaging of Fingerprints. *The Scientific World Journal*. 2006; 6: 691–699.

Wiggins K, Holness JA. A Further Study of Dye Batch Variation in Textile and Carpet Fibres. *Science & Justice*. 2005; 45(2): 93–96.

Wiggins KG, Holness JA, March BM. The Importance of Thin Layer Chromatography and UV Microspectrophotometry in the Analysis of Reactive Dyes Released from Wool and Cotton Fibers. *Journal of Forensic Sciences*. 2005; 50(2): 364–368.

Wilkinson JM, Locke J, Laing DK. The Examination of Paints at Thin-Sections Using Visible Microspectrophotometry and Fourier Transform Infrared Spectroscopy. *Forensic Science International*. 1988; 38: 43–52.

Wilson JD, LaPorte GM, Cantu AA. Differentiation of Black Gel Inks Using Optical and Chemical Techniques. *Journal of Forensic Sciences*. 2004; 49(2): 364–370.

Chapter 31

Experiment 31: Thermal Microscopy Examinations

Recommended pre-lab reading assignments:

Cassista AR, Sandercock P. Precision of Glass Refractive Index Measurements: Temperature Variation and Double Variation Methods and the Value of Dispersion. *Canadian Society of Forensic Science Journal.* 1994; 27(3): 203–208.

Grieve MC. The Use of Melting Point and Refractive Index Determination to Compare Colorless Polyester Fibres. *Forensic Science International.* 1983; 22: 31–48.

Hartshoene AW, Wild FM. The Discrimination of Cellulose di- and tri- Acetate Fibers by Solvent Tests and Melting Point Determination. *Journal of Forensic Science Society.* 1991; 31(4): 457–461.

Objective

Upon completion of this practical exercise, the student will have developed a basic understanding of:

1. the setup, operation, and use of a hot stage
2. how to determine fiber melting points with the hot stage
3. how to determine refractive index with the hot stage

Introduction

Hot stage microscopy is an analytical technique that characterizes the physical properties of a sample through the use of microscopy aided by controlled thermal analysis. This has been applied to various analytical techniques currently used in forensics. Hot stage attachments are typically used with a compound light microscope to determine fiber melting points. For

Practical Forensic Microscopy: A Laboratory Manual, Second Edition. Barbara P. Wheeler.
© 2021 John Wiley & Sons Ltd. Published 2021 by John Wiley & Sons Ltd.
Companion website: www.wiley.com/go/Wheeler/Forensic

glass samples, a phase contrast microscope can be equipped with a hot stage to determine the refractive index of the sample. Both of these analyses involve thermal microscopy. These techniques could also be applied to other forensic samples where it might be necessary to determine the melting point or the refractive index of a substance.

Fibers

A light microscope equipped with a hot stage (see Figure 31-1) is recommended for observing the effects of heat on man-made fibers. Man-made fibers are fibers that have been derived from chemical substances of either natural or synthetic origin. Most natural-based man-made fibers are composed primarily of cellulose. Synthetic fibers are composed of organic polymers that have been formed by chemical synthesis. Usually, this is a mixture of base polymers that have additives and at times finishes also applied. Since man-made fibers are composed of several chemicals instead of a single compound, they usually exhibit a range of melting point temperatures. Chemical compounds, molecular weights, and the ratio of the compounds affect the melting point of a sample. Likewise, the hot stage and how it is used may also affect results. Reproducible results can be obtained by using a slow-heating program when near the actual melting point of a sample. Observations of various types may be seen: drop formulation, contraction, softening, charring, bubbling, and melting. Melting points for common fibers are summarized in Table 31-1. Some fibers do not melt below 300°C: acrylic, aramid, azlon, fluorocarbon, glass, some modacrylics, novoloid, vinal, rayon, and natural fibers.

Complete fiber examinations involve the use of a variety of microscopes, techniques, and instruments. Initially a stereomicroscope is used to examine the fiber for macroscopic characteristics. A compound or comparison light microscope is then used to determine optical properties such as birefringence and sign of elongation (Experiment 20). At times, burn or solubility tests may also be performed during man-made fiber examinations (Experiment 20B and 20C). Additional examinations may be performed using micro-FTIR and microspectrometry to identify

Figure 31-1   A Metler Toledo™ hot stage. When used on a microscope, forensic samples can be viewed under controlled heated settings.

Table 31-1 Melting points for common fibers.

Fiber type	Melting point observations
Saran	Shrinks at 90°C, softens at 115°C, melts at 168–184°C
Polyethylene	Melts at 119–135°C
Olefin	Melts at 135°C
Vinyon	Melts at 140°C
Modacrylic	Contracts at 135–155°C, melts at 160°C; Dynel melts at 190°C; some do not melt
Polypropylene	Softens at 145–150°C, melts at 167–179°C
Nylon 11	Melts at 182–186°C
Rayon	Chars at 185–200°C, does not melt
Nylon 6	Melts at 210–216°C
Spandex	Melts at 230°C
Nylon 6,12	Melts at 217–227°C
Triacetate	Darkens at 230°C, melts at 290–300°C
Acrylic	Softens at 240°C, does not melt
Acetate	Melts at 224–280°C
Nylon 6,6	Melts at 252–267°C
Vinal	Melts at 200–260°C
Polyester	PBT melts at 221–222°C
	PET melts at 256–268°C
	Kodel melts at 290°C
Aramid	Does not melt

additional characteristics (Experiments 29 and 30). While thermal microscopy of fibers does not lead to identification, it is considered a complementary technique that provides additional information.

Glass

A phase contrast light microscope equipped with a hot stage is recommended for observing the effects of heat on the refractive index of glass samples (see Figure 31-2). This technique uses varying temperature and wavelength and is called the "Emmons double variation method" of refractive index determination. The Emmons double variation method relies on the relationship between refractive index, temperature, and wavelength of light. With this method, match points, which are points where glass particles show minimum relief, are determined at various

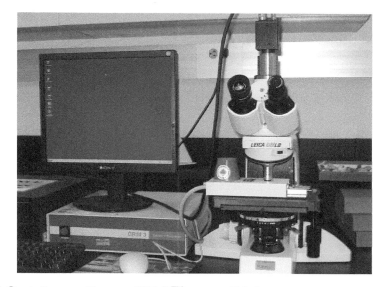

Figure 31-2   A Foster + Freeman GRIM3™ system. This instrument allows forensic scientists to acquire data from microscopic-size forensic samples. The oil immersion method can be used on a phase contrast microscope that has been adapted with a hot stage. By varying the temperature to change the refractive index (RI) of a calibrated oil, the RI of an immersed fragment of glass can be determined.

temperatures by changing the wavelength of light. Variation in the refractive index with the wavelength of light used is called the dispersion of refractive index. All solids demonstrate this dispersion, and measurement of this property can be used to assist in identification. A graph of refractive index versus wavelength is a dispersion graph. A Hartmann net is a graph of refractive index versus wavelength that also combines a series of parallel lines, and that represents the refractive index versus wavelength relationship at fixed temperatures for an immersion oil. By using the Hartmann net graph, the examiner can then plot data obtained from their sample to identify the samples refractive indices at n_c (656 nm), n_D (589 nm), and n_F (486 nm) (see Figure 31-3).

Automated instruments such as the glass refractive index measurement system (GRIM) also use a variation of this method. With GRIM, measurements are taken at different temperatures with a constant wavelength until a match point is reached. Dispersion curves, which have been calibrated for the oils and saved in the computer, are used to determine the refractive index at n_c (656 nm), n_D (589 nm), and n_F (486 nm).

Complete glass examinations involve the use of a variety of microscopes, techniques, and instruments. Initially a stereomicroscope is used to examine the glass for macroscopic characteristics. Further testing can be performed using a compound light microscope to determine optical properties. At times, the density of the glass sample (Experiment 19A) may also be determined or compared. Further testing can be performed using a scanning electron microscope (SEM) to identify additional characteristics such as elemental composition (Experiment 32). For glass, thermal microscopy allows the analyst to determine the refractive index of a single particle with a single immersion oil. For the Emmons double variation method, samples whose refractive indices differ less than ±0.0001 can be differentiated. With GRIM, differences of ±0.00003 can be determined.

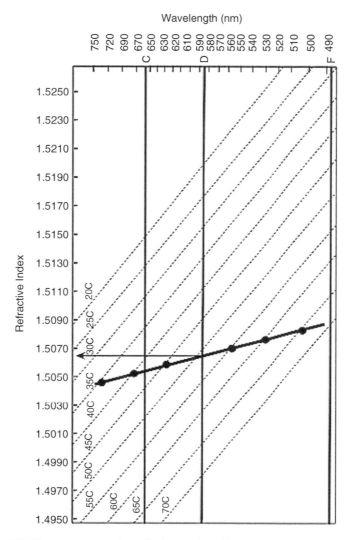

Figure 31-3 This Hartmann net produced for immersion oil 1 covers temperatures from 20°C to 70°C. Data have been plotted for a sample with matching points of 735 at 35°C, 675 at 40°C, 628 at 45°C, 559 at 55°C, 530 at 60°C, and 504 at 65°C. By following the intersecting line at the sodium D line, a refractive index of 1.5066 can be determined for this sample.

Equipment and Supplies

Compound light microscope with objectives of various magnifications (e.g., 4X, 10X, 20X, and 40X)

Hot stage and apparatus

Fiber samples (nylon 6, nylon 6,6)

Unknown fiber

Micro kit

Microscope slides and cover slips

High-temperature-stable silicone oil (for melting point)

Phase contrast light microscope equipped with a monochrometer

Known refractive index glass sample with dispersion data

Hartmann net calibrated for the oil to be used

High-temperature-stable silicone oil: Locke™ oils and Dow Corning 710™ silicone oil are recommended for soda-lime-silica glass (e.g., flat glass), Dow Corning 550™ silicone oil is recommended for borosilicate glass (e.g., headlamps), and Dow Corning F/6/7024™ for glasses with a refractive index above that of the common soda-lime glasses[1]

Unknown glass fragments

Safety

Use standard laboratory safety procedures as described in guidelines set by your instructor. Be cautious of microscope light levels to avoid eye damage. The hot stage can reach high temperatures, so the glass microscope slides will be extremely hot. Use caution when working with these slides. Dispose of glass in an appropriate container.

Part I: Melting Point Determination for Fibers

Melting point determinations are made by using either dry mounts (air) or liquid mounts (heat-stable silicone oil)

1. Using the high-temperature-stable silicone oil, make a liquid mount of nylon 6.
2. Insert the slide into the hot stage that has been positioned on the compound light microscope. Focus on the fiber under 40X magnification. Cross the polars.
3. Quickly raise the temperature to 190°C.
4. Now that you are close to the expected melting point for nylon 6, slowly raise the rate by 2°C per minute.
5. Carefully observe the fiber for changes in physical properties. The melting point range is determined at the temperature when the fiber begins to melt and at the temperature when no more change occurs. At times, viewing the fiber under crossed polars may give clearer indications of the melting point.
6. Repeat the test, using nylon 6,6. Begin at 240°C, and then slowly raise the temperature rate until the melting range is determined.
7. Obtain your unknown fiber. Since you don't know a suspected melting point, begin at the lowest temperature in Table 31-1. If there is sufficient sample, a quick temperature ramp can be run to determine an approximate range.
8. Once a suspected range has been determined, make another slide, and begin the test at approximately 15° below the suspected melting point range.
9. Slowly raise the temperature rate until the melting point range is determined.
10. Compare your findings to Table 31-1 to identify the fiber.

---

[1]Forensic Science Communications, *SWGMAT Standards and Guidelines: Glass Refractive Index Determinations*, January 2005.

Part II: Emmons Double Variation Method of Refractive Index Determination for Glass

1. Using the high-temperature-stable oil for refractive index determinations, make a liquid mount of the glass sample.
2. Place the slide containing the glass fragments in the hot stage, which has been positioned on the phase contrast light microscope.
3. Focus and align the phase contrast microscope. Adjust the phase plate and phase annulus until the rings are superimposed.
4. Set the hot stage temperature to a low temperature within the liquid's stable range. Using the monochrometer, scan the visible range to see if a match point is possible. A match point is determined when there is little or no relief between the glass fragment and oil.
5. If a match point is not found, raise the temperature 5°C, and once again scan the visible range. Make sure your temperature equilibrates each time before you begin scanning.
6. Continue raising the temperature and scanning wavelengths until 3–4 match points have been determined.
7. Once several match points have been determined, plot the points on the calibrated Hartmann net to determine the refractive index.

Report Requirements

Include all drawings, calculations, and other information obtained during the laboratory procedure. Notes and/or drawings should include the sample identification, magnification, and a complete description.

Report Questions

1. What is a hot stage? How can it be used in forensic analysis?
2. What is melting point?
3. Why are melting points an identifying characteristic for manufactured fibers, but not natural fibers?
4. Why do nylon 6 and nylon 6,6 have different melting points?
5. Describe the procedure you used to identify your unknown fiber. What is the fiber? Justify your results.
6. Explain the Emmons double variation method and how it is used to obtain the refractive index of a glass particle.
7. Why is a phase contrast microscope used for this glass examination?
8. What is the refractive index of your unknown glass sample? What type of glass would this be?
9. Why is refractive index reported at n_c (656 nm), n_D (589 nm), and n_F (486 nm)?
10. Research on the Internet to find an explanation of how the automated glass refractive index measurement system (GRIM) works.
11. What are the advantages of using GRIM over the phase contrast microscope/Emmons double variation method for glass examinations?

Recommended and Further Reading

Bennett RL, Kim ND, Curran JM, Coulson SA, Newton AWN. Spatial Variation of Refractive Index in a Pane of Float Glass. *Science & Justice.* 2003; 43(2): 71–76.

Cassista AR, Sandercock PML. Precision of Glass Refractive Index Measurements: Temperature Variation and Double Variation Methods and the Value of Dispersion. *Canadian Society of Forensic Science Journal.* 1994; 27(3): 203–208.

Causin V, Marega C, Schiavone S, Marigo A. Employing Glass Refractive Index Measurement (GRIM) in Fiber Analysis: A Simple Method for Evaluating the Crystallinity of Acrylics. *Forensic Science International.* 2005; c149(2–3): c193–c200.

Curran JM, Buckleton JS, Triggs CM. Commentary on Koons RD, Buscaglia J. The Forensic Significance of Glass Composition and Refractive Index Measurements. *Journal of Forensic Sciences.* 1999; 44(3): 496–503. *Journal of Forensic Sciences.* 1999; 44(6): 1324–1325.

Grieve MC. The Use of Melting Point and Refractive Index Determination to Compare Colorless Polyester Fibres. *Forensic Science International.* 1983; 22: 31–48.

Hartshoene AW, Wild FM. The Discrimination of Cellulose Di- and Tri-Acetate Fibers by Solvent Tests and Melting Point Determination. *Journal of Forensic Sciences Society.* 1991; 31(4): 457–461.

Hartshorne AW, Laing DK. The Identification of Polyolefin Fibres by Infrared Spectroscopy and Melting Point Determination. *Forensic Science International.* 1984; 26: 45–52.

Koons RD, Buscaglia J, Bottrell M, Miller ET. Forensic Glass Comparisons. In: Saferstein R, ed. *Forensic Science Handbook*, 2nd ed. Upper Saddle River, NJ: Pearson Education, 2002; 161–213.

Locke J. GRIM: A Semi-Automatic Device for Measuring the Refractive Index of Glass Particles. *Microscope.* 1985; 169–178.

Locke J, Underhill M. Automatic Refractive Index Measurements of Glass Particles. *Forensic Science International.* 1985; 27: 247–260.

McCrone WC. Calibration of the Mettler Hotstage. *Journal of the Forensic Science Society.* 1987; 27(3): 207.

Ojena SM, De Forest PR. Precise Refractive Index Determination by the Immersion Method Using Phase Contrast Microscopy and the Mettler Hot Stage. *Journal of the Forensic Science Society.* 1972; 12: 315–329.

Was-Gubala J, Krauss W. Damage Caused to Fibres by the Action of Two Types of Heat. *Forensic Science International.* 2006; 159(2–3): 119–126.

Chapter 32

Experiment 32: Scanning Electron Microscopy Examinations

Recommended pre-lab reading assignments:

Almirall J. Elemental Analysis of Glass Fragments. In: Caddy B, ed. *Trace Evidence Analysis and Interpretation*. London: Taylor and Francis, 2001; 65–83.

Goldstein JI, Newbury DE, Echlin P, Joy DC, Romig AD, Lyman CE, et al. *Scanning Electron Microscopy and X-Ray Microanalysis: A Text for Biologists, Materials Scientists, and Geologists*, 2nd ed. New York: Plenum Press, 1992.

Objective

Upon completion of this practical exercise, the student will have developed a basic understanding of:

1. general scanning electron microscopy (SEM) principles
2. sample preparation for SEM analysis
3. use of the SEM to examine paint samples
4. use of the SEM to examine glass samples
5. use of the SEM to examine gunshot residue (GSR) samples

Introduction

The scanning electron microscope (SEM) is a microscope that uses electrons instead of light to form a magnified image. These electron emissions can be visualized on a monitor. When used in combination with other instrumental detectors, the usefulness of the analysis increases.

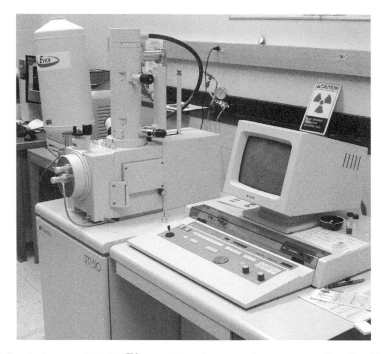

Figure 32-1 A Topcon SM-510™ scanning electron microscope, equipped with a Kevex™ energy-dispersive spectrometer (EDX). This shows the electron column, sample chamber, EDX detector, electronics console, and visual display monitor. In addition to viewing samples at extremely high magnifications, elemental data can also be obtained.

An SEM is composed of several basic systems, all of which work together to form the image and to gain information about the sample;s structure and composition (see Figure 32-1). Basically, the electron column can be thought of as a large vacuum tube with the cathode (electron gun) at the top supplying electrons and the sample at the bottom acting as a target for the electrons. There are several electron sources that can be used; however, a thermionic source is the most common. This type of source produces electrons by heating a conductive material, such as tungsten, to the point where the outer electrons gain sufficient energy to overcome the work function barrier and escape. A typical tungsten filament assembly consists of an inverted V-shaped tungsten wire that can be positioned for optimum voltage. The electrons are drawn away from the filament assembly by an anode plate that is located at the top of the optical column. Since there is a voltage difference between the negatively biased source and the positively biased anode, the electrons accelerate down the optical column. A series of electromagnetic lenses and apertures in the optical column control the path of the electrons. These lenses shape and position the electron beam to the sample. The intensity of the electron beam is controlled by the voltage and diameter of the beam (spot size), which are determined by the examiner. The electron beam causes a number of interactions near the surface of the sample. Since it is these interactions that are important to the examiner, the chamber that holds the sample also holds any additional detectors.

Most forensic laboratories use a SEM with two detectors. The first and principal detector is a photomultiplier tube for the purpose of imaging. Image formation is accomplished by dividing the sample into an x/y grid and by scanning each division of the grid sequentially.

The photomultiplier tube collects electrons, which have been deflected off of the sample for each division of the grid, and assigns a light intensity to each division. At the end of a complete scan of the entire grid, an image is obtained based on the topical features of the sample. This is viewed on a monitor. The second detector is a semiconductor, usually an energy-dispersive detector (EDX). Light is composed of photons and discrete energy levels. When the electron beam strikes the sample, X-rays are emitted. Since each element emits X-rays at characteristic energy values, the analyst can identify the elements present in a sample. By changing the location of the electron beam across the sample, it is possible to determine each element in the sample. Elements of low atomic numbers below sodium (Na) are difficult to detect because of adsorption of the X-rays by the beryllium (Be) window used by most detectors. The EDX detector is essentially a large single-crystal semiconductor. Liquid nitrogen is typically used to cool the detector so that there is little thermionic creation of charge carriers.

Acquiring data on the SEM/EDX unit is fairly straightforward. Samples can be maneuvered by an automated stage to obtain the best image. Once the sample is centered and tilted appropriately, the imaging is automated. However, at times, it may be necessary to make slight adjustments to the instrument parameters to improve image quality. For the best imaging, it is better to set the electron gun voltage as low as possible, but high enough so that you can still see an image on the screen. The spot size should be as low as possible to avoid charging. Charging is an accumulation of electrons on the surface of the sample, "bleaching" out the features. Sometimes in very non-conducting samples, the sample needs to be coated with a conducting material in order to avoid charging. This can be done by sputter coating a sample. Sputter coating deposits an ultra-thin coating of electrically conducting material such as gold, gold/palladium, platinum, tungsten, or graphite on the sample. Sputter coating will also improve contrast. Adjustments to the contrast and brightness will highlight the morphological features of the sample. The SEM has a relatively large depth of field, which allows a large amount of the sample to be in focus at one time. The SEM also produces high-resolution images, which means that closely spaced features can be examined at a high magnification. Once the image is acceptable on the monitor, further analysis can be performed with the EDX detector.

By using an SEM/EDX system, the analyst combines higher magnification (10X to 100,000X), larger depth of focus, greater resolution, and ease of sample viewing with the opportunity to determine the elemental composition of samples. Because of this varied examination, several types of forensic evidence can be analyzed on the SEM. Paint, glass, and gunshot residue (GSR) are a few of the common applications.

Paint

Examinations of paint samples are usually performed to identify a paint and then to compare a paint back to a possible paint source. Initially a stereomicroscope is used to examine the paint for layer structure and solubility properties in different solvents (Experiment 14). Paints may also be examined with the FTIR microspectrometer (Experiment 29) and the microspectrophotometer (Experiment 30). Further examination of paint by the SEM/EDX provides additional information about the composition of the paint. Pigments, additives, and fillers can at times be identified through their elemental composition. Common paint pigments are listed in Table 32-1.

Paint samples can be analyzed several different ways with the SEM. Layers can be separated and analyzed independently, or if the chip is fairly thin, the entire chip can be analyzed as a whole. For some samples, a cross section can be prepared and each layer analyzed separately.

Table 32-1   Common paint pigments.

Color	Pigments
White	Aluminum oxide, antimony oxide, barium carbonate, barium sulfate, lead silicate, lead sulfate, bismuth chloride, calcium phosphate, calcium silicate, calcium carbonate, magnesium carbonate, silicon oxide, silicon nitride, talcs, tin oxide, titanated barytes, barium tungsten oxide, iron phosphate, zinc sulfide, zinc oxide, zirconium silicate, zirconium oxide, silicate fillers, clays, micas
Yellow	Barium potassium chromate, barium chromate, cadmium sulfite, lead chromate, lead cyanamide, lead titanate, lead oxide, mercuric arsenate, strontium chromate, zinc chromate, nickel phosphate
Orange	Lead oxide, cadmium sulfide, lead chromate
Red	Antimony sulfide, cadmium sulfide, cadmium selenide, copper oxide, iron oxide, lead oxide
Green	Chromium oxide, copper carbonate, barium manganese oxide, iron oxide, zinc chromate
Blue	Iron oxide, copper carbonate, cuperous sulfide, barium manganese oxide, nickel–iron, lead sulfate
Purple	Iron oxide
Brown	Calcium lead oxide, iron oxide, manganous chromate, magnesium ferrite
Black	Antimony sulfide, iron oxide, cuprous sulfide, iron titanate
Metallic	Aluminum, copper, gold, lead, tin, zinc, iron

Glass

Examinations of glass are usually performed to identify a glass and then to compare a sample back to a possible source. Initially a stereomicroscope is used to examine the glass for physical properties such as overall color, surface features, flatness/curvature, and thickness. Optical properties such as refractive index (Experiment 19A) are used to further distinguish glass samples. Glass samples may also be examined using the SEM/EDX to compare the elements found in glass samples that can provide information about the composition of the glass. Many elements that can be identified come from the glass components themselves and not from surface contaminants. Knowing the elemental composition may assist in the identification of the type and manufacturing process used for the glass sample. The various types of glass and the common compounds and elements found in these types are listed in Table 32-2. Elements identified in glass samples may also come from colorants. Common elements associated with various glass colors are listed in Table 32-3.

Gunshot Residue (GSR)

GSR samples may also be examined using the SEM/EDX. When a gun is fired, the firing pin strikes the back of the cartridge and sparks the primer, which ignites the "gunpowder" and causes it to burn. This results in the formation of a gaseous vapor, which forces the bullet down

Table 32-2 Common compounds found in various glass types.

Type of glass	Glass components
Silica glass	Silicon oxide, commonly combined with barium oxide, strontium oxide, and calcium oxide
Alkali silicate glass	Silicon oxide, with additions of lithium oxide, sodium oxide, and potassium oxide
Soda-lime glass	Mixtures of alkaline and alkali silicates; generally, sodium oxide, calcium oxide, and silicon oxide, in addition to magnesium oxide, aluminum oxide, barium oxide, and potassium oxide
Borosilicate glass	Boric oxide
Aluminosilicate glass	Aluminum oxides, silicon oxide
Lead glass	Lead oxide
Borate glass	Various borates, commonly boric oxide
Phosphate glass	Phosphoric oxide and phosphates
Chalcogenide glass	These glasses are based on sulfur, selenium, or tellurium.
Halide glass	Zinc chloride, beryllium fluoride
Metallic glass	These glasses commonly have nickel, zirconium, palladium, iron, phosphorus, or carbon.

Table 32-3 Common glass colorants.

Color	Contributing elements
Colorless, UV absorbing	Titanium, iron
Blue	Cobalt, copper, sulfur
Purple	Manganese, nickel
Green	Chromium, iron, copper, molybdenum
Brown	Manganese, iron, titanium, nickel, cesium
Amber	Sodium, sulfur
Yellow	Cadmium, sulfur, cesium, titanium, silver
Orange	Cadmium, sulfur, selenium
Red	Cadmium, sulfur, selenium, copper, antimony
Black	Copper, manganese, nickel, iron, copper, chromium

the barrel of the gun and out the muzzle. The majority of the vapor proceeds out the muzzle, but the vapor can also escape from the cylinder gap in a revolver or the ejection port in a pistol. It is the vapor that escapes from these areas that is called gunshot residue. Gunshot residue testing examines the residues of the combustion products and any unburned primer and powder components. The analytical procedure for testing GSR starts with collection that is done by sampling the individual's hands with a sticky aluminum stub. Any possible GSR particles would be transferred to the stub, which is then submitted for SEM testing.

GSR particles have a characteristic spherical shape that is roughly spheroidal, globular, or boule-shaped. This morphology is typical for materials that condense rapidly from a vapor. However, with SEM/EDX, elemental composition can also be examined for particles. GSR contains three heavy metals: barium, lead, and antimony. With both particle morphology and elemental composition, particles may be attributed to being GSR. With SEM/EDX, the analyst can view the particle morphology and also determine its elemental composition.

Equipment and Supplies

Stereomicroscope

Paint samples

Glass samples

Prepared GSR samples

Micro kit

10×15 mm cylindrical aluminum stubs

Sticky tabs

SEM/EDX with sputter coater

Liquid nitrogen, thermos, and cryo-gloves

Safety

Use standard laboratory safety procedures as described in guidelines set by your instructor. Be cautious of microscope light levels to avoid eye damage. Use of safety glasses and cryo-gloves when handling liquid nitrogen is recommended. Refer to the safety data sheet (SDS) if necessary.

Part I: Familiarization with the SEM/EDX

Since each instrument may be operated differently and utilize different software, please refer to the operational manual of your instrument to familiarize yourself with operating the instrument.

Part II: Paint

Procedure

1. Obtain a paint sample.
2. While viewing the sample under the stereomicroscope, cut a thin slice from the top layer. This may be either a clear or colored layer.

3. Obtain an aluminum stub, and place a sticky tab onto one side.
4. Place the prepared paint sample onto the sticky tab using the forceps.
5. Following instrument specifications, obtain an image of the paint sample on the SEM/EDX. If excessive charging is observed, sputter coat your sample. *Please refer to the operational manual of your instrument.*
6. Acquire the elemental data for the paint sample.
7. Identify any elements present and, when appropriate, the pigment contained within the sample.
8. Repeat steps 2–7 for each additional layer and assigned samples.
9. Include a copy of the SEM/EDX spectra obtained from the paint samples in your report.

Part III: Glass

Procedure

1. Obtain a glass sample.
2. Obtain an aluminum stub, and place a sticky tab onto one side.
3. Place the glass sample onto the sticky tab using the forceps.
4. Following instrument specifications, obtain an image of the glass sample on the SEM/EDX. If excessive charging is observed, sputter coat your sample. *Please refer to the operational manual of your instrument.*
5. Acquire the elemental data for the glass sample.
6. Identify any elements present and, when appropriate, the elemental components contained within the sample.
7. Repeat steps 2–6 for each assigned sample.
8. Include a copy of the SEM/EDX spectra obtained from the glass samples in your report.

Part III: GSR

Procedure

1. Obtain an aluminum stub that contains a GSR sample.
2. Following instrument specifications, obtain an image of possible GSR particles on the SEM/EDX. If excessive charging is observed, sputter coat your sample. *Please refer to the operational manual of your instrument.*
3. Acquire the elemental data for the particle.
4. Identify any elements present.
5. Repeat steps 2–4 in an attempt to identify barium, lead, and antimony particles.
6. Include a copy of the SEM/EDX spectra obtained from the GSR samples in your report.

Report Requirements

Include all drawings, calculations, and other information obtained during the laboratory procedure. Notes and/or drawings should include the sample identification, magnification, and a complete description.

Report Questions

1. Explain how an SEM operates, discussing each portion of the instrument. Include a drawing of the mechanics of the SEM.
2. Explain how the EDX works. What are the advantages of this detector?
3. Which elements cannot be detected with the EDX?
4. What additional detectors are available for SEM use? What are the advantages and disadvantages of each?
5. What is the preferred method for SEM/EDX paint examinations?
6. Can elemental data vary for different locations on the same paint chip/layer?
7. What weight should be placed on elemental data obtained from a glass sample?
8. Barium, lead, and antimony are common elements associated with GSR. What can these elements be attributed to?
9. If an analyst obtains morphology and elemental data identifying barium, lead, and antimony, what result can be reached? What can be inferred from that result?
10. Why is an SEM/EDX a useful instrument to forensic laboratories?

Recommended and Further Reading

Almirall J. Elemental Analysis of Glass Fragments. In: Caddy B, ed. *Trace Evidence Analysis and Interpretation*. London: Taylor & Francis, 2001; 65–83.

Almirall JR, Cole MD, Gettinby G, Furton KG. Discrimination of Glass Sources Using Elemental Composition and Refractive Index: Development of Predictive Models. *Science & Justice*. 1998; 38(2): 93–100.

ASTM. *Standard Guide for Forensic Paint Examination (ASTM E-1610-14)*. West Conshohocken, PA: ASTM International, 2014.

Basu S, Millette JR, *Electron Microscopy Society of America, Microbeam Analysis Society. Electron Microscopy in Forensic, Occupational, and Environmental Health Sciences*. New York: Plenum Press, 1986.

Beam TL, Willis WV. Analysis Protocol for Discrimination of Automotive Paints by SEM-EDXA Using Beam Alignment by Current Centering. *Journal of Forensic Sciences*. 1990; 35(5): 1055–1063.

Choudhry MY. Comparison of Minute Smears of Lipstick by Microspectrophotometry and Scanning Electron-Microscopy Energy-Dispersive Spectroscopy. *Journal of Forensic Sciences*. 1991; 36(2): 366–375.

Dimaio VJM, Dana SE, Taylor WE, Ondrusek J. Use of Scanning Electron-Microscopy and Energy Dispersive-X-Ray Analysis (SEM-EDXA) in Identification of Foreign Material on Bullets. *Journal of Forensic Sciences*. 1987; 32(1): 38–47.

Ditrich H. Forensic Use of Scanning Electron Microscopy. *European Journal of Cell Biology*. 1997; 74: 68.

Flegler SL, Heckman JW, Klomparens KL. *Scanning and Transmission Electron Microscopy: An Introduction*. New York: W.H. Freeman, 1993.

Germani MS. Evaluation of Instrumental Parameters for Automated Scanning Electron-Microscopy Gunshot Residue Particle Analysis. *Journal of Forensic Sciences*. 1991; 36(2): 331–342.

Goebel R, Stoecklein W. The Use of Electron Microscopic Methods for the Characterization of Paints in Forensic Science. *Scanning Microscopy*. 1987; 6: 669–678.

Goldstein JI, Newbury DE, Echlin P, Joy DC, Romig AD, Lyman CE, et al. *Scanning Electron Microscopy and X-Ray Microanalysis*, 2nd ed. New York: Plenum Press, 1992.

Hawkes PW. *The Beginnings of Electron Microscopy*. Orlando, FL: Academic Press, 1985.

Houck MM, Siegel JA. *Fundamentals of Forensic Science*, 3rd ed. Amsterdam: Elsevier Academic Press, 2015; 420.

Kage S, Kudo K, Kaizoji A, Ryumoto J, Ikeda H, Ikeda N. A Simple Method for Detection of Gunshot Residue Particles from Hands, Hair, Face, and Clothing Using Scanning Electron Microscopy/Wavelength Dispersive X-Ray (SEM/WDX). *Journal of Forensic Sciences.* 2001; 46(4): 830–834.

McCrone WC. The Scanning Electron-Microscope (SEM) Supplemented by the Polarized-Light Microscope (PLM), and Vice-Versa. *Scanning Microscopy.* 1993; 7(1): 1–4.

Molina DK, Martinez M, Garcia J, DiMaio VJM. Gunshot Residue Testing in Suicides: Part 1: Analysis by Scanning Electron Microscopy with Energy-Dispersive X-Ray. *American Journal of Forensic Medicine and Pathology.* 2007; 28(3): 187–190.

Montero S, Hobbs AL, French TA, Almirall JR. Elemental Analysis of Glass Fragments by ICP-MS as Evidence of Association: Analysis of a Case. *Journal of Forensic Sciences.* 2003; 48(5).

Nesbitt R, Wessel J, Jones P. Detection of Gunshot Residue by use of the Scanning Electron Microscope. *Journal of Forensic Sciences.* 1976; (21): 595–610.

Pelton WR. Distinguishing the Cause of Textile Fiber Damage Using the Scanning Electron-Microscope (SEM). *Journal of Forensic Sciences.* 1995; 40(5): 874–882.

Pye K, Croft D. Forensic Analysis of Soil and Sediment Traces by Scanning Electron Microscopy and Energy-Dispersive X-Ray Analysis: An Experimental Investigation. *Forensic Science International.* 2007; 165(1): 52–63.

Reimer L. *Scanning Electron Microscopy: Physics of Image Formation and Microanalysis.* Berlin: Springer-Verlag, 1985.

Simpson K. Three Decades of Scanning Electron Microscopy/Energy-Dispersive X-Ray Spectroscopy at the United Kingdom Forensic Explosives Laboratory. *Scanning.* 2006; 28(2): 89–90.

Steffen S, Otto M, Niewoehner L, Barth M, Brozek-Mucha Z, Blegstraaten J, et al. Chemometric Classification of Gunshot Residues Based on Energy Dispersive X-Ray Microanalysis and Inductively Coupled Plasma Analysis with Mass-Spectrometric Detection. *Spectrochimica Acta Part B – Atomic Spectroscopy.* 2007; 62: 1028–1036.

Wagner RDC, Kiyohara PK, Silveira M, Joekes I. Electron Microscopic Observations of Human Hair Medulla. *Journal of Microscopy – Oxford.* 2007; 226(1): 54–63.

Wilber CG, Lantz RK, Sulik PL. Gunshot Residue, 10 Years Later. *American Journal of Forensic Medicine and Pathology.* 1991; 12(3): 204–206.

Zadora G, Brozek-Mucha Z. SEM-EDX – a Useful Tool for Forensic Examinations. *Materials Chemistry and Physics.* 2003; 81(2–3): 345–348.

Zeichner A, Schecter B, Brener R. Antimony Enrichment on the Bullets' Surfaces and the Possibility of Finding It in Gunshot Residue (GSR) of the Ammunition Having Antimony-Free Primers. *Journal of Forensic Sciences.* 1998; 43(3): 493–501.

ZiebaPalus J. The Use of Micro Fourier-Transform Infrared Spectroscopy and Scanning Electron Microscopy with X-Ray Microanalysis for the Identification of Automobile Paint Chips. *Mikrochimica Acta.* 1997: 357–359.

Chapter 33

Experiment 33: Case Study Scenario

Objective

Upon completion of this practical exercise, the student will have developed a basic understanding of:

1. working with others to provide analytical results
2. devising examination schemes utilizing analytical procedures learned throughout previous lab experiments
3. correctly analyzing evidence
4. reaching appropriate results and conclusions

Introduction

This laboratory experiment draws on the knowledge and skills that you have gained previously. For this exercise, the class will be divided into teams. Each team will be given a "request for examination" form. This is a form that is normally submitted along with evidence when it is brought to a forensic laboratory for analysis. On this form, exhibits are listed, and examinations are requested. Each team will obtain their evidence, inventory their samples, and then secure everything in a locked evidence locker. Each team will then divide the requested examinations and complete the analytical work. Each team will examine the evidence as they see fit. Each team will prepare a single lab report.

Procedure

1. You will be assigned to a team.
2. Obtain the "Forensic Laboratory Request for Examination" form for your team and the assigned evidence (i.e., exhibits) from an investigator.
3. Document the chain of custody (date, time, and person) and condition of the evidence (i.e., packaging and seal) on the "Report of Forensic Laboratory Examination" form and in the notes. Secure the evidence in a locked drawer when not in use.

Practical Forensic Microscopy: A Laboratory Manual, Second Edition. Barbara P. Wheeler.
© 2021 John Wiley & Sons Ltd. Published 2021 by John Wiley & Sons Ltd.
Companion website: www.wiley.com/go/Wheeler/Forensic

4. Divide the examination duties so that the analysis can be completed within the allotted lab periods.

5. Devise appropriate analytical schemes for each type of evidence from previously learned techniques so that you are able to perform the requested examinations. Make sure **all** appropriate exams are performed for each evidence type. When making a comparison, the goal is to either prove an association or prove a difference.

6. Perform the analysis of the evidence types. Document all testing performed in detailed notes. This may include drawings and photographs.

7. Combine the documentation, notes, drawings, and photographs from all evidence types.

8. Compose a combined lab report of all results.

9. Release your evidence back to an investigator.

Report Requirements

Your lab report will consist of a final lab case file containing the following information:

1. A completed "Report of Forensic Laboratory Examination" form, which includes:
   a. Chain of custody (date, time, via information)
   b. Case and lab numbers
   c. Victims' and suspects' names
   d. List of evidence received
   e. List of examinations requested (statement of problem)
   f. Clear and concise results. Using the results of all the evidence exams, state the conclusions that may be reached from the results of the testing. It is important to use short concise statements that point to a conclusion if possible. Refer to the evidence examined, using their exhibit number exactly as listed on the "Forensic Laboratory Request for Examination" form.
   g. Signature of all analysts and date

2. The signed "Forensic Laboratory Request for Examination" form.

3. Attach all documentation, drawings, and notes taken during analysis. This includes the initial exam notes, packaging details, and test procedures used. All data and/or comparisons should be compiled in the notes.

4. "Conclusions and Interpretations": A discussion stating the result for each evidence type (i.e., glass, hair, and fibers). The discussion should include an explanation of how the results and conclusion were reached, the value of each test performed, and the effect of these results on the investigation.

5. A signed evidence release form

FORENSIC LAB
Request for Evidence Examination

Investigating Officer: _____

Agency: _____   Laboratory # : _____

Address: _____   Case # : _____

City: _____ Zip: _____   _____

Phone: _____ Fax: _____   _____

Email: _____

Victim(s): _____   Offense: _____

Suspect/Accused(s): _____   Offense Date: _____

_____   Offense City/County: _____

Exhibits: (Initial exhibits received)

_____
_____
_____
_____
_____
_____
_____
_____
_____

Case History:

_____
_____
_____
_____
_____
_____
_____
_____

Examinations Requested:

_____
_____
_____
_____
_____
_____
_____
_____

Submitting Officer Signature: _____ Date: _____

For Lab use only

Received from: Received By: Date/Time:

_____   _____   _____

_____   _____   _____

Laboratory # _____   Case # _____
                                       Re: (v) _____
                                           (s) _____

Report of Forensic Laboratory Examination

Submitted By: _____

Received: Date: _____ **Time:** _____ **Via:** _____

Returned To: _____ **Date:** _____ **Via:** _____

_____

Material Submitted:

Examination Requested:

Results of Examination:

_____   _____   _____   _____
Signature of Examiner/Date   Signature of Examiner/Date   Signature of Examiner/Date   Signature of Examiner/Date

Laboratory # _____

Case # _____
     (V) _____
     (S) _____

Release of Evidence Form

Investigating Officer:_____

Agency: _____ **Date Rec.:** _____

Examiner: _____**Released By:** _____

This is to certify that the undersigned has received the following exhibits in the case cited above.

Receiving Officer:_____

Agency: _____

Received: Date: _____ **Time:** _____ **Via:** _____

Evidence Released :

Appendices

Appendix A

Optical Properties of Natural Fibers

PLANT/ANIMAL FIBER	η-Parallel	η-Perpendicular	Birefringence	Sign of elongation
Abaca	1.571	1.524	0.047	+
Cotton	1.578	1.532	0.046	+
mercerized	1.544	1.524	0.020	+
Flax	1.594	1.532	0.062	+
Hemp	1.585	1.526	0.059	+
Jute	1.577	1.536	0.041	+
Kapok	1.550	1.534	0.016	+
Kenaf	1.567	1.523	0.044	+
Ramie	1.596	1.528	0.068	+
Silk	1.591	1.540	0.051	+
degummed	1.590	1.538	0.052	+
Sisal	1.566	1.528	0.038	+
Wool	1.560	1.547	0.013	+

MINERAL FIBER	α	β	γ	Sign of elongation
Actinolite	1.6126	1.6288	1.6393	+
Amosite	1.700	*	1.695	+
Anthophyllite	1.6148	1.6273	1.6362	+
Chrysotile	1.529–1.559	1.530–1.564	1.537–1.567	+
Crocidolite	1.680–1.698	1.683–1.700	1.685–1.706	−
Tremolite	1.6063	1.6230	1.6343	+

*This orientation is not reported in literature.
Source: Based on McCrone WC, Delly JG. *The Particle Atlas*. Ann Arbor, MI: Ann Arbor Science, 1973; and Textile Institute. *Identification of Textile Materials*, 7th ed. Manchester, UK: The Textile Institute, 1975.

Practical Forensic Microscopy: A Laboratory Manual, Second Edition. Barbara P. Wheeler.
© 2021 John Wiley & Sons Ltd. Published 2021 by John Wiley & Sons Ltd.
Companion website: www.wiley.com/go/Wheeler/Forensic

Appendix B

Optical Properties of Man-made Fibers

MAN-MADE FIBER	η-Parallel	η-Perpendicular	Birefringence	Sign of elongation
Acetate	1.474 to 1.479	1.473 to 1.477		
Dicel	1.476	1.473	0.003	+
Acrylic	1.511 to 1.521	1.512 to 1.525		
Acrilan	1.52	1.525	−0.005	−
Acrilan 36	1.511	1.514	−0.003	−
Orlon	1.51	1.512	−0.002	−
Aramid	2.050 to 2.350	1.641 to 1.646		
Kevlar	2.35	1.641	0.709	+
Nomex	1.80	1.664	0.136	+
Azlon	1.532 to 1.538	1.526 to 1.536		
Vicara	1.538	1.536	0.002	+
Bamboo	1.549	1.522	0.027	+
Calcium alginate	1.524	1.520	0.004	+
Darvan				
Nytril	1.464	1.464	0	
Fluorocarbon	1.385 to 1.389	1.345 to 1.350		
Teflon	1.385	1.345	0.040	+
Glass	1.523 to 1.552	1.523 to 1.552	0	
Lyocell	1.562 to 1.564	1.520 to 1.522	0.050	+
Tencel	1.57	1.52	0.050	+
Kynol, drawn	1.658	1.636	0.022	+
Undrawn	1.649	1.649	0	
Modacrylic	1.520 to 1.535	1.516 to 1.539		
Dynel	1.535	1.533	0.002	+
SEF	1.534	1.535	−0.001	−
Teklan	1.52	1.516	0.004	+
Verel	1.535	1.539	−0.004	−

(Continued)

Practical Forensic Microscopy: A Laboratory Manual, Second Edition. Barbara P. Wheeler.
© 2021 John Wiley & Sons Ltd. Published 2021 by John Wiley & Sons Ltd.
Companion website: www.wiley.com/go/Wheeler/Forensic

(Continued)

MAN-MADE FIBER	η-Parallel	η-Perpendicular	Birefringence	Sign of elongation
Novoloid	1.5 to 1.7	1.5 to 1.7		
Kynol, unknown	1.649	1.649	0	
Kynol, drawn	1.658	1.636	0.022	+
Nylon	1.546 to 1.582	1.507 to 1.526		
Nylon 6	1.568	1.515	0.053	+
Enkalon (6)	1.575	1.526	0.049	+
Nylon 6,6	1.582	1.519	0.063	+
ICI (6,6)	1.578	1.522	0.056	+
Nylon 11	1.55	1.51	0.04	+
Rilsan (11)	1.553	1.507	0.046	+
Qiana	1.546	1.511	0.035	+
Nytril	1.464 to 1.480	1.464 to 1.480		
Darvan	1.464	1.464	0	
Olefin	1.52 to 1.574	1.496 to 1.522		
Polyethylene	1.556	1.512	0.044	+
Courlene X3 (PE)	1.574	1.522	0.052	+
SWP (PE)	1.544	1.514	0.03	+
Polypropylene	1.52	1.492	0.028	+
Courlene (PP)	1.53	1.496	0.034	+
Ulstron	1.530	1.496	0.034	+
Polyacrylostyrene	1.560	1.572	−0.012	−
Polycarbonate	1.626	1.566	0.06	+
Polyester	1.586 to 1.710	1.53 to 1.589		
Dacron	1.7	1.535	0.165	+
Fortrel	1.72	1.535	0.185	+
Kodel	1.632	1.534	0.098	+
Kodel II	1.642	1.54	0.102	+
PBT	1.688	1.538 to 1.540	0.148 to 0.150	+
PCDT	1.632 to 1.642	1.534 to 1.542	0.098 to 0.102	+
PEN	1.862	1.589	0.273	+
PET	1.699 to 1.710	1.535 to 1.546	0.147 to 0.175	+
PTT	1.586	1.566	0.060	+
Terylene	1.707	1.546	0.16	+
Vycron	1.713	1.53	0.183	
Rayon	1.542 to 1.553	1.513 to 1.523		
Cuprammonium	1.553	1.519	0.034	+
Viscose	1.542	1.520	0.022	+
Viscose (high tenacity)	1.544	1.505	0.039	+
Fortisan	1.547	1.523	0.024	+
Fortisan 36	1.551	1.52	0.031	+
Vincel	1.551	1.513	0.038	+
Tencel	1.57	1.52	0.05	+
Saran	1.599 to 1.610	1.607 to 1.618		
Spandex	1.561	1.56	0.001	+
Sulfar	1.849	1.738	0.111	+
Teflon	1.38	1.34	0.04	+

(Continued)

(Continued)

MAN-MADE FIBER	η-Parallel	η-Perpendicular	Birefringence	Sign of elongation
Triacetate	1.469 to 1.472	1.468 to 1.472		
Arnel	1.469	1.468	0.001	+
Tricel	1.469	1.469	0	
Vicara	1.538	1.536	0.002	+
Vinal	1.540 to 1.547	1.510 to 1.522		
Vinyon	1.528 to 1.541	1.524 to 1.536		
Fibravyl	1.54	1.53	0.01	+
Rhovyl	1.541	1.536	0.005	+
Vinyon HH	1.528	1.524	0.004	+

Source: Based on Palenik SJ. Microscopical Examination of Fibres. In: Robertson J, Grieve M, eds. *Forensic Examination of Fibres*. London: Taylor & Francis, 1999; 153–176; Houck MM, Siegel JA. *Fundamentals of Forensic Science*. Oxford: Elsevier Academic Press, 2015; and Textile Institute. *Identification of Textile Materials*, 7th ed. Manchester, UK: The Textile Institute, 1975.

Appendix C

Michel-Lévy Chart

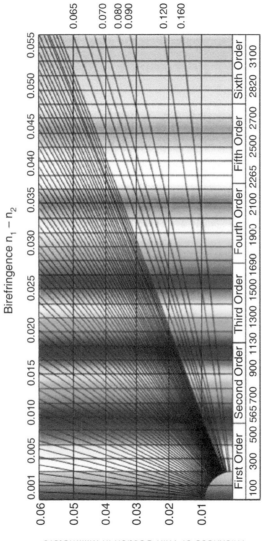

Practical Forensic Microscopy: A Laboratory Manual, Second Edition. Barbara P. Wheeler.
© 2021 John Wiley & Sons Ltd. Published 2021 by John Wiley & Sons Ltd.
Companion website: www.wiley.com/go/Wheeler/Forensic

Appendix D

Dispersion Staining Graph

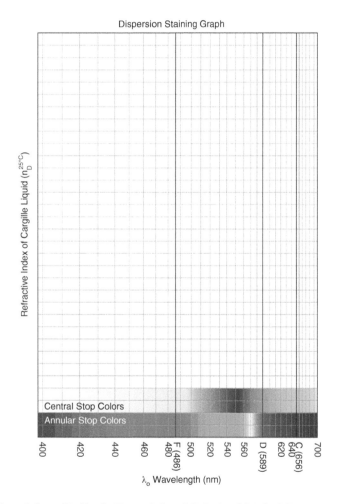

Source: Reproduced from Delly J. *Essentials of Polarized Light Microscopy.* © 2007, The McCrone Group, Inc. By permission of Hooke College of Applied Sciences.

Practical Forensic Microscopy: A Laboratory Manual, Second Edition. Barbara P. Wheeler.
© 2021 John Wiley & Sons Ltd. Published 2021 by John Wiley & Sons Ltd.
Companion website: www.wiley.com/go/Wheeler/Forensic

Appendix E

Circle Template

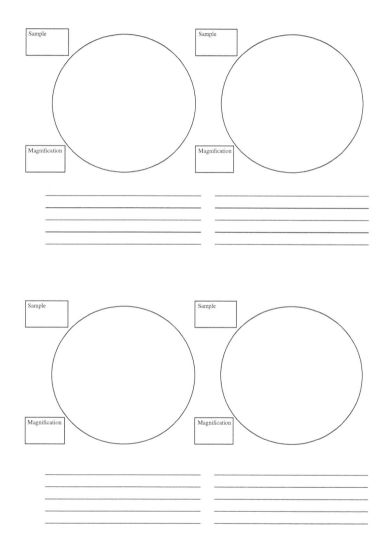

Practical Forensic Microscopy: A Laboratory Manual, Second Edition. Barbara P. Wheeler.
© 2021 John Wiley & Sons Ltd. Published 2021 by John Wiley & Sons Ltd.
Companion website: www.wiley.com/go/Wheeler/Forensic

Glossary of Microscopy Terms

Aberration	Any disturbance of the rays of light in an optical system such that they can no longer be brought to a sharp focus or form a clear image. See chromatic and spherical aberration.
Achromat	A lens that is corrected for chromatic aberrations at two wavelengths and spherical aberrations at one wavelength.
Amorphous[†]	Lacking a repeating array of crystal lattice points; amorphous materials are isotropic but may show strain birefringence.
Analyzer	A polarizing filter located above the sample and objective. Its orientation is perpendicular to the polarizer.
Angular aperture (AA)[†]	The largest angle between the image-forming rays collected or transmitted by a lens system (e.g., objective or condenser of a microscope).
Anisotropic	Having physical properties that differ according to the direction of measurement. Anisotropic samples possess order that varies along its different axes. These samples have more than one refractive index.
Annular stop	The opaque ring-shaped stop with a central opening placed in the objective back focal plane. This is utilized to give annular stop observations for dispersion staining.
Aperture	An opening, usually circular, that limits the quantity of light that can pass through the opening. See substage condenser aperture.
Apochromatic objective	A lens that is corrected for chromatic aberrations at three or more wavelengths and at two or more spherical aberrations.
Axis, crystallographic[†]	One of several imaginary lines assumed in describing the positions of the planes by which a crystal is bounded, the positions of the atoms in the structure of the crystal, and the directions associated with vectorial and tensorial physical properties.
Back focal plane[†]	A "plane" normal to the axis of a lens in which all back focal points lie.
Barrier filter	A filter used in fluorescence microscopy that suppresses unnecessary excitation light that has not been absorbed by the fiber and selectively transmits only the fluorescence.
Becke line	An optical halo caused by the concentration of refracted light rays along the edge of the particle.
Becke line test	A method for determining the refractive index of a sample relative to its mounting medium by noting the direction in which the Becke line moves when the focus is changed. The Becke line will always move toward the higher refractive index medium (fiber or mounting medium) when focus is raised and will move toward the lower refractive index medium when focus is lowered. The sample should be illuminated with a narrow cone of light that can be obtained by closing down the substage condenser.
Bertrand lens	A lens placed between the objective and the ocular; usually used to observe a magnified image of the objective back focal plane to examine interference figures. It is sometimes used to observe the lamp filament when setting up Köhler illumination.

Practical Forensic Microscopy: A Laboratory Manual, Second Edition. Barbara P. Wheeler.
© 2021 John Wiley & Sons Ltd. Published 2021 by John Wiley & Sons Ltd.
Companion website: www.wiley.com/go/Wheeler/Forensic

Biaxial crystals	Crystals in the othrorhombic, monoclinic, and triclinic systems. They have three principal refractive indices: α, β, and γ.
Birefringence	The numerical difference in refractive indices for a sample. Birefringence can be determined by subtracting the refractive indices or by using the formula: B = retardation(nm) / 1000 (thickness).
Body tube	The portion of the microscope that connects the oculars to the nosepiece that holds the objectives.
Brightfield illumination[†]	The usual form of microscope illumination with the image of the sample on a bright, evenly lighted field; or in vertical illumination, light reflected through the objective by means of prism or semi-reflecting plane glass.
Central stop	The opaque stop placed in the objective back focal plane. This is utilized to give a central stop for dispersion staining.
Chromatic aberration	The variation of either the focal length or the magnification of a lens system with different wavelengths of light, characterized by prismatic coloring at the edges of the optical image and color distortion within it.
Cleavage[†]	The property of a crystalline substance of splitting along definite crystal planes.
Comparison microscope	An optical instrument composed of two compound light microscopes connected by an optical bridge. This allows two samples to be viewed at the same time with either transmitted or reflected light.
Compensation	The result of insertion of a compensator or crystal into a light path with retardation that exactly matches the retardation of the sample. Usually conducted when the sample is in the 45° position in the NE corner of the field of view. Complete compensation is said to occur when the colors go to zero order (black).
Compensator	Any variety of optical devices that can be placed in the light path of a polarizing microscope to introduce fixed or varied retardation comparable with the sample. Compensators may employ a fixed crystal of constant or varying thickness or a mineral plate that may be rotated to alter the thickness presented to the optical path (and retardation introduced) by a set amount.
Compensator, full-wave plate (first-order red)	A layer of quartz, selenite, calcite, or an oriented polymer film of the proper thickness to produce a retardation between 530 and 550 nm. This is approximately the retardation of the first-order red color on the Michel-Lévy chart.
Compensator, quarter-wave plate	A thin layer of mica or an oriented polymer film of the proper thickness to produce a retardation of about 130 nm. This is approximately the retardation of the first-order gray color on the Michel-Lévy chart.
Compensator, quartz wedge[†]	A wedge, cut from quartz, having continuously variable retardation extending over several orders (usually 3–7) or interference colors. The retardation that exactly compensates that of a crystal can be found by pushing in the wedge while counting orders until it reaches a position at which the interference color of the crystal appears black. Retardation can be compensated only when the slow component of the crystal and the wedge are perpendicular.
Compensator, tilting (Berek)	A compensator typically containing a plate of calcite or quartz, which can be rotated by means of a calibrated drum to introduce variable retardation up to about 10 orders.
Compound light microscope	An optical instrument that forms a magnified image through the use of a two-step process. The objective forms the magnified real image of the object, and the ocular forms the magnified virtual image of the object.

Condenser	A lens or series of lenses, located below the stage of the microscope, which serve to collect and concentrate the light on the sample. There are two basic types of condensers: brightfield and darkfield.
Conjugate foci[†]	In an image-forming system, two fields are said to be conjugate with each other when one or more object fields are simultaneously in focus in a single plane (e.g., in Köhler illumination the field diaphragm, specimen, and ocular front focal plane).
Conoscopic observation	Observations of the back focal plane of the objective by the insertion of auxiliary lens, removing the eyepiece. The lamp filament, substage aperture diaphragm, objective back focal plane, and ocular focal plane are simultaneously in focus with the viewer's eye.
Constructive interference	See Interference, constructive.
Contrast	The difference in brightness between the light and dark areas of an image.
Critical angle (C)[†]	The angle at which total reflection of a light ray passing from one medium to another occurs. The angle of incidence must be large (55° to 60°).
Crystalline[†]	A substance (usually solid but can be liquid) in which the atoms or molecules are arranged in a definite pattern that is repeated regularly in three dimensions. Crystals tend to develop forms bounded by definitely oriented plane surfaces that are harmonious with their internal structure. They may belong to any of six crystals systems: cubic, hexagonal, tetragonal, orthorhombic, monoclinic, or triclinic.
Curvature of field	An optical distortion where the center of the image is in focus but the edges are out of focus. When corrected, the image is said to be flat. Lenses corrected for this distortion are said to be "Plan" or "Plano."
Darkfield illumination[†]	Incident or transmitted illumination of the specimen by indirect light whereby no direct light is admitted directly to the objective.
Depth of field	The thickness of the optical slice that is in focus at the real intermediate image of a sample.
Depth of focus	The thickness of an image at the real intermediate image plane in the microscope.
Destructive interference	See Interference, destructive.
Dichroism	The property of exhibiting different colors, especially two different colors, when viewed in polarized light along different axes.
Diffuse illumination	See Illumination, diffuse.
Dispersion[†]	The variation of refractive index with color (or wavelength) of light. The spreading of white light into its components colors when passing through a glass prism is due to dispersion that, in turn, is due to the fact that the refractive index of transparent substances is lower for long wavelengths than for short wavelengths. A measure of dispersion nu, v, is defined as: $v = \frac{n_D-1}{n_F-n_C}$.
Dispersion staining	An identification technique utilizing a specialized objective that uses the differences between the refractive index dispersion of a sample and that of the immersion liquid. A dispersion staining objective typically has three stops; annular, central, and open. Using an annular stop with the substage iris closed, a sample mounted in a high dispersion medium will show a boundary of a wavelength where the sample and the medium match in refractive index. Using a central stop, the sample will show colors complementary to those seen with an annular stop.

Double refraction[†]	The refraction of light in two slightly different directions to form two rays or vector components. Each ray is polarized, and their vibration directions are perpendicular to each other. Furthermore, each ray has a different velocity and therefore a different refractive index. See birefringence.
Epi-illumination	Illumination technique where the light source is placed above the sample, causing the objective to act as the condenser and objective.
Excitation filter	The first filter used in fluorescence microscopy, usually a bandpass filter. It produces specific exciting wavelengths from a high-energy light source that are capable of inducing visible fluorescence in various substrates.
Extinction points	Orientation of a sample where light emerging from the sample is vibrating at right angles to the preferred direction of the analyzer. These positions are 90° apart and reveal the vibration directions of each sample. These directions will parallel the vibration directions of the two polars when the sample is extinct.
Extinction, oblique[†]	Extinction is oblique if the vibration directions are oblique to the long direction of the crystal.
Extinction, parallel[†]	Extinctions is parallel if the vibration directions are parallel and perpendicular to the long direction of the crystal.
Extinction, symmetrical[†]	Extinction is symmetrical if the vibration directions bisect a prominent angle.
False Becke line[†]	A second bright line that moves in the direction opposite to the Becke line. It is usually observed with thick particles or when the refractive index difference between particles and mounting medium is large at the low index side of the interface.
Fast ray[†]	The fast ray or fast components for a crystal corresponds to the lower refractive index.
Field diaphragm	A variable aperture located in or near the light source.
Field of view	The maximum area visible when looking through the oculars of a microscope. Usually measured in millimeters.
Fluorescence Microscope	An optical instrument utilizing filter sets composed of excitation and barrier filters. These are oriented so that when used in conjunction with a high energy light source, fluorescent images can be viewed.
Fluorite objective[†]	This objective is corrected both for spherical aberration and chromatic aberration at two wavelengths.
Focal length	The distance from the center of the surface of a lens or mirror to its focal point.
Focal point	A point at which rays of light converge or from which they appear to diverge after refraction in a lens or reflection from a mirror.
Full-wave plate	See Compensator, full-wave plate.
Illumination, diffuse[†]	A good-quality illumination of lower intensity than Köhler or Nelsonian illumination because a ground glass is interposed between the lamp filament and the microscope condenser. The illuminator and lamp filament have few or no adjustments, although a field diaphragm is helpful.
Illumination, Köhler	An illumination technique that when utilized produces a bright, uniform field of view. The condenser is focused so that the conjugate image of the light source is in the back focal plane of the objective lens.
Illumination, Nelsonian[†]	High-intensity illumination is which the lamp filament is imaged in the plane of the specimen. A ribbon filament or arc lamp is required to give uniform illumination; the lamp must be focusable; and the filament position must be adjustable in all directions. Sometimes called "critical" illumination.

Illumination, oblique[†]	Illumination obtained by shading part of condenser lens or by throwing the condenser film placed in that plane.
Image, real[†]	Image formed when the incident and reflected rays converge in front of the mirror. The image that would register on a ground-glass screen or photographic film placed in that plane.
Image, virtual[†]	Image formed when the incident and reflected rays converge behind the mirror. The image would appear by construction to be in a given plane, but a ground-glass screen or photographic film placed in that plane would show no image.
Immersion objective[†]	A microscope objective that is used with a liquid of refractive index greater than 1.00 between the specimen and objective and usually between the specimen and substage condenser. Immersion objectives are used when a numerical aperture greater than 1.00 is desired, since this cannot be achieved with a dry objective.
Inherent color	The color of a sample under visible light. Often referred to as the true color of the sample. Not to be confused with the interference color of the sample.
Interference color[†]	The colors exhibited by a sample caused by removal of visible wavelengths while viewed under cross polars. If a crystal is not at extinction, the emerging vector components recombine in the vibration plane of the analyzer. Since one component is retarded, interference will cause the image to appear colored by destroying some wavelengths of light, their colors being subtracted from white light. The remaining light will consist of other colors that form the image of the crystal. These are called "interference" or "polarization" colors.
Interference figures	Light patterns that emerge from a crystal when viewed with conoscopic illumination and under crossed polars. The conoscopic pattern of extinction positions of a crystal is superimposed on the pattern of interference colors corresponding to the full cone of directions by which the crystal is illuminated, each direction showing its own interference color.
Interference, constructive[†]	The retardation of two light beams by exactly one wavelength or even multiples of one wavelength. The two waves reinforce each other, resulting in brightness.
Interference, destructive[†]	The retardation of two light beams exactly an odd number of half wavelengths, resulting in darkness as the two waves are perfectly out of phase.
Isogyres[†]	In a uniaxial interference figure, the two black bars that form a cross and represent the pattern of extinction positions of the crystals. In a biaxial interference figure, the two black curved bars (brushed) that intersect the isochromatic curves (lemniscates) and represent the pattern of extinction positions of the crystal.
Isotropic	Substances that are identical in all directions; showing a single refractive index. For example, isotropic scattering of light by a substance entails that the intensity of light radiated is the same in all directions. These samples have only one refractive index.
Köhler illumination	See Illumination, Köhler.
Lambda zero (λ_o) [†]	In dispersion staining, the wavelength at which both particle and liquid have the same refractive index.
Light microscope	A microscope that employs light in the visible or near-visible portion of the electromagnetic spectrum.
Magnification, empty[†]	An increase in size of an image with no additional increase in detail.

Magnification, maximum useful (MUM)[†]	The maximum magnification necessary to resolve detail. Magnification in excess of MUM gives no additional resolving power. It can usually be estimated as being 1000 times the NA of the objective.
Melatope[†]	The center of rotation of the isogyres in biaxial interference figures representing the point of emergence of rays that, in the crystal, travel along the optic axes.
Michel-Lévy chart	A chart relating thickness, birefringence, and retardation so that any one of these variables can be determined when the other two are known.
Micrometer (μm)[†]	The usual unit of length for light microscopical measurements ($1 \ \mu m = 10^{-3}$ mm): it is still often referred to by its former name, "micron."
Microphotograph[†]	A small, microscopic photograph, in which the image is minified; it requires enlarging or the use of a lens system in order to view it (cf. photomicrograph).
Microscopy[†]	The application of any tool or technique helpful in characterizing microscopic objects.
Monochromatic light[†]	Light composed of one wavelength. It may be obtained by the use of a laser or by gaseous discharge tubes in combinations with proper filters. An approximation is obtained by interference filters or monochromators.
Nanometer (nm)[†]	The usual unit of linear measurement with the electron microscope and of measuring ultraviolet and visible light wavelengths ($1 \ nm = 10^{-9}$ m or about 4×10^{-8} in.); replaces the former name, "millimicron" (mμ).
Negative crystals[†]	A uniaxial crystal is optically negative if $\varepsilon < \omega$. A biaxial crystal is said to be optically negative if $\gamma - \beta < \beta - \alpha$ and upon insertion of the first order waveplate, blue is obtained in the center of the interference figure.
Negative fibers	A fiber whose refractive index for light perpendicular to the long axis of the fiber, n-perpendicular, exceeds the refractive index of light parallel to the length of the fiber, n-parallel; $n_\perp > n_\parallel$.
Nelsonian illumination	See Illumination, Nelsonian.
Nicol prism[†]	A polarizing element made of two pieces of calcite specially cut, ground, polished, and cemented. A transmitted beam splits into two polarized components, one of which is refracted into and absorbed by the asphalt mount. The remaining polarized beam is transmitted.
Numerical aperture (NA)	The numerical measure of the light-gathering ability of a lens. NA determines the resolving power of a microscope.
Ocular (eyepiece)[†]	The lens that provides the second step of magnification in a compound microscope. The lens system closest to the eye, usually 10X.
Omega vibration direction (ω)[†]	Any vibration direction in the plane of the a axes for uniaxial crystals.
Opaque[†]	Material though which light cannot pass. Opaque to transmitted light, that is, 100% absorbing throughout the visible light range.
Optic axial angle[†]	The acute angle between two optic axes a biaxial crystal in the plane of α and γ. It is constant for and characteristic of any particular substance.
Optic axial plane[†]	The plane containing the optic axes as well as α and γ.
Optic axis[†]	In crystallography, the direction through an anisotropic crystal along which unpolarized light travels without suffering double refraction. Uniaxial crystals have one optic axis; biaxial crystals have two optic axes.
Optic sign[†]	For uniaxial materials, by definition, the sign is positive if the value $\varepsilon - \omega$ is negative. For biaxial materials, the sign is positive if γ is the acute bisectrix and negative if α is the acute bisectrix, or positive if $\gamma - \beta > \beta - \alpha$ and $\gamma - \beta < \beta - \alpha$.

Orthoscopic observation	Normal observations made with a microscope. When the field diaphragm, ocular front focal plane, and sample are in simultaneous focus with the viewer's eye.
Parfocal objective[†]	Objectives that are mounted so that only small adjustment of the bodytube and stage is necessary to focus after changing from one objective to any of the others. They are mounted in such a way that the second conjugate plane is in the same position on the optical axis of the microscope for each objective. Objectives used on a rotating nosepiece are usually parfocal. Eyepieces are also parfocal within any given manufacturer's series.
Phase annulus	The transparent ring at the front aperture of the condenser of a phase contrast microscope that limits illumination of the sample.
Phase contrast microscope	A form of interference microscopy that transforms differences in the optical path of a sample into differences in amplitude in the image. This produces higher contrast, allowing small differences to be easily viewed.
Phase plate	A transparent plate, located in the rear focal plane of a phase contrast microscope, which reduces the amplitude of background waves and advances or retards the phase of the component relative to the diffracted waves.
Photomacrography[†]	Photographs in the magnification range between conventional macrophotography and photomicrography, or, say, 1X to about 30X. Special lenses with built-in irises designed for small magnification ranges are usually used without an ocular.
Photomicrograph[†]	A large photograph of a small object as viewed through a microscope, the image of which is enlarged or magnified (cf. microphotograph).
Plane-polarized light	Light that is vibrating in one plane.
Pleochroism	The optical property of samples exhibiting different colors when viewed in plane-polarized light at different orientations.
Polarized light microscope	A microscope that contains a polarizer and an analyzer, which when utilized produces polarized light or crossed polars for sample viewing.
Polarizer	A filter that allows light waves to pass in only one direction. It is located between the light source and the sample.
Polars[†]	Two identical polarizing elements in a polarizing microscope. The polar placed between the light source and substage condenser is called the polarizer; the polar placed between the objective and ocular is called the analyzer. The vibration directions of the two polars may be crossed 90° to achieve "crossed polars"; slightly uncrossing one polar gives "slightly uncrossed polars"; and removing the analyzer results in "plane-polarizing light."
Positive crystals[†]	A uniaxial crystal is optically positive if $\varepsilon > \omega$. A biaxial crystal is said to be optically positive if $\gamma - \beta < \beta - \alpha$ and upon insertion of the first order waveplate, yellow is obtained in the center of the interference figure.
Positive fiber	A fiber whose refractive index for light parallel to the length of the fiber, n-parallel, exceeds that of the refractive index of light perpendicular to the length of the fiber, n-perpendicular; the elongation is said to be positive, $n_{\parallel} > n_{\perp}$.
Privileged direction (of a polarizer)	The direction of vibration to which light emerging from a polarizer has been restricted.
Quarter-wave plate	See Compensator, quarter-wave plate.
Quartz wedge	See Compensator, quartz wedge.
Real image	See Image, real.
Reflection	Light that leaves a surface at an angle equal to the incident angle.

Refraction	The change in the speed of light as it passes from one medium to another medium of a different refractive index.
Refractive index	The ratio of the velocity of light in a vacuum to its velocity in a transparent medium. Refractive index generally increases with the atomic number of the constituent atoms. A high density or atomic number elements usually result in a high refractive index. An optical property used to distinguish different transparent samples.
Relief	The degree of contrast observed between a particle and the medium into which it has been mounted.
Resolving power[†]	The ability to distinguish two small points in an image with their diffraction discs not overlapping more than half their diameter. The actual distance of one of the double refracted rays behind the other as they emerge from an anisotropic particle. It depends on the difference in the two refractive indices, $n_2 - n_1$, and the thickness.
Retardation (r)	The reduction in the velocity of the slow ray as compared to the fast ray of light produced by a birefringent sample. Often refers to the interference color produced under crossed polars that corresponds to the x-axis of the Michel-Lévy chart. Retardation is equal to the thickness multiplied by the birefringence (difference in refractive index) of the sample.
Sign of elongation[†]	This refers to the elongation of a substance in relation to refractive indices. If it is elongated in the direction of the high refractive index, it is said to be positive; if it is elongated in the direction of the low refractive index, it is negative.
Slow ray[†]	The slow vibration direction of a crystal corresponding to the higher refractive index.
Spherical aberration	An optical distortion caused because a spherical lens or mirror does not focus parallel rays to a point, but along a line. Therefore, off-axis rays are brought to a focus closer to the lens than are on-axis rays.
Stage micrometer	Usually a stage scale with divisions 100 mm (0.1 mm) apart. This is used to calibrate the scale found on oculars so that measurements can be made on the microscope.
Stereomicroscope	An optical instrument that uses two optical paths to produce three dimensional images.
Temperature coefficient of refractive index[†]	The change in refractive index (n) with temperature. The degree of variation of n depends on the composition of the substance and the state of aggregation (e.g., whether it is a solid or a liquid). It is usually about 100X larger for liquids than for solids and about $-0.0005/°C$ for liquids.
Translucent[†]	Transmission of light in such a way that image-forming rays are irregularly refracted and reflected.
Transparent	Material that can transmit visible light.
Tube length, mechanical[†]	The distance from the shoulder of the objective to the upper and of the drawtube. The mechanical tube length for biological and most polarizing microscope is 160 mm; Leitz formerly had a 170 mm tube length.
Uniaxial crystals[†]	Anisotropic crystals in the tetragonal and hexagonal systems having one unique crystallographic direction and either two (tetragonal) or three (hexagonal) directions that are alike and perpendicular to the unique directions.
Unpolarized light[†]	A bundle of light rays having a common propagation direction but different vibration directions.

Virtual image	See Image, virtual.
Wavelength	The distance of one cycle of an electromagnetic wave (the distance between two points at which the phase of a wave is the same). It is usually measured in nanometers, or formerly in Angstrom units (1 mm = 10 Å).
Working distance[†]	The distance between the top of the coverslip and the nearest portion of the objective.

[†]McCrone WC, Delly JG. *The Particle Atlas*, 2nd ed., Vol 4. Ann Arbor, MI: Ann Arbor Science, 1973.

Author's note: While many terms have been collected here, the focus is on basic microscopy terms. Additional terms are available in the online glossary available from the *McCrone Atlas of Microscopic Particles*, McCrone Associates, Inc., Westmont, IL 60559; 2005 [cited 2020]. Available from: http://www.mccroneatlas.com.

Index

A

Abaca fiber
    microscopic characteristics of,   267, 270
    optical properties of,   431
    staining of,   174–176
    uses of,   271
Abbe refractometer,   37
    procedure,   41–42
Absorbance equation,   397
Aberration,   443–444, 446, 450
Absorption spectrum,   364, 386, 388, 396
Acetate fiber
    melting point of,   407
    microscopic characteristics of,   280
    optical properties of,   433
    polymer composition of,   280
    types of,   433
Achromatic objectives,   443
Acrylic fiber
    melting point of,   407
    microscopic characteristics of,   282
    optical properties of,   433
    polymer composition of,   281
    types of,   433
Actinolite fiber
    optical properties of,   431
Acute bisectrix (Bx_a),   310
Additive retardation (addition),   64, 270, 283, 309–310
Akund fiber
    microscopic characteristics of,   266
    uses of,   271
Alumina silicate glass,   248
Amorphous,   443
Amosite fiber
    optical properties of,   269, 431

Amphetamine,   364, 365, 367–368
Anagen phase,   186, 224–226
    root,   225
Analyzer,   47–48, 50–53, 58, 258, 270, 283, 306, 309, 358, 443
Angular aperture (AA),   17–18, 443
Anidex fiber
    polymer composition of,   281
Animal fibers,   258, 268
    morphological properties of,   268
    optical properties of,   431
    uses of,   271
Animal hair. *see also* Specific animal
    deer family and antelope group, 196–197
    domestic group,   199–200
    examination of,   186–188, 195–200
    fur-bearing group,   198–199
    medulla,   188–189
    procedure,   201–202
    root,   196
    scale patterns,   186–188, 197
        coronal,   186–187
        imbricate,   186–187
        spinous,   186–187
Anions, tests for,   317, 332
    carbonate,   323
    chlorine,   323
    nitrite,   323
    sulfate,   323
Anisotropic,   51–52, 57–58, 64, 304, 308, 443
Annular stop,   38–39, 346, 348, 439, 445

Practical Forensic Microscopy: A Laboratory Manual, Second Edition. Barbara P. Wheeler.
© 2021 John Wiley & Sons Ltd. Published 2021 by John Wiley & Sons Ltd.
Companion website: www.wiley.com/go/Wheeler/Forensic